Cinderella in Arabia

Cinderella in Arabia

A Cross-Cultural Autobiography

Monika al-Amahani

Writers Club Press
San Jose New York Lincoln Shanghai

Cinderella in Arabia
A Cross-Cultural Autobiography

All Rights Reserved © 2001 by Monika al-Amahani

No part of this book may be reproduced or transmitted in any form or by any means, graphic, electronic, or mechanical, including photocopying, recording, taping, or by any information storage retrieval system, without the permission in writing from the publisher.

Writers Club Press
an imprint of iUniverse.com, Inc.

For information address:
iUniverse.com, Inc.
5220 S 16th, Ste. 200
Lincoln, NE 68512
www.iuniverse.com

Cover design by Kevin Paul Rowley

ISBN: 0-595-20116-4

Printed in the United States of America

FOR ALL THE WOMEN OF THE WORLD

Contents

Frontispiece ix
Note on the Author xi
Epigraph xiii
Foreword xv
Prologue xvii
CHAPTER ONE. CONVENT DAYS IN AUSTRIA 1
CHAPTER TWO. OFF TO ENGLAND 10
CHAPTER THREE. ABDULLA, THE KUWAITI 18
CHAPTER FOUR. LIVING TOGETHER IN CANTERBURY 44
CHAPTER FIVE. NEWLYWEDS IN ENGLAND 50
CHAPTER SIX. FIRST IMPRESSIONS OF KUWAIT 68
CHAPTER SEVEN. THE CITY OF KUWAIT 91
CHAPTER EIGHT. IMPRISONED 96
CHAPTER NINE. MAKING INROADS 108
CHAPTER TEN. WITCHES AND WASTA 118
CHAPTER ELEVEN. SEX, LIES, AND
　　　　　　　　　 THE NEXT FOUR YEARS 151
CHAPTER TWELVE. LONDON INTERLUDE 198
CHAPTER THIRTEEN. BLACK MAGIC IN KUWAIT 216
CHAPTER FOURTEEN. MONIKA'S DREAM HOUSE 232
CHAPTER FIFTEEN. MONIKA OPENS A BUSINESS 256
CHAPTER SIXTEEN. ABDULLA, THE FAMILY MAN 275
CHAPTER SEVENTEEN. TAKING UP AGAINST
　　　　　　　　　　　 A SEA OF TROUBLES 296
CHAPTER EIGHTEEN. MONIKA'S NEW HOME
　　　　　　　　　　　IS BEAUTIFUL 315
CHAPTER NINETEEN. REVENGE 324

CHAPTER TWENTY. ABDULLA AND FAWZIA &
               SO FORTH & SO ON 334
CHAPTER TWENTY-ONE. MONIKA'S FASHION
                    BOUTIQUE 349
CHAPTER TWENTY-TWO. A CANCER SCARE AND OTHER
                    CLOSE CALLS 367
CHAPTER TWENTY-THREE. BACK IN KUWAIT AND
                      SMARTER ALL THE TIME 374
CHAPTER TWENTY-FOUR. TRANSITIONAL TENSIONS ..403
CHAPTER TWENTY-FIVE. DIPLOMATIC IMPUNITIES 413
CHAPTER TWENTY-SIX. MONIKA'S EMBASSY
                    JOB AS INTERPRETER 447
CHAPTER TWENTY-SEVEN. A FEW LAST STRAWS 465
CHAPTER TWENTY-EIGHT. BYE, BYE, ABDULLA 483
Post Script 511

Frontispiece

Cinderella in Kuwait is an autobiography that exposes the tensions of intercultural marriage. Our heroine, as a naive young Austrian student, believed she was marrying a Muslim Prince Charming and found herself welded to, persecuted by, and entangled with the whole of his family and culture. Her sometimes tragic, often ludicrous, but constantly volatile lifestyle drove her to the fringes of human despair as spells thickened the air, her businesses burnt down, and infidelity reared its ugly head—again and again.

Moving from adolescent dreams under the spires of Oxford to the incestuous, corrupt, and filthy-rich milieus of modern Kuwait, this book tears away the veil of hypocrisy, misunderstanding, and myth that shrouds the contemporary Middle East. Forget about political correctness. This is a true story which takes you into the heart of 'wasta-land,' where whom you know gets you where you want to be, where haute couture garments rub shoulders with the spirit of the Middle Ages and where women are still bought and sold and consigned to a life of obedience . . . or else!

Step into the land of oil . . . and the riches it brings . . . and prepare to be shocked by what you learn.

Note on the Author

Having survived a strict convent upbringing in Austria only to find herself pitched into a turbulent marriage to a Kuwaiti graduate student bound for a future career as a wealthy diplomat, author Monika al-Amahani exposes the tensions of intercultural marriage in this no-holds-barred autobiography. This is a different sort of love story, a tale of adventure, an account of always hilarious and sometimes painful personal and vocational development. The author now commutes between Vienna and London.

A born survivor, Monika al-Amahani exults in her experiences and in her three sons, whom she adores. She lives for the moment and bears Kuwait no malice.

Epigraph

A rose planted into desert sand
Cannot survive without a helping hand.

Monika

Foreword

Cinderella in Arabia is a 'cross-cultural autobiography,' a rollicking, robust, life-affirming carnivalesque book despite its tender fairy-tale title. It is a serious critique of Gulf Arab society, revealing the really terrible crunches the author has so triumphantly survived! "Viva, Monika!"

What I especially love about the book is the author's very distinctive brand of humor. Is it Austrian, or what? This is really a hilarious book. The 'heroine' is a new sort of picaresque character: female! ... and only a rogue when (and because) she is pitted against rogues. The 'Monika' of the story sees through the pretensions and the chicanery to the essential humanity of the spectrum of people she encounters in her travels and her sojourns away from home. And all the while that this book is being entertaining, it is also sounding altogether authentic, true to the author's experience and to her Vision of Kuwait.

I think the book will have a very broad appeal. It will interest most women, whether or not they know or care especially about the Arab world, because it is the true Story of a Woman emancipating herself in many ways (vocationally, psychologically, culturally, and literally), because it gives an importantly *intimate* report on a 'cross-cultural marriage' (a subject of growing interest in this age obsessed with multi-cultural education, gender issues, and ethnic warfare), and because it is so rich in detail. I've read many ethnographies by women anthropologists and I am reminded of some of the best of them by this book—Laura Bohannon's *Return to Laughter*, Jean Briggs's *Never in*

Anger: Portrait of an Eskimo Family, and Karla O. Poewe's *Reflections of a Woman Anthropologist: No Hiding Place*—all of them groundbreaking works that changed the character of anthropology. Monika's book will also interest people concerned about the deep way childhood training in the name of religion affects individuals and the cultures to which they belong—sometimes in dubious ways. It might even become a Women's Studies classic like Zora Neale Hurston's *Their Eyes Were Watching God*.

The best thing about the book is that it is not inhibited by notions of political correctness. It weeps and laughs, grumbles and roars, and calls a spade a spade. I can't wait for it to be published so I can give copies to all my friends. I am also sure that there will be some who will think the book scandalous! *C'est la vie,* and *tant mieux*! Best wishes for success and a best seller!

R. Victoria Arana
Graduate Professor
Howard University
Washington DC

Prologue

VIVA, MONIKA!

Viva Monika! She had finally done it, put down her old baggage and walked away, straight ahead, into the bright, warm, soothing sunshine of freedom and into a more fortunate and happier future, hopefully, than her past had been.

Now at long last she could start all over again. She didn't—or, at least, her physical body didn't—have to mix with, speak to, nor look at the ugly past anymore. But what about her innermost spirit? Could it, too, along with her body, let the past be past?

No. No, it most certainly could not. Not yet. So, there remained this most important matter of freeing her spirit as well...

Something had still to be done, and what better solution than to put pen to paper and write it all down, straight from the heart and, after that, to disregard the old completely and start afresh with sound body and mind, soul, spirit—whatever one prefers to call it; for, if the spirit is ill, so is the body, and if the body is ill, so is the spirit—as we all get to know sooner or later up life's aisle.

This is why Monika determined to set down her past frankly in an autobiography, as a plaster for her hurt ego—which is much easier said than done unless, of course, you happen to be the talented Erika Jong or some such smart lady writer who knows how to shape-up a brave and sexy blockbuster of a book. To have the desired effect, Monika's narrative would have to tell it exactly as she remembered it, the fun and the frolic, the hurt and the humiliation, warts and all.

Well, I am that same Monika, and this is only part of my unvarnished life story. Well, *almost* all of it. There are innocent human beings to consider.

CHAPTER ONE

CONVENT DAYS IN AUSTRIA

As it happened, Monika didn't have much trouble writing, for at the convent where she was reared and schooled, her essays were considered rather good and, more often than not, were chosen to be read aloud in class. Only when it came to mathematics did she have any trouble. About that particular subject, she understood about as much as how to milk a mouse. The main thing is that she was boarded as a child at a convent where discipline was written with a capital D and where children learned quite a few useful life skills.

And she had hated it, having been put there by her Austrian dentist mother, who was separated but never divorced from Monika's Czech father, also a dentist. Monika's brother Werner, older by three years, was sent off, too, to a military academy. Later on, he joined his parents in the dental profession. Monika's parents had very little time for her, but they saw each other regularly in court, in front of a judge, for about twenty-five years, until her father died in a car accident on his way to court. Father wanted a divorce. Mother declined. There was no evidence of neglect on his wife's part. So, for a major part of their lives, each existed primarily in order to destroy the other.

From chubby toddlerhood, Monika had been cared for and looked after by nannies. Her little white cotton gloves were changed as many as three times on daily outings to the park, for hygienic reasons. Under

Mrs. Pavlik's instructions, cold drinks and ice creams were regarded as unhealthy and were not allowed. Then, when she was old enough for school, Monika was packed off to the convent.

Just how unhappy and imprisoned Monika felt for eight long, never-ending school years in her navy blue and white uniform with yellow brass buttons, locked up in that convent deep in the Austrian countryside, nobody ever knew nor cared. Of that, little Monika was convinced—and rightfully so. When she was ill and yellow with jaundice, it took her mother three months to turn up. Father did not turn up at all. Never, ever.

Monika and her fellow schoolmates, all children with good middle class backgrounds, agreed that they lived in a witches' coven, for the nuns, who were referred to as Sisters, were feared by the girls, who ranged from the tender age of six to an adolescent eighteen. Convent life was nothing like that lovely film, *The Sound of Music*, in which the nuns were all poetry and sweet music, full of love, and with so much love to give.

Monika's mother, Dentist Pavlik, who came to visit once a month from Vienna, thought Monika in very good hands. After all, she herself had been convent educated; and what had helped to make her such a lady was good enough for her daughter. But the Shepherdesses were extremely strict and disciplined and sometimes quite cruel, too, with their flock of sheep. Monika is now quite grown up, yet the sight of a nun still makes her stomach churn and makes her look the other way. Who says one remembers only the good times?

From the convent's inner chapel, ringing bells reminded you that prayers had to be said three times a day, on your knees. In the dining hall, you said your prayers standing up, both before and after meals, also three times a day. The children didn't think the food was worth praying for, nor thanking for.

How many times did Monika sit listlessly over her unfinished plate, with everyone else having eaten and gone!

Eintopf—a mass of potatoes, lentils, and beans, horrible big red beans—she hated it! As she stood patiently in line about to receive what she had piously prayed for, it occurred to her that Food-Sister Maria, a short, plump woman in her fifties, who knew how much the child detested that special dish on Fridays, took extra pleasure in serving her. "Oh, God, help me please," the thirteen-year-old prayed inwardly. "Holy Antonius, don't let her put a lot on my plate, please." White plate in outstretched hands, her stomach turning at the sight and smell of those beans, Monika waited for a miracle. With a wry, provocative smile, the nun plunged her huge spoon deep into the gluey brown messy mass and out came a steaming dark mountain that landed with a noisy *plop* on the girl's plate, an over-generous portion again. "Thank you, Sister Maria," she heard herself say. "You bloody, bloody bitch," she thought. "I'd love to take you like a Christmas goose and stuff that manure right down your throat three times a day, every day of the week." Her eyelids went down as she walked carefully (not to spill any of that shit and get told off as well), very slowly back to her seat to begin her ordeal. The hawk eyes of Sister Maria watched so that Monika had no chance to flip a couple of spoonfuls to her pals sitting around the table, who gave her sorry looks and would have tried to help if they'd been able.

The girls stuck firmly together. They were each other's families, and mostly got along agreeably. Monika was a leader from an early age. She was well liked by her friends, always stuck up for them, and never told on them, unlike some others who got in favor by spying and telling. No big deal. The world is full of that type, in and outside convents.

"Monika!" The dreaded voice of Sister Maria bellowed through the huge dining hall. "Stand up! Tell me, do you love Jesus? Jesus died for us on the cross, and you cannot even master the simple task of eating your food properly. Do you know how many people die each day of hunger in the world outside?" They always referred to the world as outside, as if they were not in it. "Those poor souls would love to exchange places with you. Yet, there you are, so privileged! You have food, drinks, and a bed, but you don't know how to appreciate them. Shame on you! Sit down!" And there sat Monika, a little martyr, spoonful after spoonful. It had to be gulped down, eaten up, all of it. She took the last big mouthful and ran to the toilet.

Younger nuns taught school. God help the girl who did not speak proper German in class at all times. Slang, swearing, or raising one's voice was out—was unheard of—here. But school time was loved and looked forward to, compared with life at the convent's living quarters, in the adjoining block, where the nasty older nuns had the children divided into three age groups. There was the younger set of six- to ten-year-olds, the middle group of ten- to thirteen-year-olds, and the third group of fourteen- to eighteen-year-olds, the teenagers and adolescents. When they were not dishing out punishment, the nuns preached how the human race was responsible for the end of the world, soon-to-come, sooner than we all thought. God was cross. Responsible was the human race, with its weakness of the flesh and so little will power.

At night, fully believing what the grown-ups taught, for they were grown-ups and knew everything, Monika lay wide awake and sweating under her covers, listening to the noises of the night, dreading the end of the world to come at any time. Surely such prophecies are poison for young girls' normal, inner, psychological development.

Among themselves, the children discussed and compared the nuns' behavior. The schoolgirls concluded that young nuns enter convents filled from an early age with the desire to sacrifice earthly life for God and the Catholic Church. Self-sacrifice seemed to explain why younger nuns were rather strict but kind and friendly, whereas the older, bitter ones so often acted unfairly, were so often nasty and downright sadistic. Probably, they themselves had been unable for one reason or another to master life on the outside, as other women—the girls' own mothers, for instance—routinely did. Incurable diseases, broken love affairs, husbands or children lost through tragic circumstances or death must have been responsible for the bad tempered behavior of the nuns; thus philosophized the young maidens. On the other hand, didn't the nice, young sisters grow old, too? Who in hell knows what makes a nun become a nun or what makes her nice or nasty? Children have their own theories for everything, don't they? Whatever it was that made those nuns unlovable, they surely knew how to give their frustrations the green light and let hell loose whenever they felt like it, which was often. So the children lived in the shadow of constant fear. Was it, maybe, midlife crisis that made the older nuns so harsh? Monika and her friends had wondered. Maybe it hit the old nuns twice as hard, having to come to terms with the fact that life's almost finished and it's not been what was expected; or the fact that there could be no change because it was already too late. Were some of them lesbians? Yes, probably, but women are more discreet about who or what they love than men and wouldn't need to join convents for that reason. Or did the nuns simply feel more secure in a community where one among many does not have to make life's everyday decisions? The girls had heard about priests who were closet homosexuals or who kept faithful housekeepers. Yes, the human flesh is weak, all human flesh. The girls were sure of that. How could such a Catholic priest stand high up in the pulpit on Sunday mornings and preach to his congregation how to live married life, for example, knowing nothing about it. It makes you wonder, thought Monika.

She was convinced from an early age that the Church was not for her, although she firmly believed in that greater force we call God. But not in the Church's doings. Let's face it, she would often think to herself, Catholic churches are stuffed full of worldly goods and riches. Some are museums—and viewed accordingly, and yet it is preached: do not collect worldly riches, share them with the poor. What about sharing the Church's riches with the needy and poor? How many lives could that save? She would often wonder about these things.

In Monika's convent lived one lucky man, Father Paul, the chapel's priest, young and good looking. He lectured the girls on religion, and quite naturally (but against Catholic law) most of the older girls, along with some of the nuns, lusted after him. There would be the nuns' whispered arguments about whose turn it was to take Father Paul's meal tray up to him, or their short tête-à-têtes with him in the school building in between classes, where a tall, bespectacled, darker-skinned nun seemed to be the favorite of the black-robed man. The girls used to fantasize, as young females at that tender age generally do. A long look or an extra word from the Father made them walk around on Cloud Nine. His hobby was photography, and Monika was well liked and photographed by him.

Monika was artistic, too. Her drawings were always on display. So, when a fourteen-year-old maiden had the urge to flatter Father Paul with a love letter, who better than Monika should be asked to do the art work, to draw a heart or two?

Bravely, Monika drew two hearts flaming with fire, scarlet red, in the international language of love. Shame on Father Paul, who didn't appreciate that other young girl's declaration of love. He handed the letter to Mother Superior, a much dreaded older nun, who instantly recognized Monika's artistic handiwork and pinned the letter onto her back without listening to the girl's pleas of innocence, for she really hadn't known the hearts were meant for the priest. Facing a long corridor wall, she was made to stand in shame, wishing a hole would open up and swallow her, for she never would have written a letter to the priest, not, surely, a flaming love letter. The echo of footsteps came closer and halted behind her. A female voice of God spoke: "You are the disciple of Satan, a rotten apple. You shall burn in Hell!"

"*You*, evil witch, are the worm that makes apples rotten in the first place," reflected Monika, lost in her innermost thoughts; but a tight-fingered pinch in the flesh of her right upper arm brought her back to reality, letting her know that big Sister Monika was about to let off steam, looking at that wretched letter on maiden Monika's back. Sister Monika always pinched the flesh like this with her oh-so-bony fingers.

"God no, it's not *you* again! It cannot be *Monika*!" The sister spoke in a voice of mock-surprise. "Do you know how hard you make it for me to like you? I see difficult work ahead, very difficult work to put you back on God's path. As you are my namesake, I make that promise to Jesus and will not break it." With that statement, Sister Monika seemed satisfied and, while walking away, called back: "I shall pray for you, sinner."

Accused and innocent, the poor little soul stood rubbing her arm to ease the pain. "Oh, God, why isn't my name a different one? I wish I were Jewish." Buddhists, Jews, and Muslims were all considered atheists and blasphemers whose souls would burn in Hell for all Eternity, but just then Monika would not have minded being Jewish and burning later, much later, after she had lived and then died an old woman—only, now, she so wanted to be free and happy!

A long row of children from the middle group of ten- to fourteen-year-olds on an outing in the country busily chatted and sang. The girls loved their weekly excursions on the outside—among them our heroine Monika, who was extra excited, for tomorrow was her birthday and, as happened each year, she expected her mother to visit her at the convent to wish her well with a big cake and a present, yummy yummy. Sister Magdalena in tandem with Sister Julianna made sure the girls did not step out of line nor stay behind nor take off all together, as Monika had done previously already three times. On those occasions she had used her saved-up pocket money to find her way through public transport into the unloving arms of her mother. When, after a good telling off, Monika's mother then took her back to Frankenstein's Castle, Monika got a second scolding from the nuns and a punishment to boot. On that special day some local boys, nothing unusual on such outings, made teasing remarks at the young ladies. "Hey there, you lovely birds, are you all going to become nuns? Don't you like boys? Any of you want a boyfriend? We volunteer." Diana, the girl ahead of Monika, shouted back at the lads: "You are still green behind the ears, and you all smell of your mothers' tits." As if struck by lightning, Sister Julianna turned around to shoot well-aimed poisoned looks at Monika. "*You!*" she hissed at her. "You report to me as soon as we get home." Indeed, Dentist Pavlik was never allowed to see her daughter.

The next day, March 27th, Monika celebrated her fourteenth birthday all alone on hands and knees next to a bucket of hot, soapy water, washing, scrubbing, drying, waxing, and polishing her six square meters of parquetry (the classroom floor) to the nuns' delight. Amen. Once again unjustly punished for something she had not done. Explaining herself to Sister Julianna—that it was not she who had said the rude words to the boys—would have been like trying to put toothpaste back into the tube.

Now, please, we must not forget Sister Brunhilde, another star that shone brightly in the convent's sky. She was known and dreaded for her trademark, a scepter, a wooden, round, sawed-off chair leg that, come to think of it now, very much resembled an English bobby's truncheon. When she was not fondly stroking it on her lap, she treasured it in her long black frock's pocket under the crisp, white starched linen apron. Children who displeased, or disobeyed, Sister Brunhilde earned themselves that chair leg across the palm of their young hands. Our Monika knew only too well how that wooden samurai sword felt. No feeling would return sometimes until the next day, or longer, inside her reddened palm. You always had to hold out your left hand for that punishment, unless you were left-handed, so that you could still do the assigned housework and homework; but if you played the piano, as Monika did, a swollen hand was a welcome excuse to miss some lessons. The guitar would have been Monika's musical instrument, had she been allowed to choose, but Dentist Pavlik insisted on piano for a girl—and forget the guitar.

Monika's best friend, Gretl, a petite, pretty little girl with long ash blonde neatly tied into plaits, once had the misfortune of leaking blood through her bedclothes onto the mattress of her bed. It was her first menstrual period, but with sex education out of the question, Gretl had no idea what had happened and could not have anticipated such an event nor prevented the stain from happening. Nevertheless, the accident was all the unfortunate girl needed. Sister Brunhilde came along and ordered Gretl to hoist the mattress onto her shoulders and to parade outside the washrooms for all to view. Wasn't that cruel and inhuman, too? Where were the Mother Theresas? Not with Monika!

We could continue with Monika's convent years, but that account would soon become a book all of its own, and in this one we have more important matters to attend to.

No doubt about it, leaving the convent forever at sweet sixteen was the happiest experience she had ever had, and Monika felt like punching a great big hole into the world's tummy! She didn't know it then, but she had emerged well equipped from behind convent walls to challenge this world full of rocks. It also helped to be born an Aries, with Mars for a ruling planet, and under a fire sign.

CHAPTER TWO

OFF TO ENGLAND

Now, back in Vienna with her mother, the once-chubby youngster had grown into a pretty young lady who looked fresh, neat, tidy, clean at all times, to the best of her ability, and well endowed—with enough of everything, all positioned in the right places, not to mention a tiny waist, a nice bonus. Army-green almond-shaped eyes, a full-lipped mouth, in it pearly white, healthy teeth framed by a round baby face with a high forehead and high cheekbones, her Czech inheritance. Dentist Friederike Pavlik remarked frequently on her daughter's pearly teeth, saying her smile was her greatest asset, whereas brother Werner mocked her, calling her moon face. Not completely satisfied with what God had lavished on her, Monika quietly wished for longer limbs and a fuller growth of hair. Her shoulder-length, much-too-fine, light brown hair was soon three shades lighter as she aimed towards transformation. She became a blonde. Just how much the young girl appealed to the opposite sex she was soon to find out.

    Most male clients of Dentist Friederike Pavlik wanted to know where she had hid her pretty daughter for so long, and her brother's friends made her enough compliments and offers that she was assured she had what it takes—sex appeal. Occasional motorbike rides were accepted, offhand, in the early hours of the morning. Werner and his gang of six—sometimes more—clad in black leather outfits, drove up mountain roads, through woods littered with deer, rabbits, squirrels running for cover, not to mention the occasional hedgehog crossing the road. The faster the heavy motorbikes went, the noisier and the more thrilling the ride, the more Monika relished it. The pack could not go fast enough for her. Usually the only girl amongst them, high on the pillion seat, hair fluttering in the wind, Monika thoroughly enjoyed those adventure rides, which are now firmly locked up in her memory box.

Monika well enjoyed the attention and fuss people all around made of and for her, but she took no further interest in males for the time being. It was enough for her to know she had finally arrived, that she was attractive and free. If she wanted anything, the choice was hers. Besides, after her recent release from isolation and captivity, Monika was still very shy, not being used to any male company whatsoever. She first had to work on the brother-sister relationship. Ecstatically happy and content with the unfolding of such a beautiful, exciting, free lifestyle, one that she had had no idea existed until now, Monika would jump wide awake out of bed every morning—her music turned on (usually lots and lots of Elvis Presley, if at all possible, her idol)—to live and enjoy every minute of that oh-so-free, lovely life. People everywhere were so friendly and nice, and what had been forbidden or a sin in the convent now happened to come quite naturally with everyday life. As a matter of fact, it was all part of life on the outside, and she felt warmly in tune with that atmosphere.

Applying for her first passport, in Monika's case, had nothing to do with travel, but was an urgent necessity—as I.D. She had to live with and to accept the fact that she looked much, much younger than her birth certificate stated. Her baby face was to blame. She so much wanted to look her age, if not older at that time. With her passport in hand, it turned out to be fun challenging waiters who told her she was much too young to drink wine at the *Gasthaus*. And ticket collectors at X-rated cinemas who refused her entrance, not always in the nicest manner, you understand, had to give in. From that point on she was no more to be the convent sinner, but the winner, victorious, with justice on her side.

Having acted main parts in all school plays and earned lots of applause, congratulations, and praise from fellow students, nuns, and parents alike, Monika was not opposed when proud Mrs. Pavlik took a folder with Monika's photographs to register her at a well-known drama school in Vienna. Her acting talent should be given a chance. Besides, acting lessons would contribute to help diminish the girl's unjustified shyness. A very keen Monika gave her best to the enterprise for about six months. After that, she became convinced that all attention—along with small parts on offer from film studios—was being lavished on well-endowed, tarty-looking girls, the ones who wore too much make-up and who did not leave much to one's imagination. Here again, Monika quite honestly felt, the drawback was her own much-too-young appearance. Feeling out of place anyway, a little incident went a long way towards propelling her to throw in drama school altogether.

One day an electric short of some sort cut off the main theater lights, interfering with Monika's demonstration on stage. The instructor, a bespectacled man in his forties, turned to Monika.

"Oh, blast it," he said, "I need a rubber. Do you have a rubber to fix around those wretched wires?"

"Yes, yes I do." With those words, helpful as always, she pulled on a thick rubber band that held her hair together in a ponytail. "Here," she offered.

"Not that kind of rubber, silly girl," he replied smiling. "I mean the sort you use with your boyfriend." She got the message, and with it, oh boy, did she blush! "Don't you know what I'm talking about?" he asked her, and not leaving it at that, he turned to the students and said: "Judging the book by its cover, I suppose she really doesn't know what I'm talking about"—which had them in stitches at her expense. Full stop to drama school, as Mrs. Pavlik found out, with the return of her monthly tuition check.

Now Monika, not at all academically minded, nor wanting to look up people's noses as a dentist for the rest of her life, felt drawn towards beauty and a more glamorous profession. The young miss was left with two congenial possibilities: to be a beautician, for one; or, with an eye towards the world of design, to dedicate herself to fashion, as a close second. She loved beauty and fashion, clothes and accessories and jewelry; in short, everything that could contribute to making a woman one hundred percent female. Mrs. Pavlik left the choice entirely to her daughter but did not like to see time wasted. Six months had passed already with her daughter no nearer to a decision, so she suggested a course in France or England to help cultivate her daughter's foreign languages. Besides, it was a fashionable thing to do in Austria at that time, the late 1950's. Travel would be a jolly good education for a young lady, whatever way one looked at it. Monika could only benefit. Hopefully, on her return, she would look the future positively in the eye, knowing better what she really wanted. It would he a mistake and waste of money to go into something now that later she might decide was not for her after all—like drama school. Anyway, whatever. It would not be tragic. Girls got married sooner or later. Werner's future profession was way more important.

With the help of an international students' exchange bureau, it was goodbye Vienna, hello England, for Miss Monika Pavlik. Hello Folkestone Seaside Resort, to be precise, and the Wampach Hotel, to be even more precise. Six Austrian girls served breakfast and lunch in their national costume, the Dirndel, a colorful sleeveless frock worn with a white, tight-fitting, low-cut, rather seductive, embroidered blouse. It featured a tiny waist and boobs half on show. Monika looked inviting in her outfit. Black evening dresses, black shoes, and silk stockings were worn to serve supper. Romantic attic rooms and the continuous cries of busy sea gulls accommodated the girls. Afternoons were spent at the nearby language center. Plus, generous tips and a pay packet were included every month—her first self-earned money, which she immediately spent on a red crash helmet, perfume, lacy underwear, and a transistor radio, also in red, her favorite color.

Monika was very happy, and before she knew it, it was all over. She had acquired a much improved, but far from fluent, English. Back in Vienna, she went straight to a private, English-speaking beauty school for an interview, where her place would he secure under certain conditions. First, a more advanced grasp of English was stipulated; second, a diploma in Chiropody and Manicure. The school's motto was "start at the bottom and end up on top." The Dr. Scholl's diploma was hers within a couple of months, to be closely followed by a crash course in English. And where better to do that, the second time around, than at Oxford?

Living accommodations in Oxford, arranged by her school, were with a pleasant enough English family. Sporty Sigrid from Germany was to be her roommate. They got on well together and soon were on Sigi-Moni terms. They became firm friends and, because they enjoyed each other's company, did not show much interest in Oxford's bottle-party night scene. Free time was filled visiting the local ABC Cinema once a week. They took long walks through Oxford's beautiful parks, along the Isis or Cherwell rivers, quizzing each other's English, eager to learn plenty, fast, and to go back home—Monika to beauty school, and Sigrid to be an international ski instructor on the German slopes.

One day, having accepted a party invitation, Sigrid—hardly out the door—came back in no time.

"Forgotten something?" asked Monika.

"I've just been to Jamaica," said Sigrid.

"You have not catched much sun, darling Sigi. You're as cheesy white as ever," teased Monika in her pidgin English.

"Do imagine, Moni, the room 99% full of colored men students, outnumbering the girls a good ten to one. Not my scene. And to be honest, it stank me out." With a jump, she threw her body on the bed, her legs dangling from underneath huge layers of white frilly petticoats worn in true 1950's style, two borrowed from Monika. "Listen," she carried on, "downstairs, out front, is a male person waiting for an answer. He's Irish, has tomato-red hair, and is a medical student. Not my type but very pleasant and helpful. He offered to walk me back home. To be honest, I asked him to. They were all over me in that so-called party. Someone could easily have followed me. I agreed to have a drink with him tomorrow, but only if you will join us, too. I am not going alone with him. What do you say?"

"I tell you what I say," answered Monika. "If your Bill's got red hair, ask him to bring someone for me with green hair."

Sandwiched between giggles and jokes, the two friends reached the following decision. Sigrid was to ask waiting Billy Boy to bring a respectable friend of his along for Monika, possibly someone who had a steady girlfriend to make a safe foursome for that one evening only, and forget it all the following day—said and done. They would meet the next day at 7:30 pm near the main entrance to the Randolph Hotel. Billy knew just the right person to bring along, he assured Sigrid.

Little did Monika know that, with the grand idea of a-safe-foursome-and- forget-it-all- the-next-day blind date, her well-planned future was to take an unplanned turn towards a completely different course. Or was it fate, long ago determined for her, and she really had nothing to do with it anyway? Who knows the answer to that one? The fact is, Oxford was henceforth to be a key word in her life.

On the next day at 7:30 the two girls waiting for the two boys soon noticed Bill, topped with a red mop of hair, working his way towards them through a crowd of pedestrians, in the company of—oh no!—a dark haired, dark-skinned date for Monika, who in a split second could not help whispering to her roommate, "He is unmistakably Arabic. I can tell by his nose," while not overlooking Billy Boy's huge, light-brown freckles, generously scattered all over the face—freckles that Sigrid had forgotten, or simply had not bothered to mention. No one could blame Sigrid for not wanting to have a drink alone with him. Bill wasn't Monika's type either, and nor was the one who came strolling along with Bill from some Honga Bonga land far away!

Vienna had quite a number of students like him from Iran and Arabia, but a girl from a good family was not to be seen with such a person, for those boys had the worst possible reputations. Local newspapers and magazines, too, were full of warnings and horrid stories about how they promised young, innocent girls heaven on earth but, when the girls became pregnant, dumped them, or worse, took some unfortunate souls back home to their Muslim countries, where the poor girls were forced to live a life of never-ending misery. Some, lucky enough to get away from such hell, were separated from their children, never to meet again. Some punishment! Just her luck. Of all the students in Oxford, it had to be one of them!

Disappointed, wishing she were not there, yet having to make the best of it since, thanks to Sigrid, she was there, Monika inspected her blind date rather skeptically: slim body, slim face, a little taller than her own 5'3" height; over his dark, olive-skinned forehead fell a bunch of curly black hair in a triangle. His big, alert, black-as-coal eyes gave her an overhaul, too, just lingering on her legs. He had full lips under that slightly hook-like, give-away nose of his, and there sparkled a perfect set of whiter-than-white teeth of which one could be proud or envious. To be honest, he wasn't at all bad looking for a Middle Eastern chap. And yet, generally, what a sorry picture he portrayed: hands deeply buried in the pockets of a light beige Burberry raincoat buttoned up so high it hid his neck and gave the impression he didn't have a neck at all—as if his head were screwed on between his shoulder blades. That much-too-big coat reached way down, ending a couple of inches above black, flat, rounded brogue shoes. Between coat and shoes there was just enough space left to get a glimpse of patterned, thick, very wide-cut gray flannel trousers. The stranger looked a bloody mess! In fact, he was dressed to kill altogether any possible desire a girl might have had to join him for a drink. The '50s fashion scene then current for young men decreed drainpipe trousers, Italian winkle pickers or beetle crushers, thick rubber-soled suede shoes, in true Elvis Presley style—whose then-newly-released hit song *Blue Suede Shoes* helped make them even more popular. If a coat had to be worn at all, it should most definitely not reach below the knees. A keenly fashion-conscious Monika was very much 'with it,' but that unwelcome stranger, with whom she was forced by circumstances beyond her control to associate tonight, was obviously far behind it. A young body in old-fashioned, loose-hanging gear from Grandpa's time long gone by, a lamb dressed as mutton, he would do well as a scarecrow in some field. Really, a crime to walk about like this, thought Monika; it should not be allowed.

Monika's much too harsh sentence on him was interrupted now by a slightly blushing, big nervous Bill, who came up close to introduce himself and, of course, what he had brought with him: Abdulla, from Kuwait, somewhere in the Arab world, a medical student very much like himself.

CHAPTER THREE

ABDULLA, THE KUWAITI

Monika aimed a triumphant 'you see I *told* you so, he's an Arab' look in the direction of Sigrid, who acknowledged it with a smile. Out of those ugly raincoat pockets shot Abdulla's hands to welcome and shake hands with the girls. Wow! Surprise. Here was a very energetic, live wire from a country somewhere in Arabia called Kuwait, who talked, laughed, and joked as if his life depended on it. He broke the ice for all concerned and made them feel at ease. Well, first meetings are a bit nerve wracking for each and every one of us, aren't they? But he more than lived up to Monika's expectations, who in haste had only judged him by his dull appearance, and now he was running the show. He led the way up the stairs towards the hotel bar where the staff greeted him warmly. Some addressed him as Sir, others more informally as Abdulla, and a couple of customers knew him, too. Drinks with nibbles of crisps and assorted nuts were ordered and paid for by a generous Abdulla. He, the perfect rooster, would not have it any other way: tonight was on him.

To his credit so far, he spoke excellent English and was the owner of an electrifying personality, a bundle of energy. In fact, he was 100% mercury. The scene: Cinzano-sipping girls, sitting comfortably, expectantly, with beer-drinking boys.

"Where do you come from? What do you study? For how long? Do you live far?" All that formal blah blah routine first. Monika's age came up. Surprise all around! She expected it and hated it. Bill and Abdulla assured her, no *way* did she look anything like eighteen, but more like a well-developed twelve-year-old! Some compliments she could do without, thank you very much.

No time was wasted by Abdulla in letting Monika know that, Yes, Sir, she was his cup of tea. She was bombarded with compliments and along the way he made her a most generous offer, within the first twenty minutes or so, to become his steady date. Visibly happy that she was not involved with any boyfriends, he decided and made plans then and there just how they would spend the future time together, and since it was already the week-end, starting with next week. His current girlfriend was American, and just see how nicely it coincided, for he wanted to call it a day with her anyway. She has already lost me and *you*, you lucky one, have found me just in time, he informed her. Slowly and surely, he became a bit too overpowering, demanding, and pushy. Monika did not bother to argue with him nor to reject any of his offers, nor plans, for she knew it was clearly a case of "tonight only, honey, and I never want to see you again." With that in mind, she let him talk and be. Only when he grabbed her left hand to pull a lovely 18-carat gold ring with little rubies from her ring finger and then inspected it closely only to tell her it was rubbish and that he would bring her a much nicer 22-carat one from his country, Kuwait, where they had lots and lots of gold, did she just about have enough. Touching her, getting physical so to speak, and thinking he could buy her with bribes finally put her off altogether. Didn't he live up beautifully to the Arab reputation back home in Vienna—trying to lure her like a cheap tart? Heaven and earth was not promised yet, but he might come up with that too, if she sat there much longer. Abruptly she stood up and reminded Sigrid of some unfinished homework, a good excuse in such a situation. Sigrid cleverly cottoned on to her rescue. Reaching for their jackets and handbags, they politely thanked their hosts for the "lovely" evening, said their thank yous, goodbyes, and goodnights, without counting on Abdulla's reaction. He shot up and would not hear of it. Determined, in true son-of-the-desert fashion, he was not to let his newfound prey get away that easily. Come on, Bill, he ordered, despite the girls' protests; we have to walk the ladies home safely! Oh no, *Scheisse*, get them lost, swore Monika, annoyed, to Sigrid; he sticks like glue, and I can't stand any more of him. Twenty minutes later, facing their front entrance, one more unexpected hurdle had to be overcome: the customary English goodnight kiss that both boys asked for and both girls refused.

Sigi had managed to send Irish Bill on his way with a handshake. She had rather enjoyed tonight's quiet conversation with him. Not so Monika. Left behind with a passionate Abdulla, she had to wriggle her way out of that stupid kissing business that he went for so persistently. For all she cared, he could stand on his head with a feather up his bum and no way would she give in. She was trying to avoid being hurtful, rude, or nasty; after all, he had done no harm to her. She even felt slightly sorry for him, his being so keen on her without a chance in hell. Unthinkable to associate with such an Arab and all that went with it; to think about it was not even to be considered. Here and now, this acquaintance had to end.

"Look here, Abdulla," she spoke in a very confident voice, "I've got an idea: tonight no kiss but tomorrow I'll see you at 3 pm opposite the Randolph Hotel by Martyrs Memorial. Would you like that?" As she had refused, up to the last minute, ever to see him again, he was not quite sure now—did she mean it, or not?—so he said,

"I would love that, but do you swear you will be there?" He was skeptical.

"I promise. Of course. You'll see."

"Then, I'll be waiting from 2 o'clock on," he happily replied. "Goodnight!"

"Goodnight." With a big sigh of relief, Monika ran up those stairs two at a time. Her mother came to mind. She would be mad at her for mixing with an Arab, for what people said and thought mattered a great deal to Dentist Pavlik—in diametric opposition to her daughter Monika who didn't give a damn about what certain people thought of her. Those people would be much better off minding their own business. She believed in "Live and let live," not in the never-ending gossip some people thrive on (in Austria, I have to admit, that much practiced, primitive pastime flourishes—yes, there, too).

Upstairs, Sigrid lay ready, changed already into her pink candy-striped pajamas, waiting expectantly in her bed to hear what Monika had to say.

"Shoot, what happened? Tell me about your Kuwaiti. Do you know anything about Kuwait?"

"*My* Kuwaiti? Kuwait? Never heard of it!" said Monika. "Saudi Arabia is the only Arab country I know anything of, thanks to Lawrence of Arabia. Listen, you German miss, I have only one statement to make. I can have a couple of boys waiting on each finger, but one like *that* I wouldn't want on my little toe, *capito*? And will you please change the subject now!"

"All right, all right. Don't get so agitated! Take it easy. Can I have just one more say?" asked Sigrid timidly.

Not to annoy her roommate any more, Monika gave her permission. "All right, go ahead," she said.

"I know what your opinion is of Abdulla, but I think you two make a handsome couple, him dark, you blonde. You both laugh and joke a lot. You're quite bubbly and mischievous, you know. Also, his size matches yours perfectly, and with that flair and know-how about fashion that you have, he could be transformed into a most handsome prince. Besides he seems to be very well heeled. And that he fancies you, well, as soon as he set eyes on you, that stuck out for everyone for miles on end to see!"

Sigrid had just made the statement of the year. Quickly gripping a pillow and then another from underneath an outstretched, relaxing Sigrid, Monika chucked it back at her with the words, "He's *arabisch*, don't forget, and you're crazy!" With that and her red cotton nightie, Monika disappeared into the adjoining bathroom.

On the next day at 3 pm, Monika sat like a good girl in her English class, not giving the waiting Abdulla another thought. The subject Abdulla was closed and forgotten for her. A couple of weeks later, on their way to the local shops, down Oxford's High Street, a chic motor scooter came hooting alongside the pavement to a sudden halt. On it sat a tight-jeaned, open-shirted Abdulla, sleeves rolled up, with a dark blue sweater loosely tied over his shoulders. On his feet he wore white sandals, and nothing remained of his scarecrowy past. He called Sigrid to come over to him, while Monika got tit for tat. In great contrast to their first meeting, today she was thin air for him. Yes, she deserved the slight and knew it—but she did not like being ignored! He gunned his motor to roar out of sight again. Now that was showing off!

Sigrid came back to a patiently waiting Moni and explained, "Abdulla just stopped to say hello."

"Nothing else? Did he mention me at all?" Moni wanted to know.

"No, he did not. Why? Did you expect anything else? Maybe a Thank you very much for letting me down? So lousy. When can we repeat that lovely, exciting experience again?"

"Oh, no, Sigi, not at all. I couldn't care less," lied Monika with hurt pride. No one had ever ignored her like that in the outside world. It did bother her. The way Abdulla had presented himself today and treated her somehow triggered something off, but Sigi didn't have to know that, did she now? Personal things, like this, one had to keep to oneself. And quite rightly, too.

The by now very-well-known-film *Some Like it Hot* with Marilyn Monroe was at the local cinema for the second week running. The girls had seen it twice already, but Monika came to see it a third time alone. On her exit after the 6:30 performance and into the noisy, lit up street, who but Abdulla had to catch her eye, leaning casually over his scooter, talking to a bunch of similar-aged students. He, too, had noticed her, and then looked away. Swallowing her pride, she dropped a quick "Hello, Abdulla" as she swept past him. He barely registered a look at her and, without a syllable in reply, carried on his conversation in (was it?) Arabic, for they did more shouting than talking.

Am I not a silly, silly goat! Why did I have to speak to him now! What kind of impulse on earth made me do that? She scalded herself with regret and remorse while walking home, heart pounding, away from the scene of self-inflicted humiliation. Sunk deep in her thoughts, she all at once realized she was hearing Abdulla's scooter drawing close behind her. She knew she was smiling. She felt relieved: the best medicine for that wounded ego was on its way.

"How about a lift?" offered Abdulla seconds later.

Trying hard to sound surprised, cool, and collected, her reply came: "Do you think that's a good idea?"

"Miss Austria, the best we ever had. Come on."

"Okay, but just keep in mind, whatever happens, it was *your* idea." She played it cool. Her mother came to mind again. With mixed feelings of right and wrong, but at the same time free and happy and suddenly without a care in the world, Monika stepped towards the little, midnight blue roarer.

Unaware of her destiny, Monika was now well on her way towards finding out the truth of what it's all about with people like Abdulla—finding out by herself, on her own. And good luck to her. Don't you think she might need it? That lift lasted, would you believe it, until 3 am the next morning. First, he talked her into visiting a lovely, old-fashioned, Shakespearian-type pub, one of Abdulla's habitual haunts, where his personal beer glass, engraved with sexy nude ladies and his name, stood in wait.

That he more than enjoyed his drink did not slip past her unnoticed. She even put her foot down once, rather cheekily. He wanted another drink. She thought he had had more than enough, and she won. He gave in gladly, more or less to please her really. A little bit tipsy, they strolled alongside the good old river Isis where they talked, joked, and laughed, and she almost had an accident. It was misty and quite dark. She could not much longer hold it, so she dared to go for a quick pee-pee a couple of feet down the embankment. As she sat in that awkward position to finish what she had started, the rubber soles slowly but surely (wet grass tickling bum) slid down towards the water on the slippery grass. She had to make a quick decision: fall in, can't swim, or give Abdulla the pleasure of seeing her in utter disgrace with panties way down at half mast. With a loud voice, she pleaded, "Abdulla, quick, help!"

Abdulla wasted no time running to her rescue, joking, "Has a froggie bit your bottie?"

"Bottie, froggie, pull me up, please." And saying, "Help a damsel in distress," she jokingly covered her shame. Abdulla's infectious laugh and the two gin and tonics she had just consumed helped her to overcome the awkward situation, especially when he stated the case as he saw it:

"Austrians are strange people. Where are their morals? They don't give goodnight kisses, but go straight for a nitty-gritty striptease. No, thank you very kindly, pull your pants back up please. Maybe at a later date I'll consider that offer but not tonight. Thanks for the thought, anyway." He tried his best to make her feel at ease in such a tricky situation. Slowly she took a liking to his style. It fascinated her in contrast to the European boys' behavior. The boys she knew about in Vienna usually bragged, acted unnatural, and sometimes used foul language to appear grown-up and impress the girls. Not so Abdulla. He seemed so natural, so down to earth, and soon she began to feel comfortable and safe in his company.

Having gotten humorously over that little incident, she asked for and he told her the meaning of "as well," but in return she had to promise to remember him whenever she heard or used that phrase from then on. She promised to. Always.

Her short past was of great interest to him. That her father and mother were dentists surprised him; his own mother could neither read nor write. Soon, in return, his life story was well on its way, too, a story she thought much more interesting than her own. She was all ears.

His three sisters—Diba, Sabiha, and Tamader—and their mother, a kind lady, were in deep mourning at the moment, for his unfortunate, beloved father had died most tragically only a month ago at the young age of about thirty-eight: about thirty-eight because neither father nor Abdulla himself knew their exact dates of birth. Everywhere in Kuwait at that time, long before oil—Kuwait's black gold as they called it— changed everything drastically, childbirth was very much a family affair.

At the time of Abdulla's birth there was only one hospital (that was managed by the English mostly for the English) and only one doctor in the whole of Kuwait, and native Kuwaitis were afraid and suspicious of both. According to traditional practice, Kuwaiti women helped each other at childbirth. Abdulla had arrived quickly and unexpectedly into this world on the kitchen floor, just as his mother was about to dish out the lunchtime rice on a big tray. Immediately after his birth, Abdulla was put down on a straw mat, very much like Jesus Christ, with one exception. To Jesus came three Wise Men; Abdulla's visitor was a beastly wild cat that wanted to make a meal of him. Of course, he was saved just in the nick of time, as in fairy tales with a happy ending. All his dear mother could remember about the day of his birth was, he said, the kitchen, the cat, and the weather: it was raining cats and dogs, a very wet time, most unusual for Kuwait, where it is usually 50° C in the shade and 80-100° C in the sun and where it is very, very dry most of the year around.

Mr. al-Amahani, Abdulla's father, a liver-diseased near-alcoholic, had ignored doctor's orders and advice never to touch alcohol again under any circumstances. He was warned well in advance of the possible, instant, acute, even deadly consequences, but in vain, so he had finally caused his own death. What an unnecessary tragedy for the whole family. Monika felt goose pimples coming up, as always when she heard of someone's death, although she herself was not afraid of dying, as some of her friends were. But this tasted of all the sadness, grief, and general darkness that reared its ugly head with any death.

"Abdulla, don't you think you're taking a path in the same direction as your father? You *do* like your alcohol, too. That you can't deny. You swallowed three pints in no time and even wanted more. Remember, the apple does not fall far from its tree."

"Come on, you must be joking, Monika! Today I celebrate your pleasant company."

"Yes, yes, Abdulla, sure, and snakes have armpits. Anyway, sorry for interrupting. Please, do carry on."

British people working in Kuwait were allowed a monthly ration of alcohol that, like most goods, came from Europe by ship to Kuwait's harbor, where Abdulla's father was in charge and checked the crates personally for any broken bottles. So, more often than not, he would write off a greater number than actually arrived damaged—for his own and his friends' consumption. The Holy Koran rules as law in Kuwait and keeps old customs alive. No alcohol for Muslims is a strict rule, a rule to be obeyed. Yet Mr. al-Amahani ignored religion and the law in favor of getting hooked on the (for him) deadly poison.

So now Abdulla, an only son, had become the head of his household, according to Islamic law. Of course, for the time being, until Abdulla returned home from Great Britain, his uncle Khaled was in charge of administering Abdulla's and his family's inheritance, a most considerable fortune, as his father had died a rich merchant.

Women—wives, mothers, sisters—have nothing much to say in Kuwait. They have kitchen, children, and each other for company. It's really very much a man's world, Abdulla explained. "Our women's first concern above everything else is her man, her master's comfort and well being when he is at home. In bed, too, she must be willing at all times, unless she can prove it's her period time. We might be old fashioned compared to European standards, just as I found it strange, very pleasantly strange, mind you, to mix and study as a male with females here in England."

"You and I, we really are worlds apart, Mr. Arabisch. Thank God I was born in Europe," said Monika. Now, even as they spoke, Abdulla's poor mother was obeying the Holy Koran locked in her room, confined to three months of solitude after her husband's death. Speaking to male members, even to male servants of the family, was allowed only through the keyhole, Abdulla said. Such austere precautions were taken after a woman's husband passed on to make it impossible for a widow to conceive an illegitimate son who could then still carry her dead spouse's name and with it the rights to his inheritance. If, for example, a widow has no children or girls only, with the exception of a small percentage, all of the deceased's worldly goods go to the dead husband's brother; and if the deceased has no brother, to the next male in charge within his family; and the widow, with or without daughters, is now at her in-law's mercy, which always causes family feuds. Of course, if there is a male heir, a son, nobody can touch a penny. So it would not be surprising that such an unfortunate widow, one without a son or perhaps any children at all, might be tempted to fornicate quickly with a suitable sperm donor to save her own skin and be allowed to keep on living in her house and not be sent, exactly like a divorced (and thus disgraced) Kuwaiti woman, back to her parents. A divorced Kuwaiti woman is regarded about the same as a prostitute.

"But, you know, Abdulla, if you think a bit deeper, who could blame such an unlucky woman? And, tell me, why does your mother obey such rules? She has got you, a son, as an heir."

"Sure, but there are other reasons, too. Son or no son, every widow has to follow our traditional customs under Islam's rules. As our marriages are arranged by parents, not every wife loves her husband. Some are happy he is dead and gone. Others' husbands might have been ill for a long time, and their wives could be sex starved, frustrated. And there are other reasons, too. It is all in the Holy Koran."

"Good God, Abdulla, what extraordinary, strange customs! Being a woman in your country does not seem to be much fun. It sounds to me like women exist merely to serve their men and only the men do the living. You said women wear long, black robes and cover themselves from head to toe on leaving the house, in the car, in shops. Men must not see them uncovered at any time, only their husbands?"

"Yes, but younger people like my sisters cover only if they go out and are not dressed properly. My mother, of course, does wear the black *abaya,* as it is called. Should she be seen without it, all of our small Kuwait would know within a couple of hours. Such news and all gossip travel like fire; her good reputation would be ruined. She is a widow now and an older woman, you see."

"Well, Abdulla, my sympathy is definitely with your mother, and indeed with all the women of your country."

"It's difficult for me to give you a clear picture. Every day there are changes for the better. Kuwait becomes more civilized and modernized by the hour and much freer, like Europe, really. The very old is holding hands with the very new. Whenever I fly home for a holiday, I lose my way on new roads all over Kuwait. New high buildings are shooting up. It becomes less and less the Kuwait I left a couple of years ago. Do you believe that?"

"Yes, well, I want to say something else, Abdulla. As a Muslim man, according to your Holy Koran, what have you to fulfill that will be of interest to me? Can you give me an example?"

"Let me think. I am not supposed to touch alcohol, yet as you already know I drink. I am supposed not to eat pork. I dearly love my eggs and bacon in the mornings and another thing will surprise you: I am allowed to marry four wives but personally have no intention of taking even two. I will choose only one, like my father. You see he had only my mother, but always kept a couple on the side, a bit of crumpet, as the English say."

"What do you mean—crumpet? That hot bread my landlady gives me for tea?"

"Forget it, not crumpet, no! I mean girlfriends. It always hurts my mother deeply. She endured that rather than let him bring home a concubine. Never, ever, will I be unfaithful once I am married. I made that promise to myself whenever I saw my mother suffer—which was all the time."

"Bravo, bravo, Abdulla! Can you really make such a sacrifice?" Monika laughed.

"No, no, not at all. Don't laugh. Let me tell you. My uncle, for instance, has two wives, two houses, two cooks, two cars, two chauffeurs, always two of each. If he is ill, the doctor has to prescribe for him two lots of medicine. Had he four wives, everything would need to come or be bought in fours. Whatever one wife gets or asks for, number two has to get, not smaller—and in the same color. The Holy Koran says you only take more than one wife if you can love and provide for them equally."

"Abdulla, that is impossible. Aren't they all in a harem?"

"No, our government gives a man as many houses as he has wives, and every Kuwaiti male has the same rights. Our government is second to none, and I am very proud to be a Kuwaiti. My uncle's second wife came as a gift from a friend he once helped through a tricky situation. That friend said 'Thank You' with his daughter, a great honor that he had to accept, maybe even gladly, for she is very, very young. She could have been his daughter."

"I don't believe this! Is that possible?"

"I know our customs are a bit of a mystery here in the West. My future wife will be Arabic but definitely not from Kuwait. Our own girls are so childish and spoilt. I will choose one from Bahrain or Egypt, maybe Lebanon. They are more civilized and more ladylike."

"What! You just go there, like shopping, and get one? What about love? How do you know a girl chosen like this will really want and love you and vice versa?"

"Well, you see, this does not matter so much. There is always somebody who knows somebody back home in the other country. With all the foreigners we have in Kuwait, it is really very easy. If I speak to an Egyptian doctor today, within a week I have a fair choice of photographs of eligible girls, the prettiest girls to choose from, and they kiss our feet to marry them. Believe it or not, our surrounding, neighboring Arabic countries believe money grows on trees and streets are paved with gold in Kuwait, and as for love, well, we have a saying: 'When you start eating the soup it is hot, and the more you eat the colder it gets.' Marriage is like that."

"No, no, not if one marries for love, someone you are in love with," protested Monika. "I will only marry when I am hopelessly in love. That is something I know for sure."

"Who knows, maybe I will too. I never felt such love as you are talking about," answered Abdulla.

"Neither have I, wise guy, but I know it is coming for all of us, and I am quite willing to wait for it. I have read once that within a normal life span the opportunity to fall in love with the right person presents itself seven times over."

"Miss Pavlik, where did you read that, on some toilet paper?"

"No, in an Arabisch magazine, Mr. Amahani."

Abdulla stopped and reached for her hand. She didn't object, so walking hand in hand, he continued: "My country is very, very rich. Our government pays for my education and for that of all Kuwait's male students. We can choose freely what we want to study and in which country abroad. Accommodation, food, clothes are lavished on us in double the amount our European student friends have to manage on."

Monika noticed Abdulla always referred to the Holy Koran in his narrations. The Holy Koran said so, and Muslims lived accordingly.

Well, Abdulla not only looked different, he came from a land greatly different from hers. He was one of the first Kuwaitis to study medicine and was slated to accept, once qualified, a top position in a newly built, hyper-modern hospital in Kuwait, a post that was now occupied by a foreigner—a non-Kuwaiti.

Slowly digesting the time she'd spent with Abdulla that night and into the morning, Monika lay awake in her bed for half an hour or so before the sandman came.

Eager to share everything down to the smallest detail with Sigi the next morning, she'd even tell her that this time she had given Abdulla a goodnight kiss on the cheek. He hadn't had to ask for it. And she had another date fixed, without delay, for the next day.

Monika and Abdulla saw a lot of each other, whenever possible. He would pick her up and drop her back home again on his little, handy scooter, on which dangled two big "Learner"-plates. He drove without a regular driving license because he had failed his test three times already—golly, *three* times! He didn't look *that* stupid, so why hadn't he passed? Oxford police knew him well. He was always being stopped for carrying passengers without a permit, which is an offence in England, Abdulla explained.

"I would have my license by now if I were British. English people do not like colored foreigners like me. That's why they give me such trouble to pass, and they're very rude to me, too. We in Kuwait treat foreigners with respect. I wish they would do the same over here," he complained—often.

Having first removed the L-plates, Monika sat pillion on the lookout for bobbies to avoid possible fines. Sometimes they were lucky, other times caught—like the time Abdulla shouted, "Police," gunned the engine, and spun in circles, sliding in wet rubble. A second later two arses were forced to kiss the road. Still, happy to get away with only torn trousers (Abdulla) and grazed skin and torn stockings (Monika), they got up to retrieve the scooter that had independently spun across the road in the opposite direction. By then, of course, the policemen had caught up.

"Mr. Amahani, have you got your license yet?"

"No, Sir."

"Then, tell me, when do you intend to start respecting our law?"

Fined for everything in the book and a couple of 'Yes, Sirs, No, Sirs' later, they walked away with Abdulla pushing the motorbike—but only out of the bobby's sight and around the corner, where they climbed back on and were off again. Finally, Abdulla requested from Kuwait and received an international license for motorbikes, cars, and lorries, too, without as much as passing a fart. That's one of the great privileges a Kuwaiti has in his country. Great! Monika began to see why he was so proud to be a Kuwaiti.

Slowly Monika and Abdulla, two complete opposites, began to more than like each other's company. Their meetings became highlights, with Mother Nature throwing plenty of spices into the young couple's slowly growing love, the sort of love that makes the world go round. Many refusals later, and wondering why on earth not, Monika, no prude, let experienced Abdulla, coupled with her own healthy and natural instincts, lead her on a mind-blowing sex carouse! Convents, taboos melted away, evaporating fast, and another one of life's great mysteries was most pleasantly solved.

And there was dancing. Friday, Saturday evenings were rock-'n-rolled away—all night. Both good dancers, Monika and Abdulla choreographed their own dance routines in private, ending up occasionally as the last solo couple on the actual dance floor.

Thanks to Monika, our Abdulla was now always smartly dressed, changed his underwear daily, and no longer dipped his fingers in his food by holding his knife and fork too short. He became very proud of his blonde girlfriend. His American ex-girlfriend, Carol, wrote to him to say, 'Your new girlfriend might be prettier to look at, but no way can she beat me in bed!'—or words to that effect. She was, of course, damned right, and Monika was blessed not to be like her in bed, or anyone else for that matter. For when Abdulla took Carol to the cinema, for example, they would always have to sit in the last row. Carol wanted or needed to be sexually satisfied at least three times during a film! Besides, she already had six abortions behind her at the tender age of twenty-two. Even for Abdulla, blessed with a strong and healthy sex drive, Carol became in the long run too much. Sigi was triumphant:

"Didn't I *say* you two fit like flowers in a vase! You better listen to me in the future. I am the one who saw it all coming. Will the wedding be in Austria or Kuwait? Am I invited? I was right the first time and will be again!"

"Yes, sure, Sigi. Belt up!"

"Monika, you should be able to see your eyes—your whole face—when you speak about Abdulla! And, come to think of it, that's all you speak about lately!"

Abdulla turned out to be one of the kindest, most generous, funniest human beings Monika had yet known. She knew and felt he cared for her a great deal. He always wanted to buy her things, yet she never accepted any of his offers, apart from cigarettes or fruits. She had started the silly habit of smoking along with others to be oh so cool, in Oxford . . .

And while we are talking about silly habits, let me tell you that soon Monika's pet hate became Abdulla's silly habit of drinking too much alcohol too often. He just could *not* stop once he had started, and the following day instead of seeing his private tutors or going to college, he would lie in his bed snoring away the whole morning—something Monika could not understand, nor accept. Her own father would pay for her education until she was 21. She greatly appreciated it and gave her best. Yet, Abdulla, for whom everything was laid on by his Government, made such little effort. He would meet his Iraqi, Kuwaiti, Persian friends in some pub. Come closing time—11 pm—they would all make their way to one of the students' rooms for a friendly poker game that lasted well into the early hours of the next day. Abdulla, a clever poker player and an excellent, fast bluffer, usually won, too. But his studies suffered, and while his friends would drink four pints still knowing what was going on, Abdulla started to be hyper after two. Once he lifted Monika's skirt up high, revealing her black panties and suspenders—an action that both shocked and surprised her, for his act was in great contrast to his wish that she not wear short, see-through, cut-out, or revealing clothes when in his company. It was that invisible ghost's fault hidden in that pint he drank that was playing havoc with his brains. Next day, he would hardly remember any of what had happened the night before, and he would swear on his mother's life he would not do it again. He might have really meant it, yet he never kept his promise. He drank again and again. "Even if I fail my exams, I'm in no hurry to go back home. My Government's paying for me. I will take exams until I pass."

The time came when Monika just couldn't watch him anymore. Out of five days, he slept three mornings away. Neither was she willing any longer to go around Oxford's pubs with him half cut, talking rubbish, and making a fool of himself—and, more often now, of her, too. So Miss Aries gave him options and firmly stuck to her resolve: "If you don't stop that drinking and don't attend to your waiting professors regularly from now on, I don't want to see or know you anymore." Surprised by the power she had, she found it worked. She took telephone numbers to check, and he changed drastically for the better, without cheating. Instead of card games and going for drinks, they now took long walks, went to the cinema, or drove out of Oxford, just for the ride, to have coffee and a doughnut somewhere on the way, or picnicked on a canoe with Abdulla rowing frantically—except for weekends, when he was free to quench his alcoholic thirst, all according to agreement.

Always ready for mischievous pranks, Abdulla would make bets with his Kuwaiti friends as to which of them would make a newly arrived Kuwaiti student eat pork or drink alcohol first. To eat the forbidden pork, the unsuspecting victim would be invited to a Chinese restaurant where dishes are chosen by numbers, to eat sweet and sour pork but told it was the best beef near or far. Once it was eaten and paid for, the poor skins were told what they had *really* consumed. Their faces should be seen! Some got mad. Others ran to the toilet or outside to throw up straight away. Girls, they were told, didn't go out with boys who didn't drink. So, of course, fresh from celibate Kuwait, sex-starved as they were, very little pursuing was needed. While his attention was distracted, someone would constantly top up the poor devil's glass until, well and truly intoxicated, he couldn't stand upright at all. Afterwards, the victims always saw the funny side of it. Yes, Abdulla was certainly no child of sad parents. He saw to it that Monika and his friends had masses of fun. The action always was where Abdulla was. Young and old took to him, without exception. Everybody liked Abdulla, who always gave freely because he wanted to and with an open heart, certainly never to get anything in return.

Alcohol now under control, Monika had a near Mr. Perfect and was at peace with herself and the world. She liked and admired him most when he let loose some of his jokes. He knew so many and knew how to tell them in a most entertaining manner. Not to mention music—that was another talent of his. He played flute, guitar, and the Arabic instrument the lute. Now, let's stop here, before she makes a saint of him . . .

With end of term nearing everybody would soon be on his or her way home. Sigi and Moni promised to write always. Abdulla, who had to resume studies in Oxford, said he would come to visit Monika in Vienna whenever an opportunity arose from now on, to keep in close contact. He had to go to Kuwait to sort out family business after his father's death. His return ticket was already booked by his Embassy. As it came down to the last 5, 4, 3 dates, it became increasingly difficult for both to part for good. "Why can't you try to stay a little longer?" begged Abdulla, until Monika thought, "Oh, what the heck, my beauty school can wait! I'll register for another term in Oxford. I'll wait right here for Abdulla to come back. My English could be much better anyway." Overjoyed to hear of her last minute decision, Abdulla picked her up and danced her around the floor. The idea of her going away had really upset him. Once it had even made him cry helplessly. Monika had been by no means less sorry to go, just a bit stronger, keeping her emotions well in check.

Now Abdulla was gone. Before leaving he had presented Monika with a cute, fluffy, little teddy bear that was christened "As Well" to take his place. Monika—unable to wait around for Abdulla doing nothing—went along with some other students to the local Labor Exchange for a summer job that took her to Oxford's Ratcliffe Hospital where, dressed in a crisp uniform and topped with a little white cap, she assisted nurses by dishing out food to patients in Ward 5.

Abdulla interrupted his flight home by stopping in Vienna to pay Monika's mother, Dentist Pavlik, a short visit. Anxious EXPRESS letters bombarded Monika from then on! "Is *this* the same boy you have sent me photographs of?" her mother wanted to know. "But he doesn't *look* Arabic in the photos." He couldn't have, of course, for Monika had sent her Mother black and white pictures (he wasn't that dark anyway). Dentist Pavlik asked, Did Monika *know* that Abdulla came from that country Kuwait, home to the sheikh who had recently married a German girl called Heidi? The sheikh communicated with Heidi through an interpreter! Did Monika know that that sheikh had stayed with Heidi for just two weeks and then had taken off, never to be seen or heard from again? Did Monika know that the girl's mother had to get a lawyer to secure the girl's rights and procure a divorce? The story had made the headlines in Europe's papers for weeks on end.

As fond as Monika was of lovable Abdulla, marriage had never entered her brain, not for an instant, not a single iota. He was just her first boyfriend—with more to come. After all, nobody stuck with number one. And to put Mother at ease, she told her so. We are just boyfriend, girlfriend, rather fond of each other, but nobody is getting married, I promise, she wrote back. Trying to convince Mother was fruitless. Letters, 10 to 16 typewritten pages long, plus pamphlets from the German and Austrian Embassies full of warnings against Arabs or Iranian men, reached Monika. Beware, it said at the end in full black block letters: once you are in a Muslim country no embassy has the power to help you. If anything goes wrong for you, you will be totally alone and helpless without aid from the outside. Mother's mail was not even read properly and found its way straight into the dustbin. Not so Abdulla's letters! Those she read a couple of times, and sometimes as many as three a day would arrive. In them were photographs of his car, his house, and some scenery of Kuwait. In each and every letter he pleaded, 'Please don't disappear, wait for me!' Exotic presents straight out of 1001 Nights arrived from Kuwait and took Monika by surprise: a most unusually shaped and imprinted camel-skin handbag, a golden bracelet watch with a diamond-studded cover, three wooden carved camels held together by a chain, and a silk scarf portraying belly dancers were some of the presents Abdulla lavished on her as—quite unexpectedly, out of the blue—he stood once again in her field of vision.

"Jesus Christ, Abdulla, how on earth did you do that?" she gasped. "Only this morning I received two letters from you."

"Have you ever heard of magic, oriental flying carpets, my darling? Your sweetie is back, as you see. Don't tell me you don't like surprises!"

Monika's favorite cartoon character was a cute yellow birdie called 'Tweety Pie.' Somehow it became habit. They called each other Sweetie, with an S.

Back in Abdulla's lodgings, both of them parched for lack of Amore, they did of course, first, what comes naturally, again and again, until well and truly physically worn out, exhausted, but feeling so much the better for it. Next, Abdulla had to tell her so much of what was going on back home. With coffee, beer, tea, pistachio nuts from Kuwait, gin and tonics, they kept mind and body awake well into the early hours. What fascinated Monika the most about Abdulla's recent experience back in Kuwait was hearing how his mother, according to custom, kept on the look-out for a suitable bride for—guess who?—Abdulla. As he was just about to jump into bed one night, his mother approached him with a pack of photographs of eligible girls she had collected so he could in privacy choose from among them. With each picture he was given to view, his mother offered a running commentary, saying something like, "This is Bedria. She goes to secondary school with your sister Sabiha. Her brother is married to the daughter of the Kuwaiti Ambassador in Lebanon. Her father is a merchant. The long, tall gray building on the right side of Fahad-al-Salim Street belongs to him, too. And you should see the house they live in! It is a palace clad in pink marble. They have servants crawling like ants all over the place. Last month, I was invited to a wedding and sat next to his wife. She was dripping in diamonds as big as pigeon eggs." Next came the picture of Hossa: "Now, *this* girl is an only daughter. Her three brothers study abroad like you. One, architecture in Britain, and the twins, Bader and Khaled, are in America. One is training to be a pilot. The other one studies something to do with plants." "That's agriculture, Mother." "Yes, well, whatever, her father, a good friend of your father, God let him rest in peace, imports cars from America. Her mother's sister is married to Sheik Mohammad. Our Government's Ministry of Planning has just bought a big piece of land near the sea from them at 12 million Kuwaiti Dinars, so people say. And on top of all this, they have three villas in the mountains of Lebanon. If you take her, your sisters and I, we would all have access to everything, too, so choose wisely, my son." In such manner did the mother and son sift through the photographs, but to Mother's great disappointment, without result.

    Almost all marriages were arranged this way. Abdulla's mother could well afford to be choosy and go for what she thought of as the best: Kuwait's *crème de la crème* for her only son—one of the first Kuwaiti's to study medicine abroad—would soon return to Kuwait and be sitting in a well-paid, top position with the Government. Most Kuwaitis were wealthy, but to hold a high position with the *Government*, well that was out of the ordinary, top priority! Which in-laws would not want such a son-in-law?

"I didn't tell my mother you came along and upset that apple cart, and that none of them equals you," he said to Monika, kissing her on the lips so that it hurt. "I don't want any of them, to tell you the truth. I didn't dare tell my mother that. She would have been extremely disappointed. I just let her believe that I'm not ready yet."

"Look here, Abdulla, let's be straight with each other. We are not partners for life. We never talked about marriage. And I have never thought about it. Not with you, nor anybody else either. All I know is that it won't be for a long, long time to come yet—if it ever happens. I want to travel, see the world, get to know lots and lots of interesting people like yourself and own my own little beauty shop first."

"No no," said Abdulla, "neither do I. But we stay together for now, don't we?"

"Yes, for one more semester without plans for a possible future marriage. I would really love to visit Kuwait once, but not live forever in a country where presumably foxes say goodnight. Do you quite understand, Abdulla? We will always stay good friends, for life. Come on now, don't sulk. I can tell, looking at your face, you're offended. Cheer up. It's not the end of the world, Sweetie. You're a super guy, Abdulla, and as I explained to you, it's nothing personal."

"I realized away from you in Kuwait just how much I care for you, Monika. You're my one and only, Monika. Like my heartbeat, you belong to me!"

"Let's not talk about it anymore. Sponge over it."

He sealed it all with a kiss as they started to make love again vigorously. This time Monika—too young, immature, and inexperienced—knew damn well what she wanted, but went about it the wrong way. Someone should have advised her and told her so. Why stay on any longer in Oxford after knowing Abdulla for four months if she had no intention of staying with him forever? This way their relationship would only deepen, something she did not want to happen, but happened anyway, of course.

Abdulla knew that what he wanted was Monika and talked about it at every opportunity. "You'll be dressed in designer clothes from Paris. My father left me plenty of money. You'll have lots of expensive jewelry. You're going to love all that. I'll make you Sophia Loren the Second! We build our own house entirely to you taste. And you won't need to lift a finger. Servants, cooks, chauffeurs, and a maid will all be laid on for you, my darling Sweetie." It was well meant and sounded honest, but it was not what Monika would ever want to marry for. Marriage, she imagined, would be much more mind-blowing, something that was far away out of sight right now. She loved Abdulla's company, liked to be with him all the time. Couldn't he leave things as they were now? Marriage, she had to laugh, was far out. She didn't want to stop here in life. With sayings such as "My mother and sisters will love you and adore you," he tried to win her over again and again.

"Oh, Abdulla, didn't you say you could not mention me to your mother, as I would be a great disappointment to her? How, then, is she going to accept me? Ever thought about that one?"

"Once we're married, she *has* to love you. She will have no choice."

"Abdulla, love by force never grows old, Sweetie. Your mother, sisters are none of my problem nor business. We are talking about you and me."

Monika was soon at her wits end. On the one side was Abdulla, weaving a web, and his much more frequent, unaccounted for bouts of jealousy and using her "no" to marriage as an excuse to go back to alcohol any time he felt like it. "You are playing with my feelings"—it was now *her* fault that he drank. If she loved him, she would say "yes" and he would stop straight away. On the other hand, her mother suspected something was going on and used a bit of blackmail to coerce her back to Vienna where she belonged. Father had already decided. He would no longer finance costly courses at Oxford with a place vacant at beauty school waiting to be filled by Monika, as planned well in advance. Monika found herself in a Catch 22 situation. She now had to make her life's first big decision and made a bloody mess of it. She saw the light in time, yes—yet did not heed it.

She lived to regret it instead.

At 3 pm on the day of her enlightenment, she had a date. Abdulla was to take her rowing. She brought along some salmon and cucumber sandwiches, a bottle of Liebfraumilch, and a box of Maltesers, her favorite chocolates. The girl's mind was sternly made up. Today she would tell Abdulla she had finally decided to go home and see to her career. Up to now she had been a mere nobody and nothing, while everyone around her, as indeed Abdulla himself, was progressing. But she hadn't counted on poor Abdulla's reaction. He just could not take it in.

"I can't think of another man kissing and touching you, making love to you! You belong to *me*." He cried and cried. She had never seen him in such a state! And it was all her fault. He really was breaking her heart.

She *did* love him and could no longer see him suffer, so she lied. Taking his head between her hands, kissing away his tears, she said, "Who is a silly billy then? Can't you tell I'm only playing a game? It's all a joke. I'm not going anywhere. I stay right here with my Sweetie. That was just a test. I wanted to know how much you really love me. You know that I have been to drama school. I would have made a pretty good actress, do you agree? How many points to I get out of 10, then?"

"Sweetie, you gave me the shock of my life! Never *ever* do something like this again!" He took her hand. "Feel my heart. Can you feel it pumping?" Yes, she could. Instead of rowing they went to his place to make up and make love. Still in bed, he presented her with a little red velvet box. In it was the most amazing, pyramid-shaped red-gold ring encrusted with gray-bluey-pink shimmering pearls. "This is your engagement ring, my Sweetie. I bought it for you in Kuwait, just waiting for the right moment to present it to you. Now is God's sent time. Today we tell our friends and on Saturday we celebrate. I'll arrange a party," he glowed, looking expectantly at Monika, who—still sitting on his bed in her black underwear, blonde hair untidily falling over her breasts, looking a pretty picture—hadn't said a word yet and was flabbergasted. So he had had the engagement ring, as he called it, hidden for well over two months now since he had come back from Kuwait and was just waiting for the right time! Poor sweetie. Come to think of it, he was the only human being who really loved her and that she could count on in the whole world. *He* was the somebody who unselfishly loved her! She slipped the ring on her ring finger. It was a perfect fit.

She had never seen such a ring or anything like it before—not what one would call an engagement ring, but a valuable dress ring all the same. "I suppose he doesn't understand," went through her mind, and the next thing the realization: "Oh *no!*"—recalling now what she had heard her mother say: "Pearls bring tears. If a lady desires pearls, she wisely buys them herself. Pearls given as a gift are always tears in disguise." And for me it wasn't just a gift, but my engagement ring! Surely that's only an old wives' tale! How can something so beautiful be unlucky? With that Monika dismissed all negative thoughts—and Abdulla finally had his sweetie where he wanted her, busily planning well into the future now.

She went along for better or worse, having let him make this important decision for her. What a pity. She knew deep in her heart it was not what she wanted but was too weak or did not know how to deal with the moment and go about so important an issue in the proper manner. Being weak would be much nearer the truth. At such a stage in life a youngster should be able to discuss problems and anxieties with parents or, next in line, with relatives or older friends. To whom could

Monika have turned? Yes, exactly, 00. Nor did she miss what she had never had.

Out of the blue, Abdulla was informed that he had a hospital position in Canterbury, Kent. "Sweetie, I am not going without you. Come with me," was his first reaction.

"Of course, I'll come."

"And what about your parents?" he wanted to know.

"I am over 18 now. Obeying-parents time is over and done with for me. I'll find something suitable to do in Canterbury."

"Yes, you can look after me!" enthused Abdulla, more than happy with the situation.

CHAPTER FOUR

LIVING TOGETHER IN CANTERBURY

Two rooms—Monika up, Abdulla downstairs—were chosen in a detached house in a Canterbury suburb, with a sweet, silver-haired old landlady, Mrs. Preston. Abdulla had plenty of money when Monika first met him, thanks to his father's support. With father gone, rosy financial times went, too. He had to manage on his grant. Spend-first-think-later Abdulla had to think first now. His and her money were put together and used wisely, with Monika in charge. Her good taste and know-how made friends and others believe the couple were rolling in money. Giving education the cold shoulder, Monika took a part-time job in a kindergarten, helping to feed little kiddies. She thoroughly enjoyed that pastime, and the money came in handy.

It could have been so perfect, but living so close together made Abdulla change his tune. Increasingly unreasonable jealousy, with silly arguments, crept into their relationship and overshadowed it. All of a sudden Monika's skirts, the same ones she had been wearing since she had met him, were too short. Crossing her legs in public, a habit that came naturally to her, was being done purposely with the intention of attracting men, and joking and laughing with Abdulla's friends was supposed to be a come-on signal. Things he had never objected to before became crimes, and at all times he had to know her exact whereabouts. Faithful as she was, she never gave him the slightest reason to be jealous, yet with the help of his old vice, a couple of pints later, he would start on her just for the sake of it. In Oxford, afraid to lose her, he had decreased his intake. Engaged now, living together, with everything going his way, he let himself go.

Monika was once again close to taking off. A late lecture at the hospital on a Friday evening ran on very, very late. Monika fell asleep before he got home. The next morning at 6 am she woke up bathed in a cold sweat. She had had a dream. She had dreamt that Abdulla was enjoying himself at a hospital dance where all of his attentions piloted towards a dark-haired girl, who soon sat on his knee and put her arms around his neck. His arms were around her waist and pressed her tightly close to his chest as they kissed. She saw a picture of a loving couple. She had them so close, yet could do nothing about it. Monika could see everything very clearly in her dream: chairs stood neatly around the dance floor, white tablecloths decorated with little vases. In them stood red carnations. And there on a chair sat her Abdulla in sweet harmony with another female. She couldn't wait for him to wake up.

"Did you enjoy the dance last night, Sweetie?" she reproached him as he came back from his morning leak.

"What! *Who* told you?" He was wide-awake at once.

"Told me what? That you danced last night and had that dark-haired girl on your knee kissing and squeezing? Don't worry, we'll come to that later, but first you confess to me, and do be careful not to leave out any details! I know everything, you see." She spoke with more self-confidence, knowing herself on the right track. Nevertheless, the revelation was a shock. How on earth was it possible? He had been dancing behind her back and she had actually dreamt it. Impossible! What was going on here?

Yes, Abdulla had joined the dance after his meeting (if he had ever had one!), the girl was a nurse that had had her eye on him for some time—so Abdulla's story. She asked him to join. He at first warded off her advances, telling her he was not free but engaged to be married and promised to introduce her to a good friend of his, a fellow Kuwaiti student. Now, what shocked Monika more, her dream being true or Abdulla's straying? She was in such a state and did not know quite what was what. And there was no way Abdulla believed her, that she had dreamt it all, even after she swore on all her family's death that she was telling the truth to Abdulla. What she had experienced was ESP, extra-sensory perception, something she had not known existed in this world but was to find out more about a couple of dreams and some years later.

Jealousy had always been a foreign word to Monika. She did not mind if Abdulla joked, danced, or laughed with girls. But it wasn't proper—what he had done that night. Still, she soon forgave him after he introduced the nurse in question to her, Pauline, who was going steady already with Abdulla's friend Fadel. Satisfied that he had told the truth, she soon dismissed the incident for what it was, a thoughtless slip, until not much later a more serious matter rocked their harmony and engagement.

With the last big money Abdulla had left from his now-dead father's generosity, Abdulla decided to invest in a second-hand car, a black Morris Minor that Monika kept spick-and-span inside and out. Liquid make-up, lashings of black Max Factor mascara, black eyeliner, a touch of ivy green eye shadow to bring out the green in her eyes, and we come close to Monika's daily morning face routine. She didn't use lipstick yet; therefore, to find the car's ashtray full of cigarette butts heavily coated in bright red lipstick, she naturally wondered whose they were, hoping for a harmless explanation. Maybe Abdulla gave a lift to some nurses, she calmed herself. But nurses don't wear lipstick. Definitely not that kind—at least not on duty, she remembered.

She held the ashtray well under his nose with a "Now, what's *this*, my Sweetie?"

"Oh!" he gasped, his face's expression changing to "she caught me." "I gave a lift to a girl."

"How silly of me—and I thought it was a boy! Here are at least 12 fag ends," she said with her greatly improved English. "You must have lost your way with her." After a while, shamefully, he confessed and shocked her with the truth:

"You know her, Sweetie. It was Sharon. It was the waitress from Cherry Pie." Cherry Pie was a coffee bar in Canterbury's High Street where they went often and met friends. The waitress in question happened to be a tarty looking girl with a deep sexy voice and a permanent stiff neck she always held to her right shoulder. "She stopped me in the High Street last night while waiting for a bus. She asked me for a light. So I gave her a lift. We talked. She put her arm round my neck and started kissing. Please believe me we only kissed! She's not my type for anything else. Please forgive me."

By this time Monika felt as if someone had poured a bucket of icy water over her and was heavily in tears. She never expected that of Abdulla, never *ever*. Chucking the ashtray at his feet, she told him, "Clean your own bloody car! No, better, let your Cherry Pie tart do it for you!" Running up to her room, she locked herself in and sat down to decide what to do next. She felt so lonely and let down. That surely was the biggest disappointment of her life. He was the only person she felt close to. She loved and so trusted him, even though he had become increasingly awkward of late, especially when he drank. Still, she always hoped quietly that he would change. The drinking she could deal with. But now *this*—other girls—no, *never*, she was much too proud. Abdulla did not deserve her. All of his Arabic friends were full of praise for Monika, asking if she didn't have a sister and where in Austria they could find another girl like her. It made Abdulla feel ten feet tall or jealous, depending on which mood he was in. Now was the grand finale, the end!

Under the nose of Mrs. Preston and with Abdulla knocking on her locked door, Monika threw her belongings into two suitcases without bothering to fold anything, which wasn't like her. But then, right now, she was in such a state and just wanted to be home, quick, home, away from Abdulla the louse! Unlocking the door, she made her way past Mr. A and Mrs. P down the stairs with the heavy cases, neither of them offering to help. Mrs. Preston, naturally anxious not to lose a good lodger, I suppose, supported Abdulla. In better control now, Monika got the luggage awkwardly in the car and spoke icily to Abdulla: "I'm going home. Take me to Dover."

"Sweetie, *please* don't go," pleaded a guilty Abdulla.

"Get lost! Abdulla from Kuwait can go around kissing girls and—me?—I am not allowed to cross my legs! You're jealous of everybody that breathes the same air as I do, and you say she is not your type? Am I sorry? And what if, suppose she is, your type? You are mentally deranged, off your trolley! Guys like you one can find on every corner. I'm really sorry for all the time I've wasted with you. My mother was right!" She pulled off that lovely ring she had so cherished and threw it in his pocket. She let loose: "Hold onto it. It may come in handy for your next victim. You are low on money now and might not be able to afford one so soon. Go ahead, start driving! Take me to Dover. I have paid, too, for the petrol. I'm not asking for a favor!"

A truly sorry, lip-shaking Abdulla sat in the car next to her but did not start it. "Sweetie, I swear on my mother's life, and on my father's grave, I will *never* look at another girl as long as I live, never *ever*. Please believe me and forgive me only one more time." He went on and on with all that familiar jazz. Monika now had Abdulla talking on one side and Mrs. Preston on the other. Both of them together, they managed to touch her soft nature and changed her mind. Her suitcases went back up the stairs, and with a wounded heart, she carried on as best she could. Here again it would have been nice to get some advice from a well-meaning person, someone who might have told her it's impossible to straighten a corkscrew! But would she have listened if she had gotten some good old-fashioned advice?

Life for Monika was no longer the bed of roses she had known—and had been content with—since she had left the convent. Lots of unsightly weeds had sprung up all around her.

The next unexpected major happening presented itself as a shock, though once she got over it, it became the most cherished experience of her life. Yes, as you well might have guessed: she found herself pregnant! Abdulla was solemnly in charge of pregnancy precautions. She took the pills, tablets, and whatever he suggested, for she thought him a medical student who knew about such things. She didn't think twice about it. Yet, he should have known better. The first symptoms of morning sickness told Mrs. Preston, herself a mother of six, that there was a newborn life on its way. The doctor only confirmed what Monika already knew and happily looked forward to, after coming to terms with things as they now stood.

Abdulla was scared his Embassy might find out about the situation, if not now, then later. Kuwaiti students were not allowed to get married to foreigners, nor to make babies, of course, especially not during the period of their studies abroad! Once qualified, however, they had complete freedom to marry whomever they wanted. But, should a student overlook this point, he or his family would have to repay every penny to the Government—every penny spent on him to the day!

So, along with keeping her sweet secret a secret, getting married was the next item on Monika's life's menu.

CHAPTER FIVE

NEWLYWEDS IN ENGLAND

Wedding rings were purchased out of Monika's finances and the Registrar made them Man and Wife, a legal couple, but not without first clarifying the fact to Monika that the man she wanted to marry was allowed, as a Muslim, to take four wives without asking her permission. And would she, knowing that, still want to go ahead with the ceremony? Yes? Was she quite sure? It was a little too late for such enlightenment. Her baby was on its way already, a development that could not be stopped now. Besides, Monika was determined to remain—always—Abdulla's only wife.

On her wedding day, Monika felt annoyed because Abdulla refused to wear the neatly laid out clothes she had prepared for him. Instead, he wore a white shirt with a visibly worn-out collar. So, she warned, "If you get married like this, then our future life together will be exactly like this, don't you know?"

"Rubbish," he warded off.

Keeping totally mum to her parents about baby and marriage, afraid that Father might cut off her allowance, Monika prepared herself to become the best mummy in the world. She loved children, but never in her whole life had she even held a baby in her arms. There was plenty to learn now.

Meanwhile, Abdulla had news from Kuwait. His youngest sister, Tamader, was coming to stay with him for a couple of months. It did not strike him as good news. "What on earth am I going to do with her here?" He was worried, but Monika encouraged him. "You can depend on me. It's okay. We two can easily manage a little girl. Oh, come on now, Abdulla. Besides, I'd love to meet your sister. She's only about twelve years old, isn't she? Don't let it grow into such a big problem. I shall look after her. I'll give up my job."

"But she must not find out that we are married, and definitely not a word about the baby to her," planned Abdulla, in a bad mood.

"Your family isn't the Government! So why aren't they to know?" asked Monika. He did not answer. She wasn't too inquisitive about it. Right now was not a good time to discuss such matters anyway. "I'll try to prevent her coming," were his last words that night.

But too late. The next day came a telegram with Tamader's flight number and arrival time. When the time came, Abdulla drove to Heathrow Airport and came back with a skinny, olive-skinned, cute little girl, who, except for the lovely long hair that reached well below her waist, could have been Abdulla's twin, so close was the resemblance of their faces. Her wrists were decorated with a dozen or so gold bangles, busily clicking away, and she had rings to match on her fingers. She gave a strong first impression of being a very lively girl, too, just like her brother.

"Meet my girlfriend Monika," was how Abdulla introduced his wife.

Tamader was learning English at school and spoke a fair amount. The first thing out of the ordinary that Monika noticed about Abdulla's sister was that she shouted when she spoke, as if people were next door instead of beside her.

"We are hot blooded, not cold like Europeans," snapped Abdulla when Monika dared mention Tamader's loudness to him. Unhappy with Tamader's presence, Abdulla seemed to take it all out on Monika, something she until then had only expected of him when he had had a couple of pints over his limit. Abdulla lived on his nerves. The young couple had no time left to themselves. Tamader wanted this and Tamader wanted that, and weekends arrived only to show her a good time. If Abdulla hesitated about doing what Tamader wanted, he would be cunningly threatened: "I'm going to write to Yumma (Mother)." That's when Abdulla became putty in her hands. It surprised Monika to discover a side to him so far unknown to her. Little Tamader might be only twelve years old, but she knew how to be the egg's yolk twenty-four hours a day. It soon became crystal clear why Abdulla was not overjoyed with her presence. A tense atmosphere prevailed right through Tamader's stay. She took first priority and had first rights to Abdulla's time and attention, which did not bother Monika in particular because, after all, Abdulla's sister did not know they were married; otherwise, surely, she would have been more respectful. It would be unwise to discuss the situation now with her husband as he was in need of help himself. Hopefully, soon it would all be over. So she patiently played along, except for once or twice when her self-control was being stretched a bit too far.

A weekend in Brighton would be a good idea, the couple decided. The big fun fair there would keep Tamader happy. Knowing what the weather would be like at any British seaside resort in early May, Monika was clothed in her baby-lamb coat, decorated with a cozy Lynx collar—Dentist Pavlik's birthday present to her daughter. Tamader wore a summer frock and ankle socks. On her waist shone a neat gold belt, fifteen centimeters wide, inlaid with precious stones. She had the most amazing jewelry for one so young and, understandably, wanted to show it off. She dangled a thin cotton cardigan over her shoulders, and she was ready to go.

"Let's take your coat, Tamader," reminded Monika. "It's icy cold where we are heading to. Brighton is on the seaside, you see." But her gentle coaxing did no good. Monika came up against heavy resistance. "All right, little madam. I'll carry the coat for you."

"No, no, and *no*! It is not your business! You are not my mother. Leave me alone!" Without a word in reply, for what's the use, Monika slung the coat over her arm ready to go. Tamader was even dead set against such a provision and, with a nasty expression on her face, shouted at Monika some Arabic that did not sound at all friendly to the ear. So Monika just dropped the coat. Subject closed. Good God, that child thinks she knows everything better than anybody else! What if she were to fall ill? Who would have to nurse her then? A pregnant Monika, of course. Brighton, here we come.

Exit car. A couple of minutes later, the cold wind blowing, a shaking, blue-lipped Tamader (ignoring Monika) turned to Abdulla and most of that afternoon was spent combing through shops for a suitable coat to keep Tamader warm. It had, of course, to be something that tickled her fancy as well. Stuck with her cock-up now, she tried to get back at Monika over dinner that night. But her stratagem backfired. Addressing her brother, she jabbed, "Did you tell Monika that if you two ever get married she will have to look after our Mother and do exactly as she says?" Not knowing what to make of the remark, Monika smiled in return. But a really furious Abdulla lost his cool and kicked Tamader's shin under the table so hard she cried out. Now, here, again, Monika felt sorry, for Tamader was a spoiled child. And Monika told Abdulla so.

Before their departure from the pleasant seaside hotel, Monika checked Tamader's room for anything left behind. She threw a quick glance under the bed and pulled out six little, loosely wrapped paper parcels. What presented itself to her was an unwelcome sight and she went to look for Tamader.

"Look here, soiled sanitary napkins you dispose of in the bathroom's waste basket," said Monika. "And see, here are little paper bags just for that purpose."

Tamader threw her head up and with her right hand sent her hair flying over her shoulder.

"It's not your business. My brother is paying for the room," she declared, and with that she marched off like a soldier.

As she became more and more of a handful, Abdulla located a convent nearby and was able to convince Tamader to stay there with girls her own age. The special treatment and attention she received as an odd one out held her there, but weekends were still spent with Monika and Abdulla, who could not go to parks nor dances nor adult films but were restricted to what Tamader could or wanted to join.

Only three weeks later, she arrived by taxi from the convent with all her belongings. A nun had pulled her out of bed by her long, beautiful hair for misbehaving and with a charged hand-push had sent her sliding along a well-waxed wooden floor. Memories! Monika could well visualize a replica of Austria's nunnery, but she would rather not think about it. Instead of treating the only Muslim child among Catholics with extra care and love, here, too, the nuns had failed.

A soft approach in suggesting that Tamader be sent back to her mother fell on deaf ears. Finally, Abdulla managed to find a pleasant family who had two children, where she stayed until six months of England were enough for little Miss Spoiled. After Tamader's departure, Mrs. Preston openly addressed Abdulla about Monika.

"Your first duty is your pregnant wife, you know, Abdulla. You should have stood with her—and stood up for her," she advised Mr. Amahani, who was Monika's old, joking, carefree, funny, likeable Sweetie she loved once again.

In the meantime, nothing worth mentioning happened for some time, until the baby decided it was time to introduce itself. The couple found and booked a private nursing home in Hythe, Kent, well in advance. Pregnant Monika felt a bit out of the ordinary that day and went to see her gynecologist, who, after a thorough examination, told her to go home. Baby would not be due for another two weeks yet. But her mother's instinct told her to stay that night at the nursing home, where after six hours of hard labor that same day she delivered the sweetest healthy baby boy weighing in at 5 lbs., 2 oz. She had done it! She had her own baby now, and what a miracle. She needed time to come properly to terms with the overwhelming fact.

Abdulla, informed, came rushing to her bedside with flowers and chocolates and a huge bottle of her favorite perfume, Chanel No.5. He counted baby's toes and fingers, while searching for a likeness to his family and repeating over and over again, "I have a son. I have a son! I never thought it would be a boy. I want three sons, no girls." And he fantasized, "One will study in the U.S.A., one in Great Britain, and one in Germany." He had always before said he did not mind the sex of his baby, but that must have been just to make Monika feel at ease during her pregnancy. Now he really could say what was in his heart.

Under his kisses and hugs, Monika, overwhelmed with happiness, wanted to share the experience, quite naturally, with her own mother and phoned: "Congratulations, Mother, you have become a grandmother today."

Dead silence on the line.

"Mother, Mother, are you there?"

"No, no," she heard her mother's voice. "It can't be. Tell me it's a joke! You have not *married* that Arab, have you? Oh, great God, what have I done to deserve this! I must sit down. I feel faint. Oh God, what a shock! What, for heaven's sake, is your father going to say? And the neighbors? What of the people? My patients!"

She had not a kind thought nor word for her daughter, not a "How are you?" nor a "How's the baby?" nor even a basic "Well, is it a boy or a girl?" Pissed off and disappointed, the young mother hung up the phone.

She looked at her lovely bundle of joy and spoke to the baby. "Never will I be so cold and heartless to you, my little treasure. We don't need Granny, do we?" And so she soon forgot all about her negative mother.

"Don't you worry, my Sweetie. We have got each other, and that's all that matters," comforted Abdulla. "Just wait till we live in Kuwait. It will be heaven for you. My whole family will love you, especially my mother and sisters." Monika knew Tamader now and wondered what the rest of his family would really be like.

Meanwhile two of the newly achieved threesome, back at what they called home in their two rooms with Mrs. Preston, had to discuss the immediate future now. Baby Sulaiman, named after Abdulla's deceased father of course, was living proof of their love and also a sure give-away sign of their forbidden marriage. Staying all together would be a great risk. The Government of Kuwait might find out that Abdulla had broken the marriage regulations. The time for passing as boyfriend-girlfriend was over, however much fun while it had lasted.

Never shunning work, Monika, baby in arms, marched to the local Labor Exchange and soon found a temporary home with a middle-aged business couple, where in return for room and board she helped look after their two small children plus the cutest little mongrel doggie, Twinkle.

Not long after, Mrs. Pavlik, overcome by motherly duty—or guilt, who knows?—asked her daughter to come home with the baby for the time being. All would be forgiven and forgotten. Monika quickly accepted and, once in Vienna, advertised for and employed a single, kindly faced, older nurse with good references, full-time, for the baby.

Knowing Sulaiman in good hands with the nurse with Mother keeping an eye on both, Monika then made her way back to Abdulla alone. But what she felt leaving her little mite behind only a fellow mum of a firstborn can fully imagine. She was, however, a strong, sensible, practical girl, our Miss Aries. She could always tackle life's problems by the horns as they came along. For Abdulla's sake, it was the best solution she could come up with, and he, in return, fully appreciated it, too.

"Sweetie, I will make it up to you in Kuwait! It won't be much longer now" is what he said when she fought off tears remembering and talking about her baby. With the worry about being discovered out of the way, there was no excuse for Abdulla, who could now relax and concentrate solemnly on studying. Having failed his final exams twice previously, it had to be "third time lucky" for him. Monika would see to it, whatever the cost now. Abdulla was irresponsible, not stupid. Much to the contrary, in fact, that electronic brain of his could amaze you. Only, with so many pleasant things going on elsewhere, he never found the time or concentration to study, never sat down to do some work, so how could he have passed? He acted as if he had a thousand worms dancing the twist up his posterior. Sitting still was just not Abdulla. Books were shoved aside, and concentrating on them was postponed to never-arriving tomorrows. His friends would drop in at any time just like flies. Alcohol was consumed once again, never mind the nagging wife, and never-ending poker games were again arranged. There just was no time left for dreary, gray study. But to get her husband finally through his next exam became Monika's major project and concern, for wouldn't it mean an end to her being parted from baby Sulaiman? With that positive outcome in mind, Austria declared war on Kuwait. Monika went to work on Abdulla.

Abdulla had asked his family many times over for financial help; and, with the final result in hand now, the bit of money seemed a godsend to the young couple. Till then, Monika hadn't so much as seen the shadow of any of the money Abdulla's father had apparently left him, and these 150 Kuwait Dinars were really nothing to brag about either, considering, Abdulla said, the truth of how rich he was now. Still, there just wasn't enough money to go around for both of them at the moment, with their wanting to enjoy good food and drink and to wear nice clothes, and most definitely not for the needs of their baby in Vienna. Court was held on how to stretch, how to multiply the KD 150. They finally decided on and found a cozy, four-bedroom house with the name Goldhawk on the front gate, near the sea in Herne Bay. Now a landlady, Mrs. Amahani rented out three of the bedrooms to three students—an Iraqi, a Persian, and #3 to Adam from Trinidad, who was great fun.

While getting ready for a date he would pat his dick, saying, "Easy, baby, patience please. You'll get your fill tonight." Yet, his presence in Monika's first household was short lived. Against Abdulla's wishes (Abdulla was much too soft), Monika had to give Adam his marching orders. After noticing what looked like burst-pipe wetness running down the wall from Adam's room, she investigated and found the cause: a dozen or so milk bottles overflowing with Adam's piss. He must have hovered over the bottles with his water pipe, shooting with it like a machine gun. What hit the target, good show! What didn't (just "losers luck") went on the floor, but never mind. And, to think, the toilet was right next door to his room! Monika had sometimes wondered where Adam kept the empties of his daily two pints. Now she knew.

Monika and Abdulla now had an income from the house, and Monika went out to work her mornings busily away in a coffee bar along the promenade, where she earned a good wage-packet and plenty of tips. With her father's allowance still going strong, the couple were now well off financially.

Abdulla was very proud of her, often discussing her with his friends, and insisting that a Kuwaiti girl could never compare to his Monika, who could and would do everything possible—including work—to contribute to a grander lifestyle to be enjoyed by them both. A Kuwaiti wife has to be bought, expensively; then she orders servants around for the rest of her life, but does no work herself, he would say. And, if Kuwaiti females were anything like Tamader, he seemed to be saying the truth.

Except for Sulaiman's absence and the blackmail Monika had to use on Abdulla to force him to study, a welcome fresh wind blew through Mr. and Mrs. Amahani's daily routine in their first home together. According to a newly reached agreement, Monday-to-Friday evenings were now filled with a most intensive study period. Completely cut out were visitors, alcohol, and Abdulla's notorious poker games. For the first time since Monika had known Abdulla, he did what one could call study. He sat all by himself at the kitchen table well behind lock and key, with Monika in control of the key. Every hour or so, she would open the door to let him have a tea break, during which time she quizzed him, very pleased with the results because he gave 99% correct answers. After a difficult start, Abdulla seemed even more pleased with this fruitful arrangement than his wife. Mind you, sometimes he would take off through the kitchen window for a quick pint down the road at the local Cock and Hen, to show who was boss when it really came down to it. During the week, sweet harmony existed in that little house. Saturdays were exceptions. Abdulla thought he had to make up for the five dry nights of the week. He would turn on Monika after a couple of drinks and start with the most stupid, senseless arguments; and she, not much wiser, had to reply, of course, not knowing yet never to argue with people who drink.

Pajama parties held at their house were great fun, too. Girls wore babydolls and guys came in their dressing gowns or striped pajamas. Monika, who had to look prim and proper at all times, wore long pajama bottoms and a coverall top. No babydoll for her! Anything remotely revealing was completely out of the question: Abdulla would surely have killed her after his third pint.

If they were not entertaining at home over the weekends, there was always a dance at the nearby Miramar Hotel, and, with something stupid like "What kept you so long at the Ladies?" he would start unexpected arguments: "You've been speaking to a man, haven't you? I saw that tall, blond, blue-eyed fellow take a good long look at you. He's your type, isn't he? All you Europeans are the same! Why don't you go over and go home with him. Go on!"

Unlike Abdulla, Monika had reason to be annoyed. "I haven't," she would answer, "but if I spoke to another male, it would be nothing compared to your touching Jackie's bottom all the time! Don't try to deny it. I have seen you. You hunger for her, don't you?" Jackie was a blonde, well-built regular at the hotel and, for a drink, everybody's easy lay. She wore, always, the lowest cut dresses, leaving little to the imagination. It was nothing unusual if her wobbly, big tits slipped out of her dress and into focus for more male attention to the sounds of Chubby Checker's hot twist beat. While she could so innocently pretend not to notice her bare breasts, naturally Abdulla, a red-blooded Arab stallion, could not resist her red-hot, flashing, come-on signals. If Abdulla disappeared somewhere in the huge dance hall between dancing couples, Monika knew she had to look for Jackie in order to find Abdulla. She wasn't jealous, but felt very degraded more than anything else. He neglected her for such an exhibitionist in bad taste—and it hurt.

Eight months had already passed since Monika had taken Sulaiman to Vienna—much too long a time! Monika had absolutely to have him back before his first birthday came up. Looking at proud mothers pushing their babies always stirred a slight jealousy in her. It would be sheer joy for her to take Sulaiman for walks along the seaside with Abdulla pushing the pram. She could just visualize the tranquil picture.

Abdulla, with the exams not far off now, agreed he was confident and ready this time. He would pass, so he did not care anymore if his Government found out he was married and had a son, because once he had qualified, they couldn't touch him. "And if they found out," he'd say, "what would they do to me, cut off my zip (penis)?"

For baby Sulaiman in Vienna to get used to his by-now-estranged mum would take two weeks at least, Monika calculated, during which time Abdulla would have to cater for himself. He was a cook with body and soul, a good one, something he had discovered and loved as a Boy Scout in Kuwait. Thanks to him, Monika, too, had soon learned how to prepare delicious rice and curry dishes.

Sulaiman had grown into a chubby little smasher who took to his mum as if she had always been around.

"That's because now my patients don't come to have their teeth seen to, but solemnly to visit Sulaiman. He is used to people!" So commented Dentist Pavlik.

The whites of his eyes were a light blue, and his huge, dark eyes glowed like cherries.

"He never needs to lie in the sun to get a tan. He has been born with one, an everlasting one," Monika told her mother, proudly stroking little Sulaiman's olive cheek.

Taking her baby for his daily health walk to the park in his oh-so-regal big black Silver Cross pram, bought at Harrod's of London, Her Majesty the Queen's store, became the highlight of each day. The pram had wheels as big as those on a racing bike and were only seen in Vienna in continental magazine reports with the British royal children as occupants. Mothers and grannies would stop her to ask what Sulaiman was fed on, where one could get such a pram, and how it could be possible that Monika really be the baby's mother since she was a mere child herself. And that's when Monika first started not to mind her young appearance.

Once they were back in Herne Bay, proud Abdulla spoke only Arabic with his son, while Monika, blessed with the ability to pick up languages easily, benefited a lot, too. Her Sweetie had missed her while she had been away in Vienna but had managed well enough during her absence anyhow.

There was a down side to her journey. On her return she found that the two identical rings that her mother had given her as a late wedding present were missing from the jewel box that stood on Monika's dressing table in the bedroom, where strangers never entered. The rings each had a ruby surrounded by a garland of diamonds and were very valuable. Abdulla seemed just as puzzled and swore once again on his mother's life that not a single soul had been in their bedroom while Monika had been away. What could she do but believe and trust him, swearing like that! He even convinced her to think again. Couldn't it be just possible that she herself put them in another place before her departure? At first positive, Monika was now a bit unsure. Maybe he was right. Maybe she *had* forgotten where she put them.

So, hoping that they would turn up somewhere sooner or later, she concentrated on Sulaiman, her lodgers, and the house. There was no time to sit about idle. Then, while giving the sitting room a good once over, she came upon give-away traces of a party held during her absence. Candle wax rings were scattered all over the mantelpiece above the fireplace. "Bloody hell, look at that! Abdulla held a party without me!" The realization went through her brain like a shot. She looked for and found further evidence, finding more multicolored wax droppings on all the bookshelves exactly where she always distributed the candles, but on little glass plates to protect the polished wood; these precautions Abdulla had not bothered with and that gave him away now. Typical male carelessness! He had to leave some evidence, almost as if he wanted to he found out.

Monika put two and two together. She knew now how her rings had disappeared and that he had been lying again! Naturally restless for the rest of the day, she waited impatiently for Abdulla to come home from the hospital. When he finally stood facing her, she greeted him with the words: "*So*—you arranged a party here while I fetched Sulaiman from Vienna!" She hid the fact that she knew everything, yet had not much proof to go on; she had to act doubly self-assured and in this way hoped to find out the truth without losing anything except maybe confidence in her instinct. "You see, Abdulla, I found out about it today! But I want to hear it all from *you* again. And while we are at it," she raised her voice, "don't leave out highlights like the sexy bits with Jackie, Sweetie—you provocative fucker!" We already know the notorious Jackie from the Miramar Hotel, don't we?—Jackie, who was easy game for anybody who wanted to make it with her! Girls, too, rumor had it. Why her husband always lusted after the seediest females puzzled Monika, for she and her husband fitted sexually perfectly and had it all the time. She enjoyed sex as much as he did and never refused his advances.

Abdulla's smiling face dropped, a sure sign that Monika had hit the nail on the head. Pushing his wedding ring endlessly on and off, a habit of his under pressure, he looked around the hallway as if he were searching for help. Knowing that she was on the right track, Monika, now confident, asked, "Have you lost your voice, piss artist? I'm so sorry if I gave you a shock!" Pulling up a chair for him, she went on, "Sit down and collect yourself, but don't give me any lies!"

"Who told you, Sweetie?" he asked finally with a thin voice.

"Don't you sweetie me!" She lost control. "When will your illicit sex games finally come to an end? Will I ever be able to trust you and depend on you? If that is all you care for me, jolly nice landing! You can watch my departure. *No way* am I going to Kuwait with you! Take instead an unoriginal tart like Jackie and you can fuck each other's brains out and all the Jacks and Jills that cross your path, too. You're well suited. Now I know where to find my rings! You can see to Sulaiman. I know where to find Jackie. I really, truly thought that since we got married and since you have a son, you had grown up to be a responsible, trusting, and faithful husband. But no! I had to wake up again! Nothing but sweet dreams with you, and reality stinks!"

"Please forgive me, Sweetie. If you still love me that little bit, don't look for her. Don't do it. I'll buy you *ten* rings of your choice in Kuwait! I swear on my father's grave, but don't talk to Jackie, please!"

After having thrown at him some of what was in her heart, Monika felt lighter. She picked up Sulaiman who, unused to such scenes, had begun to cry.

"I swear on my mother's death, Sweetie," Abdulla defended himself. "It was not my fault! The lodgers and some friends wanted to have a little party. *They* were the ones who invited Jackie. I was really surprised when she turned up. I only let her in the bedroom to put her coat there." The culprit tried hard to clear himself of guilt.

"Stop with your stupid senseless swearing! Just how stupid a wife to you think you have got? She just put her coat!—is that why you don't want me to talk to her? Or is it, as you bloody well know, because I might find out the whole truth—like who invited, screwed, and maybe even gave her my rings as a thanks-for-the-fuck gesture while you were half drunk! Isn't that much nearer to the truth? You bloody coward!"

But what the heck, once again Monika forgave him sincerely, hoping that *this* was the last time and the beginning of life with a faithful husband. Thank God for faith. She never understood how he could put her through the mincer all the time about a harmless smile from another guy or a skirt that twirled too high up her thighs revealing a bit of garter during a dance, for instance; yet His Majesty could go all the way with girls, and what girls! Where was the logic? Did he ever think of how *she* felt? Did it matter to him at all? Whenever she tried to talk about it, he would avoid a straight answer to her question with a joke or by switching the conversation. It was just no use. She so would have loved to understand his approach to the matter. Yet there was no way she could reach him at times like this. Instead, he became just as unmanageable as raw eggs on a glass tabletop. Of course, that's where their cultures first started to clash. Monika lived in complete ignorance that what Abdulla was up to was commonplace among Kuwaiti men folk, whose wives just had to lump it. They had no choice, as she was to find out later. The Jackies and the drinking were necessary novelties; life with her was necessary and secure. He lived in the two worlds.

Good news came in the post on a November morning. Abdulla had finally passed his exams with flying colors and top marks. He was happy: "Monika, my Sweetie, thanks to you and your patience, I have passed! You deserve an award."

"Abdulla, Sweetie, my reward is Sulaiman, and as for your passing, I knew you had it in you. But don't get big headed, Mr. Radiologist Abdulla, FSR or FRT or whatever!"

They celebrated the event with the last of their by-now-well-known pajama parties. Monika happily looked forward to a new and much better life in Kuwait, as Abdulla had promised over and over again. It was not far away now. Soon they would live happily ever after in the sunshine. His drinking days and the occasional girl would become history and be forgotten. Monika floated high above the ground on an invisible carpet of pink roses and into the unknown future. Wearing rose-tinted glasses, the overly optimistic girl thought that idle happiness was soon to be an everyday normality.

Christmas—the first for Sulaiman—they decided would be well spent in England with Dentist Pavlik as their guest. It would be a nice way to end the student-in-Great-Britain phase of their lives. Dentist Pavlik was only too pleased and eager to get to know her Arabic son-in-law. And who would have forecasted it? Abdulla and his mother-in-law got on like a house on fire! Her previous prejudice just melted away under Abdulla's charm. Monika's mother came in very handy to help with their packing, too. Besides tons of Abdulla's medical books, lots of bits and pieces had accumulated. Things like baby toys. They had a number of stately household goods: clocks, kitchen machinery, electrical portable fires, bedding, blankets, electric tea and coffee pots, good British china, radios, a record player, crystal vases and ashtrays, Wedgwood figurines. Even Mrs. Pavlik, who had a good eye for quality, had to admire their good taste. Once neatly packed in huge trunks, the first worldly possessions of the young couple went ahead to Kuwait to wait there for Monika to unpack them as was arranged.

Monika and Sulaiman traveled back to Vienna with Dentist Pavlik. Abdulla would send the air tickets to them from Kuwait within the next couple of weeks. He had to go home first. He thought he had better face his family alone and break to them gently the news that he not only was qualified now but also had a wife and son waiting in Europe for the sign to follow him to Kuwait—before his mother and sisters approached him with a new pack of photographs from which he would be urged to choose a bride. Also his steps would surely lead him to the Ministry of Health to sort out his position there as a Doctor of Radiology. He had his sights set on a high post.

Once in Vienna, Monika received letters from Kuwait about which the postman teased her. He had known her well before she took off for England, and he knew, too, how crazy she was about Elvis Presley, for he was the one who had brought her the posters and mail from the E.P. Fan Club. "So now your Elvis is in Kuwait, is he?" he joked. In every letter Abdulla assured Monika just how thrilled his mother and sisters and all the rest of his family were that he had married a foreigner. So, would she do him the little favor of staying in his mother's house for the first two weeks only? This way she could get to know them all much better, and vice versa. "In that time we can go flat hunting together. Without you, now, I might choose something that is not to your taste, Sweetie," he wrote. "And I have already instructed the servants how to prepare Kuwaiti breakfast for you. It consists of fresh liver, goat cheese, olives, and fried eggs in olive oil with onions. You will love it here. This is the piece of earth where you belong, my Sweetie."

Dentist Pavlik warned her daughter: "Be careful, Monika. He mentions his mother's and sisters' opinions all too often in his letters."

Needless to say, Monika took no notice. Abdulla's relatives were to be her new family in Kuwait from now on. Since she had no roots anywhere else. That's where she would grow new ones, along with baby Sulaiman. His relatives were of no great importance to her really. It would be a happy threesome: only Abdulla, Sulaiman, and Monika. Full stop!

By the end of February their tickets finally arrived. But, first, according to Arab custom, as Abdulla had explained in his letters, she was not to come empty handed. She had to bring presentable gifts for at least his mother and sisters, and would she make quite sure not to forget anybody. His sister Diba had a boy and a little girl. Monika's grandfather had left her some money that was put aside in the bank for a rainy day. From this she took and went on a shopping spree on Vienna's Körntnerstrasse, the equivalent of Bond Street in London, to shop for Abdulla's family. Three beautiful designer dresses were chosen for her sisters-in-law. It was not easy because, with the exception of Tamader, they all needed large sizes—from 18 to 24. Cuddly toys and sweets would do for the children. Being the kind of person who gets pleasure from giving just as much as from receiving, Monika was self-satisfied with her shopping trip.

Baby in hand, Monika's farewell in the airport from brother Werner and her mother was not at all difficult since Abdulla had promised that Monika would return to visit Europe once a year.

CHAPTER SIX

FIRST IMPRESSIONS OF KUWAIT

Sulaiman was no trouble at all on his first plane journey, and what Monika most enjoyed on her flight into the unknown was the transit in Lebanon, where she had to change planes. Walking down the steps, she found out the true meaning of the phrase "in another world." She found herself enveloped by a cloud of thick, warm, humid, intensely sweet, perfumed air. The mountains all around her, as far as her eyes could see, were of a lovely brick red color, not dark and dull as in Europe. The natives were very temperamental people who, as she had first noticed with Tamader, shouted out whatever they had to say. It's true, the darker the skin, the hotter the blood, she thought. Never had she been amid such strange people. Intrigued as to where that lovely smell came from, Monika asked a ground steward. "We have a flower called Jasmine that grows in the mountains in very large quantities in our country," he explained, and with a friendly, "Wait here a minute, please," he disappeared to return with two garlands of the whitest, hugest Jasmine blossoms. Looking deeply into her eyes, he first put one around her neck and then the other around little Sulaiman's body. A bit embarrassed and feeling the red creeping into her cheeks, she thanked him with an Arabic *Shukran* (thank you) and walked on to her connecting plane.

After getting comfortable in her seat and occupying Sulaiman with a little blackboard and some crayons, Monika took in her fellow passengers, who were staring at her in return. Was it her being clad in black leather while they were already in the most colorful summer gear? Or because she was the only white-faced European on board? Whatever. The ladies on that flight were all wearing make-up that was much too heavy, strong, overpowering; and they were wearing far too much jewelry—all in colors that did not match. The ladies looked like Christmas trees. Monika smiled.

When the plane began its descent, Monika could see the desert. It reminded her of landings over Austria's snowy winter mountains, where the wind had molded surrealistic waves and motifs in the snow. Isn't nature the most beautiful! Monika had loved snow for as long as she could remember and enjoyed noticing the desert's similarity. The plane landed and jerked to a halt, and while she was still attending to Sulaiman, the plane's doors opened and she could hear Abdulla's voice in Arabic. Abdulla was making his way towards his wife. He winked at her, snatched Sulaiman and headed for the Exit. Grabbing her belongings in a hurry, she followed him, wondering why she had gotten such a cold reception. They had always fallen into each other's arms after the shortest absence. What had happened to her sweetie?

Her thoughts were pushed aside by Tamader, who now came half way up the stairs to greet her and to kiss her. "Oh, thank God, she is at last smiling and friendly," thought Monika. Tamader told her that her mother and sisters were inside the terminal lounge. Making her way across the tarmac and towards the terminal building with Tamader, following Abdulla, they passed busy airport attendants dressed in sandy khaki-colored shirts and trousers. All the other males, including Abdulla, wore long white robes (the *dishdasha*), white headdresses (a square piece of the finest muslin folded into a triangle) with a thin, black twisted rope of silk around the head to keep it in place. Some carried the headdress on their shoulders. Others wore a red and white head cloth of slightly thicker material cleverly twisted around their heads. But most of her attention was diverted to one side of the airport, where a wire fence approximately five meters high kept back the waiting relatives and friends of the passengers emerging from the planes. Behind the wire mesh stood clusters of figures clad in black. Some of their faces showed, but most were completely covered up, either by a thin black veil or by a fancy mask (a *yashmak*) over which only the eyes were visible. Women stood in groups like bunches of black grapes, more hanging than holding onto that wire fence. So those were the Kuwaiti women . . . They were surrounded by children, most of them screaming, some of them crying. That sight—in such an atmosphere—and Abdulla's detached welcome gave Monika, momentarily, the creeps. Children climbing half way up the wires and shouting, women pulling them down again—it all reminded her very much of a zoo. Only, who were the animals and who the visitors here? She—coming from far away, looking at them in surprise? Or they—looking at her, a European woman, uncovered and free, coming out of that big bird from far away? The intense interest went both ways.

The weather in Kuwait was very humid. Just a few minutes out of the air conditioned plane were enough to transform her neat leather suit into a body-molded, skin-tight sauna suit that she was now firmly locked into, with no possible escape for the next hour or so, she guessed. She felt ever so uncomfortable and out of place, especially as every single male, it seemed, stopped dead in his tracks, unashamedly, just to stare at her.

Once inside the very noisy terminal, Abdulla pulled her into an air conditioned office, where he was greeted with handshakes and plenty of kisses on foreheads and noses by another loud, Arabic-speaking national. Abdulla handed him Monika's Austrian passport, and the officer went through it smiling at her, calling her *Um Sulaiman*, and saying what a good friend Abdulla was of his. In Kuwait a woman who has given birth to a son is not referred to nor addressed by her given name but instead is called in the name of her first-born son however many sons she may bear afterwards (girls don't count), so Monika was sometimes called *Um Sulaiman* (Mother of Sulaiman) and Abdulla was always addressed as *Abou Sulaiman* (Father of Sulaiman). The atmosphere in that official's bureau was very informal, nothing like the strict customs interviews of European airports. Spiced oriental tea was served in very small glasses, followed by thick Arabic coffee in even smaller china cups. It made her smile. What was the use of such tiny cups? One gulp and they were empty. Where was the logic? A handyman stood by in attendance to refill the hot sweet stuff again and again, until Monika could stand no more, nodding an energetic no thank you, no more. As you can well imagine, the last thing she wanted right now was a hot drink. But Abdulla forced her to accept lest she be thought rude, so against her will she gulped down a few cups of each liquid to appear polite and appreciative. She did not know it yet, but that was to be only her first taste of doing things against her will to please others and be polite in Kuwait, never mind her own feelings.

In the meantime, that nice friend of Monika's husband had discovered that Monika had come traveling on an Austrian passport that had expired three months earlier and was no longer valid. "Abdulla will get you a Kuwaiti passport, *Um Sulaiman*. Being married to him makes you a Kuwaiti, too," he said to her in very good English, while slamming a few stamps into her invalid travel document. A last handshake for her, more kisses between him and Abdulla, and she was free to leave. Abdulla was an *Aseel* (pure Kuwaiti) and so was his friend. "You see, this is Kuwait, and Kuwait belongs to us, the pure Aseel Kuwaitis," Abdulla told his wife proudly. Abdulla's family was known by everyone who was anyone in Kuwait and by almost everyone else who was not anyone besides. This was not because the family was rich, even by Kuwaiti standards. It was because the family was old and had distinguished itself by being one of the first in the country before Kuwait had became a British Protectorate. Abdulla's grandfather had won wide respect when, on his deathbed, he freed his twenty or so African slaves.

"I entered Kuwait, come to think of it, illegally just now. So would it be far off to compare you Aseel, pure Kuwaitis a little bit with the notorious Mafia? Isn't there a similarity in the system even if it's maybe not actually corrupt?"

"Look, Sweetie, the word Aseel means something like "original," "thoroughbred." It is a very significant, important word in Kuwaiti society. An Aseel is the kind of Kuwaiti, like my grandfather and father, who lived in Kuwait before the British pumped oil out here. Aseels are, to put it strongly, the superiors among Arabs in our country. We are not to be compared with the Iraqi, Palestinian, or Irani Kuwaitis whose parents flocked to Kuwait for the work that oil brought with it. After immigrating to Kuwait, they could become Kuwaitis of a lower, of a second, third, or fourth order. Even born here, they cannot call themselves Aseels. Aseel Kuwaitis like and help each other. If somebody's name comes up in a conversation and if a person is ignorant of that name, the first thing he will ask is, is he an Aseel? It is the invisible diplomatic passport within Kuwait. It has nothing to do with wealth or status. You know it is known all over the world that the Jewish people keep close and always help each other. Our Arab brothers call us Kuwaitis the Jews of the Gulf."

"How interesting, Abdulla. What about our Sulaiman? Is he not an Aseel with a foreign mother?"

"He damn well *is* as Aseel as I am, for the mother does not count. It's only important who the father is. Our Sulaiman is a first class Aseel Kuwaiti!"

"Thank God for that," said Monika, as she saw three disguised figures squatting on a settee in the terminal lounge arguing and talking loudly. They got up as Tamader called out to them to meet her half way. "Those must be my new in-laws," thought Monika. "Mother in-law and Abdulla's sisters Diba and Sabiha." They were all rolled up in the customary long, black cover-ups, which made it impossible for Monika to figure out who was who. It put her in mind of a bunch of black flies. One just as well could suspect a male under those disguises, she thought. They looked like a bunch of dark, walking mummies.

Tamader made introductions. Monika found herself shaking hands with everybody at the same time. While being kissed by one of them, she could not make out by whom, another one of the women took crying Sulaiman. He was scared, probably sensing that his Mum was feeling uneasy, to say the least, in this out-of-a-film atmosphere. Who could blame him, after the long journey, frightened by such strange faces looking at him from black tents amid all that shouting going on in Arabic. They had to shout because everyone had to have her say at the same time, and to hear any of it one simply had to shout. Their thick, musty, sweet perfume crept up Monika's nostrils. She was now truly in a completely different world. Nothing at all like what she thought it would be! Far from what she had visualized from Abdulla's narrations, back in Britain, about Kuwait. For some reason, she had imagined its people more advanced, more modern. She had expected the ladies, money being no obstacle, to be close replicas of Parisian elegance and fashion, who wore at least proper shoes, not merely flat-heeled slippers, which didn't help the grossly overweight women to walk gracefully. That women in public wore black robes so as not to arouse their menfolk sexually, she knew too, but she had imagined everything to be a bit more refined. As Monika walked amidst her new family, she was pleased that Abdulla's mother had come to the airport; it made her feel welcome. Surely, it was a gesture of goodwill and acceptance, though probably for Abdulla's sake mostly and the anxiety he had suffered over his mother's probable reaction to his having married a foreigner. His worry during the past year was surely uncalled for, a waste of nerves.

Sulaiman was handed around like a new puppy, got loads of kisses, while Abdulla didn't have a kiss or a hug for his wife yet. How strange. Mother-in-law smiled and chatted to Monika in her native tongue as if there was no tomorrow, and once outside the terminal she divided the group into two cars. Sulaiman was bundled with Diba, Sabiha and Tamader in their mother's chauffeur-driven limousine, while Monika was instructed to take her place next to Abdulla in his red automobile, and mother-in-law made herself comfortable in the back seat. Abdulla's car was a beautiful American model. Monika sank into the upholstery, not feeling the slightest motion as she was driven along in air-conditioned comfort. What a positive change from their old Morris Minor, sold for a joke and left behind in England. They now drove on a very wide, one-way road, where four or five cars could easily have driven side by side. Palm trees decorated the road, right and left. Beyond them, the never-ending desert was everywhere her eyes turned. Only now did Abdulla put his hand in slow motion on her lap, and, squeezing her thigh so hard it hurt, said, "Hello, my Sweetie, at last you are in Kuwait. I was dying for today. Is it really my Sweetie in my car sitting next to me in Kuwait?"

A weight fell off her chest. She was relieved now. He was his old self again. It must have been the strain of her arrival, a very out-of-the-ordinary thing to happen in Kuwait, that had made him act so distant. She leaned over and kissed him on the cheek saying, "Hello, stranger. I expected a knight in Arab armor on a beautiful, white thoroughbred horse, daggers dangling from your waist in true Arab fashion—like in desert films."

"Did you, Sweetie? And Sulaiman hanging onto its tail, I suppose," replied Abdulla, more at ease and with a half hidden happy-to-be-alive sparkle in his black eyes. So Monika was in Kuwait now, far away from European civilization, where for the past two years she had expected she would end up one day, and baby Sulaiman was now in the country that was his father's and would be his, too.

Monika glanced pitifully at her husband, trying to figure out his nervous behavior. He had seemed so restrained at the airport and had only a measly, lone hello for her and nothing else. His behavior had not matched his hot love letters, the letters he had sent to her in Vienna. Perhaps in Kuwait, she guessed, men did not show affection in public—at least not to women. To sons, at any rate, they did, for Abdulla had carried Sulaiman down the gangway kissing his cheek and saying things to him in Arabic and English.

Feeling exhausted after her long flight into the mysterious Middle East, the change of climate, and in particular the cold, disappointing reception from Abdulla, not to mention the first meeting with her noisy all-female in-laws, Monika looked forward to an intimate tête-à-tête with Abdulla. Up to this point she had felt strangely remote from him.

Houses that appeared in a neat row right and left along the motorway had no visible roofs and reminded her of brightly multicolored boxes topped with TV aerials galore. They stood surrounded by extremely high walls and had huge, heavy, wrought-iron or thick wooden gates. No fewer than six cars, American models outnumbering other makes, decorated the outside of these homes like ice-cream slices. White-robed nationals sat cross-legged on huge Persian carpets spread out on the wide pavements, chatting, smoking the hubble-bubble water pipe while fingering worry beads (*mesbah*). Others were glued to huge TV sets. Servant boys bustling about attended to their masters' whims, pouring out the traditional tea and coffee from huge china pots. The odd house sported one or two cows or a goat or both tethered to the main entrance.

"Do Kuwaiti menfolk live on the street, Abdulla?" Monika wanted to know.

"Oh, Sweetie, haven't I ever told you? In Kuwait, although there are no clubs, nor of course casinos, we have the busiest nightlife of all the Arab countries and that's thanks to what you see everywhere around here in action, our *douvaniahs*. Almost every house has a douvaniah. It's a room, or special quarters, for men only, with an entrance straight from the street. There men socialize from early evening into the wee hours of the next day. It's an open house for one's friends and acquaintances. Within an active night I might visit some four to five douvaniahs. That is where we hear the latest news and gossip. The douvaniah is Kuwait's news agency, its Reuter's. It's there we make friends, close friendly business deals, arrange marriages. One goes there to give condolences for a death or good wishes for a birth. In short, it is where we do our socializing, while our women and children can enjoy their freedom inside the house and its surrounding courtyards. And I must not forget the importance of the douvaniah during our two Muslim "Christmases," the *Eid* and the Holy *Ramadan*, the fasting period of 29 to 30 days that leads up to Eid. That's when we dress up in all our glory and head for our favorite douvaniah to wish our friends a happy, prosperous Eid, always starting with our elderly first."

"So, do you have a douvaniah in your parents' house?" asked Monika.

"No, I don't. I wanted to open one as soon as I came back from Europe, but my mother is dead set against it. She won't permit it. But we will definitely build one in our own house and very soon, too, Sweetie." Abdulla's mother seemed a very strong lady for a Muslim woman, who—as it is widely believed in the West and as Abdulla, too, had led Monika to believe—has not got much to say, in general. Yes, sir, Abdulla's mother certainly was an exception to the rule. And Monika did not have to be very bright to realize within the first few minutes of meeting Abdulla's family that all of his female relatives dominated him. For her, it was a familiar continuation of what little Tamader had started back in England about two years ago. Although he was at pains to show them respect and consideration, Abdulla did not at all seem to be successfully at ease around them. Monika's sixth sense told her that the poor devil had a guilty conscience around them; his crime: he had betrayed his family by marrying a foreigner. Good God, it's true what a difference a day makes! Vienna, in the heart of Europe, in the morning;

Kuwait, a step into another dimension, somewhere at the end of the world, only eight hours later. Two worlds far apart in time and culture. What a crass difference indeed.

Abdulla pulled up from the road onto a wide sandy pavement leading towards a mustard colored house surrounded by masses of cars, in all colors and shapes, some attended by chauffeurs.

"Welcome to my family's home, Sweetie. Please don't be upset. Some of our relatives and friends are waiting inside. They are dying to see you, to meet you. I hope you haven't forgotten to bring presents for my mother and sisters, have you?" he asked, probing and a bit uneasy that he had to ask.

"Was I ever unreliable? Have I ever let you down?" came her reply. A sudden loneliness and disappointment overcame her like an invisible shower. Her and Sulaiman's arrival in Kuwait seemed not to be of the greatest importance to Abdulla, after all. He seemed to be more concerned that things should go smoothly for his family. That was his central priority today. Monika didn't get the warm feeling of belonging. Instead, she felt a proper Charlie-out-of-place, an outsider-looking-in who had nothing much to do with what was going on around her because everything and all were focused on and geared towards pleasing Abdulla's family and especially his mother, whom he somehow seemed to fear. Poor Abdulla had a heart of gold, but Monika wished dearly that he were more of a man. Maybe he did not realize that emotional blackmail was being used on him. Yet Monika cottoned on straight away from the beginning with the greatest of ease. She was led by what one calls intuition.

Everyone poured out of the vehicles into the beige tiled, paved courtyard of the large ill-kept house. Abdulla jumped out of his door to help not Monika but his mother into the house while Monika struggled with the traveler's case and handbag on her lap, pulled and pressed on unfamiliar knobs and latches to free herself. After she successfully found the right latch, Sulaiman's screams reached her from the arms of some black-robed, black-skinned servant nearby; and before she could get hold of him, he was again snatched away by—oh, good!—Tamader. Monika didn't need to go into deep meditation to realize within a short time that she liked Tamader best of her in-laws. The rest looked, putting it bluntly, and acted like three incredible, walking, fat lumps with brains to match, who weren't much to write home about. Tamader was slim, bubbly, knew English and, of course, was the one that looked so like her Abdulla.

Now, people appeared at doors and peered through iron-fenced windows. They approached her chatting loudly. *Hamra, Ingilesia,* and *Um Sulaiman*—these three words kept standing out as key words. People vied with each other to talk to her and to touch her. She was surrounded by hoards of noisy kids as she stood, the center of attention amid women who had no sense whatsoever of delicacy, or privacy. They came up close, viewed her up and down, front and back. Some stood with open mouths, staring at her as if she were some creature from outer space or a slave being bought. They pulled at her manicured, long, red nails, thinking they were glued on and touched her white hands as if to see whether the color would rub off, while still others felt the texture of her blonde hair. Some took a closer interest in her leather gear, turning the hem of the skirt up to, of all things, smell it! "Soon they will be in my pants before Abdulla gets there," shot through her brain. Through all these happenings, mother-in-law kept close by her side, shouting her instructions, while Monika stood there feeling awfully uneasy not knowing—nor right now caring—what any of that huge, strange bunch was saying, with the exception of those two words-*hamra* and *ingilesia*—*hamra* meaning "scarlet woman" or "red one" and *ingilesia* meaning "English one." Monika just smiled back at them and nodded in all directions, feeling surrounded by the blind that could see.

Abdulla came to his wife's rescue, leading her inside a welcome, cool, air-conditioned, heavily sweet-scented house, a bit sickly sweet.

"All this must be irritating for you, Sweetie."

"I am a novelty here, I suppose."

Trying hard to make it up to her, Abdulla announced, "Sweetie, my mother loves you and Sulaiman very much. She will take good care of you both." Monika was sure she would, in her own way. Juma, the family's long-time servant from Yemen held a small, gold-rimmed glass of hot, thick tea like the liquid she was forced to consume at the airport, smiling broadly under her nose.

"Drink it, Sweetie," urged Abdulla. "Mother ordered it for you." So drink it she did. "It's time for the presents now," he continued. "Where are the presents? You have to present them now while everybody is watching—to show that you love my family. And don't forget to kiss my mother when handing her the gift. This way people will talk well of you."

"Anything for you, Sweetie, but would you be very sad if I told you I don't give a hoot what these people think of me?"

Abdulla's face pulled an artificial smile. He shouted instructions as servants, falling over each other like dominoes, came with the luggage. Monika carefully—all eyes watching—presented mother-in-law with her gift, accompanied by the required kiss on the thin, veiled, old cheek. The wizened old woman in her black clothes was so unlike any other women Monika had met: no more than five feet tall, very portly, her dark, wrinkled skin making her look much older than her approximately fifty years. It was as well she wore a black veil over her face for it was only close to her that you could see the black teeth and piercing eyes.

The old woman approvingly let the material run through her henna-patterned, beringed fingers, rubbing and smelling it only to hand the costly *haute couture* set into the row of on-lookers, the top going one way and the skirt in the opposite direction through the crowd. And, of course, sisters-in-law's costly gowns took the same route. It irritated Monika, to say the least, how such delicate material was manhandled in front of her eyes. Mother-in-law seemed content with Monika's formal act of homage before her friends and relatives. In their eyes, it placed Abdulla's mother above Monika. Monika realized this, but did not mind, for she could understand the old lady's misgivings that her only son should marry a foreigner.

With mother-in-law leading the way, Monika was ushered into a large, most untidy room. The furniture was a combination of traditional and modern, and everything seemed to be broken or badly chipped and scratched. Identical and look-alike golden china vases with multicolored, artificial silk roses and imaginary flowers stood everywhere. A huge elaborate Persian carpet covered the floor. There was a mighty, Western-style, sea-green glass-topped dining table with hidden lights cramped into an adjoining room that had no doors. About twenty-four chairs stood ill-arranged nearby. Yet the food was laid out on plastic sheets on the floor in huge oval-shaped china and silver trays. The meal consisted mostly of the Kuwaiti national dish, which is rice and lamb. A whole cooked lamb lay there, stuffed with chickens and eggs. Monika felt the lamb's huge eyeballs looking at her straight from their sockets: her appetite was reduced to zero. Abdulla realized it.

"Don't worry, Sweetie. You get used to it. Once you have tasted these eyes, you will want more!"

"I don't mind the eyes as much as the teeth! Don't you even bother to get rid of these filthy teeth first? That looks, and is, unhygienic with a capital U. Good God, I don't believe this although I've heard about it." No plates, nor cutlery, were anywhere in sight. The women sat on the floor cross-legged, children on their knees, and started to reach greedily for the food with bare right hands, pulling big chunks of meat out of the lamb. It was attacked as carcasses are by vultures. The sight of people eating with their hands was nothing new to Monika. It's an art to be able to eat like that, really. She herself had tried it unsuccessfully a couple of times, for one must not get one's hands soiled above the middle knuckle while eating, not an easy task. She had seen Abdulla and his friends eat rice like that before in Great Britain. Last Christmas, Dentist Pavlik had run to the toilet to throw up at the sight of six Arabs, including her son-in-law, eating with their hands. How, Monika wondered, would she react here now? Good question. Use your imagination.

Abdulla lovingly brought a plate for Monika with some rice, lamb, a little tomato sauce and handed it with a knife and fork to his now-on-her-knees wife awkwardly positioned on the floor—only to make the heavily made-up women, some of whom were breathtakingly beautiful, screech out with loud, unashamed laughter. Monika's eating habits, civilized, with cutlery, were here in Kuwait something to laugh about! Turning to Abdulla, Monika said, "You see, Sweetie, although I don't speak Arabic, I seem to have a certain knack already of entertaining your family and friends." She smiled sheepishly, as all eyes rested on her and made her feel uneasy.

"I am very proud of you, my Sweetie. One of you equals the whole lot together here. I can't wait to hold you tightly in my arms, but only to start with, of course. I am going to love you very, very much," he whispered from under his hand, indicating sex, naturally—at last something nice and positive that she too very much looked forward to as well. Then, at least, she would have Abdulla and his undivided attention all to herself. As she sat there chewing food even though she was not the least bit hungry, having been put off the food, she took in her surroundings a little more closely and discovered the beautiful crystal chandelier above her head. Not trusting her eyes, she stared. There, on a yellow string, dangled the price tag and a black and gold card on which was printed the address of the manufacturers in Dusseldorf, West Germany. Looking further around the room, she saw that all the walls, from the floor till quite high up, were heavily scratched and drawn on with everything that could possibly leave a mark. More labels and tags could be seen hanging off chairs and settees that were well worn, and the prices were still written on them. Maybe people here, being illiterate, considered price tags decorative.

The food was consumed in great haste. Quite understandably, too. With all eating from one dish, one had to see to it that the piece of meat one's eyes were fixed on reached one's stomach before some other busy hand came and grabbed it first. Holy shit, what a custom! Monika could not see herself joining their eating habits and enjoying it. People got up to wash their hands and reached for the tea and coffee, on offer once again, after which they abruptly said their goodnights, to speed away in the comfort of their awaiting limousines. The show was over.

Abdulla pulled Monika off the floor where she was still occupied with her full plate and told her to say goodnight to his mother. Then he led her up two flights of stairs, Sulaiman in one arm, into a large hall that had black and white floor tiles, like those at the butcher's in Vienna. Its green walls were over and over scribbled and scratched on by children's hands. The dining room sideboard that matched the dining table in mother-in-law's dining room downstairs stood as a lone piece of furniture in the big room. Four doors led onto a bathroom, a sitting room, a spare room, and a bedroom. All the rooms had access to dusty, sandy balconies cramped chockablock with useless household goods and broken toys. On entering the bedroom, Monika stood still for a moment, shocked at the sight that presented itself. There on a huge, pitch black, king-size, wooden double bed, which reminded her of an outsized coffin and gave her the creeps, lay the whole once-carefully packed contents of her four suitcases. All her personal belongings were littered carelessly over the bed and spilling onto the floor.

"Look at this, Abdulla! Some indoor hurricane has had a field day here, a really good go. Someone or a couple of someones have had a jolly good sniff through it all"—even trying on some of her pretty dresses, she could easily tell by the open buttons and zips; and *that* really annoyed her. What bloody cheek!

"Sorry, Sweetie. My sisters must have done it," came Abdulla's apologizing comment on the liberties that had been taken. "I'm sure they just wanted to put it all away into the cupboard, but got stuck."

"Stuck their noses into my belongings would be a more appropriate explanation, don't you agree? Now, such actions I detest. I am sorry, Abdulla, there is such a thing as privacy, and I dearly would love some of that while I am here with your family for the next two weeks we have agreed on."

"Don't worry, Sweetie. I'll see to it. It won't happen again. I tell them. Trust me."

"When are we going flat hunting, then, Abdulla?"

"Soon, soon, Sweetie, and I have already applied for a piece of land, and a grant, a financial grant to build our own house, from the Government. Every Kuwaiti is entitled to it once he is married, and we will be deliriously happy, the three of us, just you, me and Sulaiman, with a couple of servants at your disposal thrown in. I will make you very, very happy. You wait and see. I will buy you jewelry and clothes you never dreamed of. I will make you Sophia Loren Number Two."

"Your word in God's ear," she smiled back at him. Monika, a great optimist, did not easily give up on a promised happy future that always seemed to be just in sight. She firmly believed that the two of them, although complete opposites, could move mountains together. He had the opportunities and connections, and she had the in-born know-how to make it a worthwhile life together.

"What a day it must have been for Sulaiman!" Monika changed the subject, putting Sulaiman gently down to a now well-deserved sleep in his new cot, made of finest blue nylon mesh, a present from his Daddy. "I wonder what went on in his head over the sudden change of faces and language." Abdulla did not miss the opportunity. While she bent over the cot, he pressed his manhood tighter than tight against her well-formed posterior, getting more and more excited as he felt the black leather of her skirt through the fine muslin of his white dishdasha.

"Oh baby, what a turn on!" He fumbled with the buttons of her blouse and reached with trembling hands straight for the firm, white, velvety-skinned 36B-size breasts, pink nipples proudly erect, ready for action. "Oh God," groaned Abdulla. "Thank you for the ultimate, loveliest feeling on this earth with the prettiest girl in Kuwait to match it, Sweetie. I did not have proper sex since I saw you last. All I had was my right hand."

"Same here," she whispered, half gone, reaching for his erect, hard-with-blood, throbbing, hot, stiff penis as she let her now nude, garter-belted-and-stockinged body slide on the Oriental, pleading, "Let's do it three times, Sweetie. You have to promise me we will do it all night long...."

Having satisfied their sexual urges, in all positions, from all angles, to great extent, Monika should have slept through the night like her baby. Yet she could not settle down and rest in peace that first night. Barking desert dogs, squeaking rats, wild cats, strange cries, and the Mullah's out-of tune, screaming "Allah o-Akbar" (God is the greatest) from a nearby mosque loudspeaker saw to that. Really, only Mullahs with good voices should be allowed to perform such tasks. Abdulla had sometimes listened in Britain to religious programs transmitted from the Middle East, but those voices had sounded like bells, sweet music to one's ears compared to this disturbing . . .

Early the next humid, air-conditioned morning, Abdulla woke his wife with a freshly made cup of tea and pressed a smacker on her cheek. "Wake up, Sleeping Beauty. Your Sweetie is going to work, make money and help save lives."

She must have fallen asleep only in the wee hours. She had missed seeing her second half getting smartly dressed in a light beige, Italian-cut summer suit, a white shirt and matching smart silk tie that were so becoming in contrast to the national dress he wore the day before, which disfigured his good physique. She thought the dishdasha made him look unmanly and silly, to say the least, like Wee Willy Winkle with an Oriental face.

"You will spend the morning with my mother and sisters. I will be back in time for lunch at 1:30 p.m. Government employees, like myself, work only half days." Abdulla had a high position at the hospital that by coincidence his father had died in. Taking over from an Egyptian, Abdulla was now in charge of the x-ray department there. "Tamader will be here with you. Don't hesitate to ask her if there is anything you need. After lunch we usually have a siesta, but I skip my siesta today and tomorrow and the day after and I am going to eat you again and again and again. In the afternoon, I will show you the old and new Kuwait, okay? Happy, Sweetie?"

Before she could answer, a kiss was planted on her lips and her Sweetie was gone. Monika jumped out of bed, made it, and went to the bathroom. Bloody nuisance. The "cold" water was as hot as the hot! No cold running water. She was sweating like hell. The bathroom was not air-conditioned. The house's water was, she remembered, kept in big tanks on the roof. Later she learned that every so often a servant would have to cycle to a nearby water station from which a huge water truck would follow him home to refill the containers. Of course, one could not trust to drink this water. It had to be boiled first and was then kept bottled in the refrigerator. Water in Kuwait was liquid gold, worth more (though not in price) than the "black gold." It was used with care and great respect, but was not dearer in Kuwait than the oil, as some know-nothing newspapers and magazines reported, along with numerous other fantasies about Kuwait.

After douching with hot water, feeling no fresher, she slipped on some jeans, tied the edges of her pink blouse tightly together around the waist and was just about to attend to her son as the hall door opened without a knock and the exempted-from-knocking mother-in-law waltzed in, talking loudly at Monika in Arabic. She made her way to the bedroom wardrobe, where Monika had neatly stored her clothes next to

Abdulla's late last night. The old woman sifted through the hanging frocks and pulled out a yellow, v-necked cotton dress, which seemed to have met her approval. It had gold buttons down the back and sported a tight belt with a golden rose buckle. She handed it to Monika, who understood that that was what she had to wear now. Monika obeyed, hoping Tamader would come to explain what she had to dress up for.

Mother-in-law, pulling along Sulaiman, who had not breakfasted yet, led Monika downstairs, from where loud, discordant shouting could be heard and a show was to be seen. Diba, the eldest and lightest-skinned of the three sisters, and the middle one, Sabiha, lay in each other's hair, each with one hand—believe it or not—holding onto the dress that Monika had given to Diba as a gift.

"Good morning, Monika," came the voice of Tamader from somewhere in the hallway. "Take no notice of my sisters. Sabiha wants to exchange her dress with that of Diba. She thinks it fits her better."

"Good morning, Tamader. Is that why I had to change into this dress and your mother brought me down here?" A loud, high-pitched scream interrupted the conversation, as Diba now bashed Sabiha with the dress repeatedly and hard around the ears. "Pity on the material, and well deserved, Sabiha," judged Monika, secretly, as she was ushered by the teenager into "our visitors' room"—as Tamader called it.

In there, about twenty side-plates heaped with huge pieces of cake, cookies, and nuts—all piled high on each plate—were laid out on neat little side tables that stood invitingly between comfortable, gold edged, flowery lounge chairs upholstered in velvet.

"Come in here, Monika. Sabiha always starts a fight about everything. And let me warn you: she has a wild temper. I hope she gets married soon. If it's not Diba or my mother, she finds something that bothers her about me. And she always has a good go at our servants. She is the crazy one in our family. So let's forget her now. We soon will have some visitors, people who come to see you."

"Haven't they all seen me yesterday?" Monika wanted to know.

"Definitely not. All Aseel Kuwaitis are really one big family in Kuwait, and they have all heard about you. And they will all, in their own time, sooner or later, pay their respects, as one would say in England."

"Tamader, please, do me a big favor. Stay close by, for I feel like a monkey in a zoo." The word *chara* reached Monika's ears a couple of times. It was what Sabiha had shouted at Diba and Diba threw back at her. Abdulla used that word sometimes when things did not go well. It meant 'shit.' So they were giving each other a title now, thought Monika, and congratulated herself for having married into that circus. I will need an additional guiding angel here, she thought, and peered through the open windows' iron bars into a mighty cage of clucking chickens, where by the side of it on the tiled floor lay a heavily pregnant goat, her stomach digesting a costly miniature Japanese Bonsai tree, which had been a thoughtful gesture, a well-meant present from Abdulla's Viennese mother-in-law to Monika's Kuwaiti mother-in-law. The telltale evidence was the pretty white porcelain flowerpot imprinted in black with the portrait of Johann Strauss, a violin, and some musical notes from the famous "Blue Danube" waltz, in which the green had stood proudly only the night before. Its gift-wrapping of lilac silver foil lay nearby. Monika couldn't help herself: she laughed in utter disbelief!

"What is it?" Tamader wanted to know.

"I have just realized that I have flown in a gourmet delicacy for the goat out there. Sorry that I forgot the chickens!" Monika laughed, louder now.

"My mother must have thought it would do the goat good. She is pregnant, you know, and does not eat much," said Tamader.

"Do you think so, too?" Monika asked Tamader.

"Well, yes, why not?" answered Tamader.

And who in God's name back home in Austria, Monika asked that astounded brain of hers, is going to believe such happenings?

Approaching voices told her some onlookers had arrived. She expected a continuation of last night's *hamra-Ingilesia-Um Sulaiman* session to be on its way. White-skinned Europeans were automatically classified as English and rather unkindly referred to as *hamras* (the red ones, scarlet women), for their skin turned red in the scorching Eastern sun. The group of nieces and cousins now entering were making a positive impression on Abdulla's wife. These mothers and daughters had normal figures, were smartly turned out females without a hint to give away the fact that they actually belonged to the same family as Monika's in-laws. Some of them spoke excellent English, knew what Vienna was all about, had visited it; and Monika couldn't help taking an instant liking to them. They did not touch her and made polite, intelligent conversation. You could tell they knew that more worlds existed beyond Kuwait. The two eldest daughters of cousin Nabeela had studied in Lebanon, which was where civilization had ended for Monika. Such are the kind of Kuwaitis I would like to link up with and mix socially with, wished Monika, and was honestly pleased and relieved that civilized women existed after all in her new homeland-to-be. Having paid their respects and welcomed Monika as a new member of the family and invited her to come to their homes any time she wished, they all left in a mixed cloud of French perfume, amidst which Monika recognized Chanel 5 and something else.

Kuwait seemed to be the sort of place where a newcomer like Monika would have to look for the trees and ignore the forest, she theorized. Monika was more confident now that, given time, she would find compatible people and make her own friends in Kuwait. All beginnings are difficult. Doesn't every pot find a lid? she comforted herself.

"Nabeela, my nephew's mother, joked about your high forehead," Tamader immediately informed her brother's wife, unable to hide a certain pleasure in presenting the gossip straight after the visitors had left. "She said it looks like a monkey's bottom, and she, for one, can't see what Abdulla sees in you."

"In Europe, people with high foreheads are thought of as intelligent. Your cousins were so polite and friendly. I rather liked them," Monika fended off.

"Sure they are friendly to your *face*. It's jealousy, though. She would have loved to see one of *her* daughters married to Abdulla and by his side instead of you. Wait till you learn the Arabic language and understand them." With that statement, Tamader pushed a much-too-big piece of cake into her mouth.

Black-clad women came and went all morning long, on Monika's first day in Kuwait. It felt to her as if she were in a public toilet. None of them left anything near the nice impression Monika had had of her in-law's cousins and nieces. The only thing they had in common was that they were females, too. In fact, Monika's view of most of the women was that they would do well to treat their mouths to a well-deserved bank holiday. They talked endlessly as Tamader translated, but nothing worth translating was ever said, and it was a relief and pleasure to hear Abdulla's voice interrupt her thoughts. She was to get used to feeling safer and her muscles and nerves relaxing whenever Abdulla came back home from the hospital. His mere presence, somehow, made her feel secure.

According to custom, as a new member of the family, so Abdulla told Monika, she would be given some nice gifts of gold jewelry by her in-laws. The day came when mother-in-law parted with one of the bracelets she always wore, saying something that sounded like, "Well, if it's absolutely necessary, here you are," while pulling it off her wrist. It was a gold bangle that had pearls strung on a thin gold wire running along the middle. Tamader was too young to give that sort of present. Diba, the eldest, who was married to a bad-tempered alcoholic and had two children, a girl of six and a one-year-old boy, said she hadn't had time yet, but promised to buy her something later on (she never found the time to do so during the eleven whole years that Monika lived in Kuwait). Sabiha, the black sheep of the family, parted with a ring of hers that had multicolored, heart-shaped stones dangling loosely from its center, with one heart missing. To make up for the missing gem, Sabiha let Monika slip into a beautiful black velvet evening coat that her fiancé, Fahad, had brought back to her from Paris and which was a couple of sizes too small for Sabiha; and that's where mother-in-law interfered by telling Sabiha that the coat should be given to Diba and not to the "hamra."

"What's the occasion?" Sabiha wanted to know. "Anyway, Diba is much too fat and the coat won't fit her, now would it?" she contended. A mother-daughter shouting match erupted with "*Ekul chara*" offerings in between. Monika had never before witnessed anything like it in her life, and she dropped the garment flabbergasted. Why this strong resentment and dislike of her on her mother-in-law's part? Under normal circumstances she would have proudly rejected the insulting items. Only to avoid further troubles did she thank these relatives, fighting her pride and against her own grain. For intelligence had its obligations. The scruffiness of her rich in-laws' presents reflected their resentment of her. Abdulla was not tickled pink with pride either by the meager offerings and promised to make it up to her in due time.

CHAPTER SEVEN

THE CITY OF KUWAIT

Kuwait is the city of Kuwait, divided mainly into districts with names like Salmiah, Feheheel, Chaldia, Rawda, Sulaibikhat. Fate threw Monika into the Keefan area. On her first sightseeing trip, Abdulla introduced his wife to Kuwait's Fifth Avenue, the Fahad al-Salem street, named after some ruler. Tall modern buildings stood sporting unbelievable shops, crammed with out-of-this-world skilled craftsmanship from all over the globe: imported furniture, painted, carved, inlaid, anything you can think of, have heard of, and more. Bejeweled ladies—half revealing their European fashions nominally concealed beneath black covers, accompanied by spouses in snow-white dress or by their chauffeurs—moved among pricey outsized crystal ornaments glittering in dazzling rainbow colors. Vases and dishes stood in splendor among huge gold and silver tableware from the Far East, absolutely fit for kings, as the saying goes. In this case, more appropriately, for sheikhs. Monika had never seen such craftsmanship—or anything remotely like it—in Europe. While her Austrian family raved over antiques, she did not. This here was more her cup of tea: the very modern, the way out, the fantastic.

"Very few people in Europe have got the finances to purchase such goods. What European businessman in his right mind would put such exclusive stuff in his showrooms?" explained Abdulla to Monika, who was over-spilling with all that material beauty and splendor.

Next came the Old Souk (marketplace), which presented itself as a complete contrast with what Monika had just seen on Fahad al-Salem street. Little lock-up shops displayed their goods halfway across the street and were sandwiched into a long, narrow, dirty, badly paved, smelly street where the merchandise offered for sale came from China, Taiwan, or Japan. Electrical gadgets that the Japanese were so good at manufacturing were to be seen among clothes, carpets, china, Swiss clocks and watches, household goods, and everything but the kitchen sink. The shoppers in that area mostly matched the wares. Abdulla demonstrated proudly his bargaining skills. A toy plane with the price tag of 3 Kuwait Dinars landed in Sulaiman's hands for only 1 KD. Just as Monika was enjoying her "window shopping" the most, Abdulla abruptly broke it off. For all kinds of males had collected themselves around Abdulla's blonde beauty, like bees on a spring blossom, and were staring at her as if they were getting paid for it. When she moved a couple of steps, so did they, and when she stood still, so did they. Most of the unfortunate males were non-Kuwaitis, unemployed manpower that stood around waiting for work to appear—like carrying someone's shopping to the car or even a load as big as a fridge on their backs to awaiting vans, all just for the sake of an insignificant tip. They were mostly Iranians, Iraqis, or Indians—and poor—who looked and smelt accordingly in the great heat. Such men collectively rent a room and sleep, up to twenty or more, on the floor like fish in a tin, Abdulla explained. Their entire wealth is on their bodies all day—and nightlong. Money, they carry tightly wrapped around their waists in a belt. All they possess is the clothes on their backs. Poor devils, thought Monika and felt great pity for them. Such riches in Kuwait, yet some people live like rats merely to survive. One asks God, Where are You? Some of those 'men' were only boys, very young and awfully handsome looking. They had no idea that in Europe there were some girls who would go crazy over them—providing they cleaned themselves up, of course.

Homeward bound. Six camels, their front legs tied together so that they had just enough slack to take walking steps but would be unable to run away, were driven by a shouting bedouin, stick in hand, towards the slaughter house to be killed. Abdulla stopped and insisted on taking a hesitant Monika inside the foul-smelling, rat-infested building where dozens of young and old noisy camels knelt shouting and crying in line, the lower parts of their legs tied tightly to the upper parts just above the knees. The camels watched and smelt the savage slaughter of their brothers and sisters by men wielding huge, shiny, bloodstained knives. Thick, hot blood poured from the camels' necks in wide streams near the waiting camels, which must have instinctively known that their dreaded turn was soon to come. It was a sickening sight and experience for Monika. She had to turn back anyway because Sulaiman, in her arms, irritated and confused, started to cry with the camels and became very frightened. If the camels had to be killed, then why on earth not administer to them a decent death by gun or electric shock, instead of letting them suffer such inhumane treatment? The cruel suffering is inflicted, Monika learned, in the name of the Islamic religion, which forbids animals whose flesh is for human consumption to be killed by any other method. It is customary, indeed, to tie a camel outside the house where a wedding is to be held—days, even weeks, in advance—in order to advertise the happy impending occasion. The camel is then consumed at the feast. Camel meat is a bit harder and tastes sweeter than, say, a medium rare beefsteak.

The next day Abdulla drove Monika right into Aladdin's cave, a heaven for every true female that would have to be seen to be believed. Dozens of small shops were clustered under the same roof, littered with 22 carat gold and platinum jewelry, thick chains, coins in all sizes, wide bangles, narrow bangles, pearls, crowns, belts, evening bags, open velvet boxes displaying sets of king-size ruby, diamond, and emerald fantasies.

To cut it short, they had everything a female heart could possibly desire in jewelry. The sort of thing we females look at longingly, sometimes enviously, in magazines on the lucky fortunate ruling royals who possess such baubles and goodies. Wearing lots and lots of jewelry is *the* status symbol in Kuwait. A woman who sports lots of gold, diamonds, platinum, and rocks in general—the bigger the better—is telling the world, "My husband loves me. He dresses me in gold!" In Kuwait, less is not more; it is nothing. That's why so many Arab women, in their country and abroad, look like walking Christmas trees, trying hard to make the point.

In that gold market, a funny thing happened that day. Three middle aged, overweight, plump, short women in black—what else?—with Khajal applied heavily around their eyes, peeping through Kajmaks, came up to Abdulla, all shouting at him at the same time in native language: "God take pity on your *gotra* and *argal* [the headdress]. Do you *have* to take a foreigner?"

"Come closer, ladies," Abdulla invited. "Have you got daughters for marriage?"

"Yes!" they shouted, all three of them had.

"So, tell me, how much do you ask for your girls?"

They looked at each other, a bit lost for words. Then one of them recovered and said, "The usual going price!"

"Look at this pretty hamra. She is white, educated, and beautiful, and she does all the work. I need no servants. And you know what she costs me? Nothing! I got her for free. I didn't pay one *fils* [penny]." Abdulla had shut them up.

Looking at Monika and stroking her in disbelief, they chanted, as in a chorus: "God be with you, my son! God be with you!" They smiled at him and at Monika and were goners.

"People here," explained Abdulla, "are getting a bit worried. More and more educated Kuwaiti males get married to foreigners they meet while studying abroad, and our girls get left on the shelf because they can't marry non-Kuwaitis. It is not accepted. Some were daring and did, but by doing so brought shame on their families." Monika saw the point, and quite agreed. It could cause a problem in the nearer future.

Sightseeing accomplished, more than satisfyingly for one day, Monika wanted to see more—and everything—within the next few afternoons, as Abdulla had promised. She needed some walking shoes. She wore and possessed only high stilettos. What was required were a pair of white, medium-heeled sandals—to see the rest of Kuwait and the desert in comfort. Happily smiling, with Sulaiman holding onto Monika's hand, Monika entered the house. Mother-in-law yanked the box containing the white sandals roughly from under Monika's arm and inspected its contents. She looked at Abdulla while the edges of her mouth dropped towards her tits and pulled a face as if suddenly the purchase stunk.

"Mother, she bought those shoes with her own money," Abdulla apologetically lied to her. He stood before his mother, reminding Monika of a little boy who had wet his pants and was asking for a reprieve. His mother walked away, not wasting another word nor look on him. Now, Monika had understood that. She had picked up lots of Arabic words from Abdulla and his friends and from Abdulla's little talks with Sulaiman.

"Please tell me why you are afraid to tell your mother you bought me these shoes," she gently demanded.

"Sweetie, I promise I will tell you when we move out of here."

Monika had to wait seven years for that answer—as many more promises accumulated and spilled over. For that's how long Monika was kept in mother-in-law's circus tent. The first two weeks that Monika had agreed on—to get to know her in-laws—grew into the most unhappy seven years of her life, putting the miseries and indignities of convent life far behind in the shadow.

CHAPTER EIGHT

IMPRISONED

Many times Abdulla took Monika flat hunting. When on occasion she literally fell in love with some of the modern apartments that might have been suitable for the three of them, at least until their own house would be a reality, happiness seemed just around the corner. (Their own house!—at the moment, and for some time to come, just pie in the sky!) Abdulla always pleasantly, even enthusiastically, agreed if Monika had set her heart on having a certain place, only to come up afterwards with some silly excuse like, "The flat has already gone: we were too late," or "I don't like the landlord," or "I found out, in that building live too many Palestinians, and it's not fit for an Aseel Kuwaiti like me to move in amongst them!" And when he ran out of excuses, he served up the truth to Monika: "My mother is so upset that we want to leave her house. Please let's wait a bit longer, as I promised her to stay till we move into our own house."

"What, are you crazy!" Monika shouted at him, losing her temper in Kuwait for the first time. "Am I or is your mother your marriage partner, then? It's always the same. First mother, then come Diba and Sabiha and poor little spoilt-rotten Tamader, leaving me the last in line, getting the shit end of the stick. I feel like the fifth wheel on a car. Forget your mother for a moment and think of the promises you have made to me again and again! What about that? Do you get permission from them to fuck me, too, or do you only report to them afterwards? They all buy, do, go to, speak, and live altogether as they want to. You never tell them how to do anything. And let's face it, if you did, they'd tell you to fuck off! So why let them interfere all the time in our lives? If you have no pride, I've got enough for both of us. I am going back where I came from. You can find another canoe to paddle in!"

Abdulla was speechless. Monika had stood before him and given vent to all the anger and self-restraint that had accumulated in her during those first four weeks in Kuwait, all that while playing the meek role of in-laws' puppet, green light ahead.

"Sweetie, I promise you on my mother's death that we will have our own land within the next three months. Please be patient. I will take you to the gold market tomorrow, where you can choose anything you want."

"You can stick your gold where the sun don't shine! You can't buy me, thank you very much! Anyway, I would have to hide it up here in the flat because if mother-in-law gets wind of it she might get a coronary and blame it on you, and you would be the culprit on her black list once again. Don't you understand that in my case what is most essential to the heart is invisible to the eye?"

Monika realized, extremely irritated, that she had been misled by Abdulla but knew at the same time that it wasn't entirely his fault. When he had said they would move to a flat soon after her arrival, he had meant it at the time of saying it, but that was without counting on his mother's and sisters' interference. Abdulla was not completely innocent at that, for knowing what pleased them most and kept them happy, he used to tell them of all his and Monika's plans and whereabouts well in advance. He stood in the middle—on one side his ever-understanding European wife and on the other, his ignorant, backward, tricky, bitchy mother, who was backed by three jealous ill-behaved sisters. Of course, the majority always wins, doesn't it!

With his prolonged promises of "We get the land in eight (then six, then three, then six, then three) months," as much as nine horrid years passed before there was actually a house ready to move into!

Now, let's go back where we left off—to those notorious morning visits that never seemed to end—to view out-of-the-ordinary Monika in mother-in-law's house. Abdulla convinced his sweetie that that's what was expected of her, and would she please carry on with the awkward, nerve-wracking task of being viewed from all angles by noisy, simple, empty-headed, wrapped-up mummies—for his sake; and, as ever, he promised he would make it up to her. Eager to please, Monika, good-natured as she was, thought, "When in Rome, do as the Romans do." She felt unselfishly sorry for her Abdulla, who (for whatever reason) tried so hard to keep his family happy and content. Good hearted and young herself, she was yet to find out that it was she whom he was using as a tool to please and keep his family happy. She was yet to find out that, while he was very generous with way out promises that were made and forgotten at the same time, Abdulla considered her and Sulaiman the least. Someone should have told him that a lone rose planted in the arid Kuwaiti desert sand can in no way survive without a caring hand.

In the coming weeks, mother-in-law sent Monika back up to change a couple of times if what Monika wore didn't meet with her approval for the sit-in exhibitions that lasted—would you believe it?—three whole months, until every female in Kuwait who took an interest in seeing her had done so. From early morning until lunchtime, Monika did her duty in the visitor's torture chamber. When interest in her faded out, a much-relieved Monika could go back to wearing what she felt most comfortable in. Yet, the day-to-do-with-as-she-pleased was still not hers, and her in-laws saw to that, if Abdulla was not around. First of all, she did not realize what part she played, thinking naively that she was kept near them all the time because they liked her company. Down to earth, open hearted, she did not think twice when the in-laws asked her for a glass of water, to fetch scissors, or to see where some child had disappeared to in the large house. Nothing wrong, she thought, if they asked her to sew up a fallen hem or fix a button, especially as none of them could hold a needle, let alone do some sewing themselves. She was the well-trained convent girl at their disposal, doing and giving her best, polite, helpful, obliging and correct at all times, possessing virtues that her in-laws had never heard of, nor could imagine existed, nor could ever acquire. Here all the money in the world was of no use to help them, for what you don't learn in kindergarten you never catch up on in later life. Fashion- and body-conscious Monika took great pride always in her nails on her hands and feet. Of course, her in-laws wanted to have nails like hers; so she gave them, in turn, a manicure each and also attended to their neglected feet. God, what feet! She took about half a pound of dead skin off their dry, deeply cracked, uncared-for feet—the worst of which belonged to Sabiha and mother-in-law. Lots of perfume and jewelry were piled on, yet these Arab women treated their feet as if they belonged to a Jew (a pariah in Arab countries). What do their menfolk think of it? wondered Monika. After a treatment, they walked about as if newly born, showing off Monika's work of art to friends and relatives.

That reminds me! One day Abdulla came home, almost flying up the stairs and shouting, "Sweetie, Sweetie! I need your help! I want you to help me dress up as a woman. I'm going to play a joke on my friend!" Always game for a joke, Monika prepared for the occasion. She had the chauffeur take her to the female *souk* to purchase a pair of golden lady's sandals in a massive size—eight and a half. And when the day arrived, Monika considerably lightened Abdulla's facial complexion and outlined the inner rim around his eyes with black coal—*Khajal*. Long artificial eyelashes were glued close above his own. His lips glistened in bright tomato red to match the nail polish on his beringed fingers and toes. The man looked the mirror image of his younger sister Tamader! With one of his sister's black *abayas* and muslin facemask, nobody could possibly tell this creature's true sex! And so, with an outburst of laughter on his being sprayed with at least three brands of French perfume, Abdulla minced with tiny steps, swinging his hips sexily from left to right, a brown handbag dangling from his arm. He had Monika go down ahead of him to check that the way was clear, for he had of course to avoid his mothers and sisters on the way to his car. Off he drove in a rush of desert sand!

And then—guess what!—a month later Monika found out the true facts – that Abdulla did not dress up to play a joke at all. Quite the opposite, for the joke was really on *him*. His closest friend had told him that some pretty Kuwaiti *Aseel* girl fancied him and, in order to be able to meet her without arousing suspicion, he should dress up in disguise as a female. And so Abdullah drove expectantly in anticipation to a certain roundabout in Kuwait holding a white live chicken—of all things great and small! For the chicken would be the sign by which his female admirer would be able to recognize him and differentiate him from a real woman. Instead of the promised *Aseel* maiden, however, Abdulla's friends, in a cortège of cars, circled the roundabout, laughing their heads off at the sight of their victim holding a live chicken to his chest. This, in fact, was typical of many jokes played by Abdulla and his friends on one another. Abdullah was happy to confess the true facts to Monika a month later over a drink.

Slowly, it dawned on Monika that she and the slaving servants were doing all the work, while mother-in-law and her three offspring usually sat cross-legged in a room full of visitors and their mischievous youngsters, drinking tea, eating nuts, gossiping in a circle, while ordering Monika and the servants about, showing off like puffed up adders that the hamra did as they wished and ordered.

Whenever Abdulla took Monika and Sulaiman out for a ride or shopping, Monika found that her in-laws had already accommodated themselves in the car, with Monika, more often than not, having to squeeze in on the back seat—except on sightseeing trips. Then, they had to pluck their bottoms out again because Kuwait was, of course, luckily so for Monika, of no interest whatsoever to them. They had cars and drivers at their disposal, but stuck to Abdulla and Monika like Superglue, anxious not to miss out on something—or anything, really—that was none of their business in the first place. It was an impossible task for the young couple to go on a picnic in the desert or to the seashore for a swim without their breathing down Monika's neck with their stupid comments and conversations backdating to B.C.

Dentist Pavlik's words of warning came now a dozen times a day into her daughter's ears. "If you marry an Arab, you marry his whole family." Oh, Mother, how right you were! What bothered Monika more than their irritating presence was the loud, quarrelsome, screechy shouting of children and grown-ups that went right through her to the marrow. In the car, it gave her a massive headache—not forgetting their dirty habit of spitting noisily onto the car's floor, a habit they also practiced inside the house. Where in each room lay a Persian carpet, they walked up to it and slipped off their shoes to walk barefoot on the textile, but on the floor where shoes were worn, they spat as well—a sickening, most unsightly, unhygienic custom. Abdulla never did that. It was hard to believe he came from such an uncivilized family. Monika would never have guessed it, back in Great Britain. He was much better matched with his trendy cousins.

Nevertheless, in his house and his mother's limo, small children were left to crawl about. It did not seem to bother their mothers what filth and germs they were picking up while doing so. Maybe they didn't understand hygiene. As long as the outside appearance looked presentable to the eye, everything was in tranquility.

With most of the immediate, big circle of close relatives, Abdulla's mother had family feuds of one kind or another. So Abdulla took Monika in secrecy to introduce her and visit them and show her how they lived. Their generosity, coming from the heart, had no end. They were visibly knocked back and honored by the visits, offering everything edible in the house, piling it up firmly in front of Monika, the honored guest. And whatever she admired, they pressed firmly into her hands. She had to take it, too, or insult them by refusing. It sometimes got really very embarrassing. She walked out of one house with a clock that had previously hung peacefully ticking on a wall; out of another, with a massive crystal fish; another, a heart-shaped radio. She felt like a cheap beggar. Abdulla should have warned her about that custom; instead, he teased her in front of people, telling them, "She wants it; that's why she says it's nice," and so encouraged them and made her blush, all in good humor and fun. "We are not in Europe, Sweetie, where people count their pennies. Here all people have lots of money and like to give." Monika's last admiring blunder came with Abdulla's cousin Said. She praised the beautiful and elegant nine-diamond gold ring he wore on his little finger. No sooner had she said it than he pulled the ring off, insisting and swearing on his mother's head that she was meant to keep it. Everybody seemed to swear on his mother's head in Kuwait.

"Said, no, thank you. I am not a man. I can't ever wear it!"

"But you like it. So, put it on your bedside table and look at it the first thing in the morning and the last thing at night. You see, your problem is solved!"

One fine evening as Monika and Abdulla entered the house after visiting friends, mother-in-law scolded Abdulla loudly for carrying his son Sulaiman in public while walking steps behind his European wife. Friends of her who had seen them window-shopping had reported the shameful incident. In Kuwait, the women always walk five steps behind their husbands, not the other way around. Tamader had to translate that shameful incident to Monika, of course.

"You bad, old witch. You never tire of shit stirring," was Monika's unspoken comment, while for the first time—surprise, surprise!—Abdulla plucked up some courage out of the blue and dared to speak up to his mother.

"I'm a graduate of one of the best universities in Great Britain and greatly respected in Kuwait! I am not a bedouin, Mother."

For the first time Monika saw mother-in-law at a loss for words. Not expecting such a rebuff from her son, she fiddled uneasily with her mile of bracelets, searching her brain for a fitting excuse, or answer.

"I don't mind. All I want is your happiness, my son. But people are bad. They talk. Your father brought shame on us with his drinking and the women he kept in tow, and now you continue with a hamra that you have brought back to us along with your degree from Europe. The oil has ruined our lives. It would have been much better for all of us if you had never gone to study abroad. People won't stop. They will continue to talk."

Emotional blackmail was used again and again on Abdulla, and he was made to feel guilty for marrying Monika, a thorn in mother-in-law's side. Where else could you find all the nastiness you could think of all in one place? Using and exaggerating other people's gossip as an excuse, always searching for something to get at Monika with—anything was welcome to help cover the truth, which was simply that the hamra was a girl none of them could hold a candle to, and they knew it, but could not digest it. Rivalry egged them on. Being pretty and witty made Monika the object of female jealousy in Kuwait, particularly in Abdulla's family. Those women envied her looks and her trim figure. She had a good shape despite having given birth to a son. She was dressed all day long in elegant Western clothing, while they walked about the house like unmade beds. Being good hearted and a male, Abdulla didn't realize what was going on until many months of troubles later.

Sabiha, unmarried and fat, was in the hilarious habit of trying to flatten her stomach with a rolling pin after every meal. What a laugh! She seemed to be dying of surfeit. She would swear she would never eat so much again—*insh'allah* (God willing), an oath she swore every day after she had eaten. Now, here was one person who lived to eat and didn't eat to live. Her problem was not just the extra weight. She didn't know how to carry herself altogether, hadn't the faintest notion of how to walk in high heels, yet she did. While the in-laws' bodies were short and big, their legs reminded one of Popeye's Olive, especially thin at the ankles! Wearing high-heeled shoes and wobbling about made them look like Mickey Mouse, arms akimbo, trying to walk on a tightrope. When Sabiha walked, one could have fit a miniature Eiffel Tower between her open legs. And she swung her handbag to and fro like a chiming bell when she waddled from one foot to the other, like a penguin. In fact, with very few exceptions, the women Monika met in her in-laws' circle hadn't a clue about how to dress. They just put on the European designer models from Paris, London, Milano, never wore them. Monika didn't spend a lot of money on clothes. Indeed, everything she wore at the beginning she had brought with her from Europe, yet she mixed and matched well, putting the dot on the i with well-chosen accessories so that it looked as if she were always wearing something different, while her sisters-in-law would go crazy with their money, buying something new all the time, occasion or no occasion, not knowing that, in their case, less extravagance would be a plus, and they ended up looking like over-dressed turkeys. They even *sounded* like turkeys, and their big bottoms caused them to lumber along like fattened cows! While on one side despising the foreigner, they did not mind asking and taking Monika's advice on almost everything they did. Her opinion on their makeup, dress, and female beauty in general Monika gave gladly, yet there is a limit to what can be done even if you have a talent to beautify. Without taste, a certain flair, figure, and a bit of manner to match, what *can* be done? A dog fitted with a diamond necklace remains a dog. They were a disgrace to the Western *haute couture* they so unbefittingly wore. That was Monika's opinion, anyway. *Really*, she thought, you can't make a silk purse out of a sow's ear!

Monika would have needed the magic power of the genie in the lamp to achieve anything close to success in cases like Sabiha's. Her pet peeve was the way those women wore their stockings without garters! Garter belts felt too uncomfortable around their fleshy waists. And pantyhose made washing the pubic area before their prayers five times a day—a must according to the Holy Koran—complicated and difficult. So they held their stockings up, more or less effortlessly, with ordinary elastic bands, leaving generously knotted ends sticking out! Of course, their stockings always hung ruffled and loose around their calves and ankles, and what an ugly sight. Monika felt on such occasions very much like going around and pulling up every woman's stockings and pushing each one's legs together. Now, you just imagine a room full of women wearing Balmain, Dior… bejeweled, coiffed, made-up, and sitting on show with their legs spread apart wide and their primitive elastic cutting deep into the tight fat of their knees! A peep at their long-legged pants is for free, too, but not a turn on. On the contrary, it's a turn off, one hundred percent, a most unsightly sight, reducing the women in their French garments to next to nothing. If, say, those same women had had the opportunity and good fortune of attending a Swiss finishing school, what a picture of elegance and beauty they could be!

The older women like mother-in-law wore ordinary three-quarter length, Indian-tailored simple cuts in dark colors under their black abayas, with fewer jewels, because for a woman of that age, it wasn't (and still isn't) considered proper to wear flashy clothes or use any makeup, with the exception of black kajal around the eyes, not even a dash of lipstick. Monika sensed strongly that her mother-in-law would have loved to dress up and let herself be carried away by all the beauty aids available, but she had, obviously, to suppress that urge and behave according to the mandates of custom. The only accepted beauty aid for old women is the reddish brown henna that Cleopatra made popular, and that only for special occasions. It is applied on lips, nails, on the inside of the palms and the soles of the feet, sometimes drawn artfully into a pretty, imaginary pattern that looks nice until it starts to wear off, whereupon it looks dirty and untidy, just as nail polish does when it has flaked off halfway.

As Monika was forced to settle down in and fit into mother-in-law's household, Monika observed and classified people into two groups: the minus and the plus group. Her in-laws belonged to the minus; the pluses included Abdulla's nice cousins and nieces, along with the majority of Kuwaiti people she had gotten to know and was pleased existed but who didn't mix socially with her in-laws, who in turn tried their best, quite often successfully, to keep the hamra in their own circle, as if she were their bought property. If birds of a feather flock together, Monika was definitely not a bird of her in-laws' feather.

There were plenty of lovely Kuwaiti families, open hearted, friendly, sweet and kind without malice of her in-laws' kind. Deeply unhappy with her fate, Monika asked God a hundred times or more, "Why, of all the nice families in Kuwait, did you choose to send me straight into Hell and give me Medusa as a mother-in-law?"

Against her will, Monika was forced to mix with her in-laws all the time, persuaded again and again by Abdulla, who, being cowardly, had just one thing in mind: to keep his mother happy. Despite the difficulties Abdulla was facing from his immediate family for marrying Monika, he was puffed up with pride outside because of her. She was a good looker and, clearly, his friends were not averse physically or in any other way. On the contrary, most of them congratulated him, saying things like: "If you have to marry a foreigner, marry one like Monika or don't! She looks first after her husband, is a good mother, keeps her flat in sparkling order, and does not need any servants. And on top of all this, it's always a pleasure to look at her. How does she do it? Our wives have a nanny, a cook, a chauffeur, a maid for themselves, are fat and run around in the house like rag dolls. What they are best at is spend, spend, and spend our money. One hates to think what would happen if the oil, Allah forbid, were to stop overnight: no servants, no shopping, disaster!"

Abdulla throve on compliments of that type and helped to make up for his scolding, jealous mother and sisters. Of course, Monika, too, loved the nice, material things in life, but did not mind working for them. Yet, she was far away from a money-grabbing, materialistic person that begrudged anybody's beauty, wealth, intelligence, or good luck. Quite the opposite. She was happy for the fortunate. People like her are rare in this world, one has to admit.

Monika in her early twenties was a radical, orthodox person who liked to do her own, sometimes unusual, thing. The older she got, the more her individuality, which was strongly suppressed in the convent, came to light. She did not like to look or be like anyone else, or to do what everybody else around her did. She had her own style. Her personality and light coloring automatically attracted the jealousy of certain womenfolk in Kuwait, just as light attracts moths. Lively Monika stood out in the crowd without being pushy, a typical Aries ram with her moon in Scorpio, a fire sign and a water sign, all rolled into one. Around such a person there's always something doing. Rot does not get a chance to settle in easily. We know now that Monika was well aware that she would be stuck for some time to come with her in-laws. So let's look at some of the terrors she survived, nerves strained to the limit, from 1963 to 1967.

CHAPTER NINE

MAKING INROADS

In the beginning, she had to give the top half of the house, where she was to live for the time being, a drastic, thorough cleanup. The American supermarket in Fahad al-Salem Street, one of only a handful like it in Kuwait at that time and an absolute must for European and American employees in Kuwait, was a heaven-sent discovery. On entering the store for the first time, Monika was overcome. The familiar felt good. All the shoppers were foreigners like her, speaking in quiet tones—German, Dutch, English, Czech, and so on. Mixing with these people made her feel less alone. They, too, lived in Kuwait, a small but nonetheless real consolation. Full shelves offered almost the same food and articles as were available in England and an even wider choice of American and German products. Abdulla gave her the green light ahead. She could buy anything she wanted. Mother-in-law had objected when Abdulla spent on Monika, but even she had to accept that household stuff and food were necessities. The Yemeni chauffeur at her disposal would see to the bills until she was more familiar with Kuwaiti currency, for people were not immune to cheating in Kuwait. After taking in the atmosphere of the place, Monika made a bee-line for cleaning utensils, grabbing brushes in all sizes and shapes, cloths, soaps, Vim, Ajax, Fairy Liquid, Dettol, Kleenex (many boxes of Kleenex), loo cleaners, half a dozen rubber gloves, furniture polish, lots and lots of rose scented fresh air sprays, and insect killer for ants and to kill the horrible, all-over-the-flat, one-and-a-half-centimeter-long cockroaches that came crawling out of every crack, especially at night, and scared Monika and Sulaiman shitless, while Abdulla, who grew up with the repulsive insects, had laughing fits watching the two. She piled everything she needed to turn a filthy, neglected flat into tip-top condition into three shopping carts.

Back home she stood on a long ladder that she found in the courtyard and scrubbed down the doors, windows, and walls of the five rooms with Vim and Dettol. With the accumulated dirt and grease loosened, she pulled the garden hose (used by the drivers to wash cars) up through the balcony door and hosed the soapy lather off the walls, leaving them looking newly painted. She brushed the water onto the balcony, from where it found its way down. Foolhardy, she almost snuffed it, not realizing a wire that was hanging from a wall was damaged, exposed and live. When she pulled on the deadly wire to get it out of the way, she went *zig-zag-zig-zag* on the ladder and quickly let go. Mother-in-law stood below shouting and screaming hysterically and ran away. The screaming scared Monika almost more than the electric shock had done! As a remedy, Monika had a cup of coffee and a cigarette to help speed along her recovery.

Through the whole process of turning the dirty, filthy rooms into respectable chambers, mother-in-law stood close by, perplexed, watching Monika's every move, talking non-stop, making sneering remarks to herself, swaying her head and upper body like a pendulum. Whatever she was saying definitely had nothing to do with approval of any kind regarding what the white woman was doing. That much Monika could clearly make out and didn't need to speak the language to come to that conclusion. The expression on the old woman's face gave it all away. As usual, however, Monika pretended not to notice.

After Monika had finished her task, the flat was so clean you could have eaten off the floor; but she soon had to see a dermatologist, for the strong chemicals in the cleaning materials or something had promoted a severe case of nail-bed infection. She was sentenced to three months of no nail polish!

Monika never saw her mother-in-law laugh. Once in a while the woman tried to twist a false grin and grimace into a smile, but her unfriendliness was written all over her face, and her face was a photocopy of what was inside. Monika tried to stay aloof, reminding herself that she was in every way a blue-blooded superior here among the commonest of the common. Thus, any attempt to insult her—then and up to this day and far reaching into the future—would always have to remain a dream-not-come-true for her nasty in-laws. Monika knew she had what they wanted but what money could not buy: her class. They were, she now understood, deadly jealous of her.

Mother-in-law inspected the magic powders and liquids closely while shouting for her servants, ordering them to watch Monika closely and to do downstairs exactly as Monika had done in her living quarters. That same afternoon Abdulla had to make a second trip to the market for duplicate cleaning materials that his mother wanted and had to have on the spot. Thanks to Monika, the Amahani family could instruct their servants for the first time as to what and how to clean the house properly. They had merely to watch Monika and do likewise.

Before Monika's European ways were copied, mother-in-law's kitchen sink smelled nauseating from afar, as did all the toilets. Hygiene? They had never heard of it here! Corners of rooms were never cleaned because they were so crammed with junk of all sorts that no one could get at them with a broom. They had become ideal places for insects, rats, and mice to nest and to hatch. The only time Monika saw mother-in-law with a broom in her hand was when she was pushing a rat out of the room with it. Mice lived happily and undisturbed in upholstery that was never used because everybody always sat on the floor. The mice even came out at night to watch TV standing up on their hind legs! Abdulla and his family reacted with laughter to

Monika's aversion for germ-carrying pests and to her expressions of disgust.

Some things they didn't change. Rough steel wool and Persil powder were used by servants to clean plates and aluminum pots after mealtimes. The dishes and pots and pans were then piled on a big, round tray and set outside in the sun to dry on the ground, where the pile always collected a thick veil of dust that no one seemed to object to. A foul, smelly, worn-out, old towel was used to clean the gas stove, the huge gas flasks next to it, the floor, the cupboards, and the hands as well. Here people lived firmly on the floor. That is where one ate, sat, chatted, slept. For them, a house was only a small jump away from the tents they had occupied not so long ago, when they were bedouins.

Yes, Monika was, of course, married to a bedouin. She would never have guessed it of Abdulla in Britain, nor did he tell her. But once in Kuwait, there was no denying the fact; and, considering such facts, they have not done too badly. It never occurred to Monika to make discriminating remarks, nor to laugh about their primitive, ignorant, backward ways. What she strongly objected to, though, was that Abdulla's family tried to make her one of them—starting with wanting to change her name to Mona and trying to convince her that with black hair coloring she would mix in much better. But for Monika that would have meant shedding a couple hundred years or so of her modern culture, something that was—even if she were willing to go along with them—impossible. Quite naturally, she objected to being bossed about by the primitive folks. She was willing to do what Abdulla asked, in moderation, but not to overdo. As time passed, however—and without Monika's always realizing it—they made her do what they wanted, through Abdulla.

Let's go back to the kitchen where cockroaches lived quite undisturbed on some cupboard shelves and in cupboards amongst groceries. For reasons quite obvious, Monika wanted to know exactly what she and Sulaiman consumed. So she cooked her own meals for her threesome, something the in-laws could not grasp as the servants were there to do it for her. Her European dishes were daily sampled by the whole family, and for that reason she had to cook twice the amount she would have needed under normal circumstances. After licking their fingers and the dishes, too, and not leaving a trace of the European food they had consumed, Monika's in-laws thought nothing of criticizing every one of Monika's well-prepared dishes by making sneering remarks and bursting into silly laughter. They tried to give her advice on how to make her food taste better next time. She ignored it completely. Here again she was doing something they knew nothing about and the end result was the same: jealousy.

After three weeks of hard work Monika's flat was spic and span, with new curtains that hid the unsightly thick mesh wire and milky glass windows one could not see through; there were new modern lamps, spotlights hitting mighty potted plants, the latest stereo system, a king-size TV, a new, fitted, red kitchen counter in the huge hall where to start with there had been no kitchen at all. Bits and pieces of furniture were added tastefully and mirrors—plenty of mirrors—hung or stood all around the place, and—BINGO!—the unsightly shit-hole was transformed into a showpiece home. Nothing remained to remind Monika of the dirty, dark past.

Now, mother-in-law was fully occupied again and in full swing. She became a busy bee bringing in neighbors and visitors at all hours of the day to see the European-style decor, just as the fancy took her. A door would unexpectedly open and in they would walk with a hoard of kids in procession who were all over with hands and feet, stepping onto and jumping on and off settees while reaching for ornaments and anything that captured their interest. But who could blame the children? The grown-ups opened cupboards and drawers for closer inspection as if they were going to purchase the contents. Looking was not enough; they had, of course, to leave fingerprints behind everywhere and on everything. Mother-in-law and her daughters looked upon everything in Monika's flat as belonging to Abdulla or, more accurately, to themselves.

In the extreme heat of Kuwait, Monika's body craved the wet and the cold. She forgot all about food and got hooked, instead, on Coca Cola. The drinking water tasted horrible, especially since she knew the servants now and then found a dead rat and sometimes even a dead cat in the water tank. The sweet drinks only increased her thirst. Abdulla bought and stocked crates of the Cola downstairs for her. Monika didn't see why she had to go down X-times a day for a cold Coke, where she got meaningful looks whenever she opened the fridge even though she always asked politely first. Still, she went through the ritual until one day she was told there was no Coke left even though she saw two crates covered with a plastic tablecloth hidden in the corner! When she complained to Abdulla, he didn't believe her. He even got cross.

"Mother said I should store it with her for you, so why would she hide it from you?"

"Why she hid it is for you to find out, but why it is stored with her I can tell you. So that she can make me ask for it—like a subject—everyday. Tell me, clever dick, where is the logic in keeping Cola for me with your mother? Where does the logic lie? Don't you ever think for yourself without blindly following such ridiculous instructions first? You know, I think, if they suggested you poison me bit by bit, you would even follow those instructions." From then on the Coca Cola was kept in Monika's flat.

Abdulla did not have much to fear from his mother when he bought stuff for the flat because it boosted his mother's morale to be able to show it off. It was only on Monika that he was not allowed to spend any money. His mother and sisters looked upon such expenditure as treachery. Every time Monika and Abdulla carried their groceries into the house, mother-in-law first closely inspected the packages. All the years they stayed there, before they could carry their groceries upstairs, mother-in-law would have to investigate them. She would even look into the matchboxes, making sure they really contained matches! Monika detested the old woman's fingers in her cornflakes, sugar, sultanas, whatever, and the way she put her nose into every package and sometimes took a lick!

There was no getting out of it because anybody entering the house was automatically in mother-in-law's field of vision. She oversaw the main entrance, residing on a raised pillow like a well-trained police dog. If there was something Abdulla had bought and wanted to keep a secret from his family, he would have to leave it in the trunk of his car and sneak downstairs in the middle of the night like a thief to fetch it up for his sweetie. It was really difficult for him to tick both ways and act normal.

Leading out of the new kitchen hallway that Monika had designed so beautifully was a gigantic balcony measuring roughly 9 x 7 square meters, enclosed by two dirty, gray, two-meter-high cement walls that Monika cleaned and painted a fresh, bright orange gloss. Close to the walls she stood fifty or so huge green flowerpots holding different sorts of outsized, prickly, exotic cactuses from the Kuwait market. They gave the most fantastic blooms in assorted colors, and it was a great pity the flowers were so short lived. In the early morning you might see the most beautiful, delicate purple flower high up on a cactus's top and at noon there would be no evidence left that it had ever been there. That balcony became the ideal playpen for Sulaiman while Monika could sunbathe there in the nude. All in all, Monika was well pleased with her work of art.

While she had been slaving away, Abdulla—utterly unable to fix even an electric plug—took to going out to visit douvaniahs and friends, sometimes till very late in the morning, and coming back smelling of alcohol. He offered to employ a servant for her to help with her tasks, but she declined. She preferred to do things herself. Those so-called servants would have to be scrubbed down first, given clean clothes (while the old ones would have to be gotten rid of, best burnt), and after that they would need about a year's worth of training before she could let them loose alongside Sulaiman in the flat. One could tell simply by the way servants' work was done downstairs, where things looked a shambles even after they had cleaned up. One could not blame the poor servants. If the women of the house haven't the faintest notion how to hold a broom and let everything fall to the floor to be picked up by others, how are the staff to know and do better? Especially the cheap servants for whom Abdulla's mother had a preference and who were simply taken in from the street. Monika's female in-laws did not know the meaning of work, or what it might feel like to work. They were so lazy that if the impossible were possible they would have had their bottoms cleaned for them as well.

Once Monika and Abdulla were nicely settled in their new home, the clan downstairs was raving mad with envy because, compared to upstairs, their part of the house looked like a pigsty. They had all that money and servants, but no know-how, while Monika—the intruder, the hamra from the West—had it, and that just did not let them rest in peace. Not a day passed that they didn't greet homecoming, tired Abdulla with one silly complaint after another about his wife or about little Sulaiman.

"Abdulla, Monika did not put the tomatoes in the fridge. They will go bad!" "Abdulla, only yesterday your wife cooked prawns and today she cooked you fish for lunch again. Two days running fish is not proper!" "She plays her European Elvis music too loud!" "She ignores us!" "She does not like to sit with us. We ask her to come down, and she says she is busy! Busy with what? What has she got to do sitting on her own? Is she hiding something from us, or does she think she is better than we are? Aren't we good enough for her?" "Sulaiman makes noise all morning on the balcony! Mother had a headache today, and that made it worse." They also complained about Monika's foreign visitors, who were few and far between.

Those rare visitors were mostly girls who, like Monika, were married to Kuwaitis and had a lot in common to talk about. The in-laws were even jealous of that little bit of private enjoyment, anxious not to miss out on some action and the good food Monika prepared for such occasions. They held on to Monika and permitted her no privacy. Poor girl. There she was with no one to console her, nor help her, while the whole world seemed to be against her. It wasn't that way, but that's what it felt like.

Most of the time Abdulla did not take much notice of his family's mindless blather. Instead, he credited his wife with an apology. "Sweetie, I am really sorry. I can't help it. They are so very jealous of you. Given time they will get used to you, hopefully, and accept you as you are. You see, you can do all these things—occupy yourself, join in a conversation about any subject that comes up, create beautiful things out of nothing, and the main thorn is that you are a glamour puss. On the other hand, they know that they can't do a thing, and that they know nothing, and let's face it, they look a bit of a disaster, and that's all it is! Their ignorance is mingled with envy and if my mother were just another woman to me, I personally would stand up and swear, God forgive me, that she was the devil itself! But what can I do? God gave me such a woman for a mother and I have to make the best of it. I am trying, Sweetie. I am really trying, and it won't be much longer now, and we will have our own land to build on."

"If that's really the best you can do, then it's definitely doing shit!" answered Monika. "You did not tell me in England that I'd have to live with the whole bunch of your family. Please, Abdulla, please, please, let's move out now! Don't you see how I suffer? Don't you care at all about how I feel? I am even starting to lose my temper with poor Sulaiman more often lately. In this house there lingers some strangely evil atmosphere. There's no laughter. Nobody ever seems to be happy here. Your family are professional shit-stirrers!" There were tears in Monika's eyes.

Abdulla put his arms around her shoulders, pulling her close to his chest while whispering in her ear, "I know you love me. You will see it through with me because you love me, and I am the father of your most precious possession, Sulaiman. Am I right?"

Monika pushed him away. "Oh, Abdulla. Don't put on one of your sentimental records again! You're such a convincing talker, so why not go and preach to the one who, if she were not your mother, you said would be the devil! The two of us and Sulaiman are the only three happy-go-lucky beings in this house. Yet, you don't dare to show me any kind of affection in your mother's presence. And if she catches us happy together or we laugh a little louder, it's as if we sprinkle holy water on the devil. Giving your statement closer consideration, I think you hit the nail on the head! She could well be the devil in disguise!"

CHAPTER TEN

WITCHES AND WASTA

As all of them were so dead set against Monika, one might have thought that they'd have welcomed with open arms her and Abdulla's wish to move out of the house and into a place of their own. But, no! That would have been normal, civilized human behavior, something about which they didn't have a clue, something that had nothing to do with them.

Monika had already become a deep-rooted center of interest in their lives. Watching, criticizing, spying, discriminating against, and trying to change her with whatever force was available to them became their daily aphrodisiac because they had no other interest in life besides gossiping, eating, sleeping, and shopping, and no chance of a change for the better anywhere in sight. They just couldn't do without Monika any more! How true the saying: "Work is the universal panacea: without it a whole population would go insane." Monika's in-laws didn't have to work, nor did they want to, and were they sane? No, they were not! They would not have passed a test, that's for sure. Their ancestors might have been hard workers. Often, Monika heard people mention how the good old times without luxuries were changed by the British with the drilling for oil, but not for the better. Money has corrupted people; made them greedy, lazy, unreasonable, and jealous; and made them strangers, whereas before the oil they were one big, happy family.

Quite true. If Monika's in-laws had to do their own housework, they would have no time to pester her; but under the given circumstances she carried on, trying to make the best of her 'shituation' with an endlessly optimistic heart. Had she been allowed to take a quick peep into her future—as she tried to do later with the help of mediums and psychics—she would have swallowed and choked on her pride a hundred times over and gone straight back home to mother on roller skates. But, then, she was young and innocent.

Having fun with Abdulla and playing childish games like hide-and-seek didn't stop abruptly when Monika and Abdulla returned to Kuwait. Sometimes when the house was empty (except, maybe, for mother-in-law), Monika hid downstairs with Sulaiman in the big hall behind the long, heavy, olive-green, satin curtains. Abdulla knew where to look to find them. One day Abdulla sneaked quietly close, pinching her bottom. His hands worked their way around to her front and wriggled towards her breasts. Abdulla had a bit of sex in mind, not hide-and-seek. In the meantime, Sulaiman was crawling up on one of the settees and further up onto the back of the settee and reaching out with one hand for an old, broken clock that stood on the shelf above. At that moment, mother-in-law came shooting through some door and into the hall. Not suspecting that anyone was nearby, she pulled the clock forcefully out of the child's hands with such impact that his bottom hit the settee and he bounced off it, knocking his little head with an almighty bang on the hard marble floor. The baby screamed out in pain at the top of his voice. His hand was bleeding. Grandmother, not in the least bit bothered, was just about to walk off and leave him there. Monika's heart dropped with a sick feeling into her stomach. She flew to her son's rescue. She and Abdulla had both witnessed mother-in-law's cruelly heartless act. But the old witch must have experienced a mild shock on hearing Abdulla's voice shouting at her from the shadows: "Mother, what on earth are you doing! This child is your son. He is your flesh and blood. How can you be so cruel?"

"This clock is broken, and I didn't want him to hurt himself," came mother-in-law's lying excuse.

From then on, Monika took great care never to leave Sulaiman alone for a moment near his murderously nasty grandmother.

From the moment Monika first set eyes on Sabiha's fiancé Fahad, Sabiha had insisted on knowing Monika's honest opinion of him and whether Fahad or Abdulla, her brother, were the better looking. Fahad's looks were very ordinary for an Arab, nothing like Abdulla's. Unless he plastered his face in money, no pretty girl would look at him twice. He looked like a forward-leaning walking skeleton, but to make up for it he was always drenched in French after-shave and cologne. He picked at his food like a bird with his long feminine fingers, and altogether was a bit unmanly. You couldn't imagine him, for instance, changing a flat tire. Character-wise, he seemed a nice enough guy, but in general was nothing too impressive. How could Monika possibly give her honest opinion? She did not want to hurt nor to provoke her sister-in-law, neither would she ass-kiss because Monika's true nature was honesty and straightforwardness. Her pet peeves were pretense and lies, so she told a soup-eating Sabiha what she thought was a happy compromise:

"Fahad is a nice man. You suit each other. But, to be honest, he is not my type."

And how do you think Sabiha took that? I'll tell you. She pulled the spoon out of her soup, held her soup bowl in both hands, and poured the contents over Monika's head! Astounded but not angry, Monika sat with green pea soup drip-dropping down and around her. Sabiha laughed, satisfied with what she had done.

"My Fahad all women want! You, too. But you don't want to say so because you know he's special."

Monika—ready at any time to take a joke or play one back—was not annoyed at all. She was, in fact, laughing when she ran up to her flat to arm herself with last night's leftover dinner and a bottle of tomato ketchup. Sabiha was still sitting on the floor as *plonk!*—before she knew it a bundle of long, wriggly, white spaghetti sat on her head like a bird's nest.

"A bit of ketchup for the lady? And maybe a sprinkle of Parmesan cheese while I'm at it, madam?" Monika joked, and half ironically added, "And if madam has no other wishes, may I retreat, now? Do excuse me." Bowing her head in Sabiha's direction, Monika disappeared to take a shower, convinced that Sabiha would never do anything like that to her again—and she didn't. Sabiha was the closest one to her mother's heel. In the contest to minimize as much as possible Monika's love of life, Sabiha came in only second. She happened to be the least intelligent and nastiest of the three sisters.

A good Muslim makes a pilgrimage at least once during his or her lifetime to Mecca, the Holy Shrine in Saudi Arabia, where the prophet Muhammad is buried. Mother-in-law was to go and return after a two-weeks' absence, during which time Abdulla would take her place and supervise the servants. He told the cook each morning what to prepare for the day. On the day of his mother's return, he made sure that his mother's favorite fish dish was on the menu. Monika's most (and only) favorite Kuwaiti food was fish, too, but it was not Meed, mother-in-law's favorite; it was Subaidi, a big fish stuffed at home with onions, herbs, and spices and then taken to cook at the local baker's clay oven. Meed was a tiny fish whose muddy gray guts were not removed, and Monika could not stomach the smell nor sight of it. That day Sabiha, who had been shopping all morning, the fish smell creeping up her nostrils, greeted Abdulla with, "All you can think of is your foreigner. Instead of cooking for our mother today, you have her on your mind again. Shame on you. Poor mother."

"You are dead jealous," countered Abdulla, "because Monika happens to be a couple of numbers too big for you and you can't change that. That's what's bothering you. You don't give a fig for what mother gets to eat. I tell you something for free! What you smell on your hooter is not Subaidi. It is Meed, mother's favorite, and I feel sorry for the man stupid enough to take you, you useless troublemaker, for a wife; but the sooner you leave this house, the better for us all." Abdulla ended his speech at the top of his voice and spat at Sabiha for the grand finale. He felt much better afterwards. Sabiha had had something like this coming for some time now. She had given Abdulla pinches with her forked tongue once too often.

Six months had passed since Monika's arrival in Kuwait, and still there was no sign of the big trunk from London containing household goods, toys, and bits and pieces of things Monika was used to and was waiting for desperately. Whenever she enquired of Abdulla about it, he got edgy and annoyed.

"I don't know. Maybe it got lost!" he would snap back at her to avoid the subject. The question seemed to annoy him so much that, later on, Monika only dared ask about it if she knew Abdulla to be in a good mood—before a sex session, for instance, which slowly but surely after a while was to become the only time she had, and could count on, his undivided attention.

Quite unexpectedly one day while she was helping in Diba's house to prepare tea for some visitors, Monika stood in the kitchen facing—would you believe it?—her very own personal kitchen clock, the one she had bought at Selfridges in London, high up on the wall. Her inlaid tea tray leaned decoratively against white ceramic tiles, her enameled tea kettle from Austria, with the adjustable tea nut, stood on a shelf in an open kitchen cabinet, and through the opening into the Dining Hall, she was to look straight at her Swiss, creamy, lace curtains, used here as a tablecloth. Monika stood shocked, still, like a statue of stone, perspiring, her brain working overtime. See! See! That's where her trunk had found refuge! Abdulla must have known. That's why he did not want to talk about it, why he avoided the truth. Monika was on the verge of an almighty explosion, but she would never stoop to their level and let them take her "cool."

An argument with those beings would be a most welcome event for them, but too big a risk for Monika, who rightfully, cleverly, avoided disputes with them like the plague. I mean, which brainchild in its right mind would ask a bear to use the toilet? But once back home Monika let the fur fly with Abdulla, who had been all along "in the know" about the missing trunk. He explained that his mother—of course, who else?—had distributed the contents long before Monika had arrived in Kuwait, knowing bloody well whose property it was. All along he had kept this secret to himself and had lied to his wife, who, naturally, was now mad and deeply hurt, feeling utterly betrayed by her husband, the person for whom she had left Europe and her culture to come to this wicked wilderness.

Abdulla was the only man in the world for her. She considered the rest of his family unimportant, disturbed beings in her life, and she often said, God, forgive them, for they really don't know what they are doing. They knelt on their knees five times a day to pray to Allah, but as soon as they got up, mischief took over—as if that were exactly what they were praying for. Whatever her in-laws plotted, she never took to heart. Only her husband, Abdulla, could hurt her, and he regularly did so.

Abdulla badly and madly wanted Monika as his wife in Kuwait, as we now know, and he was of course responsible for her and Sulaiman. But he was much too inexperienced and weak and so allowed his interfering family to make a bloody mess of their young lives together, again and again. With "Sweetie, forget about our old stuff in the trunk. I will get you everything brand new. Let them have it," he tried to coax her into quickly forgetting the theft. But, as we all know, the material things were not at all the main issue here. It was more the point that her in-laws had done her wrong and that he had never done anything about it! Instead, if he could have insisted, he would have asked his wife to go up to them and say, "Thanks very much for pinching my stuff. I don't mind. Is there anything else you would like of mine?" That's what his reactions were, she felt. For his sake, she was already smiling when she did not feel like smiling, sat with them when she did not feel like sitting with them, talked and ate when she did not want to and shared everything she did not want to share—otherwise they would have taken it without asking. Nothing was safe from them except her sex life. And even about that they were not too coy to ask Monika if their brother was a good lover and whether he went down on his knees to please her, orally, down there. Monika tried to avoid mealtimes on the floor with the family not because of the way they ate their food, but because mother-in-law had the habit of loudly blowing her nose into the bottom of her frock when the hot peppers she ate drove tears to her eyes and caused a runny nose.

"Abdulla, don't you see? I might have given to them whatever took their fancy, if only they had *asked*. But I am treated as a non-existent here, and you, poor little mouse, want me to keep quiet and let the tomcats get on with it—until tomorrow, when something new will crop up." She added, "Your reckless mother has no doubt put the fear of God in you for whatever reason that's still a mystery to me." And when she went on to say the following, the full truth still didn't dawn on her: "I can't see how you survived so long in Europe living without her. You never, ever mentioned her there, or your sisters, except on rare occasions. So what on earth has come over you now? Have they cast a spell on you?"

Now, here, Monika had no idea how right she was in what she was saying—because spells were indeed being cast on Abdulla! Monika had married into a Kuwaiti family that cast spells and meddled regularly in witchcraft. Had she been told, then, of such activities, she would have bet her bottom dollar and put Sulaiman up, too, on a bet that sorcery doesn't work. But spells *do* work, as she was to find out.

"Really, Abdulla, I was always led to believe—by you and everybody else—that in Arabia men have the last word! It your case, it's your mother wearing the pants. And your sisters don't come too far behind. You're the last in line. Your word is very unimportant, to say the least.

Let me tell you how proud I am of my man. You are not even the last to have your say, but are only barely allowed to fulfill whatever they have ordered you to do. In other words, you are their servant, and I am the only one in this house you dare raise your voice to, the only one you force to do as you wish—correction—as *they* wish me to do. You can fetch water in a jug only until it breaks, and take note. I am slowly cracking, Abdulla. Can't you see that? Don't you see what is happening to us? We are becoming strangers."

After the slightest disagreement—like this one—Abdulla made it a habit to slam the door loudly behind him—loudly, to please his around-the-clock-spying family downstairs that throve on the young couple's arguments; and he was off, gone to some douvaniah, she guessed, from where he returned quite often intoxicated early the next morning. So Kuwait was not alcohol-free after all. One should never believe a country's propaganda. Abdulla was under stress and did not know how to act in the given circumstances. He became two-faced and played games with Monika, joining his own kind. While he told her she was the only, the most important, person in his world for him and that he did only as he did to keep that ignorant family of his in check and happy, she—the educated, cultured European—had to understand and submit to cat and mouse games for his sake and Sulaiman's. That's what was expected of her as a loving wife!

Monika's dreams of a happy and bright future were slowly sinking with the sun. Her destiny was to share life with people she had not chosen; nor had they chosen her. The horrendous interferences in her private life that she had had to deal with so far were only the tip of an iceberg yet to come. Having been well trained in a convent—and from a tender age, too—to take injustice and digest it in a sophisticated way, Monika now had an edge she had not counted on. Her girlhood stood her to advantage; otherwise she might have cracked completely, ripe for a mental hospital under the strain of it all.

Afraid that Monika might do a Daly Thompson on him, as she had sometimes under stress threatened to do, Abdulla talked her into getting married according to Islamic tradition and faith. In order to do so she would have to become a Muslim first and abandon her Catholic faith. She had no qualms about that. For her, there existed only one God and all religions whatever are bridges to God. There are no chosen ones, no favored religions. All are equals in front of that great force we call God. She was surprised to learn in the process that non-Muslim religions, other faiths, were highly despised and taboo amongst the Kuwaiti people she lived with. A small, black onyx cross with a pretty little diamond in its center, a birthday present to her from Werner, her brother, something she loved to wear, was all of a sudden an irritant to Abdulla, and he forbade her from ever wearing it in Kuwait. "We are Muslims, not bloody Christians," he'd say. Every time she opened her jewel box that pretty little cross caught her eye and made her sad, until finally she decided to give it away to a nice Czech lady employed at Abdulla's hospital, who was over the moon with it.

Becoming a Muslim and getting married according to Islam was all over within fifteen minutes. Some Mullah read out a couple of sentences from a huge Holy Koran. Not knowing what any of it meant, Monika had to repeat every word after him and so became a Muslim officially. She stuttered when he mentioned Miriam, for that was the name of Abdulla's grandmother. So she wanted to know, first, why she had to mention Granny here; and that's when Abdulla and the three male witnesses, all friends of Abdulla, could not help laughing out loud. Even the Mullah smiled. The Miriam mentioned here was the Holy Miriam in the Koran and had nothing to do with Abdulla's grandmother.

In the wedding ceremony Abdulla was asked how much he had paid for his European wife, which he, of course, answered with "Nothing." The white-bearded old Mullah shook his head disapprovingly and told Abdulla that according to the Muslim law he must pay for her, however much or little. So Abdulla pulled one Kuwait Dinar, the equivalent of £2, from his white dishdasha breast pocket and handed it to his wife. That, of course, made her and everybody else present laugh again because Arabs pay huge sums of money for their wives and, as their custom has it, women are given precious diamonds and other jewels—hence the classy jewelry shops in Kuwait. Clever mothers even draw up marriage contracts for their daughters nowadays that ask for chauffeur-driven cars, staff, a house, and money settlements in case of divorce or whatever other reason. The more a future husband is willing to give, the better for the fortunate bride and her family. Jewels resting on dark velvet in leather-bound cases, marriage contracts, and the check for the amount of her bride price are exhibited in the bride's house days before the wedding ceremony for friends, relatives, and neighbors to view and approve of, sneer at, or get a bout of jealousy over. Their reactions are left entirely to the individual. In Kuwait everybody takes part in everybody else's life. Nothing is hidden nor kept nor done in privacy. Monika realized soon that Kuwaitis lived foremost to impress society. In mother-in-law's time the bloody bed sheets were hung out by the bride's mother to show the world that her daughter was a virgin. In Monika's time a good many Kuwaiti girls took a quick trip to Cairo for an abortion or to be sewn up and transformed back into a virgin by a clever surgeon before a wedding or two, leaving Kuwait under the misleading pretense of going on a bridal shopping spree.

Yes, money brings on changes. It's like this: where there is lots of sunshine, there are also plenty of shadows. The good and the bad go hand in hand. Monika's day of formally getting hitched to Abdulla for the second time and as a Muslim, if only as a paper Muslim, ended like any other day. It had been no harder than walking into a coffee bar and ordering a cup of coffee.

The family's interference on that specific day was the clandestine decision they had made in the past, ratified in the present, Abdulla eagerly agreeing. A lamb should be killed the following day, and

Monika's name should now be changed to the much more suitable Muslim name of Mona.

"My mother is right, Sweetie. It's so much more fitting for you—as if cut to size by a tailor." Abdulla glowed all over his face, truly enchanted by his family's bright idea—while Monika, for the first time ever, surprised everyone by standing up to them on her hind legs, declining with a no-nonsense, sharp "No, never," and twirling on her heel to run upstairs. A change of name was never mentioned again. She should have acted so self-assured and positive more often. She had it in her. She might have claimed all that was rightfully hers more often, who knows. Yet, for that illumination she was going to have to wait some time. It would take a while to break out of the hammered-in suppression of her personality accomplished by the nuns at the convent. The light, for her, switched on when she was between thirty and thirty-five; that's when she woke up. But up until then her true personality lay in a deep Sleeping Beauty sleep, and she was easy material to be constantly interfered with by people with some sort of claim on her, like her in-laws.

Monika never would have suffered a fraction of the misery she experienced in Kuwait had she lived her life among her own kind in Europe; for, given the way she was brought up and trained, she had all the inner qualities to strive through life and live happily in a civilized society. Sulaiman called his parents Abdulla and Monika, just as he had heard them being called since his birth by their student friends in England; but as soon as Abdulla's family realized this, the practice had to stop. Monika was told that children who called their parents by their given names were considered bad mannered in Kuwait; and, with Abdulla agreeing, Monika was convinced to try her best to coax Sulaiman gently into saying the Arabic "Moma" and "Baba" instead. Sabiha objected the most. But all of them made it their business to re-train poor little "Monika"-"Abdulla"-blubbering Sulaiman by hitting him for his transgressions.

After all the trouble of straightening out Sulaiman, who in his right mind would have expected that, after Sabiha got married and her firstborn son started to speak, she would force-train her own baby into what had all along appealed to her (and into what Monika found out in the meantime was not bad manners at all in Kuwait, only unheard of)? No one. Nonetheless, Tarek, Sabiha's son, just as soon as he could speak, had to call her and her husband by their given names, Sabiha and Fahad, not by the traditional Moma and Baba that she had so wickedly forced upon Monika's son.

Everything unheard of or done differently, they ridiculed, were jealous of, begrudged, or imitated monkey fashion. Take, for instance, the loving way Monika and Abdulla called each other "Sweetie." Fiancés and husbands alike had to call Abdulla's sister "Sweetie" too, and vice versa. All of a sudden all these stupid sounding "Sweeties" were walking around in the same house. It would be fun to see that one on video! I guarantee you a good laugh. Monika lived among people who, say, bought a pair of new shoes and waited a week to wear them because the salesman had said that the shoes might be tight for the first couple of days. It wasn't their fault, just Monika's bad luck. Abdulla, for example, was congratulated on his polished shoes that were mistaken for new ones because shoe polish was one of the many innovations, among others, that they got to know through Monika. It was the sort of thing they couldn't do without later.

The salt and pepper shakers on Monika's dining table stirred Sabiha's interest. Now, Sabiha had learned a bit of English at school, and, after failing it twice in secondary school, thought "bugger that" and quit. Instead of S & P, she wanted initialed salt and pepper mills that sported an S & F, for Sabiha and Fahad. She refused to believe that Monika would be unable to obtain them whatever market she went to. One Friday morning when Abdulla was away for the weekend fishing, with friends, his three sisters entered Monika's bedroom, giggling and pulling on the pink sheets that covered Monika's naked body. Monika struggled half asleep but, outnumbered, she had to give in. Sitting up with her legs tightly pressed against her chest, looking into six dark, bloated eyes, she couldn't believe it.

'Tell me that I'm dreaming. Tamader, Sabiha, Diba, what on earth are you doing?"

"Take it easy," came one of their voices. "We only want to see how you look in the flesh."

Monika knew some Kuwaiti females that would give anything and everything they possessed to obtain a little lighter skin tone. Some rubbed pure lemon juice on their skin as a daily routine.

"You are very lucky, Monika, you know, with such a small waist, and you've got no stretch marks left after Sulaiman. What do you use? Tell us your secret! We want to look slim and trim like you. What shall we do? We have white marks on our thighs, stomachs, and around our breasts." Saying that, Sabiha, who claimed to be the worst off, reached into the open cleavage of her dress and fetched out one of her big brown breasts as a showpiece and evidence. Straight and broken white lines—in other words, Class A stretch marks—led to and from the dark brown, almost black, nipple and extended in all directions around it. Because their skin was dark, the white showed more prominently and reminded Monika of yeast dough that rose up high and then cracked. Monika felt sorry for them.

If Monika, not being a man, was put off by that sight, how would a man react to such a mess? Was that maybe one of the reasons why Arabs go mad for white women, and could that be one of the reasons why these women were so jealous of her? And if that's how they look now, what will they look like in ten to twenty years' time, after a couple of kids?

"There's nothing I do or use," answered Monika. "All I can advise is that you eat what you like but don't swallow. Go on a diet! If I ate everything I fancied, like you, I'd become just as big. Your skin is pulled apart because you are all grossly overweight. That's all, and I'm sorry.

But not even in the West is there a potion for such stretch marks. I'm afraid the way you look is of your own doing. If there were anything I could do, I would gladly help you." Monika could tell from their disbelieving looks that they thought she was lying. They must have plucked a lot of courage to tell her they liked the way she looked. It crossed her mind that if she were anything like them, she easily could have taken a little revenge now by telling them to rub garlic butter three times a day into their cracks. They would have done it! The thought of it amused Monika and made her smile.

"Monika, would you like us to remove your public (or what's it called?) hair down there between your legs?" offered Tamader. "Abdulla would love it. All men do when the skin is very smooth on the kiss (cunt). We have just done it to each other with a home-made paste of brown sugar, lemon, and olive oil. There is plenty left for you! It doesn't hurt. Look! Touch my arm, how smooth the skin feels now. You won't need the treatment on you arms and legs like us because you are not hairy."

Surprised, digesting an offer she had never had before, Monika ran her fingers along the young girl's arm. "Oh, yes, you are right, Tamader. Your skin is very smooth, like a baby's bottom," she blubbered, robot-like, to please them, lost for words and not having the vaguest notion how to act in order to hold on to her own pubic hair and keep the peace at the same time. "But your brother Abdulla loves hair there," she shouted at them, smiling nervously. "I would not dare touch it."

"Just try once. It grows again," begged Tamader, pulling her silky, green caftan up above her belly with one hand and Monika's hand down with the other to make her feel the clean, hairless, dark-skinned pussy. Standing full of expectation, Tamader really tried her best to get around Monika and make her change her mind. But why? This uncertain question lingered on in Monika's mind. It made her think. She didn't quite know how to rate that offer. Did she detect some hidden sexual desire amongst them? God knows!

"If I get rid of my curlies, Abdulla will be mad at me, and it will be his three sisters' fault," Monika insisted, jumping up and grabbing her dressing gown. End of story.

Listening uneasily to that story later in the evening, Abdulla was unimpressed, except for the fact that Tamader, too, had removed her pubic hair, a custom practiced only among married Muslim women for hygienic reasons. Other than that, he could not explain their actions.

Monika had the sneaking suspicion that Abdulla after all would have preferred that next time she keep such happenings to herself. He was just a chip off the old block. Whereas a couple of months before he would have comforted her, now he was starting to take things as personal attacks. He looked upon his foreign wife as a criticizing intruder, not willing to dance as was whistled. Monika was overcome once again by that now-familiar "nobody cares" feeling while Abdulla slid more and more in his family's direction.

The beginning of the end of her dreams set in, for beneath Abdulla's deceptive façade lay a hidden, deep-rooted sense of belonging to his family and his country, Kuwait. He stood between the Old East and the New West, wanting the impossible—to unite them and live the best of both worlds. Some Kuwaitis have achieved such a life, but they were equipped with stronger characters than Abdulla had and did not have to pull their archaic families in tow.

Abdulla's weakness was no bonus. He attracted the same sort of hangers-on in Kuwait as he had attracted at Oxford and Canterbury. He would go boozing with them and play poker. He'd throw parties for them at the flat, and Monika would prepare continental dishes for up to twenty hungry Arabs. For her own part, Monika would not have cared if most of the friends did not turn up. But Abdulla liked them. As always, he needed sanctioning shadows around him, and he wanted to brag, show off, glow, and impress them with his cheap, little foreign wife. He rubbed it in that his friends had had to pay a fortune for their spouses. Yet Monika saw no reason to spoil her husband's enjoyment with them. Monika had changed a lot, too. "Anything for Peace" became her motto.

What upset her most were the many fishing trips Abdulla went on, and the lonely nights she spent alone while he was surrounded by bunches of people and having the time of his life. And if he was not out fishing, he went to douvaniahs, where occasionally alcohol flowed, evidently, because he was in the habit of swaying home as high as a kite, talking nonsense and demanding sex, knowing damned well that in his state there was no business doing with his wife. He got at her with hurtful accusations, always bringing up his family and saying things like "You don't love my mother and my sisters, but let me tell you—they are all on my head and you, under the slippers I walk the floor with!" Although he apologized the next day a hundred times, often buying her a present, she bitterly detested his drunkenness. It was no use to try to take her pillow and lock herself in the sitting room to sleep there in peace because he would bang wildly on the door and carry on with his bullshit talks. Brewer's Droop, as the English say.

In Kuwait, officially, there is no alcohol. It is a dry country. There are no bars and no alcoholic drinks available in public. Monika spent New Year's in one of the big hotels with another couple—Ali, also an Aseel Kuwaiti, and his wife Aya, an extremely pretty, blue-eyed girl from Finland—and learned a pragmatic lesson. (Monika and Aya were to become—and still are to this day—best friends.) As the couples entered the restaurant, Abdulla (or maybe it was Ali) handed the waiter a white nylon bag containing a bottle of Black Label acquired on the black market as he pressed a handsome tip into the waiter's other hand.

The waiter understood and returned minutes later balancing a big tray with a huge teapot and four china cups and saucers, teaspoons, the lot, and out of the pot ran the whiskey into the thick teacups. The ice and cold water were in the sugar bowl and milk pot. Let me tell you, you people out there, there is nothing like enjoying your alcohol from elegantly formed, sparkling crystal tumblers, believe you me. It just did not taste the same out of teacups but, nevertheless, did its duty. It helped Monika to believe, for a short time, that she lived in another world. One has to expect that the waiters are likely to keep some of the booze for themselves, maybe to make an extra buck or two, topping up the pot with a little water. So, one has to watch them carefully, and one might get the Aloxe Corton looking as red as it should and sniffing the way it should sniff. The irony of it all was, of course, that almost all the other customers sitting around them were drinking spirits, too, out of teacups, giving Monika's table a well understood, brotherly smile, an unspoken "We know—we, too."

This is all part of Kuwaiti society's well played game. It's an open secret that a lot of people drink. Yet it is hushed up and never spoken of publicly because the Holy Koran forbids alcohol consumption by Muslims. Kuwait has the highest road accident rate in the world, a great percentage of it thanks to alcohol. As long as the drinking is done in one's own home, that's fine. A drunk on the streets is a rare sight. To be caught by the police is an embarrassment better avoided, although they won't give you much trouble if you happen to have the good fortune of being an Aseel—a fact easily detected from one's name and Kuwaiti accent. But God help the non-Kuwaiti!

Monika was stopped in Abdulla's big car a couple of times by the police, for no proper reason. Just because she was white, blonde, and looked good, they wanted to talk and look at this woman. It most probably gave them a hard on. With all those wrapped up, disguised, walking turnoffs, small wonder they got desperate. Monika did as Abdulla told her: "Give them your Kuwaiti driver's license and tell them in Arabic, I am the wife of Abdulla al-Amahani." After she said that, the bedouin policeman always shouted at her, "*Yella, yella!* (Go, go!)" and drove on. Monika's sweetie was Aseel, and she enjoyed the privileges that went with that status.

In Kuwait, it is very much the outward form that counts, not the inner substance, as Monika was to learn. The pretense starts somewhere around drinking whiskey out of teacups and saying that you don't drink at all, and eating and drinking during the fasting months of Holy Ramadan, when smoking is not permitted either, while you tell everyone you meet that you are not eating, drinking, or smoking and all the while have withdrawal symptoms and are dying for a fag! In personal relations between man and wife, you say you are idyllically happy when you are not and everyone knows you are not, and you know *they* know you are not. The games people play in Kuwait cut across all class barriers and are bloody difficult to understand and even more difficult to adjust to if you are a foreigner from Europe—where we call that lying. Monika should have taken a lecture course on "How to become a Kuwaiti and live happily ever after" before following Abdulla there.

Now, where were we? Oh, yes, douvaniahs, Abdulla out while his wife, left holding the baby, occupied herself with knitting as her own grandmother had done when she was eighty. Monika resorted to watching a most boring TV series broadcast on Kuwait's one channel, which specialized in nearly-non-stop religious programs, hoping to catch one of the Egyptian films that were telecast now and then because Monika learned a lot of Arabic from them. During the day, she felt like a slowly rotting cabbage, living uselessly day to day to day with nothing to look forward to. There was nothing that captured her interest, nor occupied her brain. She was not fulfilled, and a guilty conscience about wasting the day and having achieved nothing nagged at her.

Anybody could to the little housework and cooking that she did, look after a husband, and take care of one child. That to Monika was no big deal. Apart from the enjoyable free time Abdulla took for himself, his work was cut out for him. He was a full-time brother, father, son, and husband to his family, sorting out their problems—like passports, official papers, visits to the doctors, dental appointments, shopping. Although Diba had a husband of her own, Abdulla was (and felt) responsible for them and their kids, and that's how it has stayed. Even now, nearly thirty years later, he is still their robot. Abdulla was always on duty. When his sisters had their children, when they fought with their husbands, caught an infection from them, were ill, Abdulla was always there as their reliable handyman, while Monika, the fifth wheel, sensing deep down that it was impossible to break the iron bond between Abdulla and his family, hung on hoping for changes for the better. Wasn't she optimistic?

While Abdulla rolled out the red carpet for them, Monika was made to walk barefoot on nettles. His justification for that was, "I am not doing it for my sisters and their families. It is because my mother has asked me to. I do it just for her."

"I am scared of her!" would have been closer to the truth.

A brightly burning candle on Monika's dark island was the weekly German and English magazines she had discovered at a small newsagent's stall. Sometimes there was not much left of the original publication, which reminded one of a sieve with so many "confiscated" pictures and articles cut out. Out of curiosity, Monika would ask her mother to send the missing bits and pieces from Vienna. Such articles were mostly about Arabs in general, sex, or Jews—often really harmless, non-political, non-sexy stuff that could have been read out loud in any classroom in the West. There must have been a scissor-happy nut at work!

The second most important word in Kuwait—next in line after Aseel—is no doubt the powerful word *wasta*, meaning special favors from and to high places. In Kuwait, you can be made and broken by wasta coming from high places. Another name for wasta is "Vitamin WOW." If you have a wish—whether it's getting a good job or getting your son into the right school or getting your enemy chucked from his job—it can come true if you speak to the right Aseel, who speaks to the right Aseel. Kuwaitis are very, very generous and don't take too much notice of the law when they are. They always love to help each other, but they will do so freely only if the fancy hits them. You may ask for, but must never be pushy and take until it is given: the Kuwaiti despises being taken for granted, taken for a ride, used, or conned. If you are a Kuwaiti employee of the Kuwaiti Government, you will be grouped according to your qualifications, somewhere from the low grade of No.8 and on up to the top grade of No.1 or above if you are something special like a diplomat or have achieved something outstanding. Monika's Abdulla started at grade No.4 and slowly but surely worked his way up to the above-No.1 category, with a little wasta here and a little wasta there and a big wasta over there.

The lapse between first starting your job and receiving your first salary check can be months long. Paperwork takes ages in Kuwait's ministries. The saying "What you can do today, don't put off until tomorrow" is unheard of in Kuwait. Instead you hear, "*Inshallah, inshallah.*" Everything is done in the name of Allah, in slow order, and in slow motion, without hurry. Whatever goes wrong or goes slowly or doesn't happen at all is put down to the fact that that is Allah's wish. The reason must be the heat. In Abdulla's case, he waited eight months—not that he was short of money during that time (he had plenty). Monika never asked, but assumed that the money they were spending came from his inheritance. On receiving the lump sum for his eight months' salary, Abdulla managed to hurt Monika gravely.

Abdulla stated that from that point on he would have to give his mother and sisters a monthly allowance from his own salary. It surprised Monika who, since arriving in Kuwait, had seen them spending daily as if there were no tomorrow, buying for themselves all that was in fashion, head to toe. They were the sorts of people who first ordered merchandise and then asked to know the price of things. So, what was happening here? Didn't they have any money left? Yes, they had plenty. But Abdulla felt it was his duty.

"I don't understand that, Abdulla, but as long as it does not reduce nor interfere with my housekeeping and pocket money, I won't go into a duel with you over it."

"Sweetie, what do you need housekeeping money for?" came Abdulla's reply. "And you want pocket money? If you want anything, I personally or the driver can take you shopping. Anything you want will always be paid for you."

"Oh, come on, Abdulla. Stop joking and let's talk sense. Let's discuss our finances seriously now like old times to see what goes where and make the best of it as we did in England. The two of us together can make a little go far."

But Abdulla was not joking.

"I'm dead serious. This is Kuwait, not Europe where . . ."

He did not finish the sentence. She did not let him.

"What? You son of a bitch! Haven't I shared all my money with you in the past when you didn't have enough to go from A to B? Didn't I always make sure we could make it to C? I went to work like a commoner, never complaining! I worked and paid to keep Sulaiman in Vienna, with you in my ear promising me the blue from the Kuwaiti skies. You bloody well *never* cease to surprise me! Every day something new and negative comes up. You disgust me!"

Monika snapped and let loose, and when she let loose, she did it in style. She stood crying uncontrollably, shouting at Abdulla at the same time. She had taken a lot, but even for a brave girl brought up and trained to take injustice, there was a limit. And that limit Abdulla had now overstepped. To start with, she gave her cooped-up frustrations, nerves, anger, and hurt pride full rein and smashed an entire coffee set for eight made of green china and embossed with lots of gold leaf, throwing it onto the open balcony and giving her in-laws downstairs something to listen to and talk about. They were, of course, already standing on tip-toe, in line, like soldiers, and eavesdropping with all their might! Monika shouted at a shocked Abdulla that she had to break something because broken china is supposed to bring luck and she needed it. She needed lots of it now, for she was on her way out. She was not willing to take any more of his crap! This was not a marriage. She could not live life with him anymore. He could keep his money and give it all to his family—who in truth were his "wife."

"For me," she cried, "there is no place here." Monika talked and acted on impulse.

"I can't be worse off anywhere else," she thought.

Abdulla stood, a bit lost and helpless, watching his hurricane wife in amazement. She needed money to live. She was not the type to hoard or collect it, and whenever she had any she generously gave and shared it. Abdulla must have known that by now, she had spent enough on him of her money. So what had happened? What was he afraid of? Monika was nothing like his spending-crazy family. That Abdulla was once again being "doctored" by them and was doing as he was told, half hypnotized by witches' spells, did not enter her mind straight away. One has to be a witch to know one.

Feeling that he had lost his grip, trying to intimidate her, Abdulla shouted, "Why don't you go to hell!"

"I can't! If I did, your mother would follow me," she sassed. "So excuse me if I refuse your bright idea!" Pulling down her suitcases stored above the wardrobes, she added, "Instead, I'm going to go somewhere else!"

Sulaiman knew something was wrong and started to cry. Monika comforted him with ice cream and, quick as lightening, started to pack.

"Where are you going to get plane tickets from?" Abdulla asked, now in a normal tone, "because I'm not getting you any."

"Mr. Abdulla al-Amahani, MSR, RT, graduate of Great Britain, use your loaf! I know that you, with your kind-hearted, listening lot down there, keep me in prison here. Yet, you might not realize that none of you has a key to my cell. Don't overlook the fact that I am not a bedouin. If worse comes to worst, I'll make a point of sitting all day and night, too, in front of your ruling sheikh's palace until he or somebody from his entourage will give me the honor. Don't forget. I'm a Kuwaiti citizen now, something some non-Kuwaiti Arabs would kill to be, as I've heard, though I can't see why! You have lured me to Kuwait under false pretenses. Tell me what the fuck for? Was it to educate and serve your family in the daytime and to function as your sex machine at night? Big deal! Our relationship can be called everything under the sun except marriage. You take and I give, what's the name for that? Trust my hate, I'm through with you."

Her three suitcases packed and locked, Monika started to change Sulaiman, and Abdulla was convinced now that she meant business because he started to weep just as one might at a gravestone and became apology itself.

"Sweetie, forgive me! Please, can you forgive me? Just this *one* last time. Listen to me, please. Give me another chance. I swear to you, it is not my fault. Not to give you money in hand was my mother's idea. She said that you married me only for money and gold and that if you got all you wanted you would leave me and that if I gave you no money you would not be able to leave me. You know I dearly love you. I can't live in Kuwait without you. Please, don't go. I will give you anything you want."

Abdulla pleaded and cried.

She cried.

And then he reached into his pocket and threw a bundle of a thousand KD into the air. The money rained down on Monika, who stood there like Cinderella.

"Oh, Abdulla, how can a person I thought I knew so well develop such a split personality? Tell me, if you can, what money you think I am after? Maybe your lot imagines that I have the mentality of a servant? When are you going to use your own instinct and judgment about our marriage? Stop letting other people manipulate you. How do you think your mother knows how I really tick? Do you think she knows me better than you do?"

Abdulla nodded a no. "No, definitely not."

"So, stop their interfering, for heaven's sake, and let's get out of here before they part us for good. If we could live life without them, I would be one hundred percent happy."

Knowing all was well again and that Monika had once again forgiven him, Abdulla lit up like a lamp. The two of them kissed and made up and, as always, he made wild promises. Another in-law fight had been fought and gotten over. She, in her undying faith, believed in future changes for the better.

Yet, that particular incident left its scar deep inside Monika where the eye does not see. It takes it place among the other scars of the past, where many more were to join it in due time.

After confrontations of that nature, things generally went better for a couple of days. Monika always forgave but never forgot—just like an elephant. The outcome of that particular argument was that Monika got pocket money to do with as she pleased. But when she got her check she had to accompany it to the bank because it was not big enough to go on its own. It was just enough to keep herself above water. Nothing in excess. Nothing like what one might expect from an Aseel Kuwaiti husband. And housekeeping expenses? She never did get to handle them. His mother's influence was too strong. He almost never gave her any household money, and if he did as an odd exception, he always asked for the bills afterwards. Was Monika weak? Stupid? Soft hearted? Or maybe a late-bloomer in every respect?

What she was always thinking was, "I have to see it through until our own house is ready. Then, nobody—no one—can interfere." What made her forgive him time and again was a simple fact that stood out for miles and could not be overlooked: because they knew that she liked him, her in-laws, who wanted to get at her, used Abdulla as their tool. She forgave him because she dimly realized he was not wholly responsible for her misery. Hopefully, Monika might still wake up to the full reality of her life one day, but Abdulla was destined to stay asleep for a hundred years—more like Rip van Winkle than a Sleeping Beauty. By the time he opens his eyes, she will have gone. Those are my predictions.

The only service Monika required from her in-laws' servants was to empty her big dustbin once a week in the morning. It stood outside, close to the stairs. She emptied all her small wastebaskets into it each day. One day, it was already 6 pm and her big dustbin was still nowhere to be seen. Monika made her way downstairs to investigate and found it still full to the brim on an outside balcony.

"Juma, what is my dustbin doing here? Haven't you emptied it yet?" she asked the servant.

"Ameti (my aunt) has not seen it yet."

"What does your Ameti have to see my dustbin for!"

"I am not allowed to empty it without her. She has to look at everything first."

"What does she look at?"

"She collects bills and things to show to her daughters," Juma enlightened Monika.

"Well, I never! What on earth next?" she thought.

Monika waited for her mother-in-law. She had decided that her first confrontation with the old witch was ripe. She plucked up the courage without Abdulla's knowing anything about it, and about time, too, that her Arian guts should come shining through. She left the bin where it was, and then led the old homecoming woman to it. In her best Arabic, Monika asked her to look through her bin then and there and take what she wanted.

"I'll help you collect all the bills, Um-Abdulla"—Mother of Abdulla, that's how she addressed her mother-in-law. She should have been calling her "Auntie" but could not bring herself to do it, for obvious reasons.

"And, by the way, what kind of money and gold do you think your son has and spends on me? If I wanted a man with money, I would not have come here to vegetate with your son. And if you love your son a fraction of what you pretend, you need to stop interfering in our lives." That said, Monika reached into her house pajama pocket and pulled out a small, black velvet pouch. In it was the measly, second-hand jewelry that her in-laws had given her.

"Here, Um-Abdulla, some of the gold I married your son for. Take it." Monika pressed it firmly into the palm of the old woman standing surprised and speechless, at a complete loss with what Monika had thrown out at her. She had not one word in reply. No wonder. She could not hold a conversation with an intelligent person; she was just not cut out for it. From then on, Monika's dustbin was emptied punctually and—surprise, surprise!—not a word about it was ever mentioned to Monika by Abdulla.

Any evidence of Abdulla's financial inheritance, about which he had talked so much in England, was to remain invisible to her for as long as Monika lived in Kuwait. Everything that Monika's husband's father had left was invested by—and for—Monika's mother-in-law. The stingy old woman who could neither read nor write was firmly and solemnly in charge—assisted by her sister's husband, the owner of two wives, himself a clever merchant and shrewd businessman. Mother-in-law's brother-in-law was the busy one who had sent Abdulla endless documents to sign in England after Abdulla's father's death, which had occurred at about the time that Monika had first met Abdulla. It was at that time that the huge family villa in Zone B, Kuwait's then most fashionable, upper-crust neighborhood, comparable to London's Belgravia, was sold, and Abdulla's family moved into an ordinary-looking, square box in the Keefan area, where Monika was to join them.

Abdulla managed on his salary, except once, when he traveled to Jordan in mother's name to sell some oil shares. He put his share of the money aside, towards his new house, then still a dream waiting to become reality. When Monika had first arrived in Kuwait, Abdulla proudly showed her a small building with sixteen apartments, all rented out, that belonged to him and his family and told her that half of everything was his, the rest being divided between his three sisters and his mother, each of whose share should have been an eighth of the total, according to Islamic law—but not according to his mother! Good natured Abdulla never saw a penny of that rent, nor of anything else that his father had left to him.

Once, as Monika was carrying her freshly laundered clothes to hang up in the outside yard, downstairs, Sulaiman disappeared quick as a fox into the in-laws' room. Monika followed to fetch him and saw the four of them sitting on the floor in a circle with mother-in-law holding a thick bundle of crisp, green 10 KD notes that she was distributing among them, counting out loud 1-2-3-4, 1-2-3-4. Little piles of money lay in front of each of the four women. Just then, Abdulla shouted.

"Sweetie, Sweetie, where are you?" to his wife. Mother-in-law abruptly stopped counting and whispered something to her daughters as the four of them hastily stuffed the paper money under the cushions they were sitting on. By the time Abdulla entered the room, they all looked as if butter would not melt in their mouths, a cool picture of innocence itself, sitting together and drinking tea.

Monika was surprised and told Abdulla what she'd seen. Yet—would you believe it?—however hard she tried to convince him, he just did not believe her. End of story.

Deceased Mr. al-Amahani Senior had dedicated a great part of his short life, as was well known among lots of people, to drink and women; so, it was not surprising that when he built two identical houses side by side, he set up an Indian prostitute and her daughter, both exclusively his, in one of those buildings where he spent a lot of his time. He brought alcohol from the harbor to their house and regularly stocked their huge American fridge with food. Abdulla, too, became more than friendly with the daughter in question, whom he got to know while running errands there for his father. Had his father known that Abdulla had had his first sexual encounter there, too, "He would have killed me"—Abdulla's own words.

The houses stood in the Palestinian nationals' area. Kuwaitis strictly and proudly live unto themselves, while foreigners are grouped into neighborhoods according to their nationality. So, after Abdulla's father's death, this Indian woman produced a valid document, signed by three witnesses, all of them Mr. al-Amahani's drinking pals, stating that after his death the house would automatically become her personal property. Abdulla's mother's lawyer, a bearded old Mullah, stood under one blanket with the prostitute, who as it came to light later on had promised him a share of the house if things went in her favor, which they did. The Mullah told his client Mrs. al-Amahani to sign for, but not to respond to, letters summoning her to court, which she signed with fingerprints of her right thumb. With that right thumb dipped in ink, she of course lost her house.

It surprised Monika, who was in Kuwait by that time, that the case hadn't run in Abdulla's name in the first place, as he was the only son of the deceased owner of the house and positioned higher up the family order than his mother. Had Abdulla listened to his wife's ideas, he would have won that case hands down. Monika advised Abdulla to hire a clever, young Kuwaiti lawyer with a law degree from Egypt and with his help prove to the court's satisfaction that his father had signed the papers under the influence of alcohol, that he was an alcoholic (he had the papers that proved that his father had died because of alcohol), that the three witnesses that had signed the so-called valid document were drinking partners of his, and that the Indian and her daughter were both prostitutes. It seemed to Monika at the time that Abdulla could have won the case easily, especially if he had told the Muslim judges that that old fart of a lawyer on the other side—Mullah or no Mullah—had definitely tricked his mother (as well as Abdulla and his sisters) out of their property rights. With deep regrets, Monika gave up. Under the influence of his family, Abdulla firmly rejected Monika's conscientious advice. Whatever she suggested, he went and did the opposite. She had been born, Monika concluded, with practical common sense while Abdulla seemed never to outgrow his naivety.

Once, when they were on their way to the cinema, Abdulla met and greeted an Indian girl who wore much too much makeup. You could see her from afar. Abdulla was all over her like a long lost friend and introduced Monika to her, only to tell Monika afterwards that the girl was the same one connected to the case of his father's lost house.

"And what business is it of yours to introduce me to prostitutes?" was her reaction, and cynically she continued, "Did you, by the way, convey your greetings to her mother with a special 'Thank you for cheating us out of our property'? *Really*, Abdulla, I don't know what I am doing with you!"

Her first Christmas in Kuwait was something Monika looked forward to. It would provide some welcome familiarity to her, in the wilderness, far from home. Instead of snow, she now braved sand storms, sometimes such dense ones that she could not see her own hands in front of her face. Driving became a dangerous, even an impossible, challenge sometimes. Well in advance, Dentist Pavlik had posted a real fir Christmas tree from the Austrian woods to her daughter in Kuwait. A parcel of gold and silver, glittering glass and art deco ornaments, candles in their holders, sparklers, silver tassels, hooks, fairies, logs, the lot, uplifted Monika's lost spirits as she unpacked it all. The smell of it reminded her of home and brought back memories of her childhood that were not particularly happy either but, in comparison with what she had now, had not been so bad after all. In a separate box lay carefully wrapped or rolled in colorful foil what was most important to Sulaiman: chocolates, marzipan candies, sugar goodies, ready to hang in all their splendor on the Christmas tree. There were white-dotted red mushrooms, green and red parrots, golden violins, cars, pipes, watches, footballs, angels, bottles, and so on. Monika's favorite coffee chocolates—which her mother had remembered, too—were wrapped in shimmering tissue paper fringed with silver stars. For Abdulla, Mrs. Pavlik had added fine liquor confectionery. From another carton, the aroma of delicate gingerbread figures (taken from such famous children's stories as "Hansel and Gretel," "Little Red Riding Hood," and "Goldilocks") crept up Monika's nose, tickling her taste buds.

Monika had bought presents for everybody, not forgetting her in-laws. Her being nice to them was actually supposed to be an additional Christmas present for Abdulla. She would invite them up the next day. She had planned it all in advance. She would call them up after Sulaiman, Abdulla and she had opened all their presents and cleared them all away, well out of her in-laws' sight and reach—otherwise all hell would break loose.

Monika had chosen toys for the kids and for the sisters' handbags in different styles and colors, made in France; and a black mohair shawl for mother-in-law, who after wearing it would surely be surprised that anything so light could be so warm, for she really had not much of a clue what the difference was between wool and cotton or silk and nylon. Lots of parcels lay under the tree neatly wrapped in red crepe paper and tied with green ribbon. It was a most beautiful sight and greatly cheered Monika.

Diba's little girl, Selma, never far away from the fair woman, stood astonished, her huge eyes even wider than usual, staring in amazement as Monika, holding Sulaiman in one arm, gave the majestic fir tree—which was topped by a golden-haired angel blowing into a long, golden trumpet—one last approving look and a touch here and a touch there. When Monika asked little Selma what she thought of it, the girl took off shouting loudly, "Mama, Mama!" She could not keep what she had seen a secret all to herself. She had to tell somebody about it. The result was a whole curious-as-ever battalion of women visitors and family members making their way upstairs to look in on Monika. Mother-in-law was leading the troupe; behind her came a bunch of clucking females with kids in tow, as usual. To start with, they only stood around and looked at the tree; but that was not to be for long. Next thing, mother-in-law's hand reached out for something to look at. Another hand followed and another one and soon they were all shouting to each other excitedly, pulling things off the tree, and as soon as they realized that some of the pretty figures were made of sweet foodstuff, there was no holding them back. Afraid of the way the whole episode was tending, Monika shouted to Tamader, "Okay, okay, Tamader! Please tell them I give them a piece each!" But nobody listened to her, nor heard her. Tamader, too, pulled—opened—tasted along with the rest! They passed each other bits to taste—very noble—and let their kids have some. The pack was really and truly on a blissful merry-go-round. Some of them stuffed chocolates—and decorations, too—into their handbags to take home and show. They were chatting loudly and happily while, in great contrast and distress, Monika was devastated, to say the least. She was near to tears. Just then Abdulla entered to save the day (or so she hoped).

"Come, Abdulla, come quick, my son! Look what's happened here! You wife has become *megnoone* (crazy)! She hangs chocolate on a tree!" Mother-in-law shouted in Abdulla's direction, erupting into a loud *kha-kha-kha* of laughter, into which all the rest of the females joined while covering their faces in the presence of a male, Abdulla.

And what did Abdulla do? He stood there and laughed with them! Monika loathed and utterly despised her rotten destroyer of a mother-in-law. At moments like this, she could have pushed a rocket up her arse and lit it without any hesitation or regret!

That was exactly what her grandson had done to mother-in-law's chickens—the poor chickens, mind you. One day mother-in-law came to collect eggs and on seeing all the hens sitting quietly, she let them be, thinking they were all busily laying eggs for her. But when she returned a couple of hours later and found them still sitting in the same places and positions, only dead quiet, she investigated. She picked up one. Its head dropped to the side—dead. She took out another. Its head dropped down, too—dead. And that was to be the fate of all twelve of the chickens whose duty it was to lay eggs strictly for Abdulla's mother's breakfast. The chickens had all been killed identically, by Diba's son, who slid firecrackers up their bottoms and lit them. The explosions had blasted the chickens' intestines.

Left to themselves, uncontrolled and without supervision, kids in Kuwait got the craziest ideas. They didn't think twice about taking a pallet of 34 raw eggs from the fridge to smash them against a high wall just to see, or bet, which of them could produce the most interesting pattern that way. Sometimes they would stand close to the wide road, each armed with a carton of raw eggs, to throw them at oncoming cars, but not without making sure first that the vehicles were not occupied by Aseel Kuwaitis in national dress. Their favorite game was to aim the eggs straight into the window of a big truck because these were always driven by foreign Arabs, so there was no danger. Whereas a Kuwaiti might have stopped and given them all a good hiding, a Palestinian would never have dared lay a hand on a Kuwaiti child. Then, again, if a European woman happened to pass by, they might shout *gahba*, which means "prostitute." Monika was called that whenever she walked through the streets in Kuwait and was even pelted with stones by young children up to teenagers. They had been taught that every foreign woman was a *gahba*. We will come back to that subject later.

Let's go back to where we left Monika's manhandled Christmas tree. Abdulla—among all these women friends of his mother—could hardly let his mother down in favor of his wife, so he ridiculed Monika and her tree.

"Watch out, everybody! Today my wife hangs chocolates on the tree. Tomorrow she might plaster our house with chocolate, and the day after we will visit her in the mental hospital!" The ignorant women laughed and laughed at Monika's expense. Although Abdulla had said this in jest, it had a very hurtful effect on his wife. Couldn't he have instead explained to them the European Christmas custom of decorating a fir tree?

Next, Abdulla asked Monika to show him which were his family's presents, took them, and—with everyone looking on, because his old witch of a mother adored public shows of homage—proudly handed them all over to her.

Little Selma pulled on Monika's jeans and then pressed a wet kiss onto her cheek. It was a thank you for the pretty, longhaired dolly she held now tightly to her chest. That little girl—and Abdulla at times, too—did not fit in with the rest of the family.

After everyone had gone, the tree was gone, too, and looked a mess. The flat looked a mess. Monika felt a bloody mess on the inside, and tomorrow would be Christmas. What a let down!

"Come on, Sweetie. It's not the end of the world. These people have never in their lives seen a Christmas tree," came Abdulla's paltry excuse for that riot.

"All I know is that if I were a Kuwaiti woman they wouldn't dare behave as they do, and because I am European and married to a cloth like you, they do. I—Monika al-Amahani—have been made your family's favorite occupation and entertainment, without my permission and agreement. It is your duty to set them limits because their hobby is ruining my life, and they always get by with it. It's bloody amazing! How do they do it? Don't you realize, Abdulla, that you give them *carte blanche* and encouragement with your silly jokes?"

There was no possibility of *wasta* against such witches.

CHAPTER ELEVEN

SEX, LIES, AND THE NEXT FOUR YEARS

After ordeals like that, Monika usually phoned her friend Aya from Finland, who was carved of the same wood as Monika. They comforted each other when one of them had reached rock bottom. Aya had fallen for her Aseel hubby Ali in Britain, in Brighton to be precise. He had returned to Kuwait a failure. He had been sent to England to study architecture, but after he failed his exams for a third time there, even the overly generous Kuwaiti Government refused to allow him to carry on with his so-called studies.

Instead of looking for a job (which a whole year later Ali finally got, but thanks only to a *wasta* from Abdulla), Ali set straight out to seduce anything that came his way, whether in a skirt or in trousers, whether AC or DC, while poor Aya found a cheap job as a salesgirl in Kuwait and so provided their only income. Thanks to her, they had air conditioning and a fridge, the two main "musts" in Kuwait, while Ali turned out to be a bisexual sex maniac, who, towards the end of their marriage, demanded it with poor Aya from the back, under the shower. She hated it, but for peace's sake had to submit. She was in his country, and he had all the power over her that Kuwaiti husbands have over their wives.

"I just can't take it any longer," she complained. "I wish I could put a crab up there to wait for him. I found all these male-only magazines. I am sure he imagines that I'm a boy when he does that to me." It was no laughing matter to Aya. Here is a joke for the ones who don't follow: Three men met in a sauna. One was American, one English, and the other an Arab. The owner kept them company and asked, "How, I wonder, do you treat the women in your country?" First the American said, "Like a piece of chewing gum. When we're through, we spit it out." Next came the Englishman: "We treat our women like a bottle of whisky. When it's empty we get a new one. And last the Arab answered, "Our women? We use them like a record. When we finish from the one side, we turn it over!"

Aya was a true tennis and bowling queen. Everywhere Aya played, Aya walked away with the top prize. Her flat became a shrine for her trophies. Ali could well and truly have been proud of her. But, instead, on returning home from tennis for something she had left behind, she had the unexpected pleasure of viewing her little girl's 55-year-old Indian nanny's dark, wrinkled bare bottom, which made her think of a shrunken potato. The old woman was kneeling down, almost choking, while giving Ali the blowjob of his life. Next to her she had a tub of marmalade, in which she repeatedly dipped her finger to stimulate his anus with—at the same time. The two of them were so absorbed in their sex act that they did not realize Aya was standing there watching them, and just as he was beginning to have his almighty explosion, Aya made herself known. Ali's erected cock shot out of the servant's mouth, spouting sperm all over her black, neatly knotted hair and face. Any married woman can well feel for Aya and imagine what she felt—sick, betrayed, humiliated, in deep mud. The Indian ran for cover and swore to Aya later on that she had only given in to Ali's wishes because Ali had promised her a visa and a Kuwaiti working permit for her daughter in India, whom she wanted nearer, earning money like herself. Now, that is what is called a "fucking wasta" of the sort that Aseel Kuwaitis can hand out and that belongs to everyday life, too. Ali was The Classic Dishdasha Lifter, but then again he was no exception because most Kuwaitis are. Ali's father, for example, was married to fifteen women in his lifetime. He always kept four wives at a time, divorcing one for a new one instead. He died young, however. Could it have been his heart?

Aya struck it lucky with Ali's mother, who was a "with-it," understanding woman who got married again (after her marriage to Ali's father was over) and found much happiness the second time around. Ali, trying to follow in his father's footsteps, got engaged a couple of times behind Aya's back. Finally, after seven years of adulterous ups and downs, Aya left him. Ali has gotten married at least four times since. And Aya, I am sorry to say, found unhappiness with another Arab, though not from Kuwait.

One of the first other foreign girls Monika got to know in Kuwait was Helena, from France, who, unlike Monika, had seen a bit of life before coming to Kuwait. She was also married to an Aseel. Yasin was his name, a journalist and a compulsive liar, who was actually in the right field of work, come to think of it. He introduced himself to Helena as a millionaire from Kuwait, took her to the poshest nightspots in Paris, and tipped only with 1,000 Franc bills. His trick worked. Pretty, long-legged Helena was impressed. His parents vacationed six months of the year abroad, three at their villa in Geneva and the rest, mostly for shopping, at their residence in London's upper-crust Knightsbridge, where else? In Kuwait, he had just built his own marble villa, where he kept a fleet of cars, for cars were his hobby. Helena, full of expectation, was to learn on her arrival in Kuwait that Yasin had absolutely nothing. He was bullshitting! The money he had impressed her with in France was the salary he had saved up and squandered in style. He did not even own a car. He borrowed one from a friend to fetch her and her baby from the airport, still lying that it was his. She had to live for six months with his parents in an old clay hut, which was one of the first ever built in Kuwait. There Helena and Yasin had to sleep on the floor, and as her child outgrew the carrying-cot, Yasin had to save up money to buy a bigger one. Later, they moved to a rented flat much inferior to the ones she was used to in France, located in the Palestinian sector, although he, too, was an Aseel. As soon as Yasin made a bit of financial progress, he, too, started to womanize. Helena had collected massive evidence. He was selfish, too. Whenever he had aches and pains, he went and paid for private treatment in the English area of Ahmadi. Helena and her fast-growing brood of three kids had to make do with the free national health service available to all living in Kuwait, while for Yasin, only the best was good enough. But what took the biscuit in Helena's case was the cheek with which he took her, upon her arrival in Kuwait, to a public park and told her that it was his father's property and that the Government paid a high rent for it. A small consolation in Helena's case was Yasin's gentle, caring parents, who strongly condemned their son's life and actions. They brought little presents, too, for the kids and Helena. After having been through very rough times with Yasin and the skeleton of their own house finally had been erected, Yasin sent his family of four on a summer vacation to France while he took advantage of their absence and married another wife (in addition to Helena), a Palestinian stewardess he had met on some flight. Yasin told Helena she now had two choices: come back, accept and live in her new house in Kuwait; or stay in France. Helena stayed in France for good, and that after bearing patiently with Yasin for ten years.

Pia—a tall, blonde, Finnish *au pair* girl—liked alcohol and men. She bedded whatever took her fancy in London and had several abortions (various guys, including some Kuwaitis, were implicated) until she stumbled upon a wealthy, non-Aseel Iranian Kuwaiti, who fell head over heels in love with her, made her pregnant, and married her. He lavished furs and jewelry on her and traveled to Kuwait to straighten the path for his European wife to follow as soon as possible, but not without first leaving some security behind for her in the form of an American Express card. He broke off a long-arranged marriage with one of his cousins who was waiting for him in Kuwait. From the day Pia first entered Kuwait, she lived in great luxury. Her husband knew of her wild past. That's why she had to wear a headscarf and sunglasses to disguise herself in public, so as not to be recognized by some of her Kuwaiti former-lovers and thereby start nasty rumors. Her in-laws utterly despised Pia, but she was lucky, for, unlike Abdulla, her husband told them off and shut them up and stuck-up firmly for her. He gave her *carte blanche* to protect herself from them any way she felt like. She had nothing to fear from him. Monika had no idea what that must have felt like.

One day, however, Pia was taking a ride in her gleaming, white Cadillac coupe. She froze, then scrambled, screaming out of her car. In her rear-view mirror, she had seen a huge, peachy-yellow scorpion climbing up the back window, definitely put there by her desperate in-laws, who still wanted their son to marry his cousin in order to consolidate the two families' two big businesses.

Monika's friend Aya befriended Pia in Kuwait. While Pia's husband was on a business trip abroad, Pia invited Aya and Ali to stay overnight in her beautiful house. In the middle of the night Aya awoke to use the toilet and found Ali in bed with Pia, exercising and keeping alive Pia's old ways. The last Monika heard of Pia, Pia was on a bottle of scotch a day, put on weight Kuwaiti style, and showed little interest in anything else. Monika had not thought much of Pia to start with.

With such people to compare her circumstances to, Monika came to the conclusion that she, married to Abdulla and his family, was by far not the worst off of the lot. Numerous times she was glad her family was Aseel Kuwaiti in origin, and it made her proud. If they want to, Aseels can swim all the way to the top of the noodle soup, playing first (and most important) fiddle in Kuwait's society, even though they are outnumbered in their own country by foreign Arabs and Persians. Persians, she learned, were commonly referred to as *bosal* (onions). Kuwait's onions were then mostly imported from Iran, and the Iranis loved plenty of onions in their food. In fact, they smelled of onions, hence the name *bosal*. Such name-calling was mostly the result of Kuwait having become a rich country overnight while its ethnocentric natives remained insular and prejudiced. Europeans were *hamras*. Palestinians were *Samouns*, named after the small loaf of white bread they always ate with their meals.

The Kuwaiti Government does everything for its own people, the Aseels. And the ruling sheikhs and their authority are loved and greatly respected, in return, by the Aseels.

Kuwait is over, over generous to everybody living in it legally, and everyone who is thought deserving enjoys lots of privileges. A person like Monika, for example, who today holds a class 1 Kuwaiti citizenship (whose grades reach from 1 down to 5) is entitled at least to acquire government jobs, government land, government financial grants for building or otherwise acquiring a home, government health care, government everything, free of cost. No Kuwaiti really has to work very hard, and few of them do. Kuwait is a paradise for men—anyway, as close as one can come to a paradise on earth. It really is.

And for women? No! Women still have a long way to go before they find fulfillment in Kuwait. They have nothing much to laugh about. They won't be happy as long as their men prefer each other's company to the company of women and look upon the maintenance of wives as a noxious duty. Kuwaiti women have to take the initiative into their own hands, or nothing at all is ever going to change for the better for them.

Change is not coming from the inside. It was the Lebanese, Palestinians, and Egyptians who were first imported as deputies to run important jobs in the government and in private businesses alike. Engineers and technicians of other Arab nationalities have helped to put Kuwait's industry on its legs and teach it how to walk, so to speak. And now Kuwait is running all alone and has been doing so for quite some time—and how! Before the Kuwaitis successfully completed their studies abroad and took over all the major posts and positions in

Kuwait that they hold today, most jobs designated for the "schooled elite" were given to Egyptians, Egypt being the leading Arab state with its large population, semi-Western ways, and its centuries of great history and culture. Even so, the reputation that Egyptians still have in Kuwait is that they are willing to lend you their wives for their own financial gain and will do so without batting an eyelid; and that they are willing to do anything to be the proud owners of a Mercedes-Benz. In Kuwait, they are considered, as Monika eventually discovered, the *dem chaviv* (the anything goes people) of the Arab world.

In Kuwait, every true female loves to throw a party. Parties are the women's top social event, and giving them and going to them amounts to a full-time occupation. Any excuse is good enough for throwing one. For that's where a woman can be seen, where she can wear and show off her latest designer outfits and her out-of-this-world jewelry, and where she can discuss the latest gossip.

When Sulaiman's birthday rolled around, Monika decided it was time to have her first big party, a birthday party for little Sulaiman. Up to then she had arranged only small dinner parties for friends and slightly bigger do's for Abdulla's pals. Her flat was not designed for anything outrageous. Preparations were started well in advance of the date, in contrast to most Kuwaiti parties. Everything edible was homemade with great care and love—except for the cake, which was a huge wheel of black and white, made to look like a soccer ball. Enough food and drink for forty guests was laid out on two dining-room tables set in the open air on the huge terrace. Everything was artistically arranged in green and orange to complement the green cactuses and the orange, painted terrace walls. Orange and green jello wobbled on the tables, garlands of the same colors decorated the walls, lights, and doors. The end result made a pretty picture, with little Sulaiman romping about dressed to match. He wore a green short-legged silk suit with an orange bow tie, while his mummy wore a slinky, shiny, tight-fitting, cotton one-piece outfit that nipped in narrowly at her tiny waist, which was set off by a green suede belt. A thick gold chain (a gift from Abdulla) decorated her proud neck and lay suggestively between her firm breasts in that low-cut, v-necked outfit.

For parties like this one, which were for females only, one always dressed sexily. It was the only time that women could be women, that women were allowed to show that they were women, if only to each other. Abdulla's trendy cousins along with other female members of the big, al-Amahani family turned up with presents for Sulaiman that one could be truly proud of. Everybody brought an expensive toy; some guests even brought two.

When the noisy in-laws appeared on the scene, they inspected and put their fingers on and into everything. At first their eyes had been steadily fixed on Monika's new jewelry and, if looks could kill, there would have been a funeral, not a birthday party. Mind you, they, too, fitted well into the party color scheme: they were green with envy. With all their clothes, their masses of jewelry, their money, and everything in excess, it would ruin their day if they saw Monika wear something new, even as seldom as once a month. Monika, who knew how to look her best, used looking her best as a form of silent revenge on them. It was her unsung weapon, and she could use it without having to utter a single word. Sulaiman had got some rubbishy, not-worth-mentioning birthday presents from them, as usual. When Diba traveled to see her fiancé or went for a quick abortion to Cairo, for example, she brought home as a gift for Sulaiman the salt-pepper-toothpick-towelette package off the plane's food tray.

Sulaiman received and politely thanked each of the guests for his birthday presents and piled them high onto his bed, to open one by one after the party was over, or the next day. Right now he was more interested in playing excitedly and among the children with the birthday balloons, whistles, party hats, poppers, and a little puppy-dog that Monika had traded the day before with neighborhood kids for a red-eyed, white Angora rabbit.

Monika circulated among her guests, chit-chatting politely in the little Arab she had mastered brilliantly, but making sure she was well out of earshot of her in-laws, who instead of simply correcting her mistakes would ridicule her pronunciation and her valiant efforts to speak their language. Mother-in-law busied herself with offering food and showing off, as if she were the hostess. Nevertheless, Sulaiman's party ended up a big success. Abdulla and Monika had been invited for supper that same evening by a young Czech doctor and his family, and the two of them had just enough time to wrap the left-over party food and cake in aluminum foil and put it into the fridge. Everything else would have to be left as it was for the time being. But don't ask what awaited them on their return home.

Torn foil wrappings were empty, a huge chunk of cake was missing, and all of Sulaiman's presents were opened, played with—some already broken, and thrown all over the entire flat. And who knows what had been taken away? To start with there had been all these packages. What was left of the pile seemed now so little. Once again Monika's stomach did a turn.

Monika was not permitted to lock up her flat. "My family will think we have something to hide," was Abdulla's reason for that; so his family had free access to come and go and take as they pleased without ever having to think of returning anything, whereas Monika would have to go downstairs and ask politely for her stuff back if she needed it. Often none of them knew the whereabouts of the missing item—like, for instance, her makeup, or the last drop of milk she had counted on in her fridge. You can well imagine how annoying that would be to any normal human being, never mind how tolerant and patient. All those little bothers collected themselves and left their marks on Monika. But they were the least of her troubles.

On entering her flat once, she found an owl sitting high up in her bedroom, where all the windows were closed, and wondered how it had gotten there. An owl was considered a very bad omen, Monika's Kuwaiti friends told her; somebody must have put it there, somebody who was trying to warn you, they said; "be careful, we warn you." But Monika took no notice. She had no idea what they were talking about, but in the back of her head she did not stop wondering how the bird could possibly have entered the room with all the windows closed tight.

Then, while cleaning the flat after Sulaiman's birthday party, she found what she took to be a homemade toy. It was the coccyx bone of a lamb that had a face painted on it, black hair glued on, and a little red scarf knotted around it. It was made to look like a woman's face, and Monika kept it to show to Abdulla, who, electrified by the sight of it, shouted at her:

"It's evil. Drop it, drop it!"

She did. Saying Muslim prayers, Abdulla picked it up and quickly flung it as far over the balcony as he could.

"Someone is doing witchcraft on us! These faces drawn on bones carry a strong curse."

"What? Rubbish!" replied the convent girl and laughed in his face and kissed her fool of a husband, feeling great pity for him. Witchcraft did not exist for Monika, not yet.

Abdulla sat in the middle of the untidiness his family had generated after Sulaiman's birthday party, took a deep breath, and said, "Sweetie, I must say I don't blame you. To tell you the truth, I myself don't know what to do with them. I am tired and fed up with everything. I have been thinking, what would you say if I took a course for two years in England? Let's say, in extended radiotherapy? And then in those two years, we will have gotten our land. My name is on the next list. I have seen it myself."

That suggestion made Monika as lively as a bottle of champagne!

"Abdulla, Sweetie, that is the absolutely most sensible idea you have come up with since I've known you! I am willing to agree on anything that takes us out of this Alcatraz. Yes, let's do it," she replied enthusiastically, without hesitation, and with mountains of new hope in her heart. There was hope for a peaceful, normal life after all!

"That's settled then. I will apply first thing tomorrow morning in my Ministry," Abdulla promised, and Monika threw her arms around his neck, squeezing tight, almost strangling him.

"You clever, clever little Arab! Where did you keep that brilliant idea of yours hidden for so long?" she asked.

"We are not going anywhere if you close my wind pipes now," he cheerfully and jokingly replied.

New plans were made, and the two of them became substantially happier. It became easier to overlook the chicaneries that the in-laws subsequently concocted.

Sulaiman's little puppy helped to create unforeseen problems, too. In the Holy Koran, the dog is listed as unhygienic and dirty and not to be gotten in contact with. If you have washed yourself to be ready for prayer—as you must do five times a day, according to the holy rules—and a dog comes up and gives you a friendly lick, then head, face, hands, intimate areas, and feet have all to be washed a second time around, or Allah does not accept that prayer. It happened that sometimes Sulaiman would run in the garden to play with his doggy when, soon after, the in-laws' hysterical cries and loud shouts could be heard. They would run after the poor thing, shooing and kicking it away. Frightened, the doggy would come scampering back upstairs, sometimes with a bloodied, casually discarded sanitary napkin between its teeth. And *they* talked about the dog being unhygienic dirt!

During her period, a woman is unclean, according to the Koran—and therefore not allowed to pray. That's why Monika's in-laws did not bother to wash much either. The whole family and their servants, who had to clean the mess after them, knew exactly who was having her period when soiled sanitary napkins littered the bathrooms, and not a few of them, the courtyard as well.

The women moaned and groaned about this monthly interruption of their routine and got fits of the vapors, or melancholy, over them. They became ever so ill and could do even less than usual, which was precious little anyway. Mother-in-law's bathroom should have been equipped with gas masks, for it always stunk to high heaven. Anybody entering the house could find his way to the loo just by following its smell, and once you got there you found it to be cockroach infested as well.

Time and again, Monika purchased gallons of strong bleach and Dettol to pour down the drains of basin, toilet, and bath. To start with, her in-laws were enthusiastic, but the enthusiasm soon wore off. So, if Monika did not do the job herself, nobody did. And why should she have bothered anymore? Everything she did they copied at first, but their practice of hygiene was short lived and soon forgotten.

One day mother-in-law had some work for Monika to do. She told Abdulla about it, too. This time it was that Diba's new dining room set had arrived that afternoon. Mother-in-law wanted Monika to go there to help set it up, to arrange it so that it would look right. Monika, as she infrequently did, refused to go, saying she had to answer a letter from her mother. Abdulla thought her excuse was not strong enough and tried to find a better one.

"Monika has her period," he proffered.

Mother-in-law looked at Monika, astounded, in disbelief.

"What! *She* gets periods, too!"

"Mother," Abdulla said, "all females do, the black, the brown, the white skinned."

"But she can't have periods. She is never sick!" the stupid woman insisted.

"Mother, having one's period is a natural process that all women in this world, from a certain age to a certain age, go through," the medicine man explained, "but here in Kuwait it comes as a welcome excuse amongst our women and is a reason to fake disability."

"So, she gets her period just like us, and all these years she never felt ill! White people don't get pain the way we do." With that remark mother-in-law divulged the extent of her ignorance and made it worse.

Can you put yourself in Monika's shoes and imagine how she must have felt taking orders and being pushed around by people of such a low caliber mentality? Would you like to exchange places with her for all the money in the world? No? Small wonder. Of course, you would not.

Monika got on very well with kids, though, and by far preferred their company to that of Kuwaiti grown-ups. Kuwaiti kids are left to grow up naturally. They listen, mingle in any conversation, and speak their minds. They know all about sex from a very tender age, and boys at about twelve start driving cars. They are not allowed legally on the roads, but take off around the block or in the desert. Children learn to work the television set by the time they take their first steps. They don't, however, find much pleasure in toys, perhaps because they know they can and will get everything that is new on the market, never mind the cost. They have no idea how a child whose parents can't afford it feels. Being very careless because they have so much, they break their toys more often, and, since there is so much money, the driver is sent out to get replacements. Nevertheless, some of the children in Kuwait are excellent hosts. You would be surprised how welcome they make you in their homes, given the chance. Servants listen to and respect children and their wishes and orders just as if the children were adults because, if they didn't, they would be in danger of losing their jobs. Raising their hand to a child is unheard of. Kuwaitis love and pamper their children. Children always come first. Men are especially proud of their sons. Pity on the women whose bad fortune it is to bear daughters only. In Kuwait, all in all, children grow up very independent, self-assured, and secure. They are years ahead compared to Western kids, whose parents, let's face it, often train their kids more like dogs and so ruin them for life. In Kuwait, you won't hear such things as "You are standing on the

Oriental carpet. Get off it before you spill your Coke on it!" or "Where has your hair ribbon gone? Next week's pocket money is confiscated for a new ribbon!" or "Children should be seen and not heard." (By the way, that saying should be about Kuwaiti adults, not children, because if children are heard it's always amusing; but when grown-ups speak it's so often distressing.) And why are little Western children always addressed by their grown-up trainers in a silly, high pitched voice, with every other word ending in an 'ee'? Monika's attitude towards rearing children was reasonable: first should come the children, with the necessary material clutter taking a firm second place; but in the West where she grew up it was, sadly, usually just the opposite. Kuwait made her think about the whole process.

Diba's—and, later on, Sabiha's—children and huge bunch of neighbors' kids loved to play with Sulaiman, his toys, and Monika, who supervised endless games in her flat. She gave prizes and took to cooking them their first french fries, hamburgers, or hot dogs (bangers). From her they learned (and loved!) to eat their food with a knife and fork. You would be surprised how very intelligent and open-minded they were, just like blotting paper, picking it all up.

A yellow wool dress was little Selma's dream, so Monika sat down to crochet it for her, and it was ready within five days. Little Selma was over the moon watching the quick progress of the dress. Her little face lit up when she finally wore it, very excitedly, and looked at herself in the mirror. The dress was very short-lived. Careless Diba shrunk it beyond recognition in a hot washing machine.

The in-laws got so used to leaving their children in Monika's care that, when they were ready to go out one day and she, for one reason or another, couldn't or wouldn't take care of the children, they started to call her a *gahba* (prostitute). "*Shukran* (thank you)," she smiled back at them. Coming from them, it didn't feel like an insult.

Tidiness was something children and parents alike had never heard of. With a servant on hand for everything, clothes were piled high beside the bed or wherever one just happened to be standing while undressing. Jewelry and watches, whether inexpensive or worth thousands, were also dropped casually on top of that pile, and it didn't cease to astonish Monika how they then would holler and shout at innocent servants, blaming them for a mislaid shoe, earring, or some child's homework.

Tricky servants had easy game of it if they decided to steal because the owner would always be uncertain where he had left what he was looking for. Theft is rather widespread, therefore, and touches nearly all Kuwaiti residences.

Diba's little Selma wore a costly, heavy piece of ruby and pearl jewelry around her neck at *Eid* (the Arabic Christmas). When she undressed that day, the jewelry disappeared. Nobody took much trouble in looking for it either. Quite some time later, after it was more or less forgotten, the Egyptian nanny said she had found it between some upholstery. Diba was pleased and praised the nanny, who placed it, drawing considerable attention to it, on top of a big TV set and saying loudly, "Here, everybody, look where I put it this time. This time it won't get lost," after which the jewelry was to disappear and never be found again. Monika saw through the servant, that she had returned it the first time, pretending to have just found it so as to exonerate herself from being accused, then took it a second time and for keeps. The whole incident must have been well planned. She probably thought no one would suspect her. Actually, they did, but could get no proof. The fact is that servants in Kuwait often have relatives or friends working in other families, and they will all hide stolen goods for each other and lie about it. A wife can be bought at home for the price of a single piece of jewelry such as Selma lost, so, with all the wealth that servants see tossed around, it is not surprising that weakness prevails and things are lifted. It's only human.

The promise Abdulla made that Monika would be able to travel once a year to Europe never materialized. But Abdulla surprised her out of the blue with three tickets to Egypt once. The pyramids had fascinated Monika since early childhood. She remembered writing a long essay about them at the convent school and remembered the excellent mark she got for it, too. The night before taking off Monika had a terrible dream. She dreamt that their plane to Cairo went up in flames over the neighbor's house. And, because some of Monika's dreams had turned into realities before, she refused flat out to travel on the following day. They took off the day after that and stayed for three weeks in an apartment belonging to one of Abdulla's uncles.

Almost every Kuwaiti family had, in those days, a second or third home in either Cairo or Lebanon. Lebanon is now ruined, but it was then the Paris of the Middle East. Later in the 1970's, Kuwait's *nouveau riche* started to move to London, Spain, and Europe in general, while Kuwait's most elite families took off to the south of France, the English countryside, Miami, or Los Angeles.

The place where Monika and Abdulla stayed in Cairo was so cockroach-infested that when the light was switched on late at night the whole room came alive. Monika could not sleep. Well, who could have? She had had enough of Cairo after only one week, thanks to Sabiha who stayed during that visit with her fiancé only walking-distance away. Fahad was studying at the University of Cairo, so each day Sabiha joined the young couple uninvited and took charge, of course, of the daily routine. Needless to say, her presence cast a thick, dark cloud over Monika's stay in Egypt. No matter what she did, she couldn't seem to get out of her in-laws' clutches, no matter how far away she went. Gourmet Sabiha's main interests were good restaurants, shopping centers, and nightlife. If it had been left entirely up to Sabiha, Monika would not have seen anything else. She definitely would have missed out on the treasure troves in Cairo's museums and the mummies, well worth a journey to Egypt, and probably would never have seen with her own eyes nor entered one of the Seven Wonders of the World, the pyramids themselves.

Sulaiman was most impressed with the animals in the Cairo Zoo, where wheeled carts stood piled high with long-leaved, green lettuce for sale. Monika thought they were on sale for the animals. Wrong. The people sat on the grass, amongst the animals, eating the salad! To Monika they looked very funny. Different country, different customs!

Monika was whistled at all day long in Egypt.

Day in and day out, on the pavement and just around the corner from their lodgings sat the same old beggar with only one leg. On that leg, he sported a bleeding mass of pus, which, as Abdulla remarked, must have been a self-inflicted wound. It looked like the old man scratched his open wound regularly to make it bleed, again and again, in order to touch people's hearts with mercy, for that was how he earned his daily bread. Abdulla let little Sulaiman hand out a most generous donation to the old man while Monika felt her breakfast coming up. She felt great pity for the old man and for the poverty in general and the whole of it made her feel unwell. In fact, children and women would start limping on spotting the well-dressed couple in order to arouse compassion, and if Abdulla did give the poor some money, before Monika could say 1-2-3, a whole swarm of beggars would form around her and her husband.

The Egypt that Monika got to know was the Egypt under handsome President Nasser's regime, when people dared not speak about politics outside their homes, and every shoeshine boy was a political spy in disguise and on duty. One of Abdulla's friends recommended that he and Monika visit a nightclub near the pyramids. The twosome took a taxi to it and were greeted by the manager, who led them to a small, round table for two. There were only a couple of customers, males; but there were about thirty well-endowed, tarty-looking ladies of the night lining one side of the hall. They were smoking and drinking and starting to flirt with Abdulla and Monika, who got embarrassed. Sexy come-on looks were darted in their direction. The "girls" must have thought the couple was out looking for someone to make up a threesome and were vying strenuously for the job, each one trying to outdo the other. A waiter approached and put a small, glass dish of pistachio nuts on the table. Amused, Abdulla ordered a Black Label for himself and a gin and tonic for Monika. He was realizing by then that his friend had played a prank on him: he had sent him and his wife to one of Cairo's best-known brothels.

Kuwaitis—young and old—heap lots and lots of jokes on one another. In that respect, they are all very young at heart. Maybe that is what happens if one has no money worries.

Once their drinks were finished, Abdulla quickly paid, and they left with the manager close behind. He wanted extra money for the nuts, but Abdulla flatly refused to pay and told him, "Number One, we didn't order the nuts; Number Two, in all of Cairo something is always served along with drinks; it's a national custom; and Number Three, for your information, I didn't come here on a camel, you know." Abdulla did not bother to stop walking as he said these words and hailed a taxi outside. Monika and Abdulla got in, but the manager halted it and refused to let them drive off. A shouting match, with on-lookers, erupted. Monika got dead scared for her sweetie but was soon relieved at the sight of an on-coming policeman, who soon sorted out the situation. Of course, Abdulla did not have to pay for the nuts. So, imagine the disappointment when the *policeman* put his hand through the window and asked outright for a tip! Monika, still shaken from the frightening incident, could not help herself and said, "What? You're asking for money and you call yourself a policeman?" Then she spat at him and they drove off. In Egypt, wherever you went, everybody was after the easily recognizable, desert-accented Kuwaitis' money. After having seen once what was worth seeing in Egypt, Monika knew that never again would she want to go there.

Kuwait's cinemas became an umbilical cord between Monika and her Western culture. Movies were one of the few enjoyments in Kuwait she looked forward to and could dress up for. In the movie houses, classy, modern females could be seen sitting next to women who were in the same category as Monika's in-laws and simply wore their pajamas or nightgowns with plastic bathroom slippers on their feet, all of it covered by their black abayas. When the lights went out, they dropped their abayas, only to pull them up over themselves again quickly during the lighted intervals. To make up for the hidden mess, they wore heavy make-up and sported lots of jewelry.

Monika applied make-up, too, like brushing her teeth, everyday. In fact, she was never seen without it. Make-up was the first thing to go on in the morning and the last thing to come off at night—not an easy task to look your best all day in the desert heat, but, then, as every woman knows, beauty has its price. Monika could not afford to let herself go. Whenever she went out, her long blonde hair was combed back and rolled into a banana, as it was then called, on the back of her head and a fringe of bangs fell over her forehead and into her eyes in the style that was then made so fashionable by Brigitte Bardot. In fact, Monika was a bit of a look-alike for the gorgeous BB.

One time, the cinema lights went out and the film *Viva, Mana!* appeared on the screen. Monika's little boy shouted excitedly, "Daddy, daddy, look! It's mummy up there." Monika looked good, and she knew it. At the cinema, male eyes—and female eyes, too—were firmly fixed on her. She was not averse to the attention, but she didn't crave it either. In any case, that's why Abdulla's sisters hardly ever included her in their visits to the movies. As Tamader was always saying, "If she is with us, everybody looks at her, and nobody at us." Monika got used to being looked at wherever she went in Kuwait.

It wasn't her looks as much as her white skin that attracted attention. If Abdulla left her in the car for a couple of minutes, he would return to find it surrounded by non-Aseel Arabs and Persians. She did not like that at all. It made her feel uneasy, and she was really disgusted when she started to understand some of their comments and the things they said they would do to her in front of each other, things like "What if somebody comes and gives you permission to fuck this hamra up her arse?" and so on. It came as a great relief to Monika to be able to speak the language, for then she could take them by surprise. She could tell them m Arabic to go piss off or go and fuck each other! It does not sound very nice, but that was, I'm afraid, the only language they understood, and the only sort of thing that would make them back off. One cannot reason with such beastly peasants. To them you have to give what you get, fight fire with fire.

The cinema phase came to an abrupt end one day. Monika was ready to go. Sulaiman was to be dropped off at Aya's on the way. Then, the phone rang. It was one of Ahdulla's friends on the line who wanted Abdulla to join a group in a poker game.

"Come on, what kind of man are you, taking your wife always to the cinema! You are not newly married, nor engaged. Are you your wife's steering wheel? Send her with your sisters to the movies," came their sage advice.

Abdulla listened to them and proved that he was just as much male as they were.

"Sweetie," he said, "why don't you go downstairs and sit with my sisters? I have to go to my friends." And Abdulla was a goner. Goodbye cinema. Hello loneliness. Once again, Monika sat alone, tears streaming down her cheeks. As had happened so many times before, she was devastated and deeply hurt. How could he treat her like this? She felt as if he had thrown her into a corner. Where was his love for her? Even if he didn't love her, didn't he have some sort of feeling for her, some common human regard? As she sat there, she could not believe that she—herself—was the same person who took all the abuse that Abdulla doled out. He was no different from all the other Aseel Kuwaitis. He, too, saw her—his wife—merely as a duty to be attended to at certain intervals. His taking her to Cairo for a week had to make up for heaps of neglect afterwards. He acted as if she owed him something for that trip. He talked often enough about it; and when they talked, it always seemed to her that his mind was far away on other things and that he was anxious to get away to do them.

The only time now during which she held his full, undivided attention was in bed—where she was allowed to be his equal. Sex was to become the only good thing they had left over from what was slowly becoming "the good old times." The only moment he would listen to her if she had something in particular to say or if she wanted anything was before a sex session. First, Monika told herself that Abdulla was not made for marriage, but she found out in due time that what she had was a typical "marriage Kuwaiti style" and that she was by far still better off than many other pathetic Kuwaiti wife.

Men were thrown together with men and women with women—to meet up only in bed at night, where a woman was granted the honor of pleasing and receiving her master and breeding a couple of heirs for him. If a Muslim wife refused sex, Monika learned, that was a good reason to take action against her; it was grounds for divorce—the Holy Koran said so. Everything done in Kuwait was justified because the Holy Koran decreed it. For an intelligent female, marriage Kuwaiti style is a pretty degrading state. Monika's morale had hit rock bottom. She paced back and forth on the balconies and in the rooms, wearing out her mules and crying torrents, feeling truly sorry for herself. When and how could her life ever possibly change for the better? The way things stood, she was sliding down and down, and life got worse all the time.

As she stood, tears in her eyes, on the cactus balcony, straining her ears, waiting for the familiar banging of Abdulla's car door at around 3 a.m., she sighted an orange, cigar-shaped, very bright light. It was the size of a helicopter and was lowering itself very, very slowly, then held still only inches above the house across the street from her. What was it she saw there? She stood wondering. She exhausted her brain, searching through numerous possibilities. It was still there. Shaken, she looked at that unfamiliar object in total amazement.

"God, I wish Abdulla were here, to see this!" Monika ran for binoculars. It was unbelievable, an out of the world experience. A couple of seconds after she had focused her lens to get a better view—she was only allowed to take in the beautiful sight for a couple of seconds more—it took off, much faster than it had come down. It hovered and then flashed away like a Frisbee, out of sight and into the dark, dark night sky, leaving her feeling stranded and dumbstruck. She had seen something for which she had no explanation, and that was why she never mentioned it to anybody afterwards. Years later, reading in a British Sunday paper about other people's similar experiences and sightings of flying objects, some of them cigar-shaped, she realized that she was one of the few lucky ones who had actually seen a UFO (unidentified flying object). Knowing now what it was all about, she would not have minded having that experience repeated.

Abdulla came home that night about an hour later, happily intoxicated, wobbling like a Kelly Man, talking rubbish. Even if she had wanted to, what could she possibly have discussed with him now?

Monika loved the sea and Kuwait's desert. It was great fun to live in a tent among the bedouins, deep in the desert, for two weeks at a time—but only if she was lucky and the in-laws did not join in to spoil the fun. Abdulla—a well-trained, desert Boy Scout—was a great one for arranging such trips, where a compass and a plentiful supply of cold water were the items of foremost importance to take along. Abdulla took a gun along, too, "just in case someone wants to take you away from me by force," he would say.

Stories of sexual happenings in the desert were rumored about frequently. Monika's favorite meal in the tent was always breakfast, which consisted of fresh lamb's liver, deliciously spiced and crisp, on an aromatic round of Arabic bread toasted on a coal fire. Food tasted so much better after a sleep in the desert.

Afraid of scorpions and snakes (for her own and Sulaiman's sake), she made sure that absolutely all the tent openings were tightly sealed, all around, at night. Abdulla revealed himself as a first class snake catcher. He could have made his bread and butter that way. One hit with his camel-skin slippers, and the snake fought with death. Every time Abdulla aimed, he struck the snake straight on its head. He knew everything about desert life, which snake was poisonous and which lizard dangerous. Once, he caught a desert fox and brought it home for Sulaiman. Being one herself, mother-in-law did not like it, so foxy had to go! She had to reign in the house solo.

Camels and bedouins criss-crossed the sun-seared desert. The bedouins were immensely friendly folk, always stopping for a chat and ever so thankful for a drink of water, never failing to ask how the hamra came to be there. They looked her over and wanted to touch her. Old story.

All the bedouins of Kuwait were offered houses especially built for them by the Government, but they refused to live in them. They were not used to being kept between four walls, where they felt very claustrophobic, so they kept their goats and donkeys in those houses instead. Even if they had to wash their hair with camel's urine for lack of water, they much preferred the desert and loved to romp in it. It was the only way they knew how to live life, unspoiled by modern ways and technology. Bedouins, Monika learned, have very good memories and the eyesight of hawks for seeing far distances. Their tents are parted into men's and women's quarters, right down the middle, and are surrounded by horses, donkeys, pick-up trucks, American cars, Mercedes and what have you. Their cars are mostly painted red, for they believe that red goes faster. Seeing a genuine bedouin tent with its occupants, animals, and a brand new Cadillac standing beside it was an experience any European would treasure forever, Monika was sure.

Another Kuwaiti activity Monika enjoyed was the endless ladies' parties given in honor of a son's or daughter's good marks at school, to celebrate an engagement, or a recovery from sickness. People also made promises to Allah that if what they wished for were granted they would give a party in thanks. Some simply sneezed and a party was on its way. Many, many happily ending mother-in-law ordeals were celebrated with a party, too—if she happened to die or move out, or if fate got rid of her or shut her up some other way. Then, one might get to hear the most incredible stories.

Beautiful Ferial had fed as a baby on Abdulla's mother's breasts at the time that Abdulla was being weaned; and that automatically, according to their Muslim customs, made Ferial his "sister" and, just as with any other sister and brother, they would never be allowed to marry if they wished to. Strange. Real blood cousins can get together, but unrelated persons who happened to have drunk from the same breasts cannot.

Ferial's mother was a woman of Monika's mother-in-law's caliber. She married off her little beauty, Ferial, at a very tender age to a young sheikh. Ferial's striking beauty angered her in-laws, her mother in law, to be precise. So to get rid of her daughter-in-law as soon as possible before the girl had a chance to conceive an heir for her young husband, the mother-in-law made Ferial's life a misery, trying all kinds of tricks to set her son against Ferial, but nothing worked for the young sheikh wanted to hold on to and keep his pretty young wife. So the evil bitch sent a male Negro slave into the girl's boudoir and ordered him not to leave until she herself personally told him to leave. Unfortunate Ferial lay between the covers in a flimsy silk negligee, quite helpless. She could not get the slave to leave her bedroom. He would not obey her orders, only her mother-in-law's. Eventually, Ferial heard her husband's footsteps nearing the door. He entered with his mother close by.

"Here, look at it with your own eyes, my son! Now, do you believe me? I told you she is bad material. You wouldn't want your children from this woman. She is a whore! You could never be sure if they were really yours."

After that witch had finished her malicious performance, the prince chased Ferial out of his house late at night with only the clothes she was allowed to grab to cover herself. You may be asking why the servant obeyed that vile order. Well, he had been bought and so was not allowed to have a mind of his own. He had to do as he was told, or face severe punishment himself.

Abdulla's grandfather and grandmother on his father's side, with whom Monika's mother-in-law had to live for quite some time when she first got married, had kept a number of Negro slaves. Once grandmother burned a disobeying Negro woman alive in the big yard of their house while all the others had to watch that sacrifice.

"Let this be a lesson for all of you, if you value your life!" Saying that, she stood with a stick in her hand, shouting orders at those most unfortunate creatures.

Monika's mother-in-law must have been through some tough schooling. No wonder she turned out the way she did. Ferial's sheikh had spoken the crucial words—"I divorce you. I divorce you. I divorce you"—three times in the presence of three witnesses, after which Ferial was no sheikha, nor wife, anymore. Nevertheless, Ferial's ambitious mother didn't let much grass grow over the shameful accusations that circulated in Kuwait, and Ferial was married off again—against her will this time—to a very old, very ugly, but stone rich man, who married her on top of his other wives, old lecher. He granted her "every wish of her beautiful eyes," and so Ferial turned into one of Kuwait's greatest and best party givers. She had everything under her feet that this materialistic world has to offer. Yet, true love had overlooked and overstepped her as it did the majority of Kuwaiti women. Ferial was in the habit of saying, "When I have sex with my husband, I put a newspaper or paper bag over his face and think of a chunky young guy."

Marriage Kuwaiti style has nothing to do with marriage Western style. As Monika sees it, it is pure prostitution in a harness.

So, now you see? It wasn't just Monika, being a foreigner, who had a mother-in-law problem. According to Islamic law, the eldest son marries and brings his wife into his parents' house to bear him children and wait on his mother. In Abdulla's case, this only son did not bring a willing slave to his old fashioned mother, and his mother never forgave him and never ceased to use emotional blackmail to make him feel guilty. She would never let him forget he had let her miss out on the chance of being catered to by a servile daughter-in-law.

Monika with all her heart would have wished a Kuwaiti daughter-in-law on her mother-in-law, someone with the character of one of her own daughters, someone like Sabiha, for instance. Then Abdulla's mother would not have had a chance in hell! A Kuwaiti daughter-in-law would soon teach her a lesson. A Kuwaiti daughter-in-law with all her family behind her would know how to deal with her properly.

Looking at the roots of the problem, Monika saw that Abdulla's weakness of character was a main factor. Ninety-five percent of the Kuwaitis in Abdulla's age group didn't live with their parents, and nobody made a fuss about it because times had changed and the new practices, in those modern times, were willingly accepted. Abdulla's mother was not helpless, nor in need of care; she had immense power, like that of a woman seven feet tall. Her clock ran fast and overtime. She craved for someone to control. Monika was her convenient victim.

Gorgeous women, stunning clothes, exquisite jewels—Kuwait's "ladies-only" parties were adventures held in musky, thick, sex-oozing Eastern atmospheres that only filthy-rich Arab females can concoct and release. At such parties, they let their hair down and enjoyed being *femme fatales* for a few hours in that make-believe world with not a man in sight, except for the servants and a couple of musicians who played eastern instruments and helped to create the sultry atmosphere. If a husband or two were to play Peeping Toms, they might not have recognized their spouses, and if a Western man could have been so lucky as to have witnessed such a gathering, it might well have remained for him the most impressive experience of his entire life.

European women cannot create anything nearly so electrifying and mysterious. To give you an idea what is meant here, look at the two rock queens of our day, Madonna and Tina Turner. Tina's pinky is charged with more electricity than Madonna has, and that at twice Madonna's age!

The women's parties were held in residences, chalets, houses near the sea, or sometimes at a big hotel, the music usually provided by a group of hot blooded Negro women—women once bought as slaves but now enjoying their freedom singing and hitting the drums, creating a magical, spiritual music that can creep like an invisible potion of crack into the hand-clapping crowd's bones. The women would simply follow their instincts, overcome by an amalgam of happiness and dance fever. It was like a ritual. They gladly give in to the music that plays havoc with them, swaying their bodies suggestively, at first slowly, then faster and faster and faster, while the music gets louder and louder and louder. The dancers move as in a trance. The music stops. They wake up and come, exhausted, out of it, to loud applause from on-looking females sitting cross-legged in their priceless glittering gowns, gowns that would rival anything Liberace ever wore and even place his outfits in the shade, believe you me.

Sometimes famous singers from Lebanon, Egypt, or Iraq were flown in for the night, especially around the time of weddings. Most of those Arabic female artists also practiced the oldest profession in the world, as a second source of income, and were willingly flown in by the individual Kuwaiti male to perform, in addition, a skilled workout between his legs, maybe while singing him a song at some weekend "males only" bungalow, the *mezraha*. Should the wife find out about the fling, usually through a faithful or a bribed servant—in Kuwait servants often know more about what both the spouses are up to than the spouses know about each other—she would be wise to pretend she didn't know because, if she made a scene, she might run into the chance of being told, "If you don't like it, take your belongings and go back to your mother!" On the other hand, depending on the situation, her husband might feel guilty or sorry for her and make it up to her with a diamond bracelet, which usually works until the next time. Some Kuwaiti women got their nicest collections of jewelry in that way.

A lot depends on what sort of relationship the husband is caught in. If it is a long-standing affair that has just come to light, he might shut her up with a flat in London or a chinchilla. The maltreated woman has no choice anyway, because for her the choice of a divorce is out of the question, making her a branded woman. Paid off this way, she can get something to show off to her friends, at least, for being hurt.

How many naturally stunning females Kuwait has comes best to light at such parties. That's where Monika saw the most beautiful women, often without a trace of make-up—women with long black hair that shimmered with bluish or reddish lights, women with olive skin, strong, white, perfect teeth and beautiful eyes, ranging from the lightest to the darkest browns. Numerous Miss Worlds are hidden away in Kuwait.

And you just can't imagine the Eastern party food! Lambs stuffed with chickens that are stuffed with grape leaves, onions, eggplants, and tomatoes. Nuts and sultana dishes—huge silver trays of rice cooked in different ways. Curries, sauces, salads, and a heaven of sweets. Standing everywhere, outsize crystal bowls overflowing with fruits—mangoes, kiwis, peaches, oranges, grapes, fresh dates, bananas, and other Eastern fruits that are not generally known nor available in the West. The food was always fit for a king and presented on silver- or gold-rimmed platters that were—surprise, surprise!—laid out on a long row of tables. Sometimes the women were handed a fine china plate with embroidered muslin serviettes and gold or silver cutlery. The women may not always have felt at ease with the unfamiliar eating etiquette they were asked to honor, but when an affair was "Western" the hostess was able to show off all the Western-style party paraphernalia she owned and the fact that she knew how to use it correctly, too, if it came to that. On such magical nights, all the ladies put on their best acting performances and behaved and dressed, to the best of their ability, in a one hundred percent civilized, Western manner, trying hard to out-do each other.

There was usually so much food left over that even after everyone had eaten, it looked as if only a bit of it had been tasted. It seemed to Monika that the hostesses' tables were always covered with trays of food so massively heaped that the tables bent under the food's weight, and that not an inch of surface was supposed to be visible to the eye between the trays that were there laid out. Nobody, it must be said again and again, can beat the proud Kuwaitis and their generosity.

At such parties, women who feel like it and want to show their freedom, smoke freely and may gather in some room around a bottle of alcohol. Heavily restricted most of the time, on these mysterious one-thousand-and-one- nights episodes, they break out of their shells for a couple of hours and whole-heartedly enjoy and exercise their soon-to-pass liberties. And good for them—jolly good for them, too!

At such social gatherings, a suitable marriage partner may be identified for one's son or brother by finding out first, of course, if the girl in question is single, who her parents are, whether she is an Aseel, and so on, before she is seriously considered. So, appearances are crucial. Given the chance, Monika thought, Abdulla's nasty sisters would have chosen the ugliest girl in the hall for him. The most extravagant evening wear from the best-known fashion houses in Europe could be seen. It was nothing out of the ordinary to have some Champs Elysees couturier's assistant fly to Kuwait to take measurements for a certain family's females and their children, too, for special occasions, and that was how some lovelies then looked as if they had stepped out of *Vogue* or *Elle* magazine for the night. Kuwaiti parties were always breath-taking fashion shows. Women wore the latest designs. Even before they hit some European boutiques, Kuwaitis had already worn them.

It's a pity, thought Monika, that in Kuwait women dressed only for women.

To wear the same party outfit twice was considered a shame and a social sin every "with it" female in Kuwait strenuously avoided. Monika wore her black, body-hugging, silk crepe model from Vienna for a second time, ignorant of society's rules, and mother-in-law got wild.

"What will people think and say about us!" she told Abdulla. "What a scandal. All of Kuwait will talk and say that you have no money to buy your wife a dress." In principle she hated for Monika to have nice clothes, but in some cases wanting to keep up with the Joneses took priority and was much more important than keeping Cinderella in rags. In Kuwait, false pretenses counted foremost, as everything revolved around image. Indeed, Kuwaiti women know a thing or two about designer labels and surround themselves with chic extravagance. After some big party, for example, creations of white peacock feathers studded with real diamonds or a gold lamee gown decorated with thirty gold watches busily ticking away were the talk of the town. Everyone was always trying to outdo everyone else. The women worried about which designer could come up with the most outrageous, way-out creation. And to think, then, that such works of art were only to be worn once! What a waste.

The greatest pity is that those beautiful Kuwaiti girls, once married, get very careless about their appearance and let themselves go. It's somehow understandable, for they have a child within the first year of marriage and their status in husbands' eyes plunges to a level with their favorite chairs. A Kuwaiti woman takes the indignity to heart, but has not got the backbone, or the support, to fight it. Disillusioned, she eats—and sometimes smokes and drinks behind her husband's back, disappointment and grief deep-rooted inside her. Not only does she eat, she stuffs herself and becomes fat. Whatever she puts on and wears now just does not look right anymore, which makes her feel even worse. The change does not go by unnoticed by her man. The size 12 girl he married is now, only within the last two years, a stout 20 or 22. Put off by that barrel, he goes and looks for his kicks elsewhere. With so much money and power at his disposal, who would want to fuck a bomb when there are everywhere he looks around him sexy, little firecrackers available?

The jewelry worn at an average party, especially by the sheikhas, easily outshines all of the baubles worn in Hollywood at an Oscar Awards evening. It's a feast for the eyes. When you leave the party, you go home feeling you have been to the largest jewelry exhibition in the world, demonstrated on life models. It often went through Monika's head how the Western press gets away in misleading its readers about who owns the biggest, most precious rocks and jewelry in the world, when they haven't the faintest idea and know very little. Doesn't Kuwait—where women are bought with jewels and everyone has her own Aladdin's cave—belong to the world, too? Misinformation misleads Mrs. Johnson in Stoke-on-Trent into believing that Elizabeth Taylor has the second largest diamond in the world after Her Majesty Queen Elizabeth's kohinor. The press would be much more honest to report only on what they know about in the West, without mentioning or claiming to know the whole world.

The Gulfs royals and their faithful subjects—a hundred thousand or so of them—live every day in a *Dallas* and *Dynasty* lifestyle, only the royal style is very lazy and much flashier, surrounded by everything the human brain has thought of and created. Many a clever, world businessman's first stop is Kuwait. The dark joys of Kuwait reign behind high walls, in golden cages, where mail is handed on diamond encrusted gold trays by white-gloved, liveried servants. A woman is pampered in comfort and raised to get married and live life without love in the constant shadow of a husband to whom she soon becomes a habit. Meanwhile it is her duty to bear his children, and her greatest aim in life is to stay married.

All human creatures, no matter the color of their skin, no matter the religion, no matter the language, crave and need love, just as the flower needs the sun to grow. Money, even piles of it, is and can never be used as a successful substitute. A very sweet but desperately unhappy sheikha—married to a wealthy sheikh, of course—told Monika once that when she got married her mother had lectured her: "Your husband is your husband only when he is at home with you. Once he leaves the house, forget about him. Then he is yours no more until he enters your house again.

"Monika," she went on, "every night I go to sleep and every morning I wake up with the same thoughts in my mind. My husband has mistresses, I know it; yet as long as I am married to him, which is as long as I am going to live, if he does not decide otherwise, I can't do anything about it but accept it, which means I will never be happy as long as I live."

As long as women in Kuwait have this "I can't do anything about it" attitude, nothing is going to change for the better for them, and they will always be subdued by males and kept with their wings clipped.

Diba came out of the hospital with her third child, a boy, and went directly to stay with her mother because, here again, Islamic law dictates that the woman is to stay separated from her husband for six weeks after giving birth so that no sexual intercourse can take place within this time. So what does a husband do if desire comes and his own right hand is not sufficient? I can tell you what Diba's husband Ibrahim did. He phoned Abdulla one evening to ask if Abdulla could keep him company for the night. He had a bottle of Black Label he wanted to kill—and share with him. Abdulla disliked Ibrahim, who drank like a fish and regularly beat up and threw his sister out and who without permission took over and bankrupted a good, profitable Agfa film and camera agency that the deceased Mr. al-Amahani had built up successfully. But, for his sister's sake and pushed by his mother, Abdulla took his overnight bag and was on his way. It was 3:30 am when Abdulla crept back into his own bed next to Monika, waking her gently with "Sweetie, Sweetie, you'll never guess what happened to me. Ibrahim, that bloody, fucking bastard wanted to take me by force. That son of a bitch wanted to fuck me up the arse, and that pig is married to my sister! I kicked him and escaped."

Monika—at that stage of her life naive about such matters—thought that only homosexuals did that and could not believe it, but cracked a joke at him. "Don't take it too hard, Abdulla. At least he kept it in the family." Abdulla's mother and sisters, too, had a miserable life, but no more nor less than they deserved. They created so much misery for Monika and everybody else they came in contact with that some of it naturally came back to them. "What ye sow, so shall ye harvest."

To be the pusher, meaning the "man," of the two males in a homosexual encounter is not that bad in Kuwait, but to be the receiver is a great shame. Every Kuwaiti has been a pusher at one time or another in his life, and some were and still are willing receivers. Monika has met Yemeni and Omani gays with female voices whose long hair and fingernails, toenails too, were colored with henna. They would be begging explicitly for a shot up their rears, running around freely exhibiting what they were, apart from servants, deep down.

When the Beatles mania and the Beatles haircuts reached Kuwait, huge trucks drove around the streets collecting all the longhaired young boys to take them to the police station to be shaven bald. After that, those young boys showed themselves in public only with a hat on, until their hair had grown. There may have been reasons other than vanity, as Monika learned for herself.

Ignorant of consequences, Monika had not bothered to take extra precaution against Kuwait's scorching hot sun nor against the salty seawater, although Abdulla had warned her again and again. "My skin is used to the sun. It's like that of a camel. But yours is like thin tissue paper. Believe me, it will burn." Sure enough, she suffered huge blisters on her back and nose, and her fine hair broke off at the roots—to start with, just a little bit, and soon a hell of a lot more. So Monika thought, if I shave my hair off completely, a new crop will have grown within six months, and then I will know how to take better care of it. She consulted Abdulla, who listening with half an ear only while watching international soccer on TV, agreed. The impulsive Aries ram went to work, blonde locks fell under Abdulla's razor blade, and the first time he saw her bald, right after, he was so taken aback at the sight that he stood holding his face while his words got stuck in his throat. But then, when he saw her for the second time, coming back with a blonde wig cleverly arranged, Abdulla quickly calmed down, but not before giving her the name "Aziz," a man's name!

Monika told her in-laws before they would find out for themselves and make a song and dance about it, but what was the use? They made it anyway. Gaggling as if a cart of geese had tipped over, the Amahani telephone line ran hot, informing everybody they knew about what Baldy Monika had done.

At home, Monika massaged her scalp three times with a lotion of coconut oil and herbs from Lebanon given to her by the nice cousins. She kept herself presentable with the help of a variety of turbans in all colors to choose from. Sabiha found great pleasure in telling Monika that the potions stank. But that was, Monika suspected, only because Sabiha was dead jealous that the Hamra should mix with and be liked by her cousins and be always invited while Sabiha and her lot were ignored. Sabiha even pulled Monika's turbans off in the presence of Sabiha's laughing friends. If anybody stank, it was Sabiha, who smelled as if something had crawled up her arse and died there some time ago. She had the habit of wearing dark caftans that would make her look slimmer, she thought, but they exhibited the evidence of some discharge she had caught off her fiancé and that showed on her backside through the garment. It's fair to tell this because one of Sabiha's favorite topics of conversation, a topic she brought up again and again among her friends, trying to ridicule Monika, was that she could not understand how the English cleaned their bottoms simply with toilet paper and did not wash after a bowel movement. "Show us your bottom, Monika. I bet you have cling-ons," she laughed uncontrollably, rolling herself on the floor. Sabiha's bedouin ancestors cleaned themselves with desert sand and still wipe their penises dry with stones in the desert, and here Sabiha was acting as if the Kuwaitis and not the French had invented the bidet.

Omar, Abdulla's tea boy at the hospital, a young, likeable, Yemeni teenager (a Michael Jackson look-alike), approached Abdulla for an afternoon job to raise extra money. Abdulla introduced him to Monika, and she employed him to clean the sandy veranda and balconies twice a week. A month passed, and Omar did his job beautifully. He was always on time and left late. Because of the intense, sticky heat, Monika, when alone, frequently wore no more than a G-string, moving about in comfortable nudity in her flat, with a bathrobe always close at hand just in case. At night with Abdulla gone, which was almost every evening now, she took a shower, washed her hair, renewed nail polish on toes and fingers, and walked from the lit bathroom back to the lit bedroom with nothing on but an invisible perfumed veil of Joy's body silk. Her Elvis music played loud, and it was not that she heard anything, yet for some strange reason, all of a sudden, she was overcome by the urge to switch the lights on in the hall, and there by the door in the hall stood Omar, his gray dishdasha ruffled up high and tucked under his chin. He looked a completely different person, overcome by sex fever, masturbating what was raised out of his long cotton pants. The instant after the lights went on, he let his clothes drop. Monika ran for a towel wondering how many times he had watched her. Wrapped up, she came back scolding him loudly, "Omar, how dare you!"

"I am sorry, my Aunt," he said, not looking sorry at all, and he was gone.

She thought that she must have been the first woman he had seen in the nude in his life, and on top of that, she was white, an added bonus. And, let's face it, what sex-deprived, sex-starved Arab teenager could be sorry for seeing something like that? How many times had he sneaked back after work like that and into the darkened flat can only be guessed.

He was, of course, sacked from his job with her, yet what surprised Monika immensely was that Abdulla kept Omar on at the hospital as if nothing had happened. Abdulla was so strict with her that she had to button up like a nun in male company. He was overly jealous, a jealousy that bordered on insanity and which she had first mistaken for love but turned out to be more like an illness than a positive emotion. Who knows, Abdulla might even have let Omar get away with it if Omar had raped her—since looking at a woman in the nude is a major offence in Kuwait and Abdulla didn't so much as bat an eyelid about it. Right through her marriage it was always the same. Whenever she needed her man to stand up for her, what she had was a dishcloth, and she had to manage all alone. The only good that came out of this Peeping Tom incident was that from then on Monika had an excellent excuse for locking her doors against the in-laws.

Horrid crimes were often committed by comparably primitive servants all over Kuwait. Aya's next-door neighbor, to give you some idea, came home earlier than usual after an evening out, to find their five-year-old little girl spread-eagled over the kitchen table by their 7-years-faithful male servant, who had sexually molested her. It then came to light that he regularly played what the little girl believed to be games, when they were left alone together.

Then, there was a 6-month-old baby boy in the al-Amahani's circle, who after a new Indian nanny arrived, started to lose weight rapidly. The child fell ill. Doctors just could not find anything clinically wrong with him. The answer to this baby's puzzle—and maybe a life saver—was the Iraqi cook, who spoke one day without being asked: "Maybe it has got something to do with the way his new Indian nanny keeps him quiet when he cries, because that is when she opens the gas and rotates the baby slowly above it, and then he soon settles down and falls asleep." Who, for Christ's sake, could do a wicked thing like that? In order to have her peace, the stupid woman gassed the unfortunate baby to make him dizzy and go to sleep.

With the changeable climate—hot outdoors, cold inside the air-conditioned rooms—Sulaiman had developed a nasty sounding, deep, husky cough overnight while Abdulla was on one of his weekend fishing trips with his friends. All alone, Monika was worried sick and decided to take Sulaiman to see a doctor. The Health Service even then was good, but then as now, it lacked doctors and nurses properly skilled enough to use the expensive drugs and technically highly advanced equipment that the Government provided free to its people. In each section that the city is divided into, you will find a supermarket, a Tikka Bar, a fruit-seller, a barber, a jeweler, a patisserie, and a health center; that's where Monika took Sulaiman. To start with, she explained Sulaiman's condition to a bunch of Egyptian and Palestinian nurses who gathered around her, some of who spoke a bit of English. Then she was led into a big white room where Sulaiman was placed on a medical couch that sported a dirty sheet that she pulled aside straight away, and she was told to wait for a doctor who was busy right then. From behind a large screen at the other side of the room, she could hear loud female voices and a man's voice chatting and laughing as if at some tea party as she waited patiently but on needles, Sulaiman's cough getting worse by the minute. Monika could make out that there was no medical discussion going on behind the screen, so she asked loudly in English, "Excuse me, are you the doctor I am waiting for? Behind the screen?" Silence was followed by a slow, "Yeeees, patience, patience. I will be with you when I am ready." Monika could tell by his accent that he was an Egyptian. In time, the middle-aged doctor pushed the screen aside from where he sat in the company of three black-robed females. The four of them were smoking and drinking black Arabic coffee. "Sorry to have to leave you for a minute. I'll soon be rid of the Ingilesia interference," he promised them and got up.

"What seems to be the trouble?" he asked casually and let his eyes run over Sulaiman. "A cough, you say?" He reached to his breast pocket for a pen and started out to write a prescription while saying, "It's nothing, it's nothing"—without having touched Sulaiman.

"But, Doctor, I would like you to examine him first," Monika insisted, her hackles rising. "I am worried because he has got diarrhea, too."

"I don't need to examine. I have seen all I need to see." Then, the three smoking female geese giggled.

Looking straight into his eyes, with her best Arabic, Monika asked him, "Am I at the right address here? Are you . . .? Do you call yourself a doctor? Tell me, what is that stethoscope hanging around your neck for? Do you wear it for decoration?" Now, of course, he realized right away that Monika spoke Arabic with a Kuwaiti accent, which told him he had the wife of some Aseel Kuwaiti in front of him, and all of a sudden she had his undivided attention, for now he knew she could spell trouble for him. A "wasta" from her husband, and he could be out of a job. A wasta, don't forget, may be used two ways—to get someone into a position or to get rid of someone from a position. The doctor had caught on too late. Monika took the prescription he had pressed in her hand, tore it into little bits, and threw it in the man's face. "That's what I think of you, medicine man." She grabbed poor, coughing Sulaiman and made her way quickly to the door under the doctor's protest that he would be honored to give Sulaiman a thorough check up.

It worked every time. As soon as people realized she wasn't the wife or daughter of some foreign employee working in Kuwait (she still looked like a teenager, although she was in her 20's) but that she was married to an Aseel, she was treated like royalty. Monika left the Health Center and asked her way to a private doctor, telling herself she should have known better. She had heard from Abdulla that mostly bad, unprofessional Egyptian doctors who could find no post at home came to Kuwait, sometimes even with forged certificates, and get their posts there through a wasta. She thought back to the time when one of Abdulla's nephews had fallen down a flight of stairs and his mother had been told by an Egyptian doctor, after a couple of x-rays, that the boy had injured his spine and that it was quite serious. In order to make it better, he would have to lie still, strapped in plaster for three months. While the child's room was being arranged and the plaster prepared, one of Abdulla's friends, a doctor who had been educated in Britain, entered the room and as he got to talking to the boy's mother realized she was Abdulla's sister and re-examined the boy. He ordered him, "Hands up, hands down, bend forward, bend back, jump up. Now, go and get dressed. Go home and do your homework. There is nothing wrong with your spine." You know what would have happened to that poor child if that doctor had not entered in time?

Abdulla's bespectacled young Kuwaiti gynecologist friend, accredited in Egypt, who came to visit often with his wife, a very, very nice Kuwaiti girl, is another bad example. Rumor had it that he could not make it academically, so he had bribed someone for the degree. Although he knew he had to be in the operating theater first thing in the morning, he would stay on late the evening before and drink whisky on the rocks into the early hours and thought nothing of mentioning some of his well-known female patients by name, making jokes about them and using filthy language about them and their husbands. When he was not drunk, he was quite a likeable fellow with rather little up there. When Monika heard one day that one of his otherwise healthy patients had died under his hand during a Caesarean section and that all Kuwait was talking about it, for the woman had been well known, Monika was not in the least bit surprised. The opposite, in fact. She wondered how nothing like that had happened before. If you did not know better, you took a doctor in Kuwait like pot luck—and you still do, to some extent, today. Monika understood why the older generation did not have much regard for Western-style doctors. They preferred traditional witch doctor methods, like, for example, branding with hot irons to draw out evil spirits that were placed there by someone jealous who had an evil eye and made the victim fall ill. Abdulla has a big branding mark on the back of his neck and on his lower abdomen, put there by a native medicine man when Abdulla was a small child.

Sabiha got pregnant and, on a visit to her fiancé Fahad in Cairo, stayed there, and got married without any high-dee-high celebration so customary in Kuwait. Her in-laws knew that the baby boy was not premature when he arrived seven months after the marriage, but had been well on its way when Sabiha proceeded into matrimony. Her premarital pregnancy would have been considered a big shame in strictly Islamic Kuwait had it been publicly known.

Fat slob Sabiha had put on so much weight after delivery that from then on she always looked pregnant. Walking with her thin Fahad, they looked like mother and son, or like Laurel and Hardy. How could Fahad be proud of his barrel? For the next couple of years Sabiha spent her days with her mother and her nights in her mother-in-law's house. Small wonder, but she did not get on with her in-laws, who were people of a bedouin tribe. They loved Monika but not Sabiha, who did not get along with anybody. Fahad, like Abdulla, was waiting to be granted his piece of land by the Government so that he could build a house exactly like Abdulla's. Diba and Sabiha lived the life that was typical of married Kuwaiti women, but they compared themselves no end, day in and day out, with the way Monika and Abdulla lived their life. Why did Abdulla spend so much more time with his wife than their husbands did? And why did he take her out to hotel dances, foreigner's parties, hospital do's, and private gatherings? Because Abdulla told them everything, they knew everything, and spurred by jealousy, they tried their utmost to tag along, too. But because they didn't even have proper table manners, Abdulla was ashamed of their behavior, although he did not say so, and left them out of the more up-to-date social circles he moved in. Kuwait's nightlife is very busy with foreigners and modern Kuwaitis like Abdulla. Husbands like those of Diba and Sabiha left their wives behind to meet and enjoy themselves at sea, in douvaniahs, or with a bit of crumpet hidden away in a hotel or at some *mezraha* (weekend house). The four snakes in the grass sat together and held court on how to spoil life even more for the Hamra. If they were doomed to a life at home, why should Monika live hers any better? So they had a word with Abdulla.

"Abdulla, we think you should know what Kuwaiti people are rumoring about you. Our friends' husbands bring the gossip back from douvaniahs. They say your wife thinks for you and that she is in absolute control of you. Everywhere you turn up and are seen, you drag her along, too. She is like your shadow. Don't forget, my son," mother in-law urged, "a good Muslim woman's place is in her house with her children. Look at your sisters. You spoil Monika and once she is used to it, it will be very difficult to undo the damage for you, my son. If your father had lived, he would have taught you everything about how to treat a woman. Except for occasional trips to Lebanon, he never took me anywhere, and he would not have let you bring that foreigner into our house. Allah bless him and let his soul rest in peace."

Whenever Abdulla's sisters wanted anything from him, their mother was used as an in-between and had to speak up for them, for she had the most impact and power over him. But in this case they lost because their Abdulla loved to go out, dance, and show off his blondie. They were barking up the wrong tree, for a change. But, subconsciously, he registered and stored the bad influence somewhere deep in his brain. It seemed to bother him a great deal, and he was constantly torn between his four frustrated, nagging, empty, bored domestic females and Monika. After he had knocked back a couple of whiskies, he started pestering Monika—ruining the evening, every evening that he took to drink, which was more and more often—with no other subject than that of how dear and precious his family were to him and how little, or nothing at all, she really meant to him.

"My family, my mother and sisters are on top of my head and you, bloody flicking foreigner, under my slippers," he told her a thousand times over. Too stoned to drive home from wherever they had gone and where he had made a fool of her, he couldn't take the wheel. So she would drive home. Whenever the in-law problem came up for open discussion, Abdulla's friends always took sides with Monika and told him that if they had a wife like her they would be proud and treat her properly. His best and closest pals told Monika repeatedly that she was much too good for Abdulla and that he did not deserve her.

Sabiha, away in Cairo on one of her abortion trips, left her son and the Indian nanny in the care of her mother. Abdulla was away once again, fishing. Monika sat solitary while knitting on the balcony, watching Sulaiman play in the sand below just in front of the house. She saw Tamader newly coiffed in a long, frilly see-through nightgown, repeatedly running to the main entrance, looking right and left as if expecting someone, when after a while Fahad came driving up in his limousine. The nanny carrying his son settled in the car and following her close by came Virgin Tamader, black cover casually thrown over her scarlet see-through. She, too, climbed, into the vehicle that sped off leaving a cloud of whirled-up sand behind. At the time Monika smelled something fishy, for what was Tamader doing with Fahad? But she soon forgot—until Sabiha came back and her Indian had spoken. Then, one of the biggest spitting, kicking, hair-pulling, clothes-tearing, name-calling, abusive-sister fistfights raged. It came to light that Tamader had stayed the night with Sabiha's womanizing Fahad at their weekend chalet by the sea and that they had sent the Indian nanny with the baby for endless walks around the globe. Hint, hint. What goes on under Islamic law in hypocritical Kuwait behind closed doors and over the telephone—in so-called naughtiness—can easily be compared with today's naughtiest doings in any of the world's modern cities.

Not to mention the rendezvous abroad, prearranged in Kuwait, when a girl simply has to go shopping in London with a girlfriend because she finds nothing suitable in Kuwait and her secret lover is off on a quick so-called business trip and both end up at the same grand hotel—of course, in adjoining rooms. Okay, nothing's wrong. Mating is the most natural thing in the world. Birds and bees could tell you. Only, dear Kuwaitis, female and male, do wake up and revise your own doings and stop calling every pretty European female you set eyes on in Kuwait a *gahba* only because it makes you feel better and you think you can cover yourself with innocence and wash yourself clean under such remarks. It is very difficult for educated, hot-blooded Muslim females to live so restricted a life, we know, but that's your destiny. You probably can't have everything. You have got the money. We have got the freedom. Many a woman's aim, sometime in her life, is to seduce men; that's how she is universally made, and Kuwait's sex- and love-starved single and married Eves are no exception to that game. Stop acting and pretending that biologically you are made of different stuff! We have long got your numbers, honeys.

Whenever Abdulla had some kind of news, he would first rush to his family with it, while isolated Monika upstairs was the last to know or she found out from them because he did not bother to tell her at all. Her sweetie had turned into a heartless stranger led astray by his evil mother's thinking and acting around corners. Everybody else—be it stranger, friend, or relative—Abdulla treated in his usual, happy-go-lucky manner. Monika was the only one he cleaned his shoes on. At this point in her life, if the choice were Monika's again, she wouldn't have chosen Abdulla even as a friend and definitely not as a husband.

The closeness they had once shared was pushed aside by a negative, finicky attitude he had developed towards her, which firmly put her off him, like butter gone rancid. As much as he once had to have her for himself in Kuwait, lately she was being pushed aside and left on her own amidst Antarctic in-law winds blowing icily.

Abdulla had a strong urge to please his next of kin by making them feel superior and Monika their underdog, by telling them something and then swearing them to secrecy about it, especially in relation to his own wife. Afterwards, he would tell Monika what he had done and that he had just done it in order to keep them happy for a while. Something strange lived in Abdulla. After sessions with his mother, he made his frustrations air by squeezing the pure essence out of his wife as if bewitched. Just for the hell of it, he started trouble about anything within his vision. At times it got so bad, so much so that Monika got truly scared, fearing that something had snapped in his brain. If nothing else availed, he'd go to criticizing what she was wearing: her blouse was too tight, her skirt too short, and her lipstick too red. Clothes she wore the year before and that he had loved on her because they had turned him on, now on the spur of the moment he found fault with. He started calling her a *gahba* himself, a *gahba* out to arouse men. Monika—innocent—was punished non-stop, accused, humiliated. She hated his lies, immature behavior, and stupid cat-and-mouse games. Monika-the-Ram thanked God for blessing her with the skin of an elephant, for some other poor girl might have by that time been ripe for a mental hospital.

One day mother-in-law could be heard screaming hysterically, exercising her lungs and experimenting one of her new blackmail tactics as Abdulla had just confronted her with the fact that within the next two months he, his wife, and little Sulaiman would be off to London for the next two years to study new methods. So mother-in-law thought that if she faked a heart attack she could get around him and change his mind. Holding her right chest with both hands, head circling, accompanied by loud, high-pitched screams that were replaced by fast murmuring as if she were performing some ritual, she tumbled from one foot onto the other. Abdulla was not fooled.

"Stop it, Mother. Your heart is on the other side," he told her. That woman, who had given Abdulla as a tiny, new-born baby to her own mother Miriam to bring up, had no loving feelings for her son. She only knew how to take and demand, pressing him dry like a lemon, but never giving in return. She was now desperate, dreading having to face the future without the Hamra, whose life and doings had become a piece of their life, especially as the old woman had nothing—but nothing at all—to say (or interfere with) in the lives of her three daughters, who had the knack of shutting her up before she had time to open her big mouth. She did not want to let loose of what she had so much to say about and had so much control over.

Impatient Abdulla, who himself yearned to get out of restricted, artificial Kuwait for a breath of fresh air and utter freedom, lied to his mother by swearing to her that their going was solely the Health Ministry's decision and there was nothing he could change about it and, if he could, he would cancel it for her. After four years under his mother's influence and taking the easy way out, Abdulla was now a qualified, habitual liar, so much so that he wasn't even acquainted with the truth anymore. He lied to Monika to get rid of the faintest problem on the spur of the moment; and to them, if it helped him to get out of some unwelcome situation. Naturally, this way he got only more and more entwined and tangled up, which created new, even bigger, problems. Monika always knew, from the time she had set foot in Kuwait, that her in-laws were the root of all evil, and yet she never, ever seriously put down her foot to confront them simply because, to her, they were half-insane beings. Even now that she spoke their language rather fluently, she found she did not speak their language at all. Lies and deception were then and still are Monika's pet hate. She is herself always frank and open, too open for her own good some times. To her everything has to be crystal clear. Therefore, four years living amongst deceit and under great pressure naturally left its marks on her. She was now nervous, easily irritated. The slightest frustration brought tears to her eyes, and her skin broke out with some kind of acne that could have been due to the fact that she smoked now like a chimney, drank more gin and tonics than she should have, and had lost weight rapidly. Apart from all that change for the worse, she often complained of headaches, which before Kuwait she never knew existed. And worst of all, her once active brain was in danger of senile calcification. It even went so far that towards the end of her four years in Kuwait, the once headstrong, courageous Aries ram started to have doubts. She wondered if what she constantly fought for and what her inner self thought to be right was justified. *Was* she really right? Or should she maybe stop swimming against the tide, give up, and join them for the sake of peace?

The last two months of that four-year stint in Kuwait were made almost unbearable for her because she was now accused of taking Abdulla, whom she did not love anyway, to his ruin in "*Inglittara*," away from his mother and sisters who so loved him, etc.; but, since she knew she would soon be back in her own environment, she couldn't have cared less about the accusations. Up all of yours, she thought. Having long made up her mind about one thing, a thousand horsepowers wouldn't take her and Sulaiman back to disappointmentland Kuwait once they left it. And when at long last the day of departure came, Monika felt that if someone came up to her and told her she would have to stay and London was canceled she would have died there and then.

Monika left Kuwait with something she didn't have when she entered it: hate in her heart. The freedom-bound plane took off up in the air, cutting Monika razor sharp from the past's bad experience once and for all—so she thought, comfortably strapped in her middle seat, as she felt the invisible, tight, gripping hands she was accustomed to living with let go of her chest. Ah, a big sigh. *Ahhh!* How *gooood* a feeling overcame her now! She could breathe freely once again, without that heavy sort of iron sensation which had sometime in the past four years crept in on her and settled around her chest. The familiar happy-to-be-alive feeling she had experienced last about four years ago, a feeling she had forgotten existed, made itself known again and pervaded her now.

She sat comfortably thinking back to the time when she had first come to Kuwait, and a cold shower ran down her spine. Now, four years later didn't seem like four long years at all to her—more like two, really, and the reason for that must have been that she had been mainly restricted to house and car during most of that time, and all kinds of adventures that do happen to one in Europe don't at all in the day-in-day-out monotonous Kuwait.

Monika turned to her good-looking, four-plus-year-old Sulaiman and squeezed and kissed him lovingly. Right now she was ready to hug and kiss the whole world. That's how great and newly born she felt. She felt swept up by an immense zest for life and a much better future to come, hopefully. Her plans didn't really reach beyond "out of Kuwait" just yet. To her the future was far less of a problem than the past had been. 1965—and, London, here I come!

CHAPTER TWELVE

LONDON INTERLUDE

England seemed like Paradise Regained after Kuwait. Everything was arranged for Abdulla and his small family well in advance through the Kuwaiti authorities in London. For Abdulla, a place at St. Barts Hospital—which was, of course, great!—but the damp, unhealthy flat in Jewish Golders Green was more than a bit of a disappointment. Shops in the neighborhood closed on Fridays and were open instead on Sundays. Monika, concerned about Sulaiman's health, went flat hunting. Four times she was promised a place she liked, but when she turned up together with Arab Abdulla to view it and the landlords set eyes on him, Abdulla and Monika were told a polite, "Sorry, we don't take Arabs," or "The flat is already taken." As in Austria, Arabs were definitely not welcome in those days. Not the English people's cup of tea. One could not blame the reserved English, who don't take easily to foreigners anyway and least of all to the noisy Arab race with their heavily spiced cooking smells, the way they love living all together like fish in a tin, who eat by hand from dishes on newspapers spread out onto the floor, and who feel quite comfortable in clean or messy surroundings alike. Not to mention their Eastern music, which sounds like cries for help to the Western ear, blazing out loud from their living quarters and their car windows, leaving the unaccustomed quite uncomfortable or with a bit of a headache!

Haven't times changed? Nowadays the Arabs' money has long overcome such unimportant trivialities and meaningless little obstacles, for in the early 1970's, when the British media along with the whole world found out how much money the invading Arabs had and how unbelievably generous they were, arms and often legs, too, were opened wide all of a sudden to welcome the same dirty, noisy, smelly, but oh so rich race! It's true: money talks, bullshit walks.

Back in London the unbelievable happened away from his mother and sisters. A good fairy seemed to have touched Abdulla with her magic wand! He turned into an absolute Prince Charming. He was his old caring, natural, humorous self again—just as he had been when she first met him and much, much nicer and more caring, from early morning until late at night. With a reliable baby-sitter arranged for Sulaiman, Abdulla went wherever he went with his sweetie. He realized now, amongst civilized surroundings, all the wrong he had let happen to her back home and badly wanted to make it up to her the best way he knew how—which was the way all Kuwaitis made it up to their wives—by buying her luxuries. Abdulla took to lavishing on her perfumes, designer clothes, bits and pieces of jewelry, and the silkiest, prettiest underwear and nightgowns that made her feel great but at the same time guilty. She felt that she had given him the impression that the only way to win her back was to buy her back, which wasn't Monika at all. Abdulla had felt, of course, that in Kuwait Monika had grown cold and distant, with not much loving feeling circulating anymore. The only thing that hadn't changed was their sex life. That's when she pushed everything else out of her mind to concentrate on what she was doing. In sex, they still gave each other 10 out of 10. They were the perfect match.

Monika had discovered that, contrary to her prior belief, sex and love were two separate stories. Sex is not love, and love is not sex. Sex is a need of the body; love is the need of one's soul and much more important, at that. After her rude awakening in Kuwait, where her rose-tinted glasses were smashed, Monika had matured into much more of a realist, her feet closer to the ground now—but not firmly touching it yet. Not for a long time to come. Not yet.

She had long talks about the past and the future with Abdulla, and every conversation ended positively in her favor. He swore on the life of his mother that Monika was the most important being in his life and that he could not imagine living without her and that he would prove his love for her through all eternity. In these happy circumstances and cheerful atmosphere, Monika's past in Kuwait slid slowly aside. It was growing clear to Abdulla that if he wanted her to stay next to him, he would have to take root in England; for Kuwait a second time around was out of the question for her and Sulaiman. And would you believe it? Abdulla was to become the prime example of a perfect husband, and he went on like that without a slip-up for the next six months. Monika was impressed. Her sweetie couldn't possibly have been the same Mr. Nasty he was in Kuwait, or could he?

Now, quite content, Monika relaxed. Her natural mother's instinct made itself known, and anyway Sulaiman needed a brother or sister. He shouldn't grow up an only child. Even if things didn't work out after all with Abdulla, she thought, at least the kids will have each other in life.

The couple had settled comfortably in a small but lovely furnished flat consisting of sitting room, bedroom, kitchen and bath, in London's Queensgate, a stone's throw from Regents Park. Everyday London life in the 1960's was exciting, turbulent, and quite hip. Abdulla attracted new friends in no time. If they were not out hitting the town at night, pregnant Monika took care of Abdulla's poker pals' stomachs, preparing Arabic rice dishes no end—and the lamb they loved so much. She sometimes joined the game for a couple of rounds and, not at all bad at poker herself, she often won. The following day she would take her winnings to the bank or go and blow it all at Harrod's, mainly on Sulaiman.

Their flat was always an open house, a sort of home away from home, or embassy, for Kuwaiti students in London. Time passed quickly without much worth mentioning happening as tranquility reigned—up until just before Monika was due to have the baby.

It was arranged that one of Dentist Pavlik's colleagues would take over the dentistry practice in Vienna for three weeks so that Monika's mother could look after her grandson Sulaiman in London while her daughter gave birth. Everything for Abdulla's mother-in-law was ready and arranged. She was to sleep in the sitting room. Abdulla had bought a camp bed and new bedding for her as Monika's baby was now due within the next few days.

God, how time had passed! Sulaiman was already five-plus and in two months, September, he would join a kindergarten. The young couple looked excitedly forward to hugging their new baby soon.

The bell rang. Monika opened her front door. Horrid shock! She hoped that what she was seeing was a hallucination. Wishful thinking. Sabiha, her sixteen-month-old son Tarik and Tamader stood behind piles of luggage, facing Monika.

"We come to visit our brother,' announced Sabiha, pushing her way into the tidy little flat, upsetting everything and turning the place into a pigsty in no time at all, unpacking and hanging clothes in closets and taking over chests of drawers without asking, squashing Monika out of the way and to the side while Sabiha's Tarik and Sulaiman romped noisily from one room into the other, toys littering all floors.

All of the sudden the horror of her four years in Kuwait was with Monika again! Silly cow, she should have known better. It served her right. After all she had gone through, she still had not learned her lesson and probably she never would, poor skin. Her brain ticked. Now, under normal circumstances, she could have snatched Sulaiman and made a disappearance act to Vienna until the in-laws had evaporated again. But in her situation, pregnant, with the baby due any day now, hospital arrangements at the London Clinic made and paid for by the Kuwaiti

Government, Monika was stuck up a shit creek once again and without a paddle while Abdulla's sisters carried on where they had left off with Monika in Kuwait.

Never before had she had them so close! They were now breathing down her neck. Unbearable! The bed meant for Monika's mother was occupied by Sabiha, Sabiha's son Tarik was bedded on the floor next to her in a sleeping bag, and the settee was Tamader's bed. Tarik, although it wasn't entirely his fault, was an unruly child. He pulled out everything that he could reach, scratched records, and climbed over furniture. The flat for him was an adventure playground. Meanwhile Sabiha didn't even try to control her son. Her fat arse was firmly glued to the chair she sat on as if it were a throne. She gave orders to Tamader and called Monika, Abdulla, and Sulaiman, too, to run and see to Tarik if he happened to be up to no good, which he was nonstop, all the time.

Any mother can tell you that if you are pregnant in the ninth month, the last thing you want around you is what Monika had to cope with here.

Dentist Pavlik had arrived and was of course perplexed by her daughter's unfortunate fate and in effect ended up looking after son-in-law, his two sisters, and Abdulla's nephew while Sabiha was delighted to have another "servant" to bully. They had expected Monika's mother to be an old woman instead of a snappy, elegant dresser with a slim-line figure. Looking a good fifteen years younger than her actual age, she had taken them by surprise. Jealous because Monika's mother was a lady and theirs was a scarecrow, soon they were making degrading remarks.

"What for does your mother dress up every day!" they laughed. "For whom is she wearing lipstick? Did she come to London to pick up a man?"

The sisters changed Monika's routine drastically. They kept the sitting room curtains drawn and slept until early afternoon. Monika, her mother, and Sulaiman, too, had to tiptoe on pussy feet, keeping

Tarik quiet as well, or one of the sleeping sisters would shout aloud, "Chap!" (shut up!).

By the time they finally rose, Monika would already have cooked lunch for everybody, but her delicious rice dishes that Abdulla's friends came especially from all over London to consume were never good enough for the in-laws. Tamader didn't mind that much, but Sabiha much preferred to go out and eat at Indian, Persian, or Arabic restaurants. A tired Abdulla came home at 5 pm, dutifully booked tables, and picked up the bills afterwards while Sabiha, time and again, insulted pretty waitress Anita, a friend of Monika's, who often baby-sat for Sulaiman and had a Kuwaiti prince as a boyfriend.

Anita was exceptionally good looking. Sabiha looked open-mouthed at beautiful Anita; and, of course, her built-in urge to pull everything beautiful deep into the mud came through again.

"My gynecologist in Kuwait says that if he examines a Kuwaiti lady he can hardly get more than two, maybe three, fingers into her vagina, but in a European cunt he can put his whole fist because Europeans are all prostitutes." Then she started to laugh forcefully.

Monika, as always, overlooked the ignorance, which was the best way of handling Sabiha, who was now, Monika noticed, even nastier than before she was married and had a child.

Two crispy roast chickens *a la Vienna* stuffed with a lightly spiced mixture of milk, bread, eggs, nuts, sultanas, and coconut were dished up one day while Monika's mother cooked stuffed green peppers in tomato sauce and buttered potatoes with parsley.

"Potatoes, potatoes, potatoes! Those English eat nothing but potatoes. They even *look* like potatoes," was Sabiha's first comment as she plopped out of bed and sat herself at the table to grab a chicken. She tore off its neck and wings and a thigh and sampled some of its stuffing after which she licked her short, fat fingers and grabbed the next one and did the same thing there, filling her plate to the rim. Elbows resting on the table, she stuffed that gob of hers, fat running out the corners of her mouth and sliding slowly down her chin. She had to push her pajama bottoms down as her belly swelled for that's how much she had eaten. "Amazing. What an unbelievable appetite this woman has!" Dentist Pavlik mentioned to her daughter under her breath, having lost her own. Full up, just about to explode, and entirely out of breath, Sabiha turned to Abdulla, pulling a grimace as if she was just about to be sick and said:

"Tell your wife, next time she cooks chicken, not to use that much fat. It was much too greasy!"

After having had that comment interpreted, Dentist Pavlik felt like throwing the rest of her tomato sauce in Sabiha's face, wondering how her daughter could have lived for four years among these creatures.

For the ritual washing that Muslims perform before prayer, Sabiha chose one of Monika's saucepans and a teacup, which she then left in the toilet for further use and Monika marked with her red nail polish for fear of a mix up. As they did in Kuwait, Sabiha and Tamader left everything in the bathroom running and swimming in a mess. They never made even the slightest gesture to clean their own dirt away anywhere in the flat, and why should they? They had servants like Monika and her mother, who could not see straight nor endure living among such filth and therefore cleaned after them constantly.

Monika had learned—and so explained to her mother—that Kuwaitis were brought up to master life with money and that without it they could not handle anything. They were rich and yet so poor. Abdulla tried to do a balancing act between the two sets of women. He was unhappy with the situation himself and so decided to coax his sisters into staying near the seaside in Herne Bay for at least two weeks until Monika had had the baby. He was successful. Through hospital connections Abdulla located a woman who got her house ready and, being lonely, was pleased to cook meals for them three times a day, too. Perfect. Abdulla hired a car, and all seven of them left on a Saturday afternoon to Herne Bay. The sisters were satisfied with their lodgings and, thank God, agreed to stay.

Abdulla had decided to spend the night in Herne Bay, too, and had booked two double bedrooms at the main hotel there. Dentist Pavlik put Sulaiman to bed while Monika and Abdulla disappeared towards the bar for a welcome drink. A stone had fallen from Monika's chest. She was rid of the sisters and happy to go back to normal and have the flat to herself once more.

She sipped contentedly on her half pint of lager and lime, and that was exactly when Baby Number Two decided it was the right moment to start its journey into this beautiful world of ours.

At Herne Bay Hospital there was no maternity ward. Abdulla was advised to rush her to Kent and to Canterbury Hospital where he had once worked and knew everybody, which he did. He quickly arranged a private room there and, at 12 midnight, was told to leave. He should go to bed and come back the next day, for baby could not quite make up its mind.

Sunday morning Abdulla with his sisters and Dentist Pavlik, Sulaiman, and Tarik, entered Monika's empty room. It was empty because she had just been taken to the operating room. On the white sheet was a big pool of blood, which his sisters found funny. They laughed. Sabiha said, "That looks like a pig got killed here!"

Monika's mother felt tears coming to her eyes, and, crying, in her poor English, she made Abdulla understand that giving birth, even when a person is normal and healthy, is still a risk, for she herself had almost lost her life giving birth to Monika.

"If she dies, we all shit on her grave," came his comforting reply in broken German, followed by more peels of laughter from his sisters. Mrs. Pavlik was disgusted by her son-in-law's barbaric remark and those women's inhuman behavior.

The old story was repeating itself, for once again Abdulla slid slowly under his sisters' spell, and when that happened, he knew the only way to keep them happy was to ridicule Monika and try to make a fool of her—and, now, of her mother, too!

While all this was going on, beautiful Sunday child Baby Nabeel joined the al-Amahanis with a loud healthy cry. In no time Abdulla was brimming and bursting with pride. His dream always had been to have three boys; now, he already had two. One more to go. Would she? Sulaiman had been named after Abdulla's father; so, for the second child, it was Monika's turn to choose a name. She had her heart set on Sabrina if it turned out a girl, but all the Arab boy's names Abdulla came up with did not quite appeal to her. She had something else in mind. One day a male relative of Abdulla had stayed overnight with them on his way from America to Kuwait. It was a sad situation, for he was accompanying the dead body of a young Kuwaiti back home. The student had found death in his sports car, and his name was Nabeel. As soon as Monika heard that name, she knew that that name was it, should her baby be a boy.

Monika was transferred by ambulance to the London Clinic three days later, which she left with her baby after another five days. She was stunned to find the sisters back at her flat the very same day. They should have stayed another week in Herne Bay, as had been agreed on by all! Abdulla, Monika, Sulaiman, Dentist Pavlik, and the new baby—the five of them slept in the small bedroom, while the much larger sitting room was now occupied by you-know-who. After a couple of days of living so closely united, Dentist Pavlik aired her point of view.

"I would rather be stranded on an island alone than with such careless, empty-headed robots. We are all God's children, but the line has to be drawn somewhere. Here, under the given circumstances, Monika, you can safely compare yourself with the lowest, working-class wife in Austria. What Abdulla offers you here is nothing to brag about or be proud of. You would live a better life with any poor Hans or Gerhardt back home!"

You know what it is like when your best friend stays for a while. Even if she asks before she takes and helps a little here and there, after a certain time it is always nice to be on your own again. The novelty wears off. And now put yourself in Monika's place with those sisters who pulled fresh sheets and clean towels out of her dressers every day and always left sopping, dirty ones on the floor to be picked up by someone else. Monika's washing machine ran non-stop, and the iron was always hot. Shopping bags and bills littered the place after the sisters' daily shopping trips. If Monika did not pick up after them and clean the toilet and bath after them constantly, which often brought her close to throwing up, she would have cockroaches, too, in no time, she reflected. At least, Monika had her mother here to talk to and to help her whereas in Kuwait she had been entirely on her own.

Little Nabeel woke up every two and half or three hours at night for his feeding, but instead of sitting comfortably in one of her lounge settees, Monika had to feed him sitting herself down on a hard kitchen chair under occasional shouts of "Chap! chap!" coming from the sitting room should she or her baby get too noisy for the intruders—and that in her own flat. The toilet and the bathroom could only be reached by walking through the bedroom, and in the process the sisters had to open and close four doors which they often purposely did with loud bangs x-times a night! The baby cried at the slightest provocation. Waking Nabeel was a way of getting at Monika, for Nabeel's cries went like little arrows through her bones. Monika was in a state of post-partum blues anyway and always close to tears. Now that his "Bad News" sisters were around, Abdulla once again, just as he had been in Kuwait, was occupied with making life for them more tasty and digestible, never mind Monika and his, now, own two children.

Like huge octopuses, they followed and poked their long tentacles of disruption into Monika's life. However far away the couple went, the octopuses caught up. First, to Cairo. And now, to London. From the moment of their arrival, what Sabiha and Tamader wanted or needed was what took on sole importance for Abdulla. He was more of a father to Tarik than he had ever been to his own son Sulaiman, and Abdulla ignored his newest addition entirely. The week's leave from the hospital which Abdulla had long in advance arranged in order to spend it with his wife and children after the baby's birth came most in handy now to spend with his sisters, to take them shopping and sightseeing and to restaurants.

After they had eaten a massive breakfast of eggs, bacon, and pork sausage (cooked by Monika), the faithful pork-eating Muslims were strong enough to face another enjoyable day out. At around 11 am, Abdulla would casually turn to Monika as one would talk to a know-nothing Kuwaiti servant and tell her where they had decided to spend the day and ask if she wanted to come along or to stay with the baby and her own mother. Monika always stayed but sent Sulaiman along with his dad as she was pleased to see the backs of them. Even if she had wanted to join them, she could not have left her mother with the baby and a filthy flat, could she?

The whole situation blew sky high finally after about a week when the baby came down with an infection. Monika had just managed to get him to sleep in the small hours of the morning when Sabiha burst into the bedroom stamping her feel like an ox on her way to the bathroom.

"Can't you do anything quietly!" bellowed Monika, at the end of her tether for a change.

Sabiha, startled, yet had the cheek to say, "I am in my brother's home, and everything here belongs to my brother. Nothing at all, to you!"

Lights went on. Everyone congregated in Monika's bedroom.

"Abdulla, this child is ill. I have just got him off to sleep, and now he is crying again." Monika passed crying Nabeel to her mother and turned to Abdulla again, saying, "I thought they were going to be staying at Herne Bay!"

"They decided to come back. They had had enough of Herne Bay. So what!" Abdulla snarled. "I can't help it if they come back. Do you want me turn away my own flesh and blood?"

"Oh, really, Abdulla! And what about the baby? Is he less important than your bloody sisters?"

"My bloody what? Sure, he is less important. Much less important to me. He isn't even my child. Look at him. He does not even look like me!"

"I can congratulate myself, Abdulla, for now you have gone mad."

"What does he say?" Mrs. Pavlik asked in German, and Abdulla shouted at her, "You, stay out of this!"

"You leave my mother alone! She has taken enough from your damned sisters and cleaned enough for them here on the holiday of their lifetimes. Look at this place! Look at the bathroom floor, floating in water! Everywhere rubbish! And their black hair over the sink and bathtub and down the drain hole. This has become a madhouse! Tell me, why doesn't Sabiha's husband Fahad look after her? Isn't he her husband? Come to think of it, I don't blame him. After all, who wants to be seen with or sleep with a lump of fat!"

"I don't *believe* this," Dentist Pavlik inserted in German. "I just don't believe this. I must be dreaming. Is Abdulla saying the baby is not his? What's the purpose of that?"

"Even my mother is upset and has had enough."

"Abdulla," Dentist Pavlik began in broken English, "why do you not take the chemist for baby?"

"Why should I? That bastard is not my baby, and I couldn't care less if he died."

"If there is one bastard in this room, then it is *you*, you rotten bastard!" Monika spat at him, as always when words failed her. Abdulla lunged at her with his fists and caught her on the shoulder.

"*Mein Gott, polizei. Polizei, polizei!*" Dentist Pavlik managed to push herself between man and wife, repeating "*Polizei*" as she made her way to the phone and picked up the receiver.

"Who do you think you are, calling the police in my house, on my phone?" Abdulla grabbed the receiver and pushed his mother-in-law into an open wardrobe as his sisters commented, "Good, good!" By this time Monika's fists were hailing down on Abdulla's back.

"Leave my mother alone! Don't you touch her, and get them out of here. Get them out of here," she shouted at the top of her voice.

"All right. All right, they go," he conceded. "And I go with them."

For a change, even Sabiha did not have much to say within Monika's earshot. Maybe she was scared to receive a punch in her big gob after this scene. She looked glad to be going. Twenty-five minutes or a half hour later they were packed, and a cab had arrived.

"If you are going, too," Monika said coldly to her husband, "leave me some money. I might have to take the baby to see a doctor."

"Take him. You are not my family. My sisters are. And as for money, I haven't got any, not for you nor for that wretched baby. I am going to spend all my money on my own flesh and blood." And with that, he slammed the door in her face and was on his way.

"Thank God I was here. Never in a million years would I have believed Abdulla could treat you as he does," Monika's mother said. "I was sent by God to take you away from all this. I should have raised you in a pigsty. Then it might have been easy for you to blend in with them. You are not staying here. And that's final! We all go to Vienna. If that's anything to go by of what you had to put up with in Kuwait, tell me, child, why on earth didn't you leave him when you had only one child? Instead you go and give life to another poor soul! It's irresponsible. What kind of future do you expect those poor children of yours to have among people from another planet? You have to wake up. I think you are dreaming. Stop hoping. It won't get any better. With more children it can only get worse. Oh, yes, I can see it all coming. If you were married to an Austrian, you would at least have the law on your side and social security if necessary. I feel sick thinking of all the chances you could have had in Austria—lawyers, dentists, doctors, all well situated young gentlemen like the ones that kept asking about you for ages after you had left. But I did my best. I warned you in time. I saw it all coming. You are now in the situation that one warns, one frightens off, other young girls away from Arabs with," Dentist Pavlik groaned. "What a laugh. My patients and friends in Vienna congratulate me. They think my daughter is living on a silver-lined cloud in the greatest comfort being married to a Kuwaiti! I'll disappear in a hole in the ground if they ever find out how the ball really rolls."

Monika, in tears, felt absolutely rotten. She could not control herself. She knew her mother was right but told her that Abdulla away from his family was a completely different being, and Monika said this even though she had never felt a deep spiritual feeling for him deep down.

"*Mein Gott, Kind!* I hope it is not too late. I see you are completely besotted by him."

Without having slept a wink, early next morning Monika located a doctor close by, with the help of the telephone directory. The baby had developed a high temperature, was constipated, and had cried through the night. After she had spoken to the doctor, he told her to bring the baby to the clinic by taxi. But first a visit to the bank had to be made. She drew money from her account to pay for the doctor, for medicine, and to have enough to live on for the moment.

Time passed quickly. The next peaceful week with the new baby was all harmony. Dentist Pavlik's patients called her back to Vienna. It could all have been so nice, if only . . .

Monika had to promise her mother to seek her help and come to Vienna if ever she were desperate again, but Monika knew in her heart that she would never do it because Monika was too proud a person for that. She had made a mess of her life, and she would see it through to the end herself. With the sisters out of the way, Monika expected life with Abdulla to be bearable for the time being. She was right. One week after Dentist Pavlik had said goodbye to Monika and the kids, his sisters gone, Abdulla came back like a wet cat, with his tail between his legs and full of remorse.

"Abdulla, does your family practice black magic witchcraft, or do they feed you some potion?" asked Monika once again.

"I don't know what it is. Something just went wrong in my head, but, Sweetie, this is the *last* time. I am not going to promise you but show with action. None of them will *ever* come between us again! To that I swear by my mother's death, never *ever* again! That was really the last time you have seen trouble from them, Sweetie." He called her "Sweetie" again. It sounded strange because he had not done it since his sisters had entered the flat.

"I have lost count on how many times you have sworn on your mother's death, Abdulla, and every time you swore, it turned into a lie. I don't think God can hear you because your mother is still alive. You can guarantee me that it's the last time I have seen trouble from them because when you go to Kuwait in eight months' time, you will be making the journey alone. After you changed so drastically for the better once we were back in England, I was honestly quite willing to stay with you, and that's the reason I decided on having another baby, remember? But now, now I know that whatever you say and promise, you don't mean it at all! It took me donkey's years to find out. But now it is well registered. To live a half way peaceful life with you, not talking about your alcoholic escapades, I would have to wait until your mother and sisters die first, but as we all know weeds grow forever and flowers die. Only the good die young. I will be dead before them."

Abdulla and Monika got back together again, which was mostly brought about by Abdulla's winning ways.

One day he surprised her with a big, expensive-looking paper bag from Harrod's. In it was a white fox stole she had had her eyes on as a present for having the baby. A good month later, a happy, smiling

Abdulla came from a visit to his embassy, triumphantly holding up a bottle of champagne.

"Congratulations, Sweetie, we have finally got our very own piece of land in Kuwait! As soon as I get back, I mean, as we get back, we start building! You make all the designs for the house and I will have it built just for you. You tell me how you want it, and your wishes shall be my command because this is going to be your own house, that paradise I promised you in Kuwait, remember?" Abdulla hugged and kissed his wife, lifting her up as high as he could. "Sorry, Sweetie, that it took so long. Now you really need not have anything to do with my family. None of them will set foot in that house unless you wish them to. How does that sound to the ear?" Before Monika stood a proud Abdulla, and once again she was convinced he meant every word he said. But would he *really* stick to his promises once back in Kuwait and under the Bad Influence there? To be quite honest, Monika was tempted. She had often visualized precisely what and how she wanted her own house to be. The chance to make that dream come true was here now. "I have come this far. Why not try life out there in our own house?" she mused. And once again Monika threw in the towel and agreed to go back to Kuwait. Often, before, she had made up her mind to leave Abdulla, but when it came down to the crunch, she always hesitated and thought, I'll try just this one more time.

Now at least she knew more or less what to expect from Kuwait. She had mellowed and was much more disappointment- and shock-proof than she had been in the past. Courageous Monika just did not give up easily. Good luck to her!

A couple of weeks after Sabiha had gone home, her husband Fahad came to London on some business trip. He stayed at some posh hotel and came to visit Abdulla and Monika. While discussing Sabiha's previous behavior, his only comment was: "She is a troublemaker. That's why I sent her on alone. I myself try to avoid trouble with her." He made it easy for himself, didn't he?

At night the three of them went to a dinner dance. Fahad took Monika onto the crowded dance floor, where he held her and pressed her close to his body, so close she could clearly feel the process of a quickly developing massive hard-on and hated it. He had had too much to drink, smelt of it and of cigarette smoke. The farther she tried to push him, the more his grip tightened around her body—so much so that it hurt. The live band was blaring loudly. Monika looked around to catch a glimpse of jealous Abdulla, but he was out of her sight.

"Monika, you look lovely tonight! So sexy. I want you to know you can always count on me as your best friend!" Fahad shouted in her ears. "Abdulla's family, especially Sabiha, are jealous of you because you are special. Ignore them all. Even Abdulla neglects you. He does not know how lucky he is. But you can count on me. I will comfort you, give you money if you need it. Promise me that you accept my offer, please. It will make me very happy."

Monika broke out in a cold sweat and did not answer. She had no answer because he had taken her by surprise. She just could not find the right words to say. It was not quite clear to her what his intentions were exactly. Fahad—dancing vigorously and holding onto Monika with all his might—almost touched the dance floor with his back while her bottom stuck right up in the air, away from him as much as she could manage. Her body lay almost on top of him. She was pushing away from him, yet he did not let go. They looked, probably, as if they were break-dancing as one.

At last the music stopped. Monika was relieved, but Fahad did not seem to notice the music had stopped. He just carried on dancing without the music. He seemed to be in his own little world, in some kind of ecstasy, as if he was just about to come. She quickly slipped off her seven-inch high heels and staggered about, pretending she had lost her shoes. Now, he *had* to stop and let go of her. Had Sabiha known about his proposition and his behavior, what would she have done?

On the whole, after two years away from her mother-in-law, Monika felt refreshed and full of new strength for whatever was to come her way on her return to Kuwait. London had mellowed her memories of bad times in the flat upstairs in her mother-in-law's house.

How often one only remembers the good!

CHAPTER THIRTEEN

BLACK MAGIC IN KUWAIT

As Abdulla had requested, Monika once again brought from London and handed out expensive, thoughtfully chosen gifts to all her in-laws. The peace offerings had only a short-lived effect, although to start with mother-in-law did seem a bit less vindictive. Monika did not doubt, though, that behind closed doors the old woman still plotted with her daughters against Monika.

As was the case for all women in Kuwait, Monika was not allowed to get about on foot alone. So, quite often, especially when Abdulla spent his weekends with friends, Monika persuaded him to leave his car with her. As a gesture to mark a happy, new beginning, Abdulla took his wife to Kuwait's showrooms to choose her own run-about. The in-laws got wind of it, and that was it: no car. Greatly disappointed, Monika digested this piece of interference as well as she could possibly manage, telling herself it would not be much longer now before she would be moving into her own castle of peace. The workers had already started on the skeleton of the house. She would soon be her own boss again. As it happened she finally got her own car a bloody *three years* later, only after (would you believe it!) his sisters, first, took their driving tests and, second, had acquired their *own* cars. Even then, after coming home from looking for and choosing a car, Abdulla had to tell Sulaiman and little Nabeel not to tell his family where they had just been. The day

Monika finally sat in her own olive-green, beige-topped, beige-interior Datsun sports car (a very good car for Kuwait's heat), all hell broke loose in Diba's house because that's where mother-in-law was at the time she found out about it.

When the in-laws sat on the veranda below in the afternoons, they purposely used Monika's car as a trash can, laughing every time one of them scored and hit the target with their orange peels, banana skins, melon and date stones or the pips of the bamba fruit that stuck like glue to anything. Very seldom anymore did they verbally or otherwise insult Monika in the presence of Abdulla, so of course complaining to Abdulla did not help. She was not able to convince him, and he did not believe her until one day—standing on the balcony above—he saw it with his own eyes. And that's how he stopped one of their games, there and then, once and for all. Reader, if you haven't lost your appetite over this family yet, you probably soon will! I'll make a safe bet that you wouldn't even agree to a visit. Am I right?

The mother of the crash victim whose name was Nabeel didn't make any bones about it: she didn't approve of Monika's naming a baby after her dead son and showed it by being invariably unfriendly to her.

Within the first twenty months of his young life, Monika's handsome Number Two, Nabeel, had three accidents in which his life hung by a thin thread, and every time it appeared as though an invisible hand had saved him just in the nick of time, at the very last moment. The incidents all happened in Kuwait, one after the other, in quick succession.

Abdulla and Monika were amongst a picnic party of six grown-ups and their kids far away from the city on the seashore. Nabeel's round playpen was put up far above the water not too near the ends of a huge cliff and its big umbrella-shaped sun canopy was properly adjusted. Nabeel was put in and taken out—to play, to be changed, to be fed—and put back in again, soon to fall peacefully asleep. In the afternoon, a welcome breeze, getting stronger, came from the sea; and then a thundering noise interrupted a jolly game of cards. Monika's heart stopped. She looked in the direction of Nabeel. The playpen and her baby had disappeared, for what started as a breeze had developed into a strong gust of wind that had filled the umbrella and was strong enough to pull the light playpen plus baby out of sight over the edge of the cliff! Abdulla, always alert and quick to act in such situations, ran to look over the cliffs edge and see what he could do while Monika stood paralyzed and useless, only able to shout and cry hysterically. Thank God for the miracle! For Nabeel—about three meters down where the playpen had gotten stuck upside down—was swinging and smiling inside the umbrella, unharmed. He was rescued expeditiously.

Accident Number Two happened at sea. Abdulla carried a nude Nabeel into the water and jumped into a big black car tire that was floating on the surface. All of a sudden, Abdulla lost hold of the moving, wet child, and it slipped, quickly disappearing into the water. Abdulla dove frantically for Nabeel. Once, twice, a third time—only to come up empty handed. Monika just stood there and screamed! She could not swim and her Nabeel was somewhere at the bottom of that horrid sea. She wished she were dead—then she would feel better. The fourth time, Abdulla was lucky. It was the greatest relief of her life to see Nabeel come back literally from the dead as Abdulla held him up by the legs and patted his back, head down, and all the water the child had swallowed and taken into its lungs came pouring out. Little Nabeel was ever so exhausted but otherwise, thank God, perfectly okay. He healed Monika with one of his sunny smiles straight after. The biggest tragedy in life must be to lose one's child.

The third nasty accident occurred in far-out Faheheel, the agricultural area of Kuwait, where vegetables, fruit, and flowers are grown successfully. Among the small lock-up shops that Faheheel is famous for, there thrives one large Indian place that sells interesting goods exclusively from India. Taking in the carved woods, carpets, brass and leather merchandise, Abdulla and Monika were suddenly disoriented by a loud scream. Immediately after, an Indian salesman came running with a blood streaming, screaming Nabeel, who had fallen against an open, low, glass showcase and broken the glass with his arm. He had cut his little wrist on the sharp edges of the glass, deep and wide, exactly where someone would injure himself to commit suicide. Once again, clear-minded, alert Abdulla pulled the white cotra from his head and twisted it cleverly around the little arm to stop the heavy flow of blood pouring out. There was no hospital in Faheheel, and Monika could tell from Abdulla's worried face that little Nabeel needed extra care fast. Abdulla flew more than drove, tooting his horn like a madman, to Kuwait's number one hospital, the al-Sabah, as Monika pleaded (impossibly) that he go faster. At the hospital they were told that, had the cut been only one millimeter deeper, it could have been fatal because, then, the main artery would have been cut, too, and with such a long way to the hospital, there was no telling how it would have ended.

After that third accident, Monika began to think a bit more seriously about what her Kuwaiti friends had told her, about what they had advised her and believed. They were sure, absolutely convinced, that somebody had cast an evil incantation, or spell, on Nabeel—maybe Abdulla's family or the relatives of the deceased Nabeel, who in their primitive way might have said to themselves, If our Nabeel was taken from us, why should the Hamra have a Nabeel instead?

Always a bit of a skeptic herself, Monika had long felt that what had happened to her son—and all that was going on around her—was strange, even perhaps a bit paranormal, but that's as far as it went. She could not explain any of it further. She knew, of course, that evil forces existed, for in the convent she had been lectured and reared with that knowledge of good and evil. But she never seriously considered the possibility that Kuwaiti people meddled in the occult. She was advised by Kuwaitis who meant well that she ought to sacrifice a lamb, share its meat among the poor, and change Nabeel's name; or go and see a native woman who could make or break such spells as might have been cast on him and direct them back to the sender. Monika's advisers were convinced that magic would work. Monika saw no harm in killing a lamb, but meddle with any sort of witchcraft or black magic? No, not her, never! It was against her instinct and nature. It had nothing to do whatsoever with her upbringing. She just preferred to leave those sorts of nasty doings to her mother-in-law.

Only now, and slowly at that, after all these years in Kuwait, and by looking at the matter with an open mind and by watching and listening more closely was Monika to discover that her mother-in-law's family was known among Kuwait's women for practicing black magic and casting spells. Suddenly the scales fell from her eyes. She had the answer to a puzzle, and finally after fighting it for so long, it all came to her. Evil spirits called upon by her mother-in-law were responsible for Abdulla's constant, drastic changes from good to bad. She had always felt that his worst behavior was not of his own doing, not his fault; but, until now, Monika had no sound explanation for his sudden change of character although she had said quite often to him, not knowing how right she was, "You are bewitched!"

Thinking about it, she had to admit she could definitely feel the negative forces in her flat and in the rest of mother-in-law's house. Out of the house, anywhere else, she always felt more at ease, safer. Monika understood now, too, why her in-laws lived such an unsatisfied, unhappy, jealous, envious, empty life and moved about with grim faces, as if the whole world were one big lump of shit. According to nature's pattern, they only received as good as they gave, for whosoever sows evil shall receive evil.

Past occurrences that Monika had laughed off and considered mere hocus-pocus came back to her like a film flashback. She remembered the owl, a sign of death as her friends had pointed out, the lambs' coccyges that she had found on her balcony and that had shocked Abdulla (he had said they were on a mission to bring trouble and disruption and had flung them over the wall, remember?). She remembered the ash, the oil and the bones that she cleaned dozens of times from outside her front door, thinking that a child had been playing with matches there. These bits of debris were the traces of sorcery, of spells put there by who-knows-who, and the ashes were the remnants of paper burnt in the process of casting the evil spell. Putting it where they did—right in front of the door—it was a sure bet for the in-laws that Abdulla would step there, directly on the ashes every day. Such rituals, Monika learned, vary, depending on what is written on the paper, but usually the spell is meant to turn the victim against somebody whom he or she will inexorably grow to hate and despise while eating out of the very hand of whoever cast the spell. A classic example, in Monika's case. Out of the blue, Abdulla would gang up with his family and go against Monika.

Spells were also ways one could contrive to win over a lover, even if he showed no interest or belonged to somebody else, Monika was told. What's the use of getting a lover that way? she thought. The spell fades in the long run. Nobody and nothing can go successfully against nature.

Monika used to find the smallest, tiniest folded papers with tiny little writing on them, hair, even dried plants folded among Abdulla's clothes. He never knew how they got there, nor what they were, but Monika did—now. They were all spells to win him over or turn him against her. The devil could answer that one. Monika began to notice that her in-laws would dip pieces of white paper written on in pencil into water, orange juice, or milk, until the paper was snow white again. At first Monika had dismissed their doings as a bit of premature senility and had walked away, not even giving it a further thought. What would you have thought of grown-ups in their category occupying themselves with such a silly pastime? But what they were doing, in fact, was preparing a potion for someone—maybe even herself—to drink, a potion that their victim would most likely swallow unawares.

Let me tell you! They have a spell for and against everything. You name it, there's a spell for it. These sorts of practices are strictly forbidden by the Holy Koran, yet people live with black magic and practice it and think nothing of disobeying the Prophet's injunctions. On the contrary, casting spells is treated with respect and seriousness by all concerned.

Monika didn't kill a lamb nor change Nabeel's name at the time—as her friends had suggested, despite the fact that, as he strode through the perils of his young life, Nabeel seemed uncommonly accident-prone. He always survived the nearly fatal incidents and has the scars to prove it.

In the meantime, Diba had had a fourth child, her third son. Whenever unexpected visitors came, she quickly snatched her handsome offspring to hide him away in another room so that the visiting women could not get a glimpse of him. He was really such a beautiful baby that she was afraid somebody jealous of his beauty would cast the evil eye on him to make him ill or, even, to make him die.

Her in-laws regularly discussed evil spells. From then on, Monika listened and observed carefully. No longer did she consider the whole subject extraordinary rubbish. Her in-laws knew and feared the fruit of evil doings based on their own experiences with witchcraft.

At Eid, which is held twice a year and lasts three days and is equivalent more or less to Christmas and Easter celebrations, only money is handed out to children and grown-ups; no presents are given. The Eid that follows the period of 29 to 30 days of fasting called Holy Ramadan is the major holiday of the two. During the hours of fasting, nobody is allowed to be seen eating, drinking, or smoking publicly. Not even chewing gum is excused. Some fanatic people that Monika knew in Kuwait did not brush their teeth for fear that a little water might slip down their throats. Their breaths, of course, reeked accordingly. During Ramadan, getting close to people can be an appalling, utterly off-putting experience.

Children are restrained from fasting. Little girls usually start to fast when they reach puberty, and boys start at about eighteen or sixteen or even younger. Sometimes children fast of their own free will. Fasting mother-in-law complained all day long, every day, during Ramadan of bellyache and headache and, when she was not lying on the floor with an electric fan above her head, she walked around the house even moodier than she normally was, like a wound-up child's toy. Wearing one of Abdulla's white cotra scarves wrapped tightly around her head, she looked like some Japanese samurai fighter in her black dress, giving scowling orders and shouting at everything and everyone until late afternoon or early evening when food was finally permitted. Monika's in-laws sat waiting a long time before the Mullah's "Allah o-Akbar" cries came blaring out of the radio and signaled that they could start to eat. In fact, they would sit around the big tray of food with everybody ready to go, holding a date, a piece of meat, or a glass of buttermilk in their hands, just waiting for the shotgun sound that went off after prayer, which meant for them, "Go ahead! Now, stuff yourselves!" They made up for the day's fasting by eating themselves sick, stuffing themselves with the best food available, all through the night. Ramadan was responsible for a lot of people's putting on unwanted, unsightly pounds in a very short time.

After they had eaten, Kuwaitis got themselves dressed up fit for an audience with the ruling Sheikh's family to go out on visiting sprees to friends and relatives. They wandered from house to house where, again, calorie-rich dishes of puddings and sweets, black sweet saffron tea, and thick black Arabic coffee made with rose water and seasoned with cardamom were offered until 3 o'clock in the morning, which was the deadline for food consumption during Ramadan, whereupon fasting would resume again until late in the afternoon of the following day. Of course, eating so much in so short a time would help to make anybody fat and sick and bring on bellyaches and headaches, too, but many people lived without thinking a minute ahead and did not acknowledge the barest of facts. They seemed to exist only for the present moment.

Aspros and Alka Seltzers—among other remedies of the new and the old kind—were always close at hand. Kuwaiti doctors were expected to perform miracles on their overstuffed, wealthy clientele. Just before the eagerly awaited eating time, drivers in cars were sent to buzz busily from house to house on Kuwait's wide roads to deliver food delicacies in pots and on trays to families and friends, or with the compliments of their employers, often bringing back something to eat in return.

It seemed to Monika that during the Ramadan fast Kuwaiti women occupied themselves a lot—ironically—with food. They loved to eat and loved for their cooks to try out new recipes so that they could impress each other with food from their kitchens, just as they tried to impress each other with their new clothes and their extravagant jewelry.

Monika, too, had fasting periods behind her in the convent, usually two weeks before Easter, and she knew that the purpose of fasting was to give one's body and mind a little rest in solitude and to remember and sympathize with the poor. In order to put oneself in starving people's shoes, the food one ate during fasting periods consisted of very humble meals that served the same purpose as the fast did.

The feasts that were put on in Kuwait constipated and interfered with the gorgers' inner organs' daily routines. The meat of the lambs that were killed in order to be sacrificed for the dead souls of the family and that should have been given to the poor, according to Islam, always ended up within the close circle of family and friends. All they did was play boomerang with it, and very little reached the poor. They exchanged with each other very calculatingly and were sour for days if the house to which they had sent a leg of lamb sent them something less valuable in return. Not forgetting the slight, they would talk for days afterwards about it. Through the expedient of an offering, people could venture to make up with somebody they had fallen out with in the past;

if the recipient sent something in return, it meant that all was forgiven and forgotten.

To drink alcohol openly, as we know, is not allowed in Kuwait and can only be accomplished by clever stratagems. To get drunk, or even just to drink, during the holy month of Ramadan is a bit of a minus all around in Kuwait and strictly avoided. Yet, one evening during Ramadan as Monika and Abdulla were driving along, Monika spotted a man hanging out of his open car door and asked Abdulla to stop and see if he could help. It looked as though the man, an Indian, had had a coronary attack. Abdulla got close up, bent over him, stepped back, and ran to his car.

"That Poppadom [Indian bread] is soaked up with some cheap cologne! It smells to me like Pompeii, a very inferior brand that's used by servants in this country. There's nothing I can do for him! The police are going to have him in a minute or two." Yes, that's what the underprivileged poor devils out there get high on: all kinds of colognes, perfumes, and mentholated spirits. Think of their poor stomachs.

On the first day of Ramadan Abdulla would be clad in white robes and a gold-rimmed cloak, drenched in "Dehen Ooden" (an Arabic perfume), and saturated with "bochoor" (a clinging incense). Like all the Aseel Kuwaitis at Eid time, he drove first to his favorite douvaniah to wish his friends and respected elderly a happy Eid, where he quite often found himself kissing and wishing a happy Eid to some sheikh or another, who at such times mixed freely with the people. Kuwaiti sheikhs are not stuck up. With the odd exception, they are in general very easygoing, loveable rogues. In the afternoon, Abdulla dutifully trotted with Monika and his sons from house to house, greeting the many members of his large family tree, anxious not to offend anyone by leaving him or her out.

On such visits, Sulaiman and Nabeel collected bundles of Dinars. With that money Sulaiman bought a brand new red bike with all the available trimmings attached, and younger Nabeel chose a three-wheeler with a wooden cart at the back, in which he could haul his Siamese cat Fiffy, his ball, and some favorite small toys. After making their purchases, the happy, excited children entered the house overjoyed. They wanted to show off their bikes, which triggered off their grandmother the same way a bull can be annoyed by holding a red cloth in front of his eyes. Mother-in-law, old but full-of-fight, bounced at Monika, who unexpectedly had to let out a short sigh.

"You, you!" the old woman addressed Monika. "You bloody red-faced foreigner. I know this is your idea for making the rest of the family's children unhappy. You are teasing and breaking the hearts of my girls' children. That's the only reason you bought those expensive bikes, to tease and hurt our other children! I wish my Abdulla had never set eyes on you," she hissed. "Those bastards don't need more toys. They have enough upstairs."

It was true that Monika's boys had more than all the kids together, but only because they were taught how to play with them and how to look after and take care of their toys. Monika's boys did not sit down like other Kuwaiti kids and damage a new toy with the nearest hammer half an hour after receiving it.

Monika stood a while open mouthed until the accusations had sunk in. Once again mother-in-law had hurled unjust abuse at her. Monika by this time didn't much mind what came in her direction from the full-of-hate, crazy old woman. Monika turned to Abdulla, who stood close to her, and awaited some kind of action from him in her defense. But as ever, he ran after his mommy apologetically.

"I'll buy them each a bike if my sisters' children so badly want one, Mother," he offered. He begged her all lovey-dovey.

Now, that really worked Monika up! He was such an easy, willing game for the old witch's evil pranks, it was pathetic. Abdulla did not have the guts to ask where their children's money, money given to them for the Eid, had gone because he knew damn well that his sisters always took it away from their kids and spent it the next day on themselves, buying handbags, shoes, or clothes, leaving the kids with a pittance to spend on treats at the corner shop. That's why they got so annoyed: because what Monika did with her kids' money was setting a bad example. In the future, their kids might not want to give up what was rightfully theirs. They might want to do with their money what they wanted, like Sulaiman and Nabeel.

Only a day after that nasty little ceremony, Sulaiman and Nabeel were cycling to their hearts' delight up and down in front of the house with Monika's eager eye on her boys from the balcony above. Tarik, one and a half years older than Nabeel, had just pushed Nabeel off his tricycle for the umpteenth time and peddled off, leaving behind a crying Nabeel standing in the dust. Tarik did not take any of Monika's repeated warnings to heart, so finally she had to tell him, "Listen, Tarik, if you push Nabeel just once more, then Sulaiman will push you off the bike!" But her warnings were fruitless. Tarik still did not listen. So done as said, when Nabeel was sent rolling in the dust again just a couple of minutes later, Sulaiman pushed Tarik off Nabeel's cycle as he had been instructed to do by his mother, who was, of course, still watching.

Tarik started screaming his head off and ran inside the house to complain to his mother. Next thing, Sabiha came charging out of the house in her nightgown and ran with her short legs and fat wobbly body after unsuspecting Sulaiman. She reached out and her right, short, fat stubby paw landed a strong blow on Sulaiman's little back, which sent him flying off his bike and sprawling on the ground. Monika ran to her children's rescue. She flew down those stairs and stopped sharp behind Sabiha, pulling her around face to face by the shoulder.

"Don't you ever, ever, ever lay a finger on my children, or I will make mincemeat of you! If you want to hit children, stick to hitting your own!" Monika glowered.

That's all Sabiha needed. Always happy with an argument, she shouted at Monika at the top of her voice that neither Sulaiman nor Nabeel, who did not look like brothers, were the children of her brouher

Abdulla, and that Monika was a cheap prostitute and that she was not Sabiha al-Amahani if she did not sooner or later put an end to her brother's marriage.

The shouting brought out the neighbors, who came running from all directions and formed a ring around Monika and Sabiha. Monika retreated inside the gate, and fat slob Sabiha jumped at her from behind, pulling her hard onto the tiled floor. Before Monika knew what had hit her, Sabiha had yanked her blonde hair and was boxing her fleshy fists repeatedly into Monika's body, stomach, breasts, face, and neck. Sabiha went for whatever she could reach and hit wherever she could land a blow.

Monika saw red now. She blew all to the devil all of her resolve never to step down to her in-laws' level! She fought Sabiha with an iron physical strength she never knew she had. Years of frustration encapsulated deep inside her were released on hunchback Sabiha, who after a good start was flattened on the floor not much later and crying for mercy. Monika was not choosey either about where or what to hit and could not stop herself. She let Sabiha have it for all the times she had been made sad and mad by her. She now had a chance to get even, and when she finally did stop, it was only because she thought she had actually killed her sister-in-law.

After that extended bout of exercise, Monika felt really great and good, newly born, inside and out! She knew she had taken the right action for once. She felt rejuvenated! Sabiha retreated crying, and Monika went upstairs to take a shower. Most of her beautiful, long nails were now broken off, but she didn't mind because that fight had been well worth the sacrifice. Drying herself in the bathroom, she heard Abdulla coming up the stairs, shouting at her from afar in Arabic. He left the door wide open to let his family listen in, to give them satisfaction, and to prove to them that he was on their side. He scolded. Everything he said was in Sabiha's favor. He turned into an enraged lion and had easy play with Monika the lamb. He gave her the telling off of her life without listening to her side of the story. She well expected Abdulla to be on Sabiha's side, as always, but didn't expect him to be so vile.

"My sisters and my mother can hit my children whenever they feel like it! But don't you ever again dare to touch a member of my family or I kill you!" Abdulla stood there shouting at Monika, and before she could cover her nude body, he grabbed hold of her and hit her. She kicked back and pushed him out of the bathroom, locking herself in as she usually did when he was drunk and pestered her for sex and she'd take a magazine or her knitting and retreat to the loo seat. Now, Abdulla ran back downstairs to look for his innocent sons, and both got a good, unnecessary hiding from him, too. Monika could hear her poor kids crying out loud. It was a replay of the many times the in-laws had complained to Abdulla about the boys' naughty behavior, and it broke her heart. Yet, she was powerless. Had she gone downstairs, the five of them would have jumped on her.

Countless times Abdulla would come home, tired, hungry, and sweating from work and right off give Sulaiman or Nabeel or both a good bashing for something his family had relayed to him. But Monika couldn't have kept them in the flat all day either.

Thinking back now, Monika wonders endlessly how on earth she stood the abuse, why she didn't just walk out with her kinds and leave those lunatics. But where to could she have possibly turned? She had no money for plane tickets and no other home to go to, which was really Abdulla's strongest attraction. Had she had a couple of thousands up her sleeve, mark my words, he would have treated her with kid gloves; but penniless, she was cornered. Abdulla was like billions of men all over the globe—south, north, west, and east—who have kept their wives likewise. With one child it would have been much easier to leave, but with two kids Monika was stuck in deep mud, and the new house shone through in the background like a bright morning star.

That promised house gave her the strength and optimism to carry on despite all. She held on to her dream, still hoping everything would turn up roses and green grass, silly girl. God had not blessed Monika with the gift of knowing what could be achieved and what had better be left alone because it was impossible, it seemed—or was she really that naïve?

After the incident with Sabiha on the courtyard tiles, Monika never spoke to her a single word again, nor honored her with a look. For Monika, Sabiha the Witch was air.

Soon after Monika had begun shunning Sabiha, Diba fell tragically ill while bathing in the sea fully dressed as they do there. She had had a stroke. A blood clot had blocked the blood supply to her brain, and she was partly paralyzed after that. Her talk was absent-minded, and she did not even recognize her own mother.

The doctors in Kuwait were incapable of treating her. Abdulla, and not her husband, had Diba transferred to an excellent hospital in Beirut for better medical treatment in accord with the Kuwaiti Government's practice of sending difficult cases abroad. It was determined that since no one knew how long the treatment there would last, Monika and the children would go to Lebanon, too. The trip coincided nicely with Sulaiman's summer holidays. A house and its staff high up on a beautiful, jasmine-scented red mountain site, the property of one of Abdulla's generous relatives, awaited them there. Everything was arranged in a hurry. Suitcases were packed. And then, on the night before take-off, Abdulla enlightened his wife that not she and the children would be coming along as had been arranged earlier, but his mother and Tamader instead, the two of whom had unilaterally decided to take her place. Monika and her children were simply pushed aside without the slightest consideration, just like excess baggage.

"I'm sorry. It's not my fault. It's my mother's decision." That's all he had to say for himself, but, of course, Monika knew he had had no say in the matter. Monika simply did not count a fig.

Monika and her children were left alone for a month in Kuwait's heat with trouble-hunting Sabiha in charge of the house. During that time, Monika made it her main project to keep herself and her children well out of Sabiha's way. It took a lot of energy to see to it that their paths didn't cross.

Because there was nothing else to get at her with, Sabiha told Monika after the first week that the house was not a hotel and that her friend Aya and other foreign and Kuwaiti visits had to stop. Neighbors already talked, she said. (I wish you could see some of those neighbors she was referring to. One could watch them lying in the afternoon sun searching at each other's heads for lice like monkeys.)

Monika boiled inwardly but did not honor Sabiha with a reply. She simply ignored her, which made Sabiha rage like a wounded bull. Monika couldn't manage the whole pack at once, but to ward them off one by one was child's play, witchcraft or no witchcraft.

CHAPTER FOURTEEN

MONIKA'S DREAM HOUSE

During Abdulla's long absence, Monika took her two little boys to the cinema and sometimes to the seashore, where she sat fully dressed with a pile of stones at hand to throw as weapons at sex-starved males who came too close or exposed themselves to her in the water and masturbated looking at her. Sometimes she took the children where she liked it best in Kuwait at that time, to her future retreat of peace and contentment, the building site where the house that held all the hopes she had left was slowly progressing.

The building materials had to be imported from abroad, and that, of course, took time. The Iraqi and Irani workers at the building site told Monika that Sabiha had come much more often than she herself had— to check up on what was being done and to ask endless questions. Sabiha wanted to know everything about the architectural style and decor of the house on the inside and the outside.

Her Fahad was building at the same time, just down the road from Abdulla. Conscious of Monika's arty talent, Sabiha was anxious lest Monika's new home should outstrip her own. Always looking around to copy others, Sabiha had good reason to worry because Monika had long collected her designs, color schemes, and material samples from London and Kuwait. Monika had had to make Abdulla promise— and swear—not to give away any of the house's secrets. These Monika kept in a folder. Monika knew exactly how original her house would look in comparison to those of other Kuwaitis when it was finished. Lots of things she had designed herself—like, for example, the pattern for the half-meter-wide iron fence that would run around on top of the high cement walls shielding the property. Monika saw lots of smashing ideas in some of Kuwait's houses, but the majority of them looked more or less the same. If you saw one, you'd seen a thousand.

The houses were stuffed with furniture, ornaments, artificial flowers. Everything that possibly could be was gold plated or made of crystal and silver. The furnishings were overpowering, too much of a good thing cramped into one place. Nothing matched, and very little fitted, not the goods nor the colors. The overall confusion was a reflection of Kuwaiti taste, which was not imaginative. Since most women's full-time occupation and only enjoyment in Kuwait was (and still is) shopping, it was not surprising that they would buy whatever they happened to like on a given day and never mind whether or not it was appropriate, or even needed.

That is why the majority of houses in Kuwait look like shops inside. Ladies have mirrored, room-size walk-in closets adjoining their bedrooms in which they have their very own boutiques crammed full of designer models in the colors of the season. Have you every thought it possible that people who can't read or write and who eat with their fingers are some of the first ones to wear Yves St. Laurent creations? Doesn't that reduce the original image of designer clothes a bit? Well, that's how it is!

A few exceptional, outstanding villas stood here and there in Kuwait, built by people, mainly business people, who spent a great amount of time traveling abroad and had their architects and interior designers flown in from all over the world. Some of those houses were dream palaces you would not be likely to see anywhere else in the world. You might catch a glimpse of something like them in a film. But these, too, had one minus: they felt cold outside and inside. They were everything but homey. Thus was Monika occupied during Abdulla's absence.

One day Abdulla sent Monika a bottle of red wine from Lebanon with his cousin Said. The following day Said, who was married to Abdulla's cousin Laila, knocked on Monika's door, said "Hello, Monika," and made straight for her sitting room settee.

"Bring that bottle of wine and two glasses, darling. Let's have the bottle together and have a little bit of fun," he said softly approaching yet almost ordering her.

"You can have some, Said. I don't feel like wine right now," she told him, instantly sensing that he was a first-class womanizer whose wife Laila was away in Lebanon on holiday, too, and that he was up to no good. Without Abdulla around, he thought, Monika would be easy prey and an easy lay.

Monika sat down on a rocking chair, after handing Said a tray with the bottle, a bottle-opener, and one glass. Sulaiman and Nabeel's presence disturbed him, so he reached into his pocked and pressed a ten K.D. note in each child's hand and told them to go and play. He had to discuss something important with their mother "Um Sulaiman." Then Said poured red wine and made Monika the seediest love declaration of her life.

"I can't help it. I have to think all the time of you since I first saw you! Day and night! You are even in my dreams. Abdulla is in Lebanon enjoying himself and does not give a damn about you. I made the biggest mistake of my life by marrying Leila. I don't love her. I love you. Come here. Sit next to me." Said moved over, patting the seat next to him as if he were calling a dog to jump up and sit there.

"I am quite comfy where I am right now. I can swing while listening to your heart breaking Hallelujah," Monika joked to find a way around Said's cheek. He was hoping to leave her place well relieved after a quickie, that bloody bastard! Just then Nabeel entered the room.

"OUT!" shouted Said, the visibly erected bulge between his legs under the thin transparent white robe deflating slowly. "If you come once more into the room, I'll take the money from you. We will call you when we are finished."

"Nabeel, you stay here!" ordered Monika and jumped abruptly up, letting the chair swing vigorously behind her. "What you have come here for, dear cousin of my husband, we won't finish."

Said looked at her in surprise. He got up and made his way to the exit. His sex urge seemed curbed as, on his way out, he sputtered, "Please, don't tell Abdulla. I know I can rely on you."

He was wrong. She told Abdulla, who seemed to be annoyed by his cousin's action, but not enough to confront him in front of Monika as she asked him to do.

"He knows now that you are a lady and won't try it again." That was all Abdulla had to say on the matter. Yet if her skirt slipped up an inch or so above the knee in male company, he would have a go at her and give her hell! The hypocrisy of his double standard, after all these years, still had the power to stun her.

Monika couldn't wait for her own home to be finished, now that it was underway. Like everything about Monika's flat in her in-laws' house, the telephone situation there was, of course, nothing private either. The main phone was downstairs. There were two extension phones. Monika and Abdulla had one upstairs. As you may have already guessed, everybody could and did listen to her conversations all the time; and if they, downstairs, forgot to push a button on their main apparatus, Monika could listen to them, too.

On the day that the family returned from Lebanon, Monika and Tamader both lifted their receivers (one up, one down) at the same time. Tamader was the first to speak. After their "Hello" and "How are you?" the caller, a woman, asked Tamader why Abdulla had taken her and his mother to Lebanon and left his wife Monika behind.

"Because none of us wanted her to come along," came Tamader's bitchy reply. "Abdulla is really fed up with her. He would like to divorce her but only keeps her for the sake of the children. He met that darling of a nurse in Beirut. She took care of Diba. Abdulla really fancies her, and he took her out a couple of times. We are working on him. We want him to get married to an Arab like us—on top of that *gahba*. Then, we could all relax. You scratch yourself best with your own nails."

Monika had heard enough and put down the receiver. It was the first time she had actually had the pleasure of listening to one of her in-laws' smear campaigns. Except for the surprise that Tamader was also charged with so much nastiness, the revelation more or less left her cold.

Nevertheless, every time something like this happened, the fact that she had still to live among such evil energies branded deep, open wounds in her heart and soul. Monika thought it darkly funny that after finally mastering the Arabic language, a very difficult one indeed, and nothing compared to learning English, the knowledge it brought should have not only its pluses but its minuses, too. All the upheavals the in-laws caused, however, did not demoralize Monika. The opposite happened. They stimulated and induced her to remain, even more obstinately, her own distinct person. Monika had goals and saw her in-laws as an obstacle course and a challenge. One of those goals was, plainly, the Dream House under construction.

Abdulla with Monika behind the thick, high brick walls in her mother-in-law's house – her new home!

Monika's mother in-law

Little Selma cuddles close to Monika who is surrounded by the Al-Amahanis' immediate female relatives in Monika's age group.

Little Sulaiman, Monika, Sabiha (if looks could kill…)
and Abdulla in Cairo, Egypt

A fragment from the past! Musically gifted Abdulla (2nd right) is singing to the best of desert drums.

Andulla playing the flute as a boy scout in Kuwait.

Left: Monika with her brother Werner.
Right: Monika with her mother, Dentist Pavlik

Monika at her Seaclub restaurant with some of her staff

Luay, Nabeel and Sulaiman, Monika's pride and joy, at the bottom of their own new house in Rowda, Kuwait.
(Senta the Dalmatian – doggy back left)

246 • *Cinderella in Arabia*

Left: Look what became of the ugly Indian duckling! Gloom poses proudly in Western fineries, flashing his white-capped teeth.

Right: Abdulla's kind grandfather (father's side). He freed all his black slaves on his deathbed.

Left: Monika clad in a thobe, a Kuwaiti traditional gold-paletted lace robe. The costly garment is worn by females at special festivities for Arabic dancing.

Right: Monika in embroidered Arabic velvet-shift, resting by a golden douvah (charcoal fire). On it rests silver pots filled with cardomon , spiced Arabic coffee and sweet thick black tea, tiny lead crystal glasses and china cups ready to be filled.

In true Bedouin tradition, Monika in disguise under a fine black silk *abaya* with facemask woven from fine muslin

Abdulla and his friend Salam. America, here we come!

The house Monika designed and built in Kirchberg / Otterthal, Austria

Kuwait's Ambassador Sheikh Saud Al-Sabah and his beautiful wife Awatif Al-Sabah, the daughter of the Ruler of Kuwait, flanked by Abdulla and Monika

Andulla smiling from a Royal Stagecoach on his way to Buckingham Palace for an audition with her Majesty Queen Elizabeth.

Monika al-Amahani • 253

The Kuwaiti diplomat's wife poses at a Kuwait National Independence party. (Monika in white.)

Kuwait male diplomats eat their rice dishes the traditional customary way – with their bare hands. (Abdulla second from the left.)

Number 40 Baker Street, London W1 – the reason for Monika's divorce – what should have been her 'Arabic Gulf Restaurant' is today the 'Royal China' instead.

CHAPTER FIFTEEN

MONIKA OPENS A BUSINESS

Abdulla returned to Kuwait with a much-improved Diba. He acted guilty but said it was only, mind you, about leaving Monika and his children behind. To start with, he was a bit softer than any soft toy, pretending to be full of remorse. Monika knew the softness would not last long, and she also knew she would have to act fast if she wanted to use the chance to convince him that she just could not waste away idle any longer, as she was doing then, and that she simply needed to change the pattern of that monotonous day-in-day-out routine under such close and suffocating in-law observation. Her brain was starting to get rusty and her nerves were snapping like stretched elastic. She absolutely had to make a breakthrough now and do something useful with her time before she went insane, with the house (although under construction) still a far off thing.

Depression was setting in again, just as it had before Abdulla and Monika had gone to London. She badly needed a change now. Taking care of her children and the flat, this she could do with her little finger, in a jiffy. She craved the opportunity to remove herself from her in-laws for a big chunk of the day. She wanted to work, to create a healthier atmosphere around her. She knew now that depending on Abdulla for anything would get her nowhere. Besides, she had already put on unnecessary weight and had caught herself eating more and more often, out of sheer boredom and frustration, just like all the other Kuwaiti women. If she didn't step in to help herself now, nothing and no one would change anything for her and she would only sink lower, deeper, down.

During Abdulla's absence, Monika had had lots of time to consider and reconsider her unfortunate domestic position. Her first brainstorm about a job produced the idea that she should start with what she knew best. She struggled with the idea of opening a "ladies only" chiropodist and manicure salon since it had not passed Monika by unremarked that most Kuwaiti women sported feet similar to those she had treated at her in-laws' house. Monika was convinced that a salon of that sort—maybe called "Pretty Feet and Hands," the first in Kuwait—could easily take her mind off things and make a big splash, too. But Abdulla sternly rejected the idea.

"Put that rubbish out of your mind! Forget it straight away and think of something else. No way am I going to make myself the laughing stock of Kuwait. They would say, 'Abdulla al-Amahani's wife cleaned our feet!'"

Monika saw his point there. Abdulla was under continuous scrutiny because of his foreign wife—not only by his family. His name made regular rounds through Kuwait's douvaniahs. All news travels faster than fire in Kuwait. As a rule, the Kuwaiti male does not like for his wife to work, but nowadays many women are employed in well-paying government jobs and have posts they obtained with university degrees.

Monika's second bid for a bit of independence was to try to convince Abdulla of Scheme Number Two. She tried to persuade him to let her manage a restaurant that was up for rent in Kuwait's Sea Club and—Bingo!—second time's a charm. But don't ask what struggles were involved and what hurdles—what in-law hurdles!—had to be overcome first. Nothing at all came easy to Monika. Everything she had (and wanted) was (and had to be) hard earned. It seemed the pattern of her life. She was stuck with it.

Abdulla's family's reason for their opposition to the restaurant is spelled in four letters and reads E-N-V-Y. All hell broke loose when, under false pretense, the clan united and tried to convince Abdulla that any female member of the al-Amahani family who ran a restaurant like a male would stamp a devastating ill effect on their good name, so much so that the poor creatures would have to shift about hiding their faces in shame, and all thanks to the Hamra. It would be beneath all dignity, honor, and decency in the highest degree if Abdulla were to allow a foreigner to pull their Aseel heritage through the mud, and he should think in advance whether he would want his wife to come into such close contact with all sorts of men. Could he trust the ingilesia? There would not always be somebody to watch her as they had been watching her for him in the house. Had the Hamra finally won the upper hand? Was she more important to him than his mother and his own flesh and blood? And anyway, what kind of an Arab was he to dance to her fiddle?

While the in-laws were busily at work and doing overtime on weak Abdulla, bribing him and threatening him again and again with emotional blackmail, Monika, who had learned her lesson, stayed cool. She play-acted on the other side, giving the performance of her life. While she inwardly boiled and felt like squashing her spidery in-laws into all eternity, she was calm, all smiles and pure poetry itself on the outside. And when Abdulla, egged on by them, drove her nearly around the bend, she bit her tongue and treated him like royalty. It was not easy. It cost her lots of pride and nerves, but still she had iron reserves, and all was well worth it in the end. She made plenty of use of her strongest weapon and gave Abdulla sexual performances *a la carte* because that's when she had him like a ring turning on her little finger. It paid off. Monika got her restaurant, which brought her, even if not one hundred percent, at least some freedom and inner fulfillment—something she was dearly in need of.

By the time Abdulla had finally agreed, Monika was in a deep state of nervous exhaustion. The only remedy for her was to sit down and knit her frustrations out of her system. Abdulla had only been back from Beirut two weeks when he got the okay from the Ministry of Health to take Diba to England for more specialized treatment in London under the supervision of London's world-famous, Harley Street, top-notch medical doctors, all expenses paid once again by the generous Kuwaiti Government.

"This time, Sweetie, you and the kids come with me before you start the restaurant," decided Abdulla. "It will still be there when we get back. I'll help you sort it out. It has stood empty for so long, it can wait for another couple of weeks, I am sure. Diba will be taken off the plane in an ambulance at London's Heathrow airport and taken straight to the London Clinic while we stay at a hotel or rent a flat. Whatever you prefer. The choice is yours. During the daytime, we'll mostly look after Diba at the clinic and at night we'll hire a baby-sitter while the two of us paint the town bright red and pick up where we left off. We'll go to shows, cinemas, theaters, go to casinos to try our luck, and dance the night away, and . . .and I'll take you shopping at Harrod's. That will be your London highlight, Sweetie. We will do the lot. And how's that hit you, my Sweetie?" Abdulla asked his wife, who was listening brightly beaming, for it all sounded too good to be true.

"Abdulla, Sweetie, that is glam. I am fire and flame. It's brilliant. The kids and I badly need that change, and if I still get the okay for the restaurant afterwards, I love it."

Weak, immature Abdulla's proposal and goodwill were genuine, sounded great and probably really came from his heart, but once again the idea was short lived. Once the in-laws got wind of his plan, they stood united against it, and once again mother-in-law took Monika's place. Tamader could not make it this time because she had to study a couple of subjects she had failed at the end of her secondary school term so that she could re-sit the exams.

Once mother-in-law had forced her will upon Abdulla, with the help of much shouting and swearing mixed with a couple of fake heart attacks, by now quite popular, she won the day.

Abdulla had started to become a big shot in his hospital because he was kind, friendly, and very helpful and had that dynamic personality. He was always eager to please everybody—young, old, poor, rich—but had yet no say with his mother. In fact, this was so much the case that poor Monika—trailing misfortune and bad luck since she had stumbled upon Abdulla—often felt sorry for her weak husband. She herself had much more go, drive, stick-to-it-iveness, and guts. Her in-laws aside, people who took Abdulla for granted respected her in turn. Monika was a person one could steal horses with, her brother Werner had always said. He said, too, that he hoped to find a wife like her. A very good-looking, youthful, Robert-Redford-look-alike, fifty-year-old Werner, a ladies' man and successful dentist, is still single.

Monika and Abdulla were truly an ill match from the beginning. Had she grown up within her family instead of in a convent, Monika would have been much more streetwise and not so naive about what was going on; but the way it was, she did not know the first thing about life, nor love, nor marriage, nor of course any of the nastiness that some people are put together of. Still, she was not to blame, for from where was she to have known any better? She had been taught to believe that if a person is kind, honest, correct, generous, tidy, and industrious, then a prosperous and happy life is guaranteed.

Instead of waiting for a suitable match that was sure to come along in the fullness of time, she had jumped on the bandwagon and ended up married to an alien from another world almost immediately after her first close encounter with him, and a mommy's boy on top of that, someone who trod on England's soil in deep disguise as the ever-so Westernized, cultivated charmer.

Abdulla covered over his weaknesses by making tasteless jokes about his wife, jokes that hurt Monika, that made some outsiders laugh but made others (even his friends) side with her when they saw what was going on. Monika's sympathizers told Abdulla to rid himself of his mother and sisters and grow up and take responsibility for his wife and children. They told him he should once and for all put his foot down and take his wife and kids to London this time, not his mother. Abdulla just laughed it all off.

"I don't know about you, but if I go to a restaurant, I don't take a sandwich with me. London is full of pretty girls. There, I can have every night another one. After dried-out Kuwait, do you blame me? You are jealous, that's what it is."

So Abdulla went to London with his mother and left Monika behind, emotionally kicked and battered, a wallflower again. She just stored the bitterness in her large heart along with all the other sorrow and pain that had already accumulated there and squeezed it in with all the other bad memories. She soothed her hurt feelings by concentrating on and planning optimistically what to do about the restaurant.

With a good head for business and a great will to work, Monika saw the potential in that neglected restaurant location. Any money she could make there would free her from total dependence on Abdulla's fitful generosity. She would be able to buy things for herself and the kids without having to pretend that whatever money she had in her handbag was sent to her from Austria by her own mother and without having to hide from her in-laws things Abdulla bought for her and the children. She would share any profits with Abdulla, naturally.

Finally, Monika went into business, and all of Kuwait watched, especially her husband's family, who, having lost that battle, were now sniggering that the Hamra would never make a go of it.

Just as she had done when she moved into her flat, she began at the restaurant in the club by cleaning everything thoroughly with bleach and caustic soda. The kitchen was filthier than filthy, even by Kuwaiti standards. There were cockroaches by the thousands hidden in teapots and in every conceivable dark place.

Monika could not bring herself even to touch the oven, which was heavily coated in rancid oil. She had it chucked out and bought a new one. Big, fat water rats lived in the soil of the empty flower banks, and Monika felt sorry for the masses of their pink babies that had to be destroyed in the clean-up process. Outside the kitchen's back door, a huge peachy-pink scorpion nearly frightened the life out of her as she was just about to put her foot down on it. And that was one hell of a shock because Monika thought scorpions were confined to the desert. She worried about her children running about barefoot. But she was assured that her find was a rare exception. The scorpion was picked up and put in a glass half filled with sand and placed on exhibition among other rare finds from sea and shore that appeared around the Sea Club.

Monika thought back on just how often she had come here with Abdulla, to this same club, to drink tea served from those same teapots. Ugh, horrible! Better not to think about it.

Monika let loose her artistic abilities confidently in that place. The end result of her hard work was a restful, refreshing place seating 60. The club resembled a greenhouse, or an oasis, and provided a pleasant contrast to the surrounding desert that, upon leaving, one stepped into. All the empty spaces were filled with tall, green plants. Dark green, vinyl-topped tables harmonized with the orange curtains, orange lamp shades, orange candlesticks and silk flowers imported from Vienna that stood on top of each table. Yes, Monika had used the same colors as she'd chosen for Sulaiman's first birthday party. She thought green and orange very becoming for a beachfront restaurant. In the background, Elvis sang softly, non-stop. People who visited it before it opened observed that the place had a warm, continental atmosphere and complimented her on it. In fact, compliments rained down on her. She was asked repeatedly if she had studied interior decoration. Abdulla, back from four weeks in London, was congratulated on having—or better yet, on owning—such a super woman.

While Monika was busy with her children, her flat, and her restaurant—getting it polished up for the grand opening—her second half took off on a two-week holiday abroad, again. He had begged Monika to condone his trip with two friends to Egypt.

"Sweetie, all Kuwaitis travel and leave their wives behind. I let you have the restaurant," he bribed. "I want to shut them up, show them that I can do the same as they do and still be married to a lovely foreign girl like you."

Monika was deeply hurt that Abdulla wanted to go to Egypt alone. Although he tried to deny it, she and everybody else in Kuwait knew, too, that Cairo was Kuwait's mecca for cheap sex, booze, and more sex. Yet, she let him go, for what was the point of refusing and making a fuss? If that's what he wanted, her pride was not going to hold him back. She had well learned by then that by marrying a Kuwaiti one not only inherits his whole family but also has to come to terms with the fact that a husband's unfaithfulness plays a big part in Kuwait's way of life: the man who does not fuck about is scared of his wife and not a real man in Kuwait. Everybody does it. Everybody knows it. Yet, the hypocrites don't talk about it. It does not match at all the false image they represent of themselves to the outside world, sometimes quite successfully, nor the virtuous Islamic façade they utilize to their own benefit and hide behind when it's advantageous. Never mind that it drives their poor womenfolk, who are powerless to do anything about it, to illness and distraction. Those women's only consolation is that they are all in the same boat together. But never mind. They are only brainless women, created to serve the "superior, intelligent, strong" (but in reality, and in all honesty, "ludicrously weak") males. What is good for the goose is not good for the gander in their case, for in Kuwait only the gander counts. So, Abdulla went on his fucking trip to Cairo. Monika's restaurant came with a price tag attached. Nothing is free in this world, Monika reflected.

While Abdulla roly-polied around somewhere in Cairo with Fiffy, Kiki, Suzu or Nini (all call-girl names in Egypt), Monika was kept under strict observation by her envious in-laws. It satisfied them immensely that Abdulla had gone away alone and left her stranded. Under masses of criticism, their noses and fingers were again into everything concerning the restaurant. Monika's open, honest approach—and the fact that she was who she was—quickly won her the confidence and respect of the club's committee, and with their help and their Kuwaiti know-how, she soon got rid of her in-laws, who, standing around in the way, were pointedly ignored while Monika was given all the attention. Indeed, the in-laws were formally told that Monika was the restaurant's sole boss. Now, *that* they couldn't cope with. It threw them off their rails. No trump cards left to play because the trumps were all in Monika's hands, they cleared off the scene and were, thereafter, twice as nasty to her at home.

A big surprise awaited Abdulla on his return from his sin trip. Monika told him that offspring Number Three was on its way to join Sulaiman and Nabeel. The baby was not planned, but Monika—strictly anti-birth control pills—always toiled in the back of her mind with the possibility of new life. If she had been happily married, she would have wanted a whole bundle of kids. She loved them. In her questionable situation, one more to make it three would be a perfect number, but it would have to be the last, definitely. She had an oldest, a middle one, and now the youngest was to join them. From now on it would be important to take extra care of the middle one, Nabeel, she thought; for she had read somewhere that in-between children were always the neglected ones in a set of three. A gypsy on Brighton's seaside resort in Britain had once told her that she would have three boys. At the time she had only Sulaiman. So, now, she would wait and see if the gypsy proved correct. One thing Monika knew already: all good things come in threes.

Within a year Monika was to get a new restaurant, have a new baby, and move into her own new house—all positive things. Fortune seemed to be in her favor for a change. She was still a far cry away from what one might call "being happy," but taking a look around her, she never found herself to be one of the worst off among the immediate Kuwaiti womenfolk.

The first time Monika and Abdulla made love after he returned from Cairo, he looked at her 36-inch, B-cup bosoms (because of pregnancy a little bit bigger now) and said, "Gosh, your breasts are small!" With that remark he curbed her sex urge and gave himself away. It made her feel sick. He did not have to tell her outright now that he had had an Egyptian girl (or girls) with huge, outsized tits sometime in the past two weeks.

The Sea Club attracted the international foreign scene of Kuwait like a light attracts moths. Engineers, doctors, diplomats, and other highly skilled professionals with two- to four-year contracts all joined the club. Many of them were of an adventurous nature, people who came to Kuwait for the money alone—not for love, nor for culture, nor for Kuwait's charms, and definitely not for its traditions, nor its weather, but solemnly steadfastly for the lovely lolly that could be earned there, for the stuff that makes the world go round, as we all know. Foreigners stuck together in Kuwait, staying close to their own national groups. The jolliest among them were the British. The most distant and reserved were the Germans, who did not even mix with each other much because, apparently, each couple thought itself better than the next. People held countless drinking parties in each other's homes, where mostly homemade alcohol (named "Flash") that looked like water was offered to drink because the real thing, although available in Kuwait, would have annihilated their salaries. Bottles of Seven Up were filled with the precious, illegal "Flash" stuff and brought along to be consumed at the club as Seven Up. Nobody would notice. Some made an extra nickel by selling the liquid for hard cash to Kuwaitis. Loads of

Kuwaiti males of the Aseel and the non-Aseel kind were members of the club, too—but not their Kuwaiti wives.

Those Arabs loved to sit comfortably in their national dress—all white and pressed—worry beads (*the mesbah*) in hand, under the shade of a long roof, facing the sea like sparrows on a telephone wire, and to drink tea, coffee, cold drinks, or their own alcohol there, while taking in that most unfamiliar scene, at least in Kuwait: bikini-clad and swimsuit-dressed females of different nationalities, of all skin colors, of different shapes and sizes, with long, short, blonde, black, brunette, red hair. The scenery was something they had, up to then, to travel abroad to see, and it did not differ from any European beach— except for the police who stood guard in their Khaki-green uniforms to the left and to the right of the fence leading into the water, separating the club from the outside world.

Numerous unfortunate, sex-starved, frustrated males of the poor and peasant kind collected there like ants. They harassed the half-nude females, exposed themselves, and masturbated. The dishdashaed men who sat watching the goings-on in the cool sea water also discussed loudly and openly what they were looking at, and that amazed Monika, that male frankness. Probably not one of the females they discussed understood any Arabic, as she did, so it seemed to her a further insult to discuss them so openly. Their talk went, of course, towards sex, what else? She asked them once in Arabic, "Would you sit here all day long if only men and children under the age of twelve were out there in the water?" They smiled, joked back, but got the message. Monika often made little comments like that. She could not help it. She saw most men there lusting after other men's wives, sort of like dogs do after a bitch in heat. She could not get used to the primitive, cheap behavior, to say the least.

Kuwaiti males asked Monika why, as a European, she did not go in for a swim with the other foreigners. Kuwaiti women, especially the wives of an Aseel, never, ever show their flesh, not even an upper arm, to another man, not to speak of being seen publicly in a swimsuit. It would be very degrading for an Aseel if other males looked at their property's bare flesh. That was why they themselves never brought their womenfolk. Knowing all that, Monika had a smart answer.

"If you want to see me in the sea in my swimsuit, bring along your wives and sisters and mothers, too, next time, and Monika al-Amahani will gladly go for a swim with them." That shut them up.

Her answer pleased Abdulla, who loved to boast and prove to his teasing so-called friends that what he had was the best of both worlds: a pretty, clever, working European wife and mother that was a compliant and submissive servant, just like any of their Kuwaiti wives, on top of it all. They had to admit that Abdulla had a real *lulu* (pearl).

Kuwaiti women are not alone in showing jealousy and taking pleasure in running each other down; Kuwaiti men do so, too. If people taunted Abdulla about it being beneath his wife's dignity to work, he would shrug it off with, "She is European. What does your wife do and give you?"

Abdulla enjoyed the Sea Club. Many of the men at the club would have given their right arm to have a wife working like Monika—and up to the last minute of her third pregnancy at that—but none dared admit it. Abdulla realized how jealous his friends were. Because Abdulla enjoyed the Sea Club, Monika and the children saw much more of him than before, which is not to say that he stopped visiting his friends in the douvaniahs. But many people came to see him now, instead, and swam with him at the Sea Club.

Monika only employed staff that could speak Arabic and English, too. She now had a Sudanese cook, Mustafa; his kitchen help, Ramsy; two Persian waiters, Shahed and Shamsheed; and much-trusted Abou Abla, in charge of the restaurant and the money if Monika had to be elsewhere for whatever reason. Abdulla knew and trusted Abou Abla, who had previously worked in accountancy at Abdulla's hospital. Often, Abdulla would dab in a bit, too, and if he did, he mainly took charge of the till. The cook dressed in snow white, hat and all, while the waiters and Abou Abla wore black trousers, navy tee-shirts, and white sailor hats, just like the Marines. They served Arab and English meals, snacks, tea, coffee, milk shakes on silver trays with a white serviette slung over one arm—inside the restaurant and along the beach, too.

The money came rolling in, a lot of it from ice creams, soft drinks, and Monika's homemade potato chips and french fries that sold so well. English people asked that their traditional breakfast of egg, bacon, baked beans, and sausage be put on the menu, too.

Bader, a senior police officer, was in the habit of ordering a healthy breakfast of egg, bacon, sausage, and a mountain of french fries, especially after having spent weekend nights aboard his small yacht, where he enjoyed his whisky in the company of younger men. Yes, yes, you have guessed: he was gay, but that's not what we are on about here. Mother Nature put him together like that, so who are we to criticize? Bader was one of Monika's first guests to find himself on the receiving end of one of her practical jokes. Instead of the real thing, she placed two sunny-side up plastic eggs on a plate; over them she poured the hot fat in which the sausages and bacon were fried, and served Bader the prank platter personally. He was very pleased with the generous appetizing portion and thanked her politely for it by praising her. Those plastic eggs looked so real and lay so convincingly on the plate that nobody could ever have guessed they weren't real. The police chief started eating his french fries while Monika, Abdulla, and all the staffs' eyes were on him watching him expectantly. Bader dipped his fork with a french fry on it into the egg yolk. Of course, it didn't budge! A puzzled Bader looked at his egg and tried a second time, more forcefully. Then he put his fork down, picked up the saltshaker, and sprinkled salt over his eggs as if that would help. Next, he had a go with his knife, but to no avail. The eggs kept slipping off every time he tried to poke them. Bader took a closer look at the edge of the knife, put it down, and shook his head. Then, he reached for a bottle on the table and, plop, let tomato ketchup drop on those eggs; and, lifting his bottom halfway out of the chair, had a go at that plastic with all his might. What a funny sight that was! Bader's spectators couldn't control their laughter any longer. He was finally let into the secret. And the best part of the fun was that he joined in, too.

Monika's favorite trick, once in a while, was to lace the tea or coffee that was served to her friends and regular customers with salt. Once she caught out an American smoothie, a ladies man. After he had taken his first sip of salted coffee, his false teeth came out along with the coffee that he spat out—embarrassing and funny, that one!

Monika prepared her own puddings and busily baked cakes. She catered for all sorts of parties, for up to 60 people at a time. Once a fortnight a barbecue was held out in the open. For that, she charged an entrance fee and hired a talented young Indian pop group called 'Blue Flame' to play and sing the latest hit songs, to which people danced enthusiastically. Prizes (some of them funny) were handed out, too, for the best dancer or for whoever dared to stand up and do something out of the ordinary. The prizes were, for example, a toilet seat, a baby's bottle filled with milk, or black suspenders with a huge matching bra. It all contributed to a great atmosphere.

Guests could eat as much as they liked from the help-yourself buffet, which featured goulash, grilled lamb chops, Arabic rice, salads, tropical fruits, coffee, and tea. The crowd brought their own alcohol in flasks and bottles on such occasions, when everybody was friends with everybody else and all had a great time. If you did the same thing on Britain's Brighton Beach, it just would not be the same: you can't transfer an atmosphere.

Monika was happy. She had her own business well in hand, and it was absolutely booming! She was clever in business without being shrewd. While they were not present, her witch crafting in-laws managed still to overshadow her daily life, of course, for often, when

Abdulla saw her happy and talking freely or having a good laugh, he would throw in some sarcastic remark concerning his family.

"If you loved my family," he would snort, "they could all be here now, too, and have a good time. I should have married a Kuwaiti, not a bloody, fucking foreigner."

The more Abdulla drank, the heavier his accusations would flow. During the time she was expecting Number Three, he must have told her a hundred times or so that she should not forget that his family were—and always would be—more important to him than she or *her* children would ever be.

"I forgive you, Sweetie," she would answer, "for you are not speaking with your own mind. You are doctored and bewitched and, on top of that, you are drunk. Therefore, whatever you say goes into one ear and straight out the other, under the circumstances. So save your breath and shut up or go and get married to them and sleep with them."

Monika often had trouble with Abdulla's drinking at the club. The only remedy to stop his consuming more, when he had already had far more than enough, was to pour the drink away or to hide it or to frighten him back to sense by warning him that if he did not stop immediately she would phone his mother to come and take a look at her drunken son.

Looking back on it now, Monika realizes that the Sea Club and its restaurant were one long party for Abdulla, who bathed in the glory of what Monika had accomplished and was generating for him: he had all the fringe benefits and enjoyed them to the full, just like a Maharajah, while poor Monika looked upon her work as a gift from heaven that brightened up her otherwise meek and dull existence in the desert.

At the Sea Club, where she was in contact with Kuwaitis of all types (although almost all of them male, of course), Monika found they were charming and good fun. Many of them told her they preferred the company of open-minded Europeans to that of hypocritical Kuwaitis who said or did one thing while meaning or wanting to do another. She learned a lot about Kuwaiti people and their ways from her guests, and as a result she gradually developed a better understanding of her in-laws. Monika was given helpful, well-meant advice by people who knew what they were talking about. She was advised on ways to deal with her mother-in-law and discovered that Kuwait was brimming full of unfortunate females like herself who didn't need to be foreign to be treated badly by their in-laws.

Sabiha and Tamader would pop in sometimes with their friends, sit themselves in the restaurant, and expect to be fed—at no cost to themselves, of course. On those occasions, they usually had something to jeer about whenever Monika was in sight or had to pass by their table. They treated the restaurant as if it were their private property. Tamader would say that there was not enough meat in the food. "Oh, yes, there is," Monika would answer, "but even if there weren't, why complain? You don't have to pay."

Mother-in-law would come to inspect the place now and then in her black robes, her face scarcely visible beneath the black veil. She never had a single word of appreciation for Monika. Instead, she would mutter about things she thought were not done right and was always saying that what belonged to her son belonged to her and her daughters, too, implying that the restaurant had nothing at all to do with Monika, who barely existed for them and was just good enough to wait on their tables. Monika minded them less and less. She had an interest now at long last, and with it she found some independence, which to her was as important as the fresh air she breathed.

Foreign members of the club and non-Aseel Arabs always paid cash for what they bought at the restaurant. But a lot of the Kuwaiti Aseels preferred that their bills be invoiced and registered in a book laid on for that purpose. Some paid their debts at the end of each month; others after two or three or whenever they felt like it; still others had to be reminded a couple of times before they paid up

Each evening Monika would bring home the day's takings, several rolls of ten-KD notes, and count them out with Abdulla, who would then take the money. He (or someone else) had changed his mind about the original agreement he had made with his wife, which was to put all the profits in a joint account. From time to time, Monika took money for clothes and jewelry, but never put a *fils* (penny) aside for herself and her future. Silly girl. Shouldn't she have known better by then?

Abdulla said the money was much needed and would come in handy for the new house. He had to admit his wife's idea about the restaurant was a good one. In the privacy of their flat, he was all compliments; otherwise, he continued his family's puppet, increasingly so. In fact—and whose idea was this?—Abdulla would take off with his friends for long, leisure weekends while Monika managed the club and slaved away at the restaurant and looked after her kids. All her customers—foreigners and Arabs alike—were astonished to see how she made the business operate and sacrificed herself non-stop for the enterprise. She was on duty and in harness every day of the week from 9 am until late at night, while her husband did little more than brag. Nobody at the club knew, or had guessed, that for Monika the restaurant with its interesting people was therapy, a welcome getaway, sheer heaven, after her (and her kids') long imprisonment and emotional torment in her ghastly mother-in-law's house, where all alone weekend after weekend she had cried herself to sleep most nights. Now, she did not have much time left to think about her unfortunate life.

Even so, because the devil never sleeps, Monika still had to jump many high hurdles put in her course by her in-laws. One weekend, for example, Abdulla took off to Basra in Iraq for a long weekend with friends, telling Monika it was business when she knew damn well it was "business" my foot!—that, in fact, it was only the pleasure of the flesh that drew him there. Alcohol flows freely in Iraq, although it is also a Muslim country, and sex of course goes hand in hand with it and is just as easily available there. Even though Kuwaitis are not liked in Basra, they are treated like royalty because they have and are willing to spend their lolly freely there.

On that particular weekend Monika held one of her barbecue nights. Just as she was about to drive back to the restaurant after putting the boys to bed, she discovered she had a flat tire; it was punctured. She ran upstairs to search for Abdulla's car keys, but searched in vain. She could not find them. Abdulla had left his keys with her as he usually did when he did not need the car to go away, but now they were missing. She must have mislaid them. As time was pressing, she ran downstairs to the servants' quarters to take the spare keys from Mohammed the driver. Monika wondered why Sabiha and Tamader were walking about aimlessly near the servants' quarters at that time of night. She was soon to find out. As soon as Abdulla had departed, the sisters had themselves driven around all day in Abdulla's brand new, air conditioned limousine—to tease her—and now, when Monika asked for the keys, Mohammed was very hesitant to hand them over.

"You have to ask Sabiha first," he told her loudly enough for Sabiha, standing close by, plainly to hear. Monika's argument—that the car was her husband's and not Sabiha's—had no impact; it fell on the deaf ears of ignorant robot-man Mohammed, who was obviously following only the orders given by reckless, spiteful Sabiha. Monika realized at once who was responsible for her flat tire: it was, of course, Sabiha—yes, Sabiha, who stood there provocatively dangling Abdulla's car keys between her fingers! Sabiha was holding the "missing" key chain. She had taken—or, rather, stolen—it from Monika's flat and done so practically right under Monika's nose. Both sets of keys were now in the enemy's possession. The naive bitch wanted Monika to bend down to her and ask *her* for Abdulla's car. She did not know that Monika had great pride and would never in a million years do that, but sooner be absent from the barbecue than give in to that misfit.

After a brief shouting match, with the usual ingredients of filth thrown at Monika, Monika was beside herself with anger, but would show no more of it.

Monika returned to her flat and, there, lay on her bed and cried. "God," she thought, "the hundreds of times I have lain on this bed and cried because of Abdulla and his family!" She wished dearly to remember where the third set of spare keys were, the ones she had used before she had her own car. Then, she would take the car and hide it altogether until Abdulla got back, just to spite Sabiha and give her tit for tat. Frantically, she started to search again, but could not find the keys and so had to bottle up her emotions once again. It slowly but surely made her physically ill.

Monika just could not fathom the working of those Arabs' minds. The heck with it all! She phoned Aya, who came with her husband to drive her to the club. Enough of crying her eyes out for want of power to kill that bitch. How dare she!

Life continued.

Abdulla was back and Monika told him about the incident. He played with his worry beads as he listened.

"It isn't right," Monika concluded.

"I know it is not," Abdulla agreed. "She is very difficult. I know. But you put me in a vise. I am always in the middle of it all. They are my sisters, and you are my wife."

"Oh, yes, really. Thanks for telling me. I didn't know I was your wife. Thank you very much! You had better stop talking, for I can see that, like always, you are going to do nothing—so that the next time you are not here the fat, jealous, lazy slob can think of a new game to make my life continuous misery. A fine man and husband you are. I can really be proud of you. I feel so protected by you."

End of story. Monika just had to carry on living with the little things that pleased little minds.

CHAPTER SIXTEEN

ABDULLA, THE FAMILY MAN

If Abdulla was less than satisfactory as a husband, he was not a good father to his kids either—not in any conventional sense of the word, except for the fact that he had indeed fathered his sons. Now, in that, he took great pride, but he hardly ever took the boys out with him alone into the desert or to the sea, nor did he teach them, play with them, or show them anything, as fathers usually do. Instead, he compensated for the general neglect by spoiling them rotten with toys—giving them playthings to get them out of his way. The older the kids grew, the bigger their presents became—and their wishes, too; and they always got what they wanted without much trying. But when actual father-duty or husband-duty called, Abdulla would be stone deaf. Trying to make him realize how he made commitments to everybody but made none whatsoever to his own family was like spitting into a gale. As far as he was concerned, his family was his mother and sisters, and he had his hands full with them. Even his fatherly duty lay with them. If Sabiha's son would not eat his dinner, Sabiha would shout for Abdulla. If Diba's son played with matches, Diba would shout for Abdulla. And, always, the well-trained brother (Abdulla) would run up and down those stairs like a yo-yo, never complaining even though he might be completely tired out. Monika realized that in order to avoid his mother and sisters, although he would not admit it even to himself, Abdulla made an effort to spend as much of his free time away from the house, leaving Monika to take charge of her children and herself.

Abdulla was not too concerned about that, to tell the truth. He knew she could stand her ground, and he depended on her to do so if the need arose. He never asked—no one ever asked—how *she* felt. She was the one who played with the children, helped with their Arabic homework, solved their little problems, took them to the doctors, and tucked them in at night. Abdulla was never around to do any of these things. He walked in and out of that flat very much like a lodger, with the privilege of a good fuck whenever it took his fancy. In case of emergency, Monika never knew where to reach him or what he was up to. And once she had him home, usually late at night, she knew he (more often than not) had made his way home from some place where alcohol flowed freely. Drinking was in Abdulla's blood, a weakness inherited from his father, who according to mother-in-law's narrations of past experiences with her husband, was much worse while under the influence of alcohol than his son. Mother-in-law often admitted that when her husband died, it was a great blessing and relief for her. *De mortuis nil nisi bonum* (Latin, for don't speak ill of the dead); but, making an exception, one does have to mention here that the deceased Mr. al-Amahani Senior woke up his wife at 3 am to order her to cook rice and then—hold on—took a shit in the tomato sauce to consume it with his friend as rice and meat curry. Of course, the pair of them were very, very drunk, which dampened the effect.

Abdulla's father loved women excessively, too. Once he kept an Iraqi mistress. Abdulla's mother found out and, without letting her husband know that she knew, she went for an audition to the ruling Sheikh, the Emir, and told him about it. Abdulla's father was summoned and lashed twenty times across his bare back. Then, mother-in-law nursed his wounds while the mistress was sent back to Iraq. Abdulla's father swore revenge on the Judas who had given him away, but he died not knowing that it was his own wife's doing.

One thing is sure. Mother-in-law definitely had no honey-licking with her husband either. Was that maybe what made her so evil? Envious, jealous, and destructive, trying to get the injustice done to her out of her system through her actions—could it be? Or was she born with those negative characteristics like her daughters?

Once, a friend brought Abdulla home a day early from one of his weekend outings. Abdulla's arm was broken and in a cast. Abdulla was, of course, drunk.

Another time, Monika was asleep in bed, alone. She had a nightmare that the wheels of Abdulla's car had burst, and that Abdulla lay underneath the car in a pool of blood. When a noisy, totally tipsy Abdulla awoke her from that trauma and she was pleased to see that he was "alright," he told her he had just driven home at high speed away from some tent in the desert where some of his friends were gathered. He had left to avoid a heated argument about Monika, his wife.

"Some cunt asked me if you were a virgin or 'opened' at sixteen like all the English, so I asked him in return if he enjoys his Kuwaiti wife's bad smell under her black abaya and left."

He had driven home so fast and carelessly that two of his tires had burst. The car had overturned, and he had thought for a moment it was the end of his world. He had been so lucky. Cars stopped. People pulled him out of the window. He was completely unhurt, except for shock, skin grazed and a couple of bruises. Somebody had given him a lift home. He was talking a bit absent-mindedly, still tipsy, about what could have happened to him and how foolish he really was with drink. He swore on everything he held near and dear that he would never, never, ever touch that bastard alcohol again in his life. He said, too, that if he were in her shoes he would not put up with a drunk like him. And he professed how much he loved and appreciated her, his one and only Sweetie. But it was nothing out of the ordinary, for Abdulla was always full of remorse, apologies, and good will for the future after his drinking binges. And his resolve was always very short lived. He was too weak to stick to his guns and change. He might go a month without drink; and then, the next month, he would make up for his abstinence by indulging in excess all over again.

After that particular incident, however, Abdulla went out with his mother's driver and searched for two whole days before he found his overturned limousine. He just could not remember where he had left it. Monika was sure Abdulla had a guardian angel. Otherwise, how could he have driven home safely under the influence of alcohol so many, many times?

In Kuwait, people drink to get drunk. There, they don't say, "Let's have a drink tonight." They say, "Let's get drunk tonight," and that's, I'm sure, because its forbidden to drink openly. If Kuwaitis grew up with legal liquor around them like people elsewhere have, they would give alcohol far less importance than they do—and that goes for sex, too. By the way, tell me, what do the Gulf Arabs go for first thing in the West? Yes, liquor and sex—why? Because, where they come from, they lack both.

Monika put up endlessly with Abdulla's drunkenness. Before they left the house to go to dinners, dances, parties, or other invitations, he would swear to her that he would stick to three whiskies for the night. But he never did. And what had promised to be an enjoyable evening for both, 99 out of a 100 times turned into a traumatic experience again and again. It made Monika wish she could snap her fingers and quickly disappear, for when Abdulla drank he was overcome by an urge to ridicule his wife and reduce her in public to nothing. Why was that? Could it have been because she reasoned and sensed things? As she grew older, Monika realized the only person he really reduced though that behavior was himself.

Sometimes he would even raise his hand against her, and she also learned never to argue with a drunk. But before that happened, she often had arguments with him while he was in a drunken state. In such a state he once threw a large wooden laundry basket at her. It caught her under the knee, on the shin. God, was that painful! And just as Monika was about to take revenge and knock him into the middle of next week, the banging and shouting aroused mother-in-law's attention. She came hurrying up the stairs with Tamader to investigate. Abdulla held strictly to one commandment. And that was at all costs to avoid letting his mother or sisters see him drunk. So, as they entered the flat, he quickly cupped both his hands over his testicles and bent like a willow, half crying to distract them from the fact that he was drunk.

"*Yumma, yumma* (mother, mother), the *Ingilesia* hit me in the balls!" Abdulla stood there, crouched over, head hanging down, acting as if he were in great pain—pain that was non-existent, for Monika had not touched him with a finger yet, although he had thrown the basket at her. If the in-laws had not burst in, she would have let him have it. He had it coming. She always hit back, but never anywhere near his balls. He was such a liar. To cover himself, he was always throwing her to the wolves.

Tamader jumped at Monika, pulling bushels of her hair and shouting hysterically.

"Don't you lay hands on my brother, you bloody foreigner! You *hamra gahba*! Go eat your shit!"

And mother-in-law boxed her in the back with clenched fists.

Freeing herself from the clutches of the two hyenas and telling them to smell and take a closer look at their drunken Abdulla, Monika ran for refuge to her poor children's room, where both lay crying, and locked herself in. Through the door, she could hear the women comforting Abdulla, bringing crushed ice to put on his injured private parts, while swearing at that foreigner for daring to accuse him of drinking alcohol, of all things!

At times like this, with the whole world seemingly against her, Monika felt devastated. The walls seemed to crush in on her. She was the loneliest person in the world, helpless, with no one to talk to. To whom could she admit stuff like that? Following that episode, she sported a huge, round, dark blue, 8" x 8" bruise on her right leg for a good month after—caused accidentally, if anybody asked, by the slamming of a car door.

Abdulla's pattern repeated itself quite regularly, like clockwork. He'd be drunk. He'd be remorseful. He'd be so sorry, be very kind trying to make it up to her, and the next day be drunk and abusive. Same story all over again.

But Monika solved something that had puzzled her for a long time. Abdulla loved to swear. He swore on his dear father's grave, on his unborn child—even when he damn-well knew he was telling a lie. She wondered how he could be so callous, bold, and cold-blooded—until a friend enlightened her about Muslim promises. For a Muslim to swear truly, his body has to be completely pure and clean from head to toe. If you want him to swear meaningfully, let him step out of a shower and make him do it then. If he indulges in sex, passes wind, or takes a leak afterwards and then swears, his swearing does not count, for he is unclean. Yes, that of course explained Abdulla's false swearing. Monika was rather relieved to learn about it, for she knew he was not that bad! Abdulla was not bad at all, really; he was only weak, very weak, too weak for his own good. She told him he could forget about swearing to her—for one—in the future.

Just as Monika had taken to her charming future-hubby at Oxford, the Sea Club's members found extrovert Abdulla extraordinary, great fun to be with. Everybody who met Abdulla took to him, especially as he wasn't particularly choosy in picking friends and acquaintants. He firmly believed in giving everybody, anybody who felt like it, a good time. Abdulla was always the life and soul of the party, whoever he was with. He loved to entertain and to be a showman, and he was jolly good at it, too, a natural, as natural as they come. His being financially generous, too, always attracted two-faced hangers-on who needed wastas or were after one thing or another from Abdulla, who had the silly habit of bringing home or to the restaurant all sorts of rubbishy people who happened to cross his path. He brought them in the way cats bring mice.

Monika never had any privacy in her home, and she could easily see through people for what they were and sometimes even told them so, which always greatly annoyed Abdulla and also caused fights. Again and again, Monika tried unsuccessfully to open his eyes in time and to convince him of the fact that he was being used. But Abdulla took no notice of her warnings. He was always coming back to her later on to tell her that she had been right and that he had been silly not to have listened to her in the first place. Yes, well, you can lead a mule to water, but you can't make it drink. The point is that Abdulla let such people, people he hardly knew, become more important than his own wife and kids. Monika, Sulaiman, and Nabeel stood, first, in his mother's and sisters' shadow and, secondly, in the shadow of every Aziz, Ali and Mohammed he met virtually in the street. He would often ridicule her in order to give those shitty people she would never herself associate with a good laugh and made sure to give them the impression that he was in charge and that she was merely a slave any Arab man would be proud to possess. He ordered his kids to greet politely and to kiss the "uncles." It drove Monika up the wall. But the more she opposed something like this, the more he did it just to force her into submissiveness, to needle her. The children were some of his favorite weapons. He used them freely, without consideration for the poor souls.

Monika's Kuwaiti husband was now transformed into a completely different person from the one she had fallen for in Oxford and married in Canterbury. How true. People do change their personalities. Abdulla was the best proof of that. All the evidence that he had once been a gentle, kind, charmer had blown away with the desert wind. She was now bound to a silly show-off who had shed all that she had liked and loved and that was European and civilized about him. His medical certificates and his wife were the only things he was left with from

Europe. In Kuwait there prevails a certain inbred confidence and pride in being an Aseel Kuwait. Abdulla had now joined that fellowship.

It's funny. However much women, for instance, might try to lighten their skin and hair and copy Western fashions and however much men might study abroad (as Abdulla had done) and try to impose more-or-less Western values on Kuwaiti society and wear Western business suits, the pride of being an Aseel Kuwait will always run very deep, and the polite chit chat with foreigners, the sorties to the fleshpots of Europe in magnificent Western clothing, and that sort of thing are nothing but an elaborate veneer, let's face it. Beneath Abdulla's façade lay a deep-rooted sense of belonging to simple, unsophisticated, easy-going Kuwaiti life, his home, his country, his people—a sense that surfaced increasingly, although Monika, for one, thought he'd been much happier in England than he had ever been in Kuwait. But that happiness obtained away from home was, in the last analysis, reluctantly admitted, deeply resented, and now even ridiculed. It failed to bring the same ease that he and other Kuwaitis felt in their own land. Kuwaitis always felt the call of their homeland soil, or homeland sand rather. The better off, upper-crust Kuwaitis verged on schizophrenia about it, longing to be in London or California but always hankering after their roots, which they felt had been seriously disturbed by the wealth brought by oil. Kuwaitis are a bit like the apocryphal insurance salesman in England who at the age of twenty-three throws it all in to set up his own business and after years of work ends up a millionaire. When he has made it, he never feels altogether at home with his money and success and reminisces about the good old days, which deep down he knows weren't really good at all.

At about the same time as Monika opened her restaurant, she heard mother-in-law repeatedly mentioning Fawzia, a girl who kept calling Abdulla on the telephone and leaving messages for him. Mother-in-law was very inquisitive and impatient. She wanted to know who Fawzia was and what she wanted.

"Oh, it is nothing. She is just a girl who works with me at the hospital. It's about a patient," Abdulla replied.

Monika took no notice at first but started to show a little interest when Abdulla, himself a patient, lay at the hospital with acute appendicitis. After his successful operation, Monika came to visit as often as she could, alone or with the children. On one of her visits, an already present mother-in-law was busy spinning one of her poison webs. Doubtless, to make Monika jealous, she asked Abdulla in an extra loud voice if that pretty girl Fawzia who had just left his room was the same Fawzia who had left him all those telephone messages. A bit ill at ease, Abdulla tried to change the subject, but his mother rattled on telling him that if he had not been so hasty in taking an English wife he could have brought her someone like Fawzia. While she spoke those beady black eyes were firmly fixed on Monika, who quickly made a short cut to Abdulla's loo to escape the old, uncultivated goat and not to give her the satisfaction of letting her see how the blood had rushed to her head, thanks to her shit stirring. But from then on Monika was all ears when the name of Fawzia would pop up again, for now she was curious and wanted to find out what really connected Abdulla to Fawzia.

After an especially successful day at the Club, where Monika had cashed in on a farewell party she had arranged for a popular person, she visited Abdulla at the hospital; and there, full of pride, she emptied her handbag stuffed to the rim with the day's rich takings. The money spilled all over Abdulla's bed, and he, delighted at the sight of it, praised and kissed her, telling her what he always said to praise her: that a spoiled Kuwaiti wife would never, even in her wildest dreams, know how to do, or want to do, half the things that Monika did—and be pregnant on top of it. At that point, great horror! in walked mother-in-law, saw the money scattered about, and burst into frenzied, obscene language, swearing like a trooper and calling Monika names.

"Crazy, crazy girl! Who taught you to throw money about like that! Not your parents, that's for sure, because they did not have any to do it with! What if visitors come now and see your money-mad wife, my son! We don't have to advertise it that she came to Kuwait for money. The shame! The shame, my son. Here now is the living proof of what I told you, of what I warned you about. She only married you for your money! I have always said it, and I was right!"

Monika gave her a hateful look, which earned her some more vitriol in return.

"Shame on the cunt of your mother that let you escape, you daughter of a dog! Go eat your shit!" she hissed at Monika, who once again stood there speechless, eight months pregnant, while the most primitive of the primitive made no secret of the way she felt about Monika. Abdulla's mother thought that Abdulla had given Monika all that money there and then. After the witch got off her chest what was bothering her, she dropped into a chair and play-acted one of her fake heart attacks. It killed Abdulla's mother to see Monika, the gahba foreigner, with money that she thought should go to herself or her daughters. The old woman was money greedy and money ill. Instead of letting her son take over his inheritance as she should have done according to Islamic law, she put herself firmly in change of the fortune Abdulla's father had left behind; and, still, that fortune was not enough for her. She had her eyes fixed on every single *fils* (penny) whether or not it had anything to do with her. She never spent any of the expropriated money on herself either. If she wanted something, she ordered Abdulla to buy it for her with money of his own. Abdulla—not once, but a hundred times—said to Monika, "Never mind, it will all come back to me one day if my mother dies, God forbid. I will be a multi-millionaire overnight. Then, I will roll in it and enjoy it."

And what did Abdulla do sitting up in his bed like a rabbit, not interrupting his mother while she had that unjustified go at his innocent wife? Yes, he took his mother's side, as usual!

Monika abandoned the money where it was and left the claustrophobic room, but not before turning around and asking the old witch in the most polite Arabic, how the old witch thought Monika should eat her shit, with a spoon? by hand? or was a knife and fork allowed? But, again, on her way home, she felt the loneliest person under Kuwait's blue sky. She did not mind the beastly woman, but Abdulla's action hurt her deeply. He could have just *once* openly defended her. As soon as she reached home, Abdulla started to phone non-stop; and hurt as she was, she just kept hanging up the receiver on him, until the ringing telephone got on her nerves. She gave in, and he asked her for forgiveness. Eight months pregnant, with two kids! What else should, or could, she have done?

With "No woman in the whole world equals the dirt under your finger nails, my Sweetie," said over and over, he got around her. "Please forgive me. Once we are in our own house, we start a whole new life. Just you, me, and our lovely children." Abdulla had a way of raising Monika up to the stars with one hand and pulling her down deep with the other—or rather, up with his mouth and down with his mother. Why couldn't he let her walk side by side with him, as equals? Come to think of it, does any man do that?! Gentle Monika didn't harm a fly, yet she constantly had to swim against a heavy tide.

Through friends at the Club, Monika heard of and employed Sakia, an Egyptian maid from Cairo, to help her with the kids and the baby who was due any day. Sakia was a friendly, clean-cut, 35-or-36-year-old good worker, but whenever Monika came home from the Club, her maid Sakia was occupied with work that mother-in-law or her daughters had ordered Sakia to do while Sulaiman and Nabeel were left to themselves upstairs, or all of the family's children were left in Sakia's care. The in-laws took to bribing her into telling them things they wanted to know about Monika, by giving her chocolates and sweets, or by inviting her to drink tea with them and eat nuts. Sakia understood very well what was going on. She stayed faithful to Monika and did not talk. Those in-laws were like dumb children breaking everything that Monika built up. Monika knew only too well that if she talked and forced the issue, the in-laws would start another *blitz krieg*; so, instead, she changed their daily routine and kept Sakia and the children for a great part of each day at the Club with her. The new house was almost ready now. Monika had steadfastly held on to her hope of freedom in that house. It was her towering strength; it gave her the power to carry on when she was panic stricken. Sakia could not stand Abdulla's family and disliked taking orders from them. Even for an Egyptian servant, this kind of Kuwaiti was too primitive.

And where was Abdulla through all of this? Your guess would have been as good as Monika's.

The only one of Abdulla's children born in Kuwait was his third and last child, and that baby's birth was sheer hell for Monika. She hadn't been scared at all to start with, for she knew that the first was usually the most painful to produce. The second came much more easily. So the third should be no problem at all. Of course, it would be painful, but then Monika was never one to complain and always took her pain bravely. Well in advance, she had asked her doctor, who was chosen by Abdulla, for oxygen to be ready when her time would come, for it had helped her greatly during her first two confinements. She would breathe in the oxygen deeply and push, breathe in and push, no problem. Monika thought herself well prepared. At 3 am, aware that the time had come, she got dressed. Her suitcase—including lots of lovingly hand-knitted baby clothes along with her own stuff—stood by ready. She was full of expectation. A boy or a girl? It would not be long now.

Just the night before, Abdulla had been drinking. He demanded sex. Because she had not let him touch her since he had been drinking, Abdulla declared how much more lucky his friends were. Their Kuwaiti wives never dared to refuse their husbands' sexual urges, drunk or not drunk. Then, he grew abusive, as always, and told her, too, that he was not really in need of her.

"I don't need you. I've got Fawzia, whose black hair reaches down to her waist. And she has big black eyes like almonds. I am sick of your green cat's eyes."

The name Fawzia registered now in Monika's upper chamber, and again Monika thought, "The next thing I do will be to find out who she really is and what is up with her." Monika promised that to herself.

Now, Abdulla did not want to get up, so she prepared him strong black coffee. As she kissed Sulaiman and Nabeel goodbye, the pair of them demanded, "Make it a boy, Mum. Make it a boy! We don't want a soppy girl. We want another boy for a football team." She promised to do her best, but personally thought and felt that this time the baby would be a girl. It had better be, for she already had a baby's wardrobe full of frilly knickers and cute little velvet dresses in all pastel colors. On seeing it all, Abdulla had said, "Don't prepare the medicine until you fall down." He hoped, of course, for another boy. It would give him higher prestige to be the father of three sons than of two boys and a girl; and, yet, in the West the saying goes, "It takes a man to make a girl."

Abdulla drove Monika to the hospital, from where he phoned her doctor at his home. The doctor told Abdulla not to worry, to leave it all to him; he would give the hospital's maternity ward further instructions. Abdulla should leave his wife there in care of the nurses and go home. So Abdulla kissed his wife goodbye and Monika was led into a big white hall that was noisy and busy, like a pressroom in London's Fleet Street. A Kuwaiti wife bears an average of six children or more. Abdulla's mother had had many miscarriages, or Abdulla might have had more brothers—and, just think of it, maybe even one who would have had the guts to stand up to his mother and sisters, thus taking the burden off Abdulla's shoulders. Who knows?

Monika was stripped of her clothes and rudely told off by two nurses for not having shaven her pubic area before coming to the hospital. They shaved her.

"You should have done that for yourself. It's unclean to keep one's pubic hair. Doesn't your husband mind?" they wanted to know.

Monika had no word in reply as she lay there under the blade in a slaughterhouse, so to speak. Next, she was led into an adjoining room and passed on to another two nurses—one Egyptian, the other Iraqi. The two of them—Monika could not believe her ears—started a loud argument about whose turn it was to take a patient into her care.

"You take her. I've got three already," said one.

"No, you take her. I had three yesterday, remember? And I took on a fourth one while you only had two."

Monika, with only a short little white apron on, open at the back, stood in the middle of the room, feeling the contraction, and none of the nurses wanted her. Can you imagine how she must have felt—half nude and shivering, clothes over her arm, in pain, her baby on its way? Not unlike being in a concentration camp!

Then, just like an angel, a sweet, smiling, gentle Indian nurse came along and rescued her. She said, "Don't worry yourself. I have four patients already, which is our limit really, but I'll take you as well." She spoke with a kind, warm voice in good English and led the way to an empty bed, leaving the two bickering nurses (who had obviously chosen the wrong profession) to their now pointless argument. "Your doctor will soon be here," she comforted Monika and helped her into bed, checking her pulse rate and listening to the baby's heartbeat.

Monika lay next to a Palestinian countrywoman who, just about to have her baby, was in great pain and was being told repeatedly and most rudely to "Shut up" by nurses passing by. All this woman was doing was to call out "Yumma, Yumma" (mother, mother), which did not disturb Monika, who could feel with her. But the rude, heartless nurses greatly annoyed and bothered Monika. What really took the cake was when a very young nurse of 18 or 19, who wore a pink striped uniform and glasses and her hair in a ponytail, stood herself in the doorway while putting on surgical gloves and had the cheek to echo each of the poor woman's labor cries of "Yumma" with a loud *Miaauww, miaauww* like a cat. If Monika hadn't thought she might endanger her baby and drop her baby onto the floor, she, mark my words, would have gotten up there and then and slapped that insolent girl's face, and nobody could have stopped her. The Palestinian woman had to give birth to her baby without a doctor. She was shouted at, inhumanely slapped, told off, and shown no mercy by the cold bitches who called themselves nurses. A horrible, horrible experience to witness, while you are lying there helpless and can only hope and pray for better treatment for yourself.

Monika dreaded and worried herself sick over what stood before her. She was trembling and freezing like an autumn leaf when the sweet Indian nurse said goodbye and left her at the end of the night shift at 7 am. An Iraqi, freezer-cold bitch took over; she talked to Monika in a short, sharp tone as if Monika were a prisoner and told her to shut up saying it was hers, the nurse's, business and "not the patient's" when Monika had dared to ask where her doctor was because she was feeling the baby emerge under unbearable pain—pain she had not experienced with her first two babies. Monika was near desperation and just about to pass out when her doctor stood before her. He took one look between her legs and shouted at that rotten nurse and the sister in charge who stood by his side. He wanted to know why he had not been immediately informed of his patient's advanced state and why his telephoned instructions to put her in a private room had not been obeyed. He tore more than pulled the oxygen mask that hung at the head of the bed and put it on Monika's face, ordering her to breathe in as deep as she could and push. She breathed in and in and in until it hurt, but was not able to push for it was much too painful, while the doctor kept shouting at her, "Breathe deeper, draw the oxygen in, breathe and push, breathe in, you stupid woman, you have to help, you know!"

"I can't, doctor. I have no oxygen coming."

The doctor checked the oxygen tank's meter. It was empty! The doctor swore at the nurse and the sister and told them they were unprofessional in the highest degree. Didn't they know that it was not permitted to wear nail polish on duty! Then he raged:

"You are sacked, both of you. Leave the ward at once! I will make sure personally that for the pair of you there are no jobs in all of Kuwait. This, here, is work, a matter of life and death, not an amusement park."

While he was telling them off, he was already holding the baby's head in both hands, and helped it out with a strong, hard push on Monika's belly with his elbow. Under the doctor's shouting at the staff, Boy Number Three was born. The baby was of an ink blue color, and Monika agonized.

"Oh, no, God, please. Oh, no, please. Don't let my baby be dead!"

The baby was taken away hanging upside down by his little legs, like a plucked chicken, while the doctor shouted instructions. It was awful. There are no words in the dictionary that can describe Monika's feelings at that time, in that hellhole. The doctor poured out a whole, huge bottle full of red disinfectant all over his patient's lower body, and he was furious. He apologized to Monika. She hardly heard him. Her only concern right then was for her blue baby. The doctor was assuring her that her newborn boy would be all right, but his words were meaningless to Monika, who felt awful, like a corpse whose intestines were pulled out. She lay shivering with cold, aching inside and outside, all over her body. Even her brain hurt. What a difference to have a baby in Europe under loving care and to have it here in bloody Kuwait. Nothing went right for her in Kuwait, nothing at all. It was as if she lived her whole life there under a curse.

At long last her baby was brought back to her, wrapped in a white sheet. She was loaded onto a trolley with her baby in her arms and taken in an elevator up to a private room. Monika's most traumatic hospital experience was behind her. It had seemed like a bad dream, but it was over. That birthing, without so much as an injection or a little oxygen, had felt like brutal slaughter in comparison with her first two experiences, which were like tea parties.

Abdulla was over the moon. He was now the father of a third son! Now, he had what he had always wished for: three sons, for whom he had big plans. Each one of them should acquire a prestigious profession abroad, in three different major cities. Sulaiman and Nabeel were happy, too, with little Luay—for that's what Monika named her third son, and not, like Sulaiman and Nabeel, after a dead person this time.

Mother-in-law came to see her grandson after five days and, with her visit, changed the family custom of presenting a newborn baby with a gift of gold jewelry. She came bearing a box of tea biscuits worth a quid or two, which Monika gave to the cleaning staff. Monika couldn't bear to look at that box. She had to have it out of her sight, for it was a painful reminder of her real situation. The sisters-in-law hadn't even bothered to bring a roll of toilet paper, ha ha! Instead, they came to insult Monika by arguing and giggling over what the baby resembled more, a rat or a monkey.

"This foreigner shits only boys," Sabiha said. Sabiha the Cow, as Monika mentally referred to her, broke all boundaries of accepted womanly Kuwaiti bitching. Everyone outside the family said of her that she was a madwoman—*magnoon*—simply crazy, moonstruck. She had big ideas and the smallest of minds. She liked being with highly positioned people who did not like to be with her. She was that stupid. Sabiha was not alone: there was lots of jealousy on the part of the in-laws, again, as Monika was now the mother of three boys. Now, that should have made her position much stronger, under normal conditions that is, but Monika's circumstances obviously were not normal.

On first entering a Kuwaiti lady's maternity room, a foreigner might well think he had blundered into a wedding reception instead because he'd find himself in a princess's boudoir. For Kuwaiti women, giving birth is one big ceremony, a well-deserved, long party/fashion show held in bed among sets of silk nightgowns and feathered robes and Cinderella sandals (designer labels, naturally). Hairdressers and manicurists at hand, the new mothers rest in their own Swiss hand-finished, embroidered, silk and muslin bed linens and coverlets. In the bathroom hang, likewise, matching sets of embroidered towels with matching bath mats. Gold plated tissue boxes, full silver fruit bowls, elegant flasks of the latest popular French perfumes, powders and colognes and boxes of fine Swiss chocolates decorate the dressing tables. The whole room is pleasantly scented with "bochoor."

Bochoor and Aseel Kuwaiti go hand in hand. Bochoor is an incense imported from India. Specially grown rosewood tree roots are chopped small and boiled with rose oil and the natural oils of other pleasant smelling, fragrance-producing bushes and flowers. Every Kuwaiti family has one or more incense burners standing beside the popular rosewater sprinklers in silver and gold urns of different design. The incense burners have a small opening in the middle for inserting a piece of lit charcoal on which a tiny piece of bochoor is then placed; and up climb the heavy, magic fumes, pleasantly overpowering one's senses. In fact, Kuwaitis scent their houses while intoning Islamic prayers, thereby getting rid of evil spirits with the incense-fragrance before visitors arrive and so that everybody who enters is powerless to cast an evil eye or other negative vibes; and then they all treat themselves by standing over the scented coal letting the precious smoke waft and climb up their skirts and dresses and abayas—and, lastly, by bending their heads over the precious fumes to soak them up deep into their hair. Men stand like women with open legs over the container to let the smoke creep in their white dishdashas, then bend over it to drench their headdresses, too. Arab men do a lot of kissing of foreheads and noses, so it is nice to smell pleasant. As with cigars, though, both cheap and expensive varieties of bochoor exist. A handful of expensive bochoor can be purchased for around a thousand British pounds (or more, for the very best), but the cost is well worth it. A sheikh may pass though some corridor; and when you come by an hour later, the smell of his bochoor still lingers on. It is fabulous. No French perfume can do what bochoor does. Now, bochoor is truly the mystic Middle East. Monika always lit up some bochoor, even in her car, and still does so; she loves it. The equivalent liquid scent to bochoor is "Dehen Ood," and that's the most expensive essence of perfume oil in the world. Every Kuwaiti woman has at least a tiny flask of it hidden away somewhere. There is so much kissing going on and being done—by men to men, and women to women—that one feels so much more confident with a whiff of "Dehen Ood" behind the ear. But let's go back to those princesses' boudoirs.

Persian rugs are laid out around the bed with soft pillows for visiting bottoms that find chairs much too uncomfortable and on which the maid then sleeps, close by, at night.

Coffee and tea are brought in thermal flasks at least twice a day and offered with nuts and sweets to visitors and their children who come and go noisily, flowing steadily like a stream of water, steadily and endlessly. Small Kuwait has very large families. Everybody seems to be related to everybody else, so the maternity room ends up looking like some flower boutique with heaps of neatly wrapped packages, gifts, piled in one corner. Every visitor comes with full hands; one simply has to outshine the others. For the visiting women who have nothing else better to do, it's an enjoyable day out, for they come to see, to hear, and to be seen. Once back home with her baby, the new mother and her visitors continue to discuss—within the close family circle and over tea and nuts—everything that they observed in the maternity ward, down to the smallest detail of the hair clips that so-and-so wore.

It's no wonder that young women put on so much weight after their first child. The traditional dish of *cabut*, a very rich curry of meat and dumplings mildly spiced with herbs is especially prepared at home for the new mother and brought to her bedside every day for two to three weeks after her delivery and eaten in the belief that it will strengthen slack muscles and help to close and tighten the over-stretched vagina.

Now, here at least, Monika was in luck because nobody cared about her. Nobody forced that stuffing into her, thank God.

Soon after having recovered from giving birth to Luay, Monika made her way longingly to her almost finished house. On her way there, she had to pass by Sabiha's new house. When she saw Sabiha's house, Monika slammed on her brakes and stopped the car, hot sweat pouring from the pores of her skin as her stomach did a turn. Monika sat there in disbelief, looking at the pretty iron fence that stood proudly all around Sabiha's house. It was Monika's very own original wrought iron fence, the one that she had taken so much care and skill to draw and that was, of course, nowhere else to be seen in Kuwait because Monika had designed it for her own house and because it had come out of her fantasy world. The first thing that went through Monika's head was, "I wonder what other ideas of mine sister-in-law has copied?" Doing stuff like that was typical of Sabiha! She must have stolen it out of Monika's folder, where all the new-house material was kept tidily together. Untrustworthy Abdulla must have been the one who showed the plans to his sister behind Monika's back because Monika kept the folder well hidden on top of the wardrobe under a suitcase where only Abdulla knew its place.

Monika turned around nervously, agitated, and drove back home, boiling, to check her folder. Of course, that drawing was missing altogether! Abdulla was sorry for showing it to his sister (after which he added, "Big deal!"). Monika asked Abdulla to find out from Fahad where Fahad had gotten his fence idea, and Fahad said it was Sabiha's, that Sabiha had seen it somewhere in Europe! So tell me, what was there left to do but for Monika to shut up, give in, sit down, and think of a new design? If Sabiha had only asked, maybe through Fahad or Abdulla (because Monika and Sabiha did not speak anymore), Monika would probably have obliged. She was always willing to advise and to help every member of the al-Amahani family, as she had been doing for years on end. But, here, to steal from her!—she could have exploded with anger to think of the cheek of it.

Monika was submitted to such unpleasant manipulations constantly, and they finally got her down. She had no one to talk to, no one to turn to. She was the innocent party and, automatically, the one who had to give in to injustice again and again. So, slowly but surely, although she had been born a strong ram, the stress more and more got the better of her. And so, as any expert might have predicted, Monika went physically and mentally downhill. Abdulla, her "husband," the father of her sons, was never any help. The opposite, in fact, was true. He was the one who pulled her down.

CHAPTER SEVENTEEN

TAKING UP AGAINST A SEA OF TROUBLES

Not her once-bright spirit, nor her sparkling mind, nor her body—nor anybody else's—could be subjected to such barbarous life and get away unscathed.

Sulaiman's doggy Twinkle, the puppy he'd gotten at his first birthday party, was passed along to an English couple in Kuwait a couple of days before Abdulla and Monika had taken off to England for his two-year course. On their return to Kuwait, Monika, who loved animals and wanted her children to grow up with them, bought Fiffy, a female Siamese kitten, thinking that a cat could cause much less bother with her in-laws than her dog had in the past. As soon as Fiffy was old enough, she had been taken to Aya's Siamese male to mate and was now successfully expecting. Monika put a padded cardboard box under Luay's baby-crib and picked Fiffy up frequently, putting her into the box so that she could get the feel of it and learn that this box was the spot in which to have her babies. Fiffy, like so many animals, had an almost human understanding and was extremely lovable. The only thing she didn't do was speak. She would wake Monika punctually in the mornings at 7 am by nibbling her ear lobes and licking her nose, which tickled. And, when Monika was really down and out (which was a lot of the time) and was having a good cry, Fiffy would jump onto her lap and look her straight in the eyes as if to say, "Hey, don't worry. I am here to comfort you," and she would press her body forcefully against Monika's.

One day when Monika, Sakia, and the children came home from an outing, Fiffy miaowed impatiently and led the party proudly to her box, in which four woolly, fluffy, nutshell-colored bundles of kitty cat slept peacefully rolled up. Fiffy got praise no end and was rewarded with a hefty portion of fresh liver on top of it, but as soon as the in-laws found out about the kittens, they started pestering Abdulla with horrid stories about the sorts of illnesses that cats in Kuwait were contaminating babies with. They carried on saying that Monika was irresponsible to keep five cats in such close contact with baby Luay. Abdulla—what else?—agreed with them and put pressure on Monika. The more the in-laws pushed, the more Monika got worried for her baby, and when poor Fiffy, who must have sensed something, kept trailing her young from one place to another and they ended up in Luay's baby dresser amid his diapers and vests and then on Luay's pillow, close to his head, Monika just had to put Fiffy and her babies out on the balcony. She did it thinking, "Just for now, till they have grown up a bit," but it was winter in Kuwait and icy cold, and although Monika fed them well, they all got sick and died, one after the other, with Fiffy the last to go.

Monika will never, ever forget the last glassy reproachful look that Fiffy gave her from her ill, multi-colored eyes before lying down to die, too. Monika knelt by her side on the cold tiles, crying and stroking her, pleading repeatedly, "Forgive me, Fiffy. Please, forgive me, Fiffy. You are much better off now. You have been a good girl."

Today, Monika knows better. She knows, first of all, that the in-laws were simply jealous of her having (and being able to look after) beautiful animals and, second, that their stupid saga about cats spreading illness to babies in Kuwait was all made-up poppycock. If it had really been true, the evil lot would not have said anything.

Monika had never had any experience with animals prior to doggy Twinkle and the cats and therefore knew nothing much about pets; but to this day Monika still can't believe that she was the cruel human being who allowed those poor, faithful, lovely cats she loved to die such a miserable a death. It just shows the impact of the forces she was constantly subject to. She was not allowed to be a person in her own right. They took over her mind. Instead of being a fish that swam against the tide, as she had done in the past, Monika became weaker and weaker under the constant pressure. She became increasingly submissive, to the extent that she even started to think, "Maybe they are really right and I'm wrong."

Two weeks after little Luay was born, Monika was back in full charge of her restaurant. Some members were surprised she had had a baby, for they had never even noticed her bulge. Others praised her tiny waist, tiny so soon after having given birth. The praise was well earned because Monika had resolutely starved herself to get back in shape.

Sakia, dressed in a nurse's white uniform, imported from Vienna, complete with a cute little cap and white shoes, walked Luay in his pram. Copycat Sabiha was soon to adopt that idea and had her maid, too, walk around wearing white.

Abou Abla, the trusted man who was left in charge of the restaurant when Monika was absent, like any average hot-blooded Kuwaiti male, had a weakness for pretty, foreign ladies who came to the club. A Club committee member told Monika he had noticed that Abou Abla gave away ice creams and alcohol-free beer free of charge to a German lady who wore a yellow bikini and who came into the restaurant every day before she left the Club. Monika didn't really believe it. She had to find out the truth behind this accusation against her trusted Abou Abla. So, she made a plan. She had to see for herself, with her own eyes. She borrowed a long-haired, black wig and pretty clothes from Neshur, one of her Kuwaiti friends, smudged layers of dark make-up all over her body, put on lots of black mascara and eye liner to make her look

Eastern. She put on a straw hat and carried a straw bag. Huge owl glasses covered most of her face. All ready to go on a spying trip in a first-class disguise, Monika was highly pleased with the way she looked in the mirror. She didn't recognize herself. When she tried to slip through the club's reception area, she was caught. Hassan asked for her membership card! So to her great amusement and laughter, she divulged herself to Hassan and explained what she was about to do. He complimented her on her fabulous disguise and brilliant idea. Monika walked down the beach, looking out for the German lady in question, spotted her, sat fully dressed (as Arab women do) not far from her, and began looking through Arabic magazines. Abdulla would not have allowed Monika to undress—remember?—so she sat there and fried in the heat a good two hours or so, sweating like a pig, before the bikini-clad, long-legged German woman's husband turned up to fetch her. The woman got up, collected her things, and made her way (together with her husband) towards the restaurant. While she went in, her spouse waited outside. Monika was quick to enter the restaurant and to order a Coke from Abou Abla before the woman could get to him. Abou Abla handed Monika the bottle, took her money, politely thanked her, and did not recognize his boss when he handed her the change. Abou Abla was all eyes for the fair bikini-maid, who stood close behind Monika. He clapped his hands together loudly, smiled at the lady in question, and stood two bottles of beer in front of her; then he made his way to the ice cream fridge and came back with four cups of Coffee Cream Whirl, Monika's favorite.

"This is very good! This is the best ice cream we have. This is from me to you, pretty lady," he serenaded the lucky German as his sparkling, lusty eyes followed the curves of the well-proportioned, almost nude body right down to her toes. Monika, pretending to be busy with her Coke, stood close by watching their every move through her glasses and took in the visual pleasure Abou Abla got out of doing what he was doing. The German—whose husband didn't move from his spot outside and who must have known that there would be nothing free coming their way if he stood by her side—held her money purse in her hands, yet made no gesture to open it and to pay for what he had received while sly Abou Abla opened the till and let his fingers run noisily through the clicking coins that lay already in the till. He did that so as not to arouse suspicion among the rest of the staff. He didn't know he was already sussed out. And then Monika spoke.

"Abou Abla, why doesn't the lady pay?"

A shocked Abou Abla looked up to where the familiar voice was coming from, straight at Monika, but of course he didn't recognize her. His head shot from right to left, front and back, searching for Monika, saying, "Madam, madam, where are you?"—searching even underneath the counter while Monika started stripping off her disguise, her hat, glasses, and black wig. She asked the now speechless Abou Abla (who stood dumb struck in front of her) and the German for how long this had been going on. The German girl said she thought the restaurant belonged to him. She was lying, trying to take advantage of the moment, for every member of the Club knew it was Monika's. The German girl never showed her face in the restaurant again, and Abou Abla was ever so remorseful. He admitted that only by giving something away for nothing could he get the attention of a pretty female.

Monika, getting wiser and wiser about how male brains in Arabia clicked from her experiences with Abdulla, his friends, and the other Club members, understood Abou Abla all too well and forgave him. Doesn't everybody have his weakness? For instance, Shamsheed, the new Irani waiter, had developed the bad habit of cleaning away guests' glasses at barbecues and parties held at the Club when they were still half full of home-made Flash while the guests went onto the dance floor. He drank it himself, hidden in the kitchen, sharing it with Mustafa the cook, who turned out to be a crook, too.

Mustafa's kitchen helper, who peeled potatoes and cleaned the vegetables, always left earlier than the rest of the staff. One day, while

Monika (who made all her own puddings) stood over a hot stove stirring cream caramel, she was surprised to see black Mustafa, a bear of a man and always very proud, carrying the garbage can out to the back yard, which was not his job and which he'd refuse to do if he were asked or ordered to. Monika sensed something fishy was going on here; and, while letting a couple of possibilities for his voluntary action run through her brain, she kept her eyes fixed on the trash can through the kitchen window. She was rewarded by a glimpse of the long-gone kitchen helper, whose head was popping up right over it. She knew instantly what was going on. She told unsuspecting Mustafa to take over stirring her cream caramel while she went to spend a penny, walked slowly out of the kitchen, then ran to the first person she could find in charge of the Club. Soon, six men were running towards the trashcan. They caught the kitchen helper red handed, walking away with an onion sack full of stolen frozen meat on his back, like Santa Claus. In that sack there were two of everything, one for each of them (him and Mustafa): two chickens, two packets of liver, two packs of fish fingers, two steaks, two boxes of hamburgers, 12 dozen each, two legs of lamb, two packs of sausages. The kitchen helper admitted there and then that what he was doing had been going on twice a month ever since he had first started his job upon the recommendation of Mustafa, six months earlier, and that Mustafa was the master brain behind the thieving. The police were called. Mustafa was arrested and put in prison, only to be let out the following day upon the orders of some sheikh in whose kitchen Mustafa's cousin worked and who got him the wasta. Mustafa was free to go and do his thieving elsewhere, supported by the mighty, unofficial, yet very official "wasta law" of Kuwait

A well-known Kuwaiti VIP—a sheikh and friend of Abdulla and Monika—had killed his non-Kuwaiti mistress with a gun when he caught her leaving another man's house, where she had been making love, so he thought, but the well-known man was only symbolically jailed and was later found living a life of luxury in Beirut. The Aseel

Kuwaitis always manage to work something out between themselves to avoid the law and the police. That's great, right? It makes you feel the country you were born in really is your country so long as it does not overstep its mark. It's usually the poor non-Kuwaiti devils who feel the hand of the strict Kuwaiti Islamic law the hardest, often quite cruelly and unjustly. Take, for instance, the case of one of Abdulla's friends. He was a highly respected Palestinian gynecologist, who in the line of duty reported to his directors at the hospital that a certain police officer, whose duty it was to stand guard outside a pregnant, unmarried bedouin girl's room to prevent her brothers from killing her, spent the night inside a female ward where a nurse he fancied worked. That doctor and his pregnant wife, on their way home from a visit to friends late one night, were stopped by three policemen on motorbikes who appeared out of nowhere. One of them was the officer in question, who was out to give the doctor tit for tat. The couple was ordered out of their car and brutally assaulted by the three policemen, who took turns. They repeatedly kicked the pregnant woman's stomach with their boots until she lay unconscious. The doctor found his glasses broken in a thousand splinters, as he scrambled to his hurting legs. To cut the story short, the woman lost the baby, the doctor resigned, and they immigrated to America. He sent his Kuwaiti nationality, achieved through honors, back to the Ministry of Justice. Kuwait lost a fine doctor. And there are numerous cases like it.

Kuwait's army and police corps consist almost one hundred percent of Kuwait's bedouins. Those are the only two institutions in which foreigners have no access to jobs. Even so, being a mere policeman is a bit degrading for an Aseel or educated Kuwaiti, so the only option left for the Government is to hire Kuwaiti bedouins, who often misuse their power out of sheer ignorance but are very faithful to their rulers. The police would never, ever dare to treat an Aseel Kuwaiti the way they treated the Palestinian doctor.

Once again, as had happened so many times before, Monika's restaurant had run out of bread rolls. It was scorching hot when Monika jumped in her car, drove to and pulled into a parking space near the bakery out of which a Kuwaiti's car had just driven. A policeman on a bike stopped next to her, his arm waving.

"*Yella, yella!*" he shouted at her, meaning "Go on, go on, move!"

"Why should I move on?" she demanded in Arabic, which took the officer by surprise.

"You can't park here."

"Who says that?"

The policeman looked flustered, especially now as shoppers, shop owners, and laborers from nearby were beginning to gather around to hear this row in Arabic between a bedouin and a European.

"Who do you think you are?" Monika asked. "Just because you think I am European, you think I am scared of you? You are taking advantage of your uniform. You think I am a foreigner ignorant of the law, like so many European women to whom you can show off. Well, I am sorry, but today is just not one of your days because I am not one of them. My husband belongs to the al-Amahani family. He taught me the law, which doesn't say anything about a Kuwaiti's being allowed to park here and *not* me because I am a white woman; so find yourself another fool you can play silly games with, or better, go and do something useful. *Masalama* (goodbye)!" Monika turned on her heels, the small crowd parted, some bystanders clapped for her, and she went to buy her bread rolls. The meddlesome bedouin had picked on Monika to exercise his power in public over a white woman. Maybe, Monika speculated, it gave him a hard-on.

Like many white women in Kuwait, Monika was followed in her car at least once a week by one Aseel Arab or another, who had only one thing in mind—sex, of course—even when she was driving with her children. It became routine for protective Sulaiman to sit in his mother's car well prepared with a packet of eggs or small stones close by, which he would aim at the cheeky drivers' cars. His mother often had to keep him forcefully from using big bricks and other materials of self defense, for accidents could be caused that would be much worse in outcome than those ignorant men's advances. If those men drove up close making their suggestions verbally or in sign language, Monika could not help spitting in their direction or telling them in Arabic to go fuck their mothers and sisters, first, before talking like that to a respectable woman, or she would say, "You really don't think that I am a prostitute like your mother and sisters are known to be all over Kuwait, do you?" She knew that that was the right medicine to treat them with, and they took off like tornadoes! Monika kept a special pad and pen in her car just for writing down the license plate numbers of men that gave her more than a meaningful look and bothered her on the road. The men addressed her always as English in English, and when she answered them in Arabic with a Kuwaiti accent, they just knew she was the wife of a Kuwaiti and took off at high speed.

Abdulla would give the numbers, after Monika had collected a few, to a police chief friend of his, who would find out the identity of the guilty drivers who had bothered his wife and given them a good telling off, but only if they were of no big, well-known Aseel family. And if they were, *forget it!*—nothing would be done.

A bedouin taxi driver followed Monika once, right bang into the middle of the Sea Club after he had chased her for fifteen minutes, driving up on the right, staying back, driving up on the left, passing her, and so on. She drove up right to the restaurant's back entrance and jumped out without bothering to switch off the engine to give alarm. Abdulla, who sat playing cards, ran outside and had no difficulty in catching up with the bearded, brown-toothed bedouin, who now looked scared and knew he had made a big mistake. He was trying desperately to reverse in a hurry, but got stuck in the desert sand. Abdulla walked up to him and found him to be a patient he had recently treated.

"Why do you follow my wife?" he asked him in a sharp voice.

"Oh, I thought she was a girl I knew," came his excuse, scared shitless.

"Now tell me, you live in a the desert in a tent. How do you happen to know a white woman?" asked Abdulla. And by saying, "I will take you to the police station for a good whipping," Abdulla only meant to frighten the middle-aged bedouin, who turned into apology itself before Abdulla let him off the hook with a stern warning and helped his taxi's back wheels into motion.

Another time, Monika was driving together with Aya on one of Kuwait's lovely wide roads when a white, gold-plated Cadillac (like so many cars in Kuwait!) drove up close beside them and a voice said in perfect English, "Hello, darlings." A fat-faced, mustachioed man in his fifties, wearing diamond rings and a diamond Rolex watch, addressed the girls.

"Would you like to follow me?" he offered. "You can name your price, just name it. Money is no object. Or do you prefer gold? Maybe a present of gold? The choice is entirely yours if you follow me and be nice to me."

Monika at such times almost always blew her top. She could have smashed her car into his out of spite, for she just could not get used to the fact that every male who set eyes on her and who did not know her identity took her for a prostitute in Kuwait. While Monika searched her head for a fitting answer to give to that fatty in his big limo, who in the meantime had driven up on the right to look at Aya, and then back over to the left again, to get a closer look at Monika while maybe fantasizing who would be doing what to him, Aya shouted at him in Arabic.

"We are both at your service for free. Do you want it from the back or the front? Follow us to the police station. We will do a threesome there." After which, the white Cadillac took off like a torpedo. Monika and Aya laughed their heads off. They did not even bother to write this man's license plate number down, for judging by the look of it, his identity would surely never be divulged to Abdulla. And even if it were, what—tell me—would Abdulla do anyway?!

Monika had not been brought up with and, as a girl, did not know any foul language. She only started to use it in England—where she had learned some from Abdulla—in quarreling with him about his constant pursuit of other girls or his drinking—and because *he* used it. Yet, in Kuwait, using harsh and foul language in Arabic is the only way a white woman can protect herself from the insults and advances of Arab men. So she had to learn, and learn she did. Arabs did not expect her to use such strong language. The effect of Monika's responses, then, was to cause the offensive men to recoil in shame and embarrassment. Swearing oaths in Arabic is quite different from, say, swearing in English. Bad language is put to use rather than just dropped in as the odd word here and there, as in English. It revolves generally around an insult to some member of the offensive person's family. "Go screw your mother." "Crawl back into the cunt of your mother." "Eat mother's shit." "You son of a dog." "Go shit on your father's grave." And so on. On the other hand, oaths are common and not always designed to insult. If an Arab wished to impress an acquaintance with his truthfulness, he might say, "I cut off my penis if I am telling a lie. I swear on my mother's life if what I say is not true. If what I say is not true, then my mother is a whore and I am her bastard." Because of the importance to an Arab of his immediate family, insults and promises are made on their honor or lives, whether they have any honor or not.

Kuwait's sea has taken many lives: in the old days, those of pearl divers and fishermen; and more recently, those of pleasure boat riders in their luxurious yachts, taken by surprise by sharks or the weather while out at high sea; those of Iranis, seeking illegally to work in Kuwait, the promised land, where they think money grows on the desert cactuses. Those poor chaps pay high sums of money to boat owners in Iran to be taken across the gulf at night, but if spotted by Patrol Police, they are forced to jump into the sea and then have to swim for their lives. They die by drowning when they get tired or can't swim properly or their dishdashas are washed above their arms, which hinders them as they swim. And they drown before or after sharks attack them. Their bodies would sometimes be washed up on the Club's shore. Sometimes Monika could not resist taking a look at them, and afterwards felt sick for the rest of the day.

The hanky panky, the bit of nooky, such goings-on as Monika witnessed at the Sea Club took her a big step closer to understanding why Kuwaitis called "*Gahba!*" after every European woman they saw in the street. Monika was sad when she heard her own two offspring, hanging out of her car window, calling, "*Gahba, Gahba,*" at a white woman walking along. It was something they had learned from other kids. Of course, they did not know what it meant then; they just imitated. European women had a bad name because some of them really did behave like prostitutes in Kuwait, and their husbands, of all people, eagerly encouraged them, too. Where there is smoke there is fire. When a party to which Monika and Abdulla were invited was held at a middle-aged English couple's home, Monika could not believe her eyes and ears. The hostess was everybody's. While the host, a respected engineer working for Kuwait Airways, offered homemade Flash and walked around making the guests feel at home, the hostess disappeared with one Arab chap, one after another, into her bedroom, where her skirt must have gone up and down like theater curtains.

Monika was in no way prudish, but those goings-on overstepped the mark and disgusted her, especially when she overheard the Arabs afterwards, who, not realizing that Monika understood what they were saying, openly discussed like heroes their various positions and the ways they had had their kicks with the English woman. One would brag, "I let her suck my cock." Another said, "So did I. I came in her mouth," while another beamed, "I didn't do it from the front because she stank, so I fucked her up the arse."

Once, Monika asked an older engineer, whose wife appeared to be a very upper-crust, respectable looking woman in her forties but who was known to be a tart, if he didn't mind what his wife was obviously up to. "No, not at all, my dear," he replied. "She is a couple of years younger than me. I want her to have her fun. Why shouldn't she? She gets lovely gifts, like the priceless gems she is wearing now," referring to a set of diamond-and-ruby-encrusted jewels that decorated his wife, "which I could never, ever afford to give her because we have been saving to buy a pub (back in the English countryside) for as long as I can remember, but now, another year and we go back home and no-one there is going to be any the wiser."

The old, old story! It was money, the root of all evil, that led many a respectable person or couple into degrading behavior that they would be ashamed to own up to back home. Monika could not swear to it that most of those women—and their husbands, too, mind you—didn't get more than money out of it. But, come to think of it, money was the main reason for which all those foreigners were in Kuwait in the first place. And Monika observed how they spoke in awe to the Aseels (the money bags) and almost with bowed heads.

European couples swapped partners at home and played tootsie on the beach out of sheer boredom, having nothing much else to do, while others drove out to the sea to exchange partners in their boats, where a woman might jump into an Arab's boat for a quickie while others lay in wait in their boats, getting kicks out of spying on them with binoculars and then coming back to the Club to report like journalists on whom they had caught and with whom. It was a colorful life at the Sea Club. A couple of people were dismissed for misconduct, which usually had to do with sex. The naughty, sexy, exhibitionist group was, of course, in the minority, and Monika kept her distance from them: so much as a cup of tea with them and she knew she would be labeled as one of their kind.

Sex plays a major part in the lives of the outwardly strict Kuwaiti Muslims, just as it does all over the rest of the world, if not more so because it is forbidden and so much energy is required to keep it well disguised behind an almost fanatically religious fake front. The majority of Kuwaitis, Westernized and illiterate alike, live a useless life that's food, drink, and sex, with a little work done in between. Although as a rule a single girl or woman won't get (or will have trouble getting) a visiting visa to enter Kuwait alone for just that reason (sex), hundreds of pretty, pleasure girls from all over Europe are solicited and flown to Kuwait weekly or monthly. They enter with wasta visas from Kuwaiti VIP's in high positions. Those girls stay a short time at some big hotel, or they land on some rich man's yacht or in one of the mazrahas of men whose unsuspecting, non-person wives sit at home while the men leisurely enjoy the skin and flesh of their white crumpets and quench their sex libidos to overflowing—after which the girl or girls (who come through some agency, are stewardesses on some Middle Eastern airline, or are passed on by some friend from abroad) are sent back where they came from with a tidy sum of money and usually with a generous gift or gifts of beautifully crafted jewelry. Some girls come away with 5,000 pounds sterling for the weekend, plus little or big designer trinkets.

It has captured Monika's attention that Kuwaiti men in general look rather youthful for their age while their women usually look much older than they are. Is the reason for that eternal male youthfulness maybe the fact that so much money and time is dedicated to extra-marital affairs? It could be. Love, after all, is the fountain of eternal youth. Or is it sex? Arab men seem to be insatiable when it comes to sex while their wives get it only when their masters fancy them with what strength they have left over after the side kicks. Kuwaiti women are raised to show no interest whatsoever in sex, even if they feel like and fancy it, because (they are taught) it is bad to admit to wanting and enjoying sex. It can't do them much good, either physically or mentally, to hold back, to suppress nature that way. Especially not when so many younger women are aware nowadays of Western ways, including feminism.

Children with European mothers don't have it easy at school either. Little Sulaiman was called out of class once and asked by his teacher—male, of course—if it was true that his mother was European.

"Yes, sir," said Sulaiman.

"Does your mother shave her hair down there?" The teacher pointed toward his crotch.

"No, sir," answered poor Sulaiman, ashamed and disgusted, for he knew it was not right for his teacher to ask him that.

Monika took the children on a drive along the seaside one afternoon, passing a couple of cars on whose tops young men sat on carpets, tea or coffee flask at hand, smoking and chatting and looking about aimlessly to pass the time. Those young men took pleasure in looking inside passing cars and giving the girls they saw going by, foreign and Kuwaiti girls, that is, the eye and a whistle. The much-restricted Kuwaiti girls, in return, toured the streets in twos and threes, more or less for the same reason, to look at the guys and do a spot of flirting. Little folded bits of paper with telephone numbers written on them kept flipping in and out of cars passing by each other on the road. It was an everyday Kuwaiti scene in the afternoons. On that particular day, Monika was whistled at and spoken to in English. One especially enthusiastic young man shouted at her from the top of his Chevrolet, "Hello, darling. How about us two? Take the children home and come back to me. I'll be waiting." Before Monika could do anything, Sulaiman put his head out the window and spat at the cheeky guy, but his spit did not reach that far up and landed bang in the middle of the window. Little Sulaiman pulled himself in and sat down like lightning, feeling very sorry about what he had just done, for he realized that the man up there was his religion teacher. That was all Monika needed to know. She turned the car around under heavy protest from Sulaiman and gave that teacher a mouthful, a bucketful. She told him she would report him to the

Minister of Education, who was a close friend of her husband. The teacher was scared. He apologized then and there and again by letter afterwards because she had indeed reported him. Kuwaitis only dare to treat foreigners, especially women, so shittily (to use the vernacular!) because foreigners don't know what to do about it; and, anyway, foreigners are regarded as parasites who just come to their country to take away money. They should be given a short course before departing to Kuwait by somebody like Monika.

Sulaiman and, later, Nabeel, too, had far from happy childhoods in Kuwait, even apart from their bitchy blood relatives at home. The poor souls would tell their friends at school that their mother was Lebanese, which although not good was still much better than the truth. To have an Arab mother, any sort of Arab mother, was preferable to having a European mother, for they were trying to avoid being told, "Your mother is an Ingilesia, a gahba." Little Sulaiman said one day to Monika, "Mum, I love you very, very much, but please don't come to fetch me anymore from school. They call me and you—always!—such horrible names the next day." Sulaiman had to deny his mother, and that hurt Monika very much. But, for Sulaiman's sake and from then on, only the driver transported Sulaiman, and later Nabeel, to and away from school. Children can be much more cruel than adults, although it is very hard to out-do Monika's in-laws in cruelty.

The last nasty stroke wielded by the in-laws before Monika moved finally into her own castle was caused by a fight over Nabeel's red, sit-in toy car. Monika had bought it for him recently, and as usual Saud, Sabiha's son, demanded by force to play with it when Nabeel was sitting in it and enjoying it on the big veranda upstairs. Fed up with not getting what he wanted, Saud hit Nabeel hard in the face. Monika didn't stand for that, of course. She told Saud the car belonged to Nabeel and that if Nabeel wanted to he would lend it to him and if not, bad luck—he would just have to wait until Nabeel did—but, in any case, that he could not have his way by force of hitting the younger boy. A crying Saud took off downstairs to complain to his grandmother just as Abdulla was coming home.

Monika could smell a rat as, united with his mother and Tamader, the three of them came hastily up the stairs as they had so many times before. Abdulla headed straight for the poor little innocent Nabeel and took over where Saud had left off by hitting him hard across the face, ordering, "Get out of the car! Let Saud play with the car." Then he pulled his own flesh and blood out of the car by force. Nabeel's little legs got caught between the pedals, and he cried out loud. But his enraged, wound-up father kept pulling even harder. Monika ran to screaming Nabeel's rescue, freed his legs, and then pulled him out of Abdulla's arms while Abdulla quickly lifted Saud, who was much too big and fat for the car, and squeezed him into the seat to the accompanying approving remarks made by mother-in-law. When Monika saw a thin stream of blood running down Nabeel's little leg, she could not hold herself back.

"I hate you, you bloody savage bastard!" she shouted at Abdulla. "I can't wait till my kids grow up and can protect themselves from you and your mad tribe for themselves, you two-faced chicken!"

Mother-in-law told Monika to shut up, that in Kuwait women don't shout at men, but show them respect, that it was not Monika's house to boss about in, and that her children's toys were bought with Abdulla's money, which belonged to everybody in the family, and that if Monika did not like sharing she could go back to Europe where she belonged. Tamader, among other nasties, called her "Gahba" again and again. Monika was in tears when she responded.

"If there is a gahba present, then I am afraid it is *you*, Tamader."

The next thing happened very fast. Abdulla picked up a small wrought-iron table that stood minding its own business and threw it mightily at his wife to impress his mother and sister and to give them satisfaction. Blood poured from a gushing wound, which scar Monika sports to this day on her upper arm as a reminder of that last scene in the Horror House of Keefan. Yes, that's how Abdulla al-Amahani, who was well-liked, even loved, by everybody he met, treated his sons and the mother of his three children when he was under the influence of his mother and sisters. Had people been told, they would most likely never have believed that kindly Abdulla was capable of being such a cruel person. Street Angel, House Devil.

It was high time for Monika to leave that evil house because she was just about to lose her grip on her own reality. She was starting to look for faults within herself each time she was victimized. The atmosphere had completely deteriorated. It was rotten. More jealousy had grown because Monika was soon to live in her own new, modern house and because it had really turned out a dream. From the workers, she had found out that the in-laws never ceased coming regularly to inspect progress. Sabiha had said there was some hidden secret in the house on which she couldn't quite put her finger. What she was talking about was probably taste, simply Monika's good taste, which neither Sabiha nor anybody else in that family had and which none of them was likely to acquire with all the money in the world because, like charisma, either you have it or you don't and nothing in this world can change that. Now, whenever mother-in-law heard Monika's car drive up, she would busy herself somewhere in the big entrance hall of the house; but when Monika walked in, greeting her, the old woman would never reply. Monika would have bet her bottom dollar that if *she* had walked past the troublemaker without saying a word of greeting Abdulla's mother would then have complained vociferously to Abdulla that his wife had passed by and insulted her by ignoring her.

At a Palestinian wedding to which the al-Amahani family was invited and at which men and women mingled, Monika and Abdulla sat close to a good-looking Indian banker. The official ceremony over, people got up to help themselves at a sumptuous buffet. Monika took a little on two plates—one for herself and the other for Abdulla—walked back, and was just about to sit down when her ear caught what that banker was asking Tamader, who was standing near by but bent over so that her long, black hair blocked her view to left and right in such a way that she could not see that Monika was back at her seat and could hear her, too.

"From where—and who—is the pretty, blonde foreign lady with your brother?" the man asked Tamader.

"She is his wife, but she is nothing. She comes from Austria and is very naughty. She gives my mother lots of headaches, and all of us don't like her. My brother thinks of divorcing her," etc., etc.

The food got stuck in shame in Monika's throat. Monika felt rushing blood flushing her cheeks while Tamader was in her element, just jumping at the chance to degrade her sister-in-law.

Monika told Abdulla what she had heard, but Abdulla—what else?—said he did not believe her. So Monika dared him to ask the Indian what Tamader had just said. It took her a hell of a lot of convincing, after which Abdulla finally did ask, and the Indian, a gentleman, confirmed the story.

"Please do not worry. Don't take it to heart. We, as you know, have the same trouble in India. Jealous family feuds are fought in all Eastern families. It is part of our culture, but may I congratulate you on your pretty wife, Mr. Abdulla?"

"Never mind, Sweetie. Tamader is a child. She is only behaving that way because she is jealous"—that was Abdulla's total reaction concerning the incident. It would not have occurred to him to confront his sister nor to defend his wife because he knew he would only have gotten a foul mouthful from Tamader.

CHAPTER EIGHTEEN

MONIKA'S NEW HOME IS BEAUTIFUL

Monika's new home stood at long last proudly ready for her and the kids to move into and thus leave all the misery of the past seven years behind. The house was built on one thousand square meters of grounds adjacent to the area's mosque, whose loud "Allah-o-Akbar" screams—day and night—from loudspeakers attached to all four sides of the dome took some getting used to. Two stories capped the ground floor, which accommodated the servants' quarters as well as a big kitchen, designed for entertaining, and opening out directly onto the garden. On the first floor were two open sitting rooms—one, ultra modern, decorated in white and electric blue, with wine-red accessories and comfy pillows on settees and spread out on the floor; the other was more distinguished, with its antique clocks, huge crystal chandeliers, crystal wall sconces, and Persian carpets with horse and rider motifs on the beige marble floor. Long rows of low windows with hidden lights were swathed in heavy, gold-threaded brocade drapes with massive gold tassels over thin, cream net lace curtains. The walls were plastered in gold-patterned, real silk wallpaper, the latest from Italy; and the antique chairs were covered with hand-stitched tapestry from Thailand. Large crystal ashtrays, cigarette boxes and bowls stood on tables in gold-plated dishes and trays. Golden-bronze angels, carved in wood, decorated the built-in marble units which, along with the long, creamy-colored, wood-covered cement pillars, held up the ceiling. Sulaiman's, Nabeel's, Luay's, Monika's, and Abdulla's photographs stood gold-framed among other gold and silver knickknacks. That room with its golden ceiling was fit to be a monarch's reigning temple. Only in her dreams would Monika have envisioned calling a place like this her own one day, but working twice as hard as she thought she could, she had it now and knew she well-deserved it all. For the first time since she had come to Kuwait, she wished her friends and family from back home could see her now. Wow! Would they be surprised!

In Kuwait it is necessary to have two sitting rooms when entertaining Arabs, for, after greetings are exchanged, men automatically retreat into one room and women into the other. If there is only one room, then the atmosphere and conversation are usually very, very restricted and superficial.

Abdulla had abandoned the idea of building a douvaniah into his house because, being married to a foreigner who did not run for cover at the sight of a man, all his friends could come straight into the house and sit there with him any time of the day or night.

Abdulla and Monika both loved to entertain most generously. Some of the garden parties they were to give in that house in Rawda made it into Kuwaiti newspapers and magazines, along with photographs of the events featured. The house had been built with entertainment in mind, more or less from the very beginning, for there was little else to do in Kuwait, especially for the women.

Three stair steps led up from the "antique" room into a huge dining hall decorated in gold and jade green, which seated twenty-four people and was nicely livened up by masses of hanging greenery to match the palm trees adorning the four corners of the room. The dining hall's furniture of heavy oak was a present from one of Abdulla's close friends, a multi-millionaire, Yasim Kharafi. Nearby, a few steps through the dining room door, on one side, was a turquoise powder room with double turquoise yellow, gold-plated wash basins and a toilet and bidet of the same colors. Towels, Kleenex boxes, soap—everything designer-made and color-matched in true Kuwaiti fashion. Big flasks of French cologne and perfume stood invitingly nearby on crystal and golden trays, one for the ladies and one for the men; for, after meals, visitors usually splashed themselves generously. Hosts were expected to provide those little pleasures of life. The last big room on the floor was, of course, the important main kitchen. It was a bright, friendly mustard yellow. That room was to become the heart and soul of the house, with a homey sitting accommodation across one corner where the family's daily meals would be consumed. From the beginning, the children had a soft spot for the huge, ice-making freezer.

On the next floor up, each of the three boys had his own room and toilet to himself, furnished in the colors of his choice. Sulaiman chose green, Nabeel blue, while the baby Luay's room was a typical baby's room, with lots of soft toys, diapers, and not much else. The large hall upstairs between their rooms served as a TV lounge for the kids. It sported a fridge filled with cold soft drinks; and Monika kept her gin and lime (it helped her escape reality and was absolutely necessary) hidden away in there.

The house had an entry phone and room-to-room intercoms. Until they got used to the system, the children hung on the line for hours on end.

Sakia occupied the servant's room next to Luay, and across the hall, on the other side, lay the master bedroom and a walk-in, mirrored changing room, in shades ranging from the lightest lilac to the deepest purple. The adjoining bathroom and laundry room opened up in soft pink and gentle grays.

The whole house was stuffed with house plants which did wonders for the eyes of those who were used to living for years on a big sand carpet with nothing but beige to look at wherever the eyes roamed.

Monika was responsible for the way the house had turned out, for the way it looked, inside and out. Abdulla, of course, had taken care of all the legal and contractual business necessary. She should be very proud of what she had achieved. Despite the jealous in-laws and numerous fights with Abdulla, Monika had gotten all her wishes concerning the house. For example, Abdulla had wanted to scrap the ground floor with its servants' quarters and kitchen because it took up only a third of the space and the other two-thirds stood empty on pillars and because he had to pay the builders the same amount as if it had been finished and bricked up solid. Abdulla wanted to build the servants' quarters against one of the surrounding walls and scrap the kitchen altogether, but finally Monika got through to him that his idea, first of all, would take up too much space from the garden and, second, there was no way she was going to live so close to the ground level in cockroach- and rat-infested Kuwait. As it turned out the empty space under the house, set off by black-mirrored, shining pillars and cactuses planted close to the wall, was to become the only place where the children could retreat to play without risking sunburn and where grown-ups could sit comfortably in the cool breeze, day or night.

Just before moving in, Monika had worked at her restaurant by day and in her house by night; and although she was getting very little sleep, her work, especially on the house, revitalized and rejuvenated rather than exhausted her. That was because, as she saw it, she was working her way out of prison and into an idyllic future with Abdulla and her three lovely children. At long last there would be no more confrontations and there would be no more being spied on by her in-laws, and that was all she longed for. She wanted with all her heart to be happy and free. She hoped that once she was alone again with Abdulla, he would be the person he had been when they had lived in England outside the influence of her in-laws. Abdulla, she knew, had his faults, and she was human, too; but even so, they could easily live alone and be happy as in

England, just—please, God—no more outside interference. No more in-law troubles.

One of Abdulla's friends, an artist who had viewed the new house, suggested, rather impressed with what he saw, that Monika should say goodbye to the restaurant and set up business as an Interior Decorator and Designer in an office that he would be only too pleased to open for her before her talent wasted away unused.

"Kuwait needs talented people like you. We import designers from Europe with hard cash. Do you know the money you can earn here?" he said.

While Monika was considering the suggestion and toying with the possibility, chronically jealous Abdulla had already made up his mind in favor of a stern "No" because, as he said, "My friend is not interested in your artistic work, but in the anatomy of your body. That is what he is after." Well, again Abdulla's friends congratulated him on his workaholic, super wife. And the friends they had known since their Oxford days even suggested that Abdulla erect a statue in Kuwait's main square in Monika's honor, for they knew her true worth and sacrifices. Just as it had been when Monika set up the restaurant, Abdulla proudly sponged up all the compliments, which went a little to his head this time. He started to develop an exhibitionist's tendencies and to abuse Monika's good nature, bossing her around to do this and that, without as much as a Please or a Thank You, and even whistling at her if a friend's whisky glass was empty and needed a refill. He became such an exhibitionist, such a show-off!

Monika closed her eyes to his showing off and played along with his little immature games because she knew Abdulla was always out to impress people, never mind which walk of life they came from. Worse—she even knew he wouldn't hesitate to hurt his own wife and children to stand ten feet tall in someone else's admiration for a minute.

Monika never got to the root of Abdulla's inferiority complex. He wasn't tall, but then Arabs aren't anyway in general; otherwise he could be proud of everything he had stood for and achieved. His sex machine worked properly; it's size was impressive, so much so in fact that Abdulla often joked, saying he had cut the tips off his rather short fingers and added them onto his willy. His job at the hospital took him from one promotion to another. He climbed the ladder of success fast and incessantly. There was no holding him back. Enthusiastically watching, Monika had predicted: "Before long you are going to end up somewhere in a top position. You are going to be a 'top dog' one of these days," and her prediction proved psychic.

Abdulla often himself acknowledged that Monika deserved a couple of medals for helping to iron out some tricky situations that he found himself in when he had put his foot in it and then did not know how to get himself out of the mess by himself. Many a time he would thank her for having so intelligently helped to solve some problem of his. Then, he would say, "How did you know that? Where did you learn that?" or "Without hour help and advice, I would not have known what to do."

Monika was Abdulla's backbone. It was she who pushed him right up the ladder, sensing the endless opportunities he had in his homeland as one of its first highly qualified professionals.

Not a single penny from Abdulla's inheritance was put into the new house because, instead of Abdulla's getting his hands on some of what was his, his mother still sat like a vulture on its eggs and held resolutely onto what was not hers, living a life of luxury with her daughters and apportioning all to them and absolutely nothing to anyone else. The old bird even had the bloody cheek to dress down Abdulla like a schoolboy every time she discovered something that was newly bought for the house.

"You are wasting good money behind my back," she would shout at him, not caring who could hear, while Monika knew that everything she shouted at Abdulla was really meant for Monika. It was all part of twenty-two carat jealousy because Monika's house had turned out so much better with so much less money than Fahad and Sabiha's house had cost—theirs being dark and stuffed full of pricy clutter since they had no money problems and, like typical Kuwaitis, they had acquired whatever they happened to see, not what was necessary and fitting. It was Monika's sweat and hard earned cash that had helped to make her new house what it was: a show palace.

Whenever friends or relatives mentioned the money Abdulla's wealthy father had left to him, Abdulla would change the subject so that Monika would not be any the wiser. Yet, he would put all of the restaurant's cash that Monika had earned into his own basket, telling her, "For your house, my Sweetie. Every penny goes towards your house." After considerable persuasion by Abdulla, stupid, slow-witted Monika even parted with a box of jewelry she had bought for herself from the restaurant's profits when now and then she had felt she needed some uplift. The trinkets hadn't helped make her happy anyway and made no difference. To buy beautiful furniture for the lovely house, Monika even threw in her most prized possession, a diamond ring her mother had spent 1,500 pounds sterling on and given to her. Monika had had numerous second thoughts about doing that because that particular diamond was this Aries' lucky stone and she did not have another one. But, then, Abdulla had said, "Sweetie, I could not have done any of it without you. Definitely not if I had taken a Kuwait wife. With one of them, my monthly salary would not be sufficient for keeping up with the Kuwaiti Joneses—in dresses and jewels." And then Abdulla told Monika a true-life story.

A friend had recently confided to Abdulla at the hospital that, like Abdulla, he had lived on his salary while building a nice house with a Government grant. His house was finished, too, but he had no money left to spend on his wife. She stayed away from parties and social gatherings to which she had been invited rather than turn up in a dress that everybody had already seen once. We talk here of designer dresses that cost four or five or six hundred pounds sterling and on up into the five digits, not to mention the designer label handbag and shoes that have to match, too, and the hairdresser and so on. This amounts to something like three months' salary for the average Englishman or American—just for one Kuwaiti woman's night out with her women friends. Some so-called friends of his wife got wind of her poverty and made insinuating remarks. Talking about money and not having money are considered bad manners in Kuwait and frowned upon. It does not matter about your personality. The poor girl was so unhappy about losing face among her friends that she developed a stomach ulcer. So Faisal, her husband, had moved with his wife and kids back to his parents' home and rented his new house to an oil company to be able to give his wife her health back and *carte blanche* into Kuwait's fast spending, artificial society. Hallelujah! The big day.

The last possessions were moved from Keefan's miserable flat into the new house. Monika's little family could sleep there for the first time: freedom day had finally arrived for ever-so-patient Monika, who had been growing uncharacteristically impatient of late. For the first day or two in her own palace, Monika's heart beat at twice its normal rate—out of sheer happiness! Life started there very idyllically, just as she had expected and planned. Abdulla spent all his time at home and, to Monika's surprise, took great interest in the garden, planting fig, olive, date, orange, and palm trees around the latest of Monika's works of art, a cleverly designed barbecue center with separate spaces built in for plates, cutlery, and pots. The barbecue center gleamed through the young trees, standing in the corner of the garden amid the white garden furniture and leisurely hammock from Great Britain. Two workers, especially hired, had built the barbecue oven (directly under Monika's supervision) out of bricks and cement; it was then glazed in orange glossy paint and topped by a modern long-legged garden lamp, whose orange vinyl shade had the shape of a festive umbrella.

Dark shadows fall where bright light shines. Things as they now run were too good to be true for long-suffering Monika, who was afraid to wake up one day and find that her hard-acquired, well-deserved peace had been just a dream. The fear was not unfounded. She was a bit psychic, really, for only a couple of weeks later she stood shattered and discouraged—this time, as never before.

CHAPTER NINETEEN

REVENGE

The new house made Monika's problems even worse and brought on some new ones—which did not come instead of the old, but as extra ones. Except for Sabiha, who mostly had kept out of Monika's way since their fist fight (good riddance!), her in-laws walked in and out, showing off the new house as if it were theirs and Monika just a servant at their disposal. Mother-in-law took the greatest interest; she was ever so anxious to know exactly what was happening in that new house. She came at all hours of the day and night, walking in like the Queen of Sheba, pulling half of Kuwait's female population and their kids in tow, to show off her son's new house. She would make her way directly to the fridge, where she would inspect and choose from its stores. She had no qualms about opening every drawer and cupboard in the house to sift through their contents.

Mother-in-law had decided to use Monika's home as her own private coffee and tea place, as a favorite, new found gathering site for herseff and her noisy, messy friends, ordering Sakia and the newly employed cook Reda to prepare whatever took her fancy. Mother-in-law tried to take charge of the kitchen by issuing commands on what to cook the following day, and she even gave orders to Sakia to put dirty laundry that lay nearby into the washing machine. Scared of Abdulla, the servants did exactly as they were told by the old dragon, and Monika stood helpless against her. All she could do was feel sorry for herseff, her last dream and hope for freedom and a bit of happiness lying broken into a thousand splinters all around her feet.

She knew this time that things would stay forever irreparable. Her feelings about her unrealized hopes were the hardest emotions she had ever had to deal with, and she didn't know how to act, now that there was no light left at the end of the tunnel.

So she carried on. She had to. But don't ask how. The circumstances she found herself in required the skin and nerves and strength of an elephant; yet, don't forget, she was only a Ram who could only take so much and then would crack, and crack she did. She felt thwarted on all sides and became much less resistant than she had been before when she still had the dream to hold onto. She didn't expect any help from Abdulla, who stood united with his mother.

"Be tolerant, Sweetie. It won't be long before my mother will get tired of coming here. She is just excited about our new house. You don't expect me to throw her out of my house, do you?" he asked provocatively.

"I don't mind if they come here and behave as guests—but not as your mother does, taking over as the owner, pushing me forever into the shade. I haven't put all I've got, all my money and sweat, into this house to step back once again and roll out the red carpet just so that your family can come and give me hell. Tell me, Abdulla, what on earth happened to your promise? Didn't you swear to me repeatedly on your mother's death and your father's grave that my kids and I were going to have peace from them behind my own four walls here, for fuck's sake? Why don't you, for your own peace and quiet, stand up for what is right and proper! Does your mother mean *all* and I nothing to you?"

All of Monika's pleading and trying to knock some common sense into Abdulla fell on dead ears. It was just as it had always been—to no avail at all, just a waste of time and a waste of nerves. Mother-in-law came and mother-in-law went as she pleased, always creating and leaving a rotten, foul atmosphere behind.

It had taken Monika years, but now she was finally convinced and gave up. There was no way she would ever get away from the in-laws' clutches. As long as she was Abdulla's wife, they all stayed with her as well. That fact gave her the creeps and the shakes and drove her nearly insane. Now, she had nothing left to look forward to. Now, there was no way left to get out. Like a drowning person holding onto a twig, she had held on with all her strength to that house and invested everything she had in it. She knew now that she had reached the end of her long road. She stared in cold reality at her problem, her in-laws. The problem was here to stay, and she was desperate, completely drawn and exhausted with nothing left to hold onto. Monika now lived in her golden cage, surrounded by this world's wealth and servants, miserable as ever, just like so many, many typical Kuwaiti wives.

And, as if that were not bad enough, bad luck struck in yet another form.

Early one morning the police phoned Abdulla to tell him that the restaurant, which had not been insured, had burned down completely overnight. The cause was either an electrical fault or sabotage.

Numb, Monika thought only of the little bird she had kept there. She cried for her bird, Bimbo, burned to death in its cage. It had been a tame skylark that had sung beautifully through the day and that she had fed from her mouth.

The restaurant had burned down just a day after a brand new, two-meter-long aquarium with colorful, sweet-water fish had been installed. The aquarium hadn't even been paid for yet. Monika felt sure the fire was sabotage, for jealousy is widespread and works overtime in Kuwait. Envy is part of Kuwait. It is the Kuwaiti disease. Today, Monika knows one thing: the more money people have, the more they crave. They never have enough and are never satisfied with what they have. Let's face it, the restaurant was a gold mine, and everybody knew it. People often enough mentioned the fact. It is worth mentioning here that not one of the Kuwaiti Aseels, not a single one of the twenty or so millionaires and two or three billionaires who had unpaid accounts with the restaurant, came forward to pay up his old account. The ledger book was lost to the flames and with it, it seemed, went their honor and their memories.

So, now, Monika was back at square one. She was a housewife and mother kept under close inspection in her own house. The delight of the in-laws was obvious now that the restaurant was gone. As she had not salted away any of her own wealth, she now sat with no money of her own. Abdulla continued tightfisted towards her but spent lavishly and openly on the house. He put a gardener on the payroll and was overcome by the sudden urge to turn his garden into a zoo. He brought in a carpenter and had cages built to accommodate two big Aara birds (parrots) and a monkey; and one day, believe it or not, Abdulla even came home with a donkey. Monika had already acquired a new Siamese cat and another baby skylark when, her father having died accidentally in a car crash in Austria, her mother, Dentist Pavlik, shipped one-year-old Senta, father's lovely Dalmatian, to Kuwait because she thought the children would be thrilled to have a new doggy. The children were thrilled, but not so their father, who staged a tantrum, saying that because of Senta his family and friends were teasing him unmercifully, saying, "Your wife's inheritance from her father is an unclean dog!"

"Tell your family and friends that from your own father's inheritance you and your children didn't even get to *see* a dog," was Monika's reply. In her situation, what did she have to lose? She was at the end of her tether, as the English say.

Slowly, Abdulla developed his own daily pattern, which took him to work in the mornings. At 1:30 pm he came home to eat—and beware if the food was not ready to be dished out just as he entered the kitchen, or he would go crazy and blow his top. After eating he would lie down on the electric blue settee to read his paper and fall asleep—until

Monika woke him gently at 4 pm with black tea, after which he went on his daily visit to his mother's house. Often, he forced Monika or one of the kids, who all hated it, to go along with him. Usually when Monika was there (in mother-in-law's house), everyone ignored her; that's probably why they wanted her there in the first place. As for the children, they always came back filthy, crying, or wounded, blood gushing from a leg, a face, or some other part of their bodies, sometimes needing stitches, because neither Abdulla nor anyone else in that household would take care of them. Once little Nabeel came home with the bottom of his trousers burnt out. He had sat accidentally on mother-in-law's *douvah*, the glowing, low-rising, coal-fire contraption on which hot coffee and teapots stand and around which people sit cross-legged on the floor, warming their hands in winter, and on which the incense *bochoor* is sprinkled.

If Abdulla missed a visit to his mother's house just one day, all hell broke loose, and his mother would perform crying fits and heart attacks. On one of Abdulla's very rare lucid moments regarding her, he once said to Monika, "I wish my mother loved animals. Then I would get her a cow, twenty goats, and a couple of sheep to occupy her, and I would have her off my back."

After visiting his mother, Abdulla would go on to douvaniahs to see his friends, do bits and pieces of errands for his family, or come up with other excuses to stay away, often coming back home just in time for bed or way past bedtime, as always, demanding sex, waking her from a deep sleep, and so looking for trouble, especially when he was drunk and knew damn well that she would refuse his advances anyway. On the weekends, Abdulla would go fishing or away on hunting trips in the desert. What one calls married life or family life in the West was, for this family, non-existent. The three boys saw nothing of their father, spent no time in his exclusive company. But, at any rate, she knew by then, of course, what Kuwaiti marriage was all about.

Although Monika had lived in Kuwaiti society for many years and had mingled in it, especially in her restaurant, she was really not a part of it. She felt she could look at it with objectivity, as an outsider but who had the benefit of dearly acquired personal experience and the knowledge she had gained from many years of being put down and very nearly crushed by it. What she saw of Kuwaiti society convinced her that it was, in general, sick. Kuwaiti men lived their own lives, and their women resented it but didn't dare rebel. It wasn't that they resented their husband's friends and outside interests; it was that those friends and interests completely excluded the home; wives were expendable and knew it. Men treated their homes as places to sleep and, if their wives were still capable of bearing children, then as a place to breed. If Kuwaiti women were treated respectably, as proper marriage partners, they could be happy, Monika theorized; they might then not feel frustrated and jealous to the same degree, which led inevitably to the mindless bitchiness of which Monika had herself been the butt for so long. Many Kuwaiti women did not even know why they were so restless, yet right through the row they all were. It is really Kuwait's national disease, still.

A this point in her story, Monika had already spent eleven years with Kuwaitis, and she thought that 95% of them needed psychiatrists, herself included. Having one could well become such a fad that a couple of enterprising psychiatrists could make millions setting up their practices in Kuwait. All those beautiful, super-rich Californians absolutely need their psychiatrists and simply can't do without them, poor darlings; it could be the same in Kuwait, thought Monika. But then, on the other hand, she thought, those quacks seem to be needed everywhere on earth where people have the fewest money worries, where people are spoiled rotten by good luck and wealth and beauty combined. One can't see a down-to-earth, levelheaded coal miner in Newcastle stretched out on a psychiatrist's couch, can one? And if you look it up, it's almost always people who come into money, power, or fame more or less overnight—very seldom the ones who were born into it, like royalty, for example—who can't master life. Monika felt empty, useless, and lonely with such thoughts. While she hungered for a better relationship with Abdulla and the boys, she couldn't enjoy her new house or anything else, not from the heart. The only real diversion Monika, a born hostess, could look forward to in that house was entertainment. She could still throw parties for Kuwait's VIP guests. Because she was a foreigner, lively photographs of those parties often appeared in Kuwait's society pages and gossip about them showed up in the daily papers, as had been the case in the past with events held at her restaurant. The attention she received in this manner and the jealousy it caused ate at her in-laws.

At party time, noisy, fat Sabiha, who had no pride whatsoever, was not ashamed to drive up in her car and struggle up to the top of its roof to get a good eyeful of what was going on in the brightly lit garden and house. Or she would drive past in her husband's white, gold-plated Rolls Royce and honk to attract attention and be seen driving in that exquisite machine. Mother-in-law always passed by, too, and made sure she got a big tray full of all the party food to sample.

One night after a garden party, Monika dreamed that her new house was on fire. She woke up sweating to see real live flames shooting up outside her bedroom window on the top floor. Good grief! She woke Abdulla and the kids and together they all raced down and out into the open. Reda had put the coals from the barbecue pit into the garbage disposal unit, where they had started a fire that had already gotten hold of a wooden bench on which Monika and Abdulla sometimes sat until late into the night shooting rats and betting money on who would catch the most. Thank God no real damage was done, but what a frightful shock those two-story-high flames had caused, coming so soon after the restaurant had burned down!

The big speaker on the side of the mosque facing Monika's house was one day replaced by a much larger one, twice its size, on the orders of the Islamic Association; and the loud screeching that came out of it five times a day deafened the family's hearing systems and sent them running for cotton wool to put in their ears. The new sound system had been installed especially to awaken the Kuwaiti sinner Abdulla (and his European wife) to the voice of Islam. At the same time that it had upgraded its speakers, the Association had placed an article in their religious paper, not mentioning his name but saying that the British-educated Kuwaiti living in Rawda who had betrayed his culture by bringing home a white non-Islamic woman from Europe preferred the sound of the devil (meaning European music and rock and roll) to the voice of Allah. Very annoyed, Abdulla took two shotguns and went onto the roof of the house with Sulaiman, who was 12 at the time, to shoot a couple of holes into the offending loudspeaker, keeping themselves well hidden behind the water tanks. The next day, Abdulla went to the Ruler of Kuwait himself for an audition to complain about the matter, and one hour later the holey, ear-shattering loudspeaker was removed and replaced by the old one. The Islamic Association has a high percentage of Kuwaiti followers; and, so, of course, they were represented in Parliament. Most of the time, this religious sect interfered with or opposed the Government's modern decisions. For example, when the first university to be built in Kuwait was officially opened, members of the Islamic Association marched in protest, long-bearded and short dishdashaed, holding the Holy Koran high above their heads and shouting their opposition. Another time, the walls surrounding the Islamic Association's headquarters were plastered all over during the night with clippings taken from the most explicit of Western sex magazines—in revenge, Monika supposed, by a couple of persons like Abdulla. Set off by the Ayatollah Khomeini, the Islamic fundamentalist movement is getting larger and stronger and more powerful by the day, in all of the Islamic counties.

Monika's house stood on a corner, with only one family for next-door neighbors, the Doulies, real bedouins who after generations in a tent lived for the first time in their lives in a house. They had a big douvaniah where Abdulla was often a guest. Like all genuine and upright bedouins, they were the sweetest, most good-natured people one could know. They kept sending dishes of homemade food to Monika. One day Monika, busy in her kitchen fabricating a chocolate cake, heard the bedouin woman's hysterical shouts. When Monika looked through the window, she had a loud laughing fit. On the neighbor's kitchen window, right smack on top of the poor woman's enormous, wide open, red watermelon sat Abdulla's monkey, stuffing its face with the fleshy, fresh fruit. It was the shock of that discovery that had prompted Monika's neighbor to scream.

Across the road from Monika's house was a newly built home—a pretty little house—of a young Iraqi Kuwaiti, who was a well-known TV sports commentator, and his wife, a teacher. Like so many people in Kuwait, that young man had a drinking problem. But his was enormous. He got drunk every night on a bottle of scotch, after which he could be heard beating his wife senseless, and then the echoes of her screams would follow. Sometimes he threw her into the street and, as the dust whirled around her slender body, invited passers-by to "Fuck her—that's what she wants, that is what she is good for." Monika and other neighbors offered the poor soul shelter, but she always refused, thanking them and saying, "If I accept, my husband will break your door and give you trouble." And to the question why she didn't leave her drunken man, she always said, "Oh, I would, I would, but then he frightens me and threatens that if I walk out on him he will kill our two small children and believe me I know he is capable of doing this when he's drunk. He would really do it." He sometimes came out to throw stones at her, some of which were huge and struck her face, leaving bruises for days after. She sat like a tattered ball of old clothes by her gate, never daring to move until ordered back by the alcohol-crazed man.

Once, that drunk exposed himself on the street to a group of children, among them Sulaiman and Nabeel, saying to them, "Come on, look at it! Do you like it? Come and suck it." Monika phoned the police, who came in 15 minutes, four men with guns in a Jeep, but the Iraqi (who brandished a shotgun) must have had a big wasta, for he shouted at the police to fuck off or he would shoot them, and the policemen jumped into their Jeep and quickly disappeared. That poor unfortunate woman's kids did not get killed, but she did—a couple of years later—by a gun whose trigger was pulled by her husband, after which he shot himself, too. Poor kids. What a waste!

CHAPTER TWENTY

ABDULLA AND FAWZIA & SO FORTH & SO ON

Deprived of the exercise of moving and running around in the restaurant after it burned down, Monika felt she needed something else to do to occupy her body and mind, so she disguised herself as a Kuwaiti male in one of Abdulla's headdresses and a long white dishdasha and went cycling with Abdulla at night. The children's favorite pet, Senta the Dalmatian, ran excitedly alongside their bicycles and enjoyed those outings tremendously. Senta was the only Dalmatian in Kuwait. People stopped and gathered about to gape at the beautifully built dog, while some of them kept asking again and again, "Did you paint those black spots on her white fur?"

A few Kuwaitis kept dogs they had imported from Harrod's in London or through some other foreign source when a fashion fad to keep pretty dogs hit Kuwait. Of course, the doggies were not allowed to enter their masters' houses and were left untrained and unkempt more or less to themselves in their yards. A few doggie owners flew in Barbara Woodhouses from abroad to train their newly acquired novelties, but the razzmatazz soon would wear off and, in the end, all the dogs ended up with more or less the same fate. After the children's series *Lassie* flickered over Kuwait's TV sets, every child wanted a dog, not knowing what work and care was involved. Inevitably, the dogs would run out of their main gates, be pinched on the streets, or run into the desert to join a pack of wild dogs that used to roam the streets at night looking for food and barking ceaselessly. Not used to animals, Kuwaiti children are often very cruel and sadistic to dogs, which they keep on short leashes. They get a kick out of pushing articles into the yelping dogs' bottoms and even lighting their willies with matches since the dog is listed as unclean in the Koran. The children know no better, and no one stops them.

In Kuwait, one is one minute exposed to scorching hot sun and the next one cools off in air-conditioned rooms and freezes. Monika's tonsils couldn't stand the extremes. Little by little over the years, Monika's condition worsened. The dusty bicycle excursions probably didn't help. She developed chronic tonsillitis, and her doctor told her that, as septic as her tonsils looked, they would have to be removed without delay.

So, there she was in a private room at the hospital where Abdulla worked, surrounded by a professional nursing staff who knew well what they were doing this time and were very friendly as well, especially an elderly Palestinian nurse, who for reasons not yet known to Monika seemed to take a special interest in her. The nurse was rather well informed about Abdulla's life, except she didn't know he was married to a pretty, intelligent foreigner from Austria and *that* fact, as she admitted to Monika, really took her by surprise.

"I didn't realize Mrs. al-Amahani would turn out to be someone like you," she ventured. "You are such a nice person. I thought Abdulla was married to one of those typical Kuwaiti women, maybe even to his cousin, as it is so customary among the Aseel Kuwaitis here."

"Whatever gave you that idea?" asked a smiling Monika. And after a very long pause, the nurse answered.

"I am sorry, but I better not say, Um Sulaiman. I can't say more." But something was clearly fishy.

Monika was mystified but instinctively knew there was more to this revelation than just a polite bit of nurse-patient chit chat, and it wasn't just nosiness that induced her to pursue her curiosity.

"Please, tell me what you mean," she pressed.

"I can't. I blame myself." A few moments later the nurse added, "Oh, my! Look, if I do tell you something, do you swear on the life of your son Sulaiman that you will never divulge your source of information? Because, believe me, I only do it to help you. I want you to look upon this as a favor from one caring woman to another. You are such a nice girl, and I feel sorry for you. I don't want you to walk in the dark."

"Of course, I promise."

"You know it is quite serious. You must never, ever tell, or I would lose my job."

"I will never tell. I am a European whose word you can depend on, not a Kuwaiti. I know how to keep a secret." Monika sat up straight in bed like a rabbit in the morning dew, not knowing in the slightest yet what the nurse was on about, nor suspecting. The Palestinian sat down on a bedside chair and took a long, deep breath before she began to speak.

"Well, to start with, I thought Mr. al-Amahani's wife was a different person," she almost excused herself. "A little while ago we had a woman patient here. Her name was Fawzia. There was nothing organically wrong with her. She lay here for a couple of days just for check ups, while your husband regularly visited her, and I helped him to do it. Oh, I am so sorry now . . ."

"Oh, please, don't be silly. Don't worry. I have heard that name before in connection with Abdulla. So, what happened?" Monika wanted to know, more impatiently now.

"Mrs. al-Amahani, they were—I mean, are—for all I know, lovers. Your husband stayed for hours every day while on duty and came back again in the evenings. She is an attractive Kuwaiti girl, but nothing like you. She is unhappily married to her cousin, who is an influential, well known, very wealthy, much traveled Aseel Kuwaiti. I only participated, I only helped them because I imagined that Abdulla was married to a horrid Kuwaiti woman and that he had been forced into marriage with her by his family as so many young people here are. So I helped them to meet. We all rather love al-Amahani here, you know. I never knew that he was married to a European. We talked a lot, yet he never mentioned it. My only excuse is that I love people and like to see them happy. So many marriages are arranged and then partners just exist side by side without love. Being a hopeless romantic, I thought I was helping and doing good for Mrs. Fawzia and Abdulla. I wanted to help them to a bit of genuine love. I saw no harm in it, to tell you the truth, if you were (as I imagined) like most of the other women here. But now I see I was wrong. And I don't know what to say in my favor. I can only hope my confession will help you and do good."

Suddenly a veil fell from Monika's eyes. Now, at long last, after a good year or so, she knew the truth that stood behind the name Fawzia. Now the puzzle was solved.

"It is not your fault. And I thank you very much for bringing up the matter. It must have taken you tremendous courage to tell me. As I said, I have heard the name Fawzia many times in the past in connection with my husband, and I always suspected something, but just could not put my finger on it," she told the worried nurse softly. "And don't lose a minute's sleep. Your secret will stay between us. No one will ever know how I found out."

The nurse, visibly relieved, went back to her duties, and Monika was left alone to digest the disclosure. It felt like the final cut of the last strand that held her to Abdulla, the young charmer she had fallen for at Oxford. Monika thought back and let the whole Fawzia affair run through her head like a film. All good things come in threes, and all bad things, too. First, the disappointment with her new house; then, overnight, the restaurant was wiped out; and now this, a whole new situation. She felt like a prostitute. It had disgusted her in England to see

Abdulla drunk, chasing after some pretty girl. Now, he wasn't able to do that sort of thing openly in Kuwait. And she had often wondered what he might get up to in private. It was anybody's guess. She went back in her mind almost a year—to when she had first started hearing the name Fawzia. It had been a couple of months before she was pregnant with Luay. She recalled the time she first took a little interest in the name that kept popping up; but with the restaurant, in-laws, kids, new house, the matter hadn't appeared to be of really great importance, and so she had not thought it worthwhile to try to find out who Fawzia was and what her connection to Abdulla was all about. But now she knew. Up to this very moment, Monika had never known the feeling of icy coldness towards Abdulla that suddenly overcame her, crept into her heart then and there, and has never, ever left her.

Now there was nothing, nothing at all left between her and him, except two marriage certificates, and paper was patient.

Of course, she had the three children, and for their sakes, she wished dearly that she had chosen another father.

Monika did not hate Abdulla. She pitied him for his weakness and for the way he dealt with her and the children, always treating them as mere afterthoughts. Now that she was on to him, she hit rock bottom. She felt like dying—not committing suicide—just lying down and never waking up. Right now she was in the proper place for that. After getting a hold on herself, she summoned the pluses and minuses she had left in her liaison. There were no pluses, only massive minuses.

"How could I have been so blind and, let's face it, weak for so long?" she scolded herself. She recognized that the Fawzia affair was no one-night stand. It had been going on for a good year or more.

This time her problem was much bigger than herself and too much for her to handle. The only thoughts racing through her head were, How the hell do I get out of Kuwait with my children? What possibility have I got? Will I be able to manage them on my own? Monika ended with the sad facts: that without someone's help, such feats would be impossible for her. She saw no choice but to carry on being the doormat for the in-laws and a willing front-and-back betrayed servant to Abdulla. Oh, God, what a bleak outlook for the future! And she got annoyed with God.

"Why on earth am I singled out to live through so much misery while doing only good myself?" she asked. "While trying so hard? Wishing everybody only the best?" Questions like this cannot be answered. There's a saying, "We come alone and we leave alone, and everything in between is a gift"—but so far for Monika, the in-between bit was one long hectic fight for survival, with hardly any relation to a gift, whatever way one looked at it, with the exception, of course, of her three lovely kids, in whom she took great pride.

Monika decided to confront Abdulla about Fawzia in the privacy of their own home, not to give the nurse away and, secondly, because she needed time to think how to handle the matter properly while in the meantime observing him a bit more closely. She watched him when he came to visit her, greeting her with a false "Sweetie this and Sweetie that" after which he probably just went away and fucked Fawzia.

What Monika found hard to understand was why Abdulla had needed an affair. He was the one who came home disgusted, telling her about just such goings-on all around him at the hospital. It had been, as she now knew, his way of distracting her from the bare fact he had to hide. Presumably, he felt more for Fawzia than he had felt for the casual sexual relationships he had dallied in when he was in England and which Monika never doubted he was having in Kuwait. Monika had never refused him sex, unless he was drunk, not even when he came in the middle of the day, nor even during her three pregnancies, all during which they relished normal intercourse up to the time each child was born. She had not been like a Kuwaiti, who refuses herself weeks before the birth and weeks after and is more or less on a nine-month sick leave with complaints of pains and aches everywhere in between. Monika hated such unfeminine behavior in Kuwaiti women. Abdulla's sisters were the best example of it. And Monika often wondered what their husbands were making of it, but she didn't wonder why their husbands looked out for other women, and she didn't blame them either. She believed in the adage that a wife should be a lady in the parlor, a cook in the kitchen, and a whore in bed. She now realized that, as in her own case, that little bit of wisdom did not work with Arabs. Maybe it only applied to Westerners, in which case she should have no trouble in finding her match the second time around.

Abdulla noticed the frosty gesture with which Monika cut short his hello kiss that evening when he visited her at her hospital bedside. The last bit of flame left of the fire that had burned healthily had finally gone out. Coolly, she assured him that nothing was wrong—just post-operation blues. Monika was a good actress, remember, even if it cost her her nerves.

The day Monika decided to confront Abdulla about his lover Fawzia came two weeks after Monika left the hospital. She was all poised and calm when he came rushing home, hungry, from the hospital, or maybe after a quickie with Fawzia. Monika made Abdulla lose his appetite. She waited—it was well planned—purposely all dolled up, ready for the showdown of her life, black cigarillo in hand, looking her best, sitting in the modern "antique" room. She did it in style, drawing in overwhelming bochoor incense. She had lit the slim long cigar only because Abdulla did not like his wife to smoke and even though—her tonsil wounds were still sore—smoking caused her pain. All the chandeliers and lights were switched on. The light reflected in the pure magic glitter of the lead crystals on walls and tables. It burned intensely all around her in the brightest, clearest rainbow colors. Monika was surrounded by beauty and, despite her misery, she felt beautiful, too; and that gave her self-confidence and strength, strength to fight the last battle over the emotions she had lost. She felt she had no more to lose from now on: everything was gone, had evaporated.

"I am here, Sweetie," she shouted, as she heard him enter through the front door.

"Oh, hi! What's going on here, Sweetie? Are we celebrating something I don't know about?" he asked surprised. Samsonite briefcase in hand, he stepped into the beautiful parlor.

"How did you guess, my Sweetie. Surprise, surprise! We're celebrating Fawzia, your lover, together, just you and me. Tell me, isn't it a nice surprise? Am I not a very thoughtful and good little wife, just the way you would always wish her to be? I'm awfully sorry. Fawzia tried, but she just couldn't make it."

Abdulla let his case slip onto the carpet. His olive skin turned beige.

"Come, come, make yourself comfortable, and before you get a heart attack, tell me *all* about her, please. I'm dying to know what has been going on, darling. I know a bit, but not quite everything." Monika spoke a teasing tone.

Abdulla, his lips trembling, could only stammer: "Who told you, who told you?"

"Now my—oh, sorry—*our* Sweetie, we won't get anywhere with 'who told you, who told you.' You don't need to be so worried because, as you can see, I don't mind and don't give a fuck what you do anymore and in whose cunt you dip your cock. For all I care from now on, you can have a go and fuck all of Kuwait's cunts. I can swear to you on the death of my three children that if I were to see you screwing a woman right here in front of me it would leave me cold, just as if you were my brother Werner, because I have no loving feelings left for you whatsoever. In their place is now Antarctic ice, that's what. That's exactly what I feel for you now, and to tell you the truth, somehow I'm relieved it has happened because now I'm completely free from you, body and soul. You're not worthy of having a decent wife like me. I'm much too good for you, and you know it!"

Abdulla cried and cried and begged her for forgiveness. He didn't let Monika leave the room until she was willing to sit down and listen to his side of the story, with which he hoped to wash himself clean. He came up with an excuse that was not very original. It was the saga most overused by unfaithful men: it had been all Fawzia's fault! *She* was the guilty party. She was the one who had persuaded him when he was minding his own business.

"A friend of mine asked me to look after Fawzia because I have good connections at the hospital. Feeling unwell for sometime, she had seen x-number of doctors. Nobody found what was wrong with her, so I arranged for a psychologist for her. He told me there was nothing wrong with her and that all she needed was a man who would give her attention. She is married to her cousin, a very rich and influential man. They have two children, but no love is lost between them. She is a very physical woman but hates sex with her husband, who forces her and even pays her to have sex while watching hard core sex films. The husband travels a lot and Fawzia knows that he fucks around a lot. The last thing he did, for instance, was to bring a well-known Lebanese movie starlet to Kuwait and set her up here in a hotel. Fawzia told me that apart from my physique, it's that I am married to a foreigner that turns her on. People here think that we, the ones married to foreigners, are a cut above the rest. I am not the first and I won't be the last Kuwaiti she has gotten involved with. She only associates, though, with Aseel Kuwaitis like me, who are very careful and afraid for their reputations. She is afraid that if her husband finds out he will kill her. With an Aseel she feels safe and sure not to be blackmailed afterwards. Fawzia has a nanny who has taken care of her from the time she was a small child. This faithful old woman covers up for her and misguides her husband by telling him she is with a girlfriend, gone to the cinema or on some visit, when in fact she was with me. The first time I met her was at the hospital after my friend had introduced us, and after that she came to see me in my office non-stop. I was afraid people might get suspicious and realize what was going on, so we started to meet outside Kuwait near the desert, where she would drive up with a girlfriend in her car and then jump into my car. I would then drive a bit further away . . .

"Spare me the juicy bits," intervened Monika.

"Yes, and then I drove her back to her car. And when her husband traveled, I parked my car on the main road, not to arouse suspicion among neighbors, and walked to her house."

"To sum it all up, because her husband took little interest in her, you thought it was your duty to take a lot of interest in her. Isn't that what you're trying to tell me? Isn't that what it really boils down to? Well, that is really very, very Good Samaritan and thoughtful of you. Do you believe I never knew I had a husband with such noble qualities? Why, how come you never thought of going out of your way to be kind and protective to *me*—and our children? For us, you never have any time. You're so full of irresponsibility that it makes one's hair stand on end. You have finally signed the death certificate of our marriage." Monika paused.

"I love you all," he sobbed.

Pleased with the way things were going and feeling she had the upper hand, Monika drew a deep puff from her cigarillo and blew the smoke right into Abdulla's face.

"Then you have a strange, invisible way of showing it, carrying on with another woman, giving her healing, while you are destroying me, not thinking nor giving a fuck what effect it has on your children."

"It does not mean a thing to me! It was only a game, and, please Sweetie, don't smoke."

"Don't you 'Sweetie' me! From now on I will do exactly as I please, taking orders from no one, just as you and your family have done since I first set foot in your shitty country. And if you don't like it, bad luck. But you will have to live with it. I have realized, Abdulla, since I can't win, I am going to join you. When in Kuwait, do as the Kuwaitis do! That faithful, obedient, hardworking, shortsighted Monika that served as a punching bag is a thing of the past. You better get used to that fact.

Please spread it around thick and make sure it gets far enough to reach that monstrous mother of yours."

Abdulla's guilt about the affair was to become Monika's strength. She had decided that from then on she wouldn't give a hoot about anybody, for what did she have to lose? Where did her modest patience get her?

The next morning, as soon as Abdulla left for work, she couldn't wait to reach for the telephone to find and dial Fawzia's husband's office number, and she had no trouble getting it. He was the owner and head of a well-known daily newspaper. She didn't blame Fawzia, the other woman, for (given Fawzia's conduct) if it hadn't been Abdulla, it would have been some other Kuwaiti, especially if what Abdulla had related was even partly true. Monika did not blame Fawzia for going astray, given what her own husband was up to. After all, it says in the Holy Koran that men and women are equals, doesn't it? Fawzia would not have had a chance with Abdulla if he hadn't been ready and willing, or if he had told Fawzia that he was happily married and loved his wife, for then Fawzia would have turned to somebody else's body. It was far more likely that poor "neglected" Abdulla had complained about how unhappy he was and told her that he was still married only for the children's sake. That is the simple, primitive excuse generally given by unfaithful men all over the world, and women of all colors and nationalities fall for it. Although Monika did not blame Fawzia, she somehow felt she had to let off steam in her direction, too, and found herself much better off afterwards for having done it.

A secretary answered. The conversation was held in Arabic.

"Your name, please?"

"I cannot give you my name. Would you please put me through to your boss, Mr. al-Sadam? It is very important," demanded Monika.

"Mr. al-Sadam is in a meeting at the moment, and I cannot put you through if you don't give me your name," she insisted.

"Thank you," said Monika and put down the receiver. Hell hath no fury like a woman scorned. Five minutes later she tried again, very restless. She just *had* to get through. This time she put on a posh English accent, gave a name she had made up, and was through to the big man himself in no time.

"Good morning, Mr. al-Sadam. You don't know me but I know you. I come straight to the point. For the past year or more, your wife has been very close—too close for both our tastes—to my husband. She has been so close, in fact, that according to your Islamic law here she should be barbarously stoned to death."

"Listen, whoever you are, I have no time to play silly games with you. We know how to deal with the likes of you. Our telephones are tapped. We will catch you and make more trouble for you than you think possible."

"Mr. al-Sadam, will you cool it please? I have had my trouble already, thanks to you wife Fawzia. If your telephone is tapped, I have nothing to fear, but it should prove very embarrassing for you because I speak only the truth. Listen, I don't want to harm you. You have done me no wrong, but your wife has really been having an affair with my husband. I am not playing games with you."

"What? Impossible!" he said.

"I wish it was," answered Monika. "It is not only possible, but it has actually already happened. And it has been going on for a long time. So you understand when I am quite blunt about it." Monika could hear a sigh at the other end of the line. She said, "I am sorry that I have to upset you; you have been married for some years now, have two children, even if you won't admit it. But now I know as well as you that love between you and your wife does not exist. I know that you are cousins and that your marriage was arranged. You are abroad a lot and also have mistresses. Please let me finish. That's all your business, of course, and I would not care, except that Fawzia has decided to have a relationship with my husband. She has done this sort of thing several times before, but with different men, always careful to choose only Aseel Kuwaitis to protect herself for reasons best known to you. Only this time she has not chosen too wisely. You can tell her that she has been found out by me, a foreigner married to an Aseel. Her old faithful nanny helped and covers for her. When you think that the two of them are chaperoning each other, they are in fact plotting assignations; and at the moment it is my husband's turn with Fawzia, who, don't misunderstand me, is of course, not an innocent party. This is why I telephoned you. I just had to."

"This is monstrous!" Mr. al-Sadam replied. "It cannot be true."

"Mr. al-Sadam, I can't really see why you are so speechless. After all, what she did was only to follow your example. Do you mind my asking, does the word *gahba* apply to your wife now or do Kuwaitis use that term only for white skinned women?"

Mr. al-Sadam's voice hollered down the line, "We have to meet! Can we meet to discuss this further?"

"No, I have children. I don't want a feud between you and my husband. You are an important man with that newspaper of yours and God knows what revenge you would take. You would probably ruin him."

"You mean you still care?"

"I care for my children only. There would be no useful purpose served by telling you who I am. If you have the slightest doubt in believing what I have just told you, I suggest, the next time you go abroad, hire a detective to watch your wife and on your return he will tell you what I have told you. But if you believe me, save your money and confront your wife. And now, goodbye. I have said all I wanted to."

"Wait, please, wait! You can't leave it at that. Please don't hang up. We have to meet."

"No way, Mr. al-Sadam. I am going to put down the receiver now and wish you luck."

"Thank you for letting me know, whoever you are. I wish you good luck, too. Goodbye."

Infidelity was a social grace that brought lots of unhappiness. Yet, of course, a husband who is unfaithful—as 99% of them in Kuwait are—could hardly expect his wife to love and obey him blindfolded. The absurdity was—and is—that all Kuwaiti men, whatever they are themselves up to, expect their wives to be obedient, pure angels, which is against all natural human instinct. Even the Koran puts women on an equal footing with men. The Islamic woman is not at all meant to play an inferior role to men. Still, Muslim women are being tricked into servility by their fervently traditional menfolk and not by the teachings of the Holy Koran. Chauvinistic medievalism is still sweeping and ruling the Middle East and clashes heavily with modern, educated ideals. Monika's case is a classic example.

Marriage in Kuwait is a depressing, childbearing institution for women. Men spend their time with men and women with women, except for sex, and that is matter of fact, done in the same spirit as you might go and fill up your car because it has run out of gasoline. Women, even those kept in isolated comfort, know that after a couple of children they will be consigned to the scrap heap and be allowed to exist in luxury, maybe, but be inwardly unhappy, at the mercy of their owners, who if the fancy strikes them take a new wife or mistress or travel the world to experience sex at every available gas station, without a sign of guilt or remorse. Kuwait's men live well in their male-created world, which is not going to change for a long time to come, if ever.

Herself a victim, Monika understood Kuwait's love-and-affection-starved women and greatly sympathized with them and thought it great the way some daring, modern-thinking and -acting females sometimes secretly clubbed together, rented a flat in a foreign-populated area of Kuwait where nobody knew them or their cars, just to find a bit of privacy from their big families, their husbands, and their husbands' families, where the modern Kuwaiti female heart could give free rein to the natural instinct she had otherwise to suppress or hide away from judgmental guardians in the artificial life she lived. There, among the sisters of one mind, she could smoke, dance to the latest European and American popular songs, drink, watch sex movies, meet a secret lover, and so on.

Given that women are separated from men and forced so close together with other women, it is not surprising that so many Kuwaiti females develop lesbian tendencies, either. Most daring womenfolk we talk about here woke up in the early 1970's, only to imitate what their men folk had been doing for donkey's years, and jolly good luck to them, too! If nobody cares for—nor understands—you but only ignores you, you have to help yourself and cater to your own needs. After all, this is your life, isn't it?

CHAPTER TWENTY-ONE

MONIKA'S FASHION BOUTIQUE

Over the years, Monika's gatherings with the wives of fifteen of Abdulla's closest friends developed into a fairly regular once-a-week meeting, and except for a bit of bitchiness and jealousy which erupted among the members of the group now and then, those women were all rather pleasant. All of them, though, complained—through the row—of being neglected, abandoned, and treated as non-existent. None of them liked the way their husbands went off together for weekends near the sea, where they had a chalet. Yet, there was nothing, it seemed to them, that they could do about it. What are they up to there? Why don't they take us along, too? Why not the children—do they have female company? Okay, we know they drink alcohol there, but then they do that at home, so why don't they want us there? I would give anything to be able to see what goes on there! Those were just some of the many questions that strained the poor women's brains, left as they were in the dark. Monika was no wiser herself about what Abdulla was really up to when he went off with those women's husbands; so, to her girlfriends, she proposed what she thought was a brilliant suggestion.

"Why don't we hire a big van with a driver and a big tent, which is all very easy to come by in Kuwait, and dress up like bedouin women, black covers, face-masks, the lot, not forgetting to take along our most important weapons: our binoculars. We'll come close up and alongside them for one night. They won't know who we are, and we'll be able to see what is going on. Either that, or we will be sitting here not knowing until our dying days."

All the women were fire and flame for Monika's ingenious idea, and for the next three meetings things were planned. Nothing else much was spoken of besides the forthcoming spying expedition. Everybody was so excited! Almost over-excited. Monika had the van and tent already arranged and everything else, too, down to the smallest detail when, just a week before the departure date, slowly, one by one, all of the women chickened out for one silly reason or another until only Monika was left like a spare prick at a wedding. She had to cancel everything. The poor souls did not admit it, but they were scared of their husbands, their masters, and Monika understood. End of adventure!

During all her years in Kuwait, Monika had not met a single female who was happily married for long. Only the newly married and the single still had stars in their eyes. Kuwait has many spinsters. Some of them were victims of true love, women who had fallen for the wrong guy—either a foreign Arab (marriage to him would have brought disgrace upon the whole family) or a man whose family did not approve of her, or vice versa. Instead of entering an arranged marriage, the girls stayed single. In many a Kuwaiti woman's face a thick book of sadness is written. Take it from the experienced: money and material goods, however abundant, cannot make up for freedom, love, and happiness. The adrenalin that sets your body aglow and your soul, too, is related to these. Long, long live love!

Something clicked in Monika's head the day she found out about Fawzia that made her see her past and future and the bloody mess her life was in with Abdulla. It's true—if a marriage is on its final rocks, you find the rocks in bed. Sex from then on would never, ever be the same for her again—with him, that is. The only reason she stayed near him was her kids, and she told him so. From then on, she was completely turned off. Making love, as she was used to calling it in the past, became from that point something more like a rape session. It left her unsatisfied, irritated, and, of course, frustrated. She just could never again bring herself to let go with him. How could any wife enjoy fulfilling her husband's sex drive anytime he fancied it if he had betrayed her for so long with another woman, apart from all the other troubles he gave her? It got so bad that she could not even stand his hands on her body anymore. Instead, she wished the Berlin Wall were between them. Yet, she had to submit for peace's sake—every time, one hundred times, and a thousand times to come—all for peace's sake. Until when?

Monika didn't put on an act. She quite honestly and repeatedly told Abdulla that she did not love him anymore, and that made Abdulla turn into a sex maniac, demanding sex from her and forcing sex on her at every given opportunity, to break her pride and her "thorn," as he would call it. He could not digest her rejection. He wanted his little slave girl back with body, mind, and soul, but she had slipped this time for good. It was something Abdulla would not acknowledge, nor could understand. Men think differently from women, and they feel different. He would say, "I know you love me. I know you still love me, but you don't want to admit it."

Rather nasty scenes were now played out in that new house, which turned out to be everything that it was planned not to be. Everything that Monika had expected to avoid by living there happened there, especially when Abdulla drank.

A couple of days after Monika lifted the veil on Fawzia, Abdulla presented her with a gold-rimmed, small, black leather case. In it sparkled a diamond solitaire ring much bigger than—twice the size of— the one she had sold some time back to help pay for the new house's furniture. Abdulla just didn't seem to understand that a wife's disgust on discovering that her husband had another woman could not be assuaged by an expensive gift. In Kuwait, many if not all wives sooner or later receive similar peace offerings. The women then show it to their friends and pretend the presents are marks of their husbands' affection for them. They find satisfaction in the charade although everyone knows exactly how the cookie crumbles.

It saddened Monika even more to think that Abdulla hadn't thought her worth such a grand present sooner, hadn't given her the ring just for being who she was—on her birthday or for some other occasion—in all the years they had spent together in Kuwait. It was obvious he had always been able to afford it. Instead, it was used as a bribe to iron out an affair and to win her back. Abdulla had begun marriage showing her love and affection openly, but once he had returned to Kuwait, everything changed drastically. He joined his friends in the belief that respecting one's wife was unmanly and turned a man into a cowardly sissy. The drastic negative change was getting worse for Monika by the hour, and it was turning the once bubbly, full of life, fun-loving Monika slowly into a bitter, ill being who sat for hours on end doing nothing but straining her brain, thinking about her messed up life. She had no hope in hell for a positive change.

Her destiny had taken its toll. She was now regularly plagued by headaches, sleepless nights, and an unhealthy urge to swallow everything edible, anything she could grab, although she was not hungry and, as a matter of fact, had no appetite at all. And, of course, she put on weight rapidly. Her size 10 figure became a 14-plus. She knew exactly how so many poor Kuwaiti women felt; she was having a bitter taste herself of what ailed them. With servants for everything at her fingertips, she felt useless and wasted, without much "go" left.

After crocheting a cover in the appropriate color for each of the beds in the house, after painting each ceiling in an original pattern of appropriate tints, and after creating some fine, imaginative surrealistic and abstract oil paintings, including a fabulous one of her mother-in-law (which showed her in her true colors: a red cancer spitting green poison—a masterpiece expressing all Monika's anger and frustration)—after all that, nothing more could (or needed to) be done to the house. With the last strength and will-power that flickered low in her, Monika approached Abdulla and talked him, coaxed him, sex-played him into acquiring a boutique that stood empty in a busy shopping area. The resistance from him and his family was great, but Monika finally prevailed and landed in her boutique "Domino," which took her mind off things a bit and filled a big hole in Kuwait's fashion market scene for the very large and the pregnant ladies who up to then had been overlooked and walked around, like Monika's mother-in-law, in ill-fitting Indian-tailored frocks.

Domino's clothes were imported from Fa Hauser in Austria, and business went as it always did with wise-woman Monika's know-how. She wouldn't have thought it, but Monika's own hand-knitted and crocheted shawls, dresses, and jumpers sold like hot cakes. Fashion jewelry was added according to demand, and Monika was in business again. But the boutique did not do what the restaurant and the new house had done for her psyche. It didn't pep her up. Instead, seeing no meaning to her life, she went further down, way down. Her resistance was very, very low. She found no pleasure in anything that life in Kuwait had to offer. Her general outlook was very, very bleak. After starting and trying again so many times, she was physically and mentally exhausted, washed out.

Her new house had proven unlucky. What had started so well, with so much enthusiasm on her part, had turned into the worst nightmare of disappointment. The house was no help. The opposite. It irritated the in-laws and seemed to possess the same bad omens that afflicted the house in Keefan. Monika was more or less convinced now that mother-in-law's practice of casting evil spells had bound Abdulla closer to the witch and created havoc for his wife. The witchcraft had had an impact and had a lot (if not everything) to do with the way things always turned out disastrous for Monika. It is so difficult to believe in something one cannot see! What helped to convince Monika in the end that the occult was no myth was the evidence that she and her servants had collected in the new house. They had found enough written material and mysterious potions—pressed between small pieces of red, white, or black silky material, drenched in strong smelling liquid, with spice, black hair, and herbs—to open a small museum. Sometimes the stuff they found wrapped up tightly stank to the blue heavens of Kuwait! Monika collected and took all her findings to her Kuwaiti neighbors' friend Laila, whose mother seemed to be quite an expert in witchcraft. Laila's mother confirmed Monika's fears that she was a victim of black magic, but the way in which the woman advised Monika to respond to protect herself against those powers was a bit out of Monika's line.

"Collect every day a bottle of your urine and wash your body from head to toe every morning or night, as you prefer, before your shower: by doing this you clean yourself of all evil that may be cast upon you."

"Okay," Monika responded. "Let's say doing that takes care of me, but what about my servants and children? They are affected, too. I can't possibly order them to wash in their urine. And what about Abdulla?"

"The way you explained Abdulla's behavior to me sounds as if he is doctored by his mother on his daily visits to her. She must feed him something," Laila's mother said. "I can't help you with him unless you would like me to put a spell on him to love you only and not his family."

Monika declined and thanked her politely. *No way* was she going to go into that bit of Kuwaiti culture. It was sad enough to find herself in such a low position as she had already slid to so helplessly, thanks to her cruel fate. She only wanted the spells stopped, wanted things made better, to go back to being halfway human again. Besides, she knew that if she did evil in this world it would sooner or later snowball and return to her and her children. Puzzled, Monika sat next to Laila's mother on the thickly carpeted floor, discussing witchcraft, and a thought shot through her mind. What if her friends or family in Austria were to hear her speak, ever so convinced, about demons the way others talk about a cooking recipe? They would write her off, declare her gone insane. She would be the laughing stock of Vienna, and she wouldn't blame them.

It took her years and a hell of a lot of self-convincing before she started to believe in any of it. When she had first come to Kuwait, she used to laugh about such nonsense and feel pity for believers. Until she felt the results again and again on her own body and mind, in her own house, only after witchcraft had destroyed her life completely did her common sense (or what she had left of it) tell her that what had happened here was indeed of a paranormal nature. What a deeply mysterious world we live in!

Monika asked Laila's mother—an old, wrinkled, but kind looking woman in black—to give her an example of how one puts a spell on somebody.

"What you need to learn most urgently, first of all, my child, is how to win back your husband. If you do as I tell you, it won't be too big a task for you. Now listen carefully. Here, take a pen, and that's the paper, and write it all down. You take a three centimeter square piece of red silk material (red is for love), place a teaspoon of sugar in the middle of it, pick up the four corners of the material, and, careful not to spill the sugar in the middle, place the corners together, wrapping a red silk thread tightly around it. Then, you go to a private place and push it deep into your vagina. After two or three hours, it should have drawn enough of your juices to be fully drenched. The next tea or coffee you prepare for Abdulla you sweeten with that love potion, as we call it. But, don't forget, you have to think of him and keep him lovingly in mind, imagining him doing all the things you want, while you perform the procedure. And I can guarantee you, my child, that that man will love you and only you, devoted, as he has never loved you before. And if you are the daring woman I think you are, you're best off masturbating while the sugar is in your vagina, always keeping Abdulla in mind, and nothing can go wrong. This I guarantee you."

Monika expected strange news from that lady but nothing near what she had just been told. Good grief, how primitive! How utterly despicable! She did not have enough time to let that bit of grotesque advice sink in before the woman offered her another method, which was to take a bit of one's excreta, dried in the sun and minced with red pepper and salt, and sprinkle the mixture over one's lover's fried eggs or soup or whatever.

"As long as he consumes it, it does not matter what he eats it with, I tell you. That man will eat out of your hand and forget about his mother and sisters. I will pray for you—and take this with you and rub it in your hands before you start the ceremony." Having said that, the old woman gave Monika a small bottle containing a thick, yellow oily substance.

While the old woman was telling her about these voodoo-like rites, Monika automatically had to visualize her in-laws sitting together in secrecy brewing up similar things. "Good God," she thought to herself, "I've been under their spell ever since I came here, doing what they wanted me to do for such a long time. I just hope I haven't been doped into obeying by eating their shit!" A sickening, nauseating feeling made itself known in her tummy region. As a cold chill ran down her spine, she had to shudder at that possibility like a wet dog. "From now on," she told herself, "I'm not going to eat in my in-laws' house, and that's law!"

"If that's what I have to do to get Abdulla back to normal, if that's the only possibility, I don't want to know more. He's not worth my doing these rituals," she told Laila's mother and thanked her. What she did not tell her, though, was that she thought the old woman a tool of the devil, too, for how could somebody pray five times a day and then go and indulge in such sinful doings? How backward are those people? They haven't even learned to think for themselves. There is no common sense at all: on the one side, the religion; on the other witchcraft. It never ceased to surprise Monika how some Kuwaitis, like Laila, were very open minded, Europeanized, and university-educated, and yet their brains were still firmly rooted in the Middle Ages.

The atmosphere Monika now lived with in her house was one of constant fear. Everything grew much worse than it had been in her in-laws' house. There was no sunshine with Abdulla anymore, only rain, and that, by the bucketful. She was living in an even more unreal world than she had in Keefan. She could not explain any of it otherwise, except that she now believed she was living under a spell, a constant, never ending spell. She found herself in a haze, feeling like a shooed away chicken. She could not think clearly for long. Her mind, her brain just gave in and failed her. She was helpless, without stamina, not caring anymore, just letting it all happen.

Every time the in-laws appeared, they left trouble behind. Fights between the servants—something that had never happened in Monika's household before—started to erupt. The illnesses among the children didn't seem to end. As soon as one was getting better, the next fell ill. It was one out of the hospital, the next one in. Sulaiman and Nabeel broke their arms within a short time of each other—as new evil joined the bloody mess. The telephone started and never stopped ringing: anonymous callers wanted Monika to know of affairs that Abdulla supposedly was having at the hospital. Monika told them rudely that she had given him the okay to have those affairs and that she didn't care a fart. After talking to certain people about Abdulla and Fawzia, Monika had found out that Abdulla had flirtations with nurses and the female staff at the hospital to brighten his short working days and hours there, too.

Non-Kuwaiti females from poor Arab countries working close to Aseel males in Government jobs were usually easy game and fire and flame for the men, never mind their ages because being nice to an Aseel man could mean working permits in Kuwait for their relatives or other wastas like that, including better jobs for themselves. The number of beautiful non-Kuwaiti Arab girls married as number 2, 3, or 4 wife to

Aseels old enough to be their grandfathers is unbelievable—and all for the sake of money. A sixty-year-old man with two or three wives just decides on the spur of the moment to go to Egypt and buy himself a new wife there. His sons might try to prevent him, might ask him to think it over first, but if he can convince them he is still as randy as ever and nothing much is doing with their mothers because he has lost his appetite for them, then he goes shopping with his sons' blessing. Sex, food, and money are so very important in Kuwait—sex for the men, food for the women. Both the men and the women quench their depressive blues by letting their taste buds run wild, typical creatures of habit.

Despite being discovered with Fawzia, Abdulla did not reform his ways. Instead he went absolutely mad. It might not be long before he snapped completely; he was almost ripe for the mental hospital—so much so, in fact, that Monika already was worried, even before Abdulla snapped, about what would become of her and her children. The Russians couldn't have done a better job of brainwashing than the in-laws with their witchcraft. Abdulla did not speak much, but if he did, the subject always centered about his poor mother and sisters whom he had to leave behind. He hurled at Monika that she, the bloody fucking foreigner, had taken him away from his family, that if he had married a Kuwaiti he would still be living with his poor mother and be able to rent out the new house for a tidy sum. Abdulla—whose face began to look as black as the Ace of Spades he loved to play poker with—didn't close the doors anymore; he just slammed them shut. He was going mad, and getting madder by the day. When he came home at night after enjoying himself enormously somewhere—probably at a *mezrah* where he had had his way with some girl—and if Monika had the English radio station turned on, Abdulla would order her to turn it off immediately or switch it to an Arab station, saying, "We are not bloody fucking English here!" In the new house only Arabic was allowed to be spoken. If he heard an English or a German word from Monika or the children, he would hit his fist hard and loud against a door or on a table, and if one of the kids were the sinner, he would get a slap for it. Mother-in-law's waters and poison seeds, well planted in Abdulla's system, sprouted healthily. What is described here is only a fraction of all the possible ways to prepare, to fix, and to plant a spell. Monika only got to know a fraction due to non-interest.

The new house's sector didn't have its own post code and street numbering yet, so Monika's mail was delivered to Abdulla's hospital address; and when he came home and handed her the post, she often retreated to the toilet to read her letters there because he would not let her read them in peace anywhere else in the house. He pestered her saying, "It is all about me, isn't it? Your mother hates me. It's all about Abdulla . . . Abdulla this and Abdulla that . . . what she writes. I know she is the one who turns you against me." Sometimes he would stand outside the loo door and bang against it so fiercely that she thought he would come crashing through any minute. Monika retreated hundreds of times to the toilet for a bit of peace and quiet from Abdulla when he was drunk and pestered her, or when he was drunk and wanted sex, or when she felt like a good cry and didn't want to give him the satisfaction of seeing her so low.

Her greatest tonic during her worst times—something she often indulged in now—was going on a solitary drive with Elvis singing her favorite songs on big cassettes. She kept her cassettes well hidden from Abdulla. When they had met at Oxford, Abdulla loved Elvis, too, and knew all his songs by heart. He even played them on his *o'ud*, and now she had to count on the possibility that in one of his mad fits he might destroy those Elvis cassettes that meant everything to her. For reasons unknown to her, Abdulla had grown to hate everything English and foreign. He was obsessed. So, Monika, driving aimlessly, circled around and through Kuwait, tears streaming down her face, not knowing or much caring anymore what was what. Or she would get quite high on a gin and tonic, her favorite tipple, and then her general outlook never seemed real, nor so bleak. Only those cures did not last long. Have you ever thought of the power that lies in a tumbler of whisky? Amazing, isn't it, the strength it has!

Although Monika did a roaring trade with her shop, Domino didn't much help her morale. Nothing available in Kuwait did, or would.

After feeling more often unwell or downright ill of late, Monika employed Christian Um-Mohammed, an elderly Egyptian saleswoman, for her boutique. Monika got on well with her. When she caught on to Monika's ill fate with her in-laws, Um-Mohammed got into the habit of blessing the shop daily, first thing in the morning, with incense and prayer, cleaning it of all possible evil spells, as she said.

One day, Monika was busy sewing Domino labels into the newly arrived stock and, after greeting them politely with a smile, took no further notice of the two abaya-clad, yashmak-faced, heavily bejeweled and perfumed Kuwaiti women who entered the shop chaperoned by a Negro woman. Monika was far away in her thoughts—as she always seemed to be lately—and only started to pay attention and to listen to what was being spoken after Um-Mohammed tapped her foot gently against Monika's shoe, which meant, Listen to that! Monika listened and was taken aback, mystified by whatever it was that was being played out here in front of her eyes and ears. The woman who had bought two long expensive dresses without trying them for fit or size said to the other, "Don't you think the red flower Abdulla has given me will go well with this cream gown?" "Oh, yes, of course, Abdulla's flower will look really great on it," came the reply, after which the black servant chipped in, too: "Oh, yes, my aunt. Mr. Abdulla's flower is so beautiful. It must have been very expensive." (Servants address their employer's family members respectfully as uncle and aunt.)

Um-Mohammed, who was more on the ball than Monika was, sensed something and asked, "Which Abdulla is Madam talking of? I take it, of course, it is your husband?"

"Husband? Me? Husband? Abdulla al-Amahani, of course," shot out of the woman's mouth—as if from a gun. "I'm not married, you know. I am just shopping around for fun."

Monika sat on her chair, flabbergasted, not knowing what to make of it, nor how to deal with it. Either it was a well set-up plot against her, staged by her in-laws, or it was really another lover of Abdulla he had ditched, and she, typical woman, craved revenge. Either way, Monika didn't care much anyway. While she might still have blown her top a couple of months earlier, she let it all pass now. The saleswoman was more shocked and upset than Monika.

After the mysterious Kuwaiti woman—who had beautiful, big eyes outlined in black khol—paid for the purchase, leaving Um-Mohammed a £140 tip, she asked for the telephone number of the boutique. She said she needed it to let her staff enquire when new stock would be available.

"We will gladly inform you, Madam, if you leave us your number," countered Um-Mohammed.

"I am not in the habit of leaving my telephone number with strangers," she replied at the top of her voice. Having snatched the business card out of Um-Mohammed's hand with her long, fuchsia-red, painted fingertips, she whizzed through the door with her friend, the black woman trailing behind and carrying her bags. As a long black limousine with dark golden-mirrored windows drew up, a black driver jumped out to open doors and the enigma disappeared.

Monika never bothered to get to the roots of what that was all about.

The turquoise telephone in the pleasant, pastel, bright little shop started to ring in the morning and rang all day. Frustrated sex-starved males are desperate to talk to females in Kuwait. Either they'd start politely by asking Monika to hang on and just talk to them because they had seen her and fancied her, or they'd talk filthy from the start, whispering imaginary sex positions and sex acts down the line, saying things like "Help me, my milk is getting sour" or "I have cut your picture from a magazine, which is always with me. I am now holding my prick, looking at it and thinking of you. You turn me on. Shall I tell you how many times I have fucked you? Every day, my love . . ." —and so on. There was the third kind: men who tried to talk her into a meeting because they so adored her. They would say that Abdulla had other women behind her back and wasn't worthy of her. Then, there was the female kind: the mystery woman calling Monika who wanted her to know that Abdulla had all kinds of tidbit affairs she should know about; a couple of females calling out of bitchiness or jealousy to tell her, among other bullshit, that she should get out of Kuwait or they would break her legs if she wasn't careful, and so on. It could have been a fat and jealous wife who had found one of Monika's magazine photos in her husband's possession and gave the matter much more importance than it actually deserved. Kuwait is very small and close knit. News travels fast, and every male and female in Kuwait soon had heard about "Domino."

One of the big drawbacks of Kuwaiti life is that Kuwait's people have no hobbies to fill time, as Westerners do. So, not knowing what to do with themselves and having whole days at their disposal, they love to think up and get into mischief. If Um-Mohammed answered the telephone, the caller asked for Monika. If Monika was not in the shop, the caller just slammed down the receiver. That annoying telephone business got so bad and so out of hand that Monika taped some conversations and gave them to Abdulla. He didn't know what to do with them and had the telephone number changed, and when that did not make any difference, he had the telephone officially tapped by the Ministry of Post and Telephones.

But here, again, as was the case with the car license plate numbers, the offensive VIP Kuwaitis protected themselves through wastas and were only ticked off. Nothing happened to them, and Monika never got to learn the identity of any decent, or filthy, admirers. Once the perverts were apprehended and rebuked (probably only slightly), they just started to be more careful about calling.

"I know your phone is tapped, but no one can trace me a second time," was what one of them kept saying.

So much for what reporting the matter had accomplished for Monika.

Young and old men, some not even able to read, entered the ladies' boutique and stood there like the man in the moon, just staring at Monika or maybe starting a conversation and talking rubbish, asking if she sold cigarettes or some other ridiculous item like 'Durex' that turned them on and had nothing to do with her boutique.

Others came and clumsily bought an item of clothing, taking their time, just to get a chance to talk to a pretty white woman, to look at her close up—and then they probably went and masturbated with her in mind or made one of those obscene phone calls.

All of it contributed to Monika's soaring temperature, high already in that hot and humid climate. It was awful!

Young boys would drive their cars past the shop again and again, tooting their horns, smiling and waving. In Kuwait there is no law against hooting one's horn, and everybody hoots it all day long.

It didn't happen just to Monika; it happened to all the girls and women in Kuwait's shops. It could have been that Monika tickled their fancies more. Because she was pretty, because she was an uncovered, white blonde, because some people in particular wanted to bedevil her, she seemed to attract double the attention in Kuwait. Whatever the reason, she felt she was singled out for a rougher ride.

In the huge building in which Domino was situated, Domino's door stood out because it was decorated to look like an outsized black domino, white dots and all. An Iraqi tailor (a woman) had her business two floors up. When Monika ran out of certain garments or her stock from Vienna was late in arriving, she bought material and patterns from the market and had some garments sewn by that tailor. Everything was fine in that quarter until the day that, on her way to her boutique, Monika's eye was arrested two shops away from Domino in front of a newly painted store that had previously specialized in all sorts of exquisite and expensive presents and now had changed its name to "Bambino" and was unaccountably showing Monika's maternity garments in its display windows. The sly Iraqi woman had opened a maternity and large sizes store exactly like Monika's.

Monika entered the new shop to confront its owner, who blushed like a beetroot and didn't know where to put her face.

"You could have told me and discussed what was on your mind, if you were half-way decent. We probably could have come to some agreement—like, for instance, to open one big shop together as partners, or we could have agreed that you would sell the large sized and I only the maternity wear. But to go and do exactly like me—and that, next door—and have the audacity and cheek to use my designs, too, that really stinks, and you should be ashamed. I wouldn't like to be in your skin." Monika said what she had to say and left. Whereas in the past the guilty one had always said "Now the sun shines" when she met Monika, now she had not one word to say for herself.

She had to have known that what she was doing was indecent in the highest degree. "Domino" was regularly advertised in all of Kuwait's magazines and newspapers. Even people who could not read and came to find Domino by word of mouth walked, of course, into Bambino by mistake. A drop in sales was imminent.

Only three months later, Monika drove early to the shop and beheld all of Bambino's contents lying strewn over pavement and roadside. The landlord, an Aseel Kuwaiti, had evicted the Iraqi personally with the help of two workers because the Iraqi had taken over the lease from the previous owner without the Aseel's permission and had not evacuated the shop after repeated warnings.

The moral of that story was, for Monika, that God is just and that it is true that whatever you do wrong in this world you have to pay for in this world, too. "So," she prayed, "when—God, oh, please, when—will it be the in-laws' turn to pay?"

The moment was sure to come, just as day follows night! Seeing all those garments strewn about made Monika wish for greater justice.

In that boutique of hers, one had to have the eyes and ears of an eagle and the brain of an elephant to hold on to one's stock, not to let clothes slip unpaid for through the door unnoticed. It was never the Kuwaiti Aseels who shoplifted. They are very proud and honest. No, it was the non-Kuwaiti Arabs who were the thieves and sometimes, much to Monika's surprise, bedouins, as when one fine day a frail, small, white-bearded older bedouin entered with his three very young wives. They smelt a bit of camel, to put it mildly, and the first thing they did was to go for Monika's blonde locks, touching her hair for texture, and admiringly stroking her hand's white skin.

"Now, you have examined me, let me see your face. Remove your masks for me," demanded Monika.

"No, that's a sin. *Haram. Haram.* Nobody, only our husband, is allowed to see our faces," the trio giggled. One of the three was swollen with pregnancy. All three squashed into the dressing room. Refusing assistance, they tried on fifteen different styles, after which they finally decided on a maternity trouser suit. Monika liked bedouins. To her, they were such a mystery, just as she was to them. The bedouin husband sat proudly erect, drinking Arabic coffee, which was offered to all customers, as he watched and listened to his wives. After he had paid and the wives walked behind, leaving the distance required by custom between them and their husband, to show respect, Monika realized that of the fifteen items they tried on she had only thirteen left now. Hurriedly, she sent Um-Mohammed out to trace and bring them back. Two of the wives had split the missing trouser suit between them. One had put on the top, and the other, the bottoms—all easily hidden under their loose black robes. The frail-looking bedouin had a hell of a lot of go in him. He reached for his *Argal,* the black silk rope around his headdress, and used it to whip his wives, now screaming, pregnant or not. You would not have believed the strength that little man possessed.

He made the women run screaming in all directions for cover, like chickens hiding behind the clothes, the curtains, and the chair. Um-Mohammed and Monika had to intervene here or run the risk of having to call an ambulance to the shop because the man had taken off his camel-hide slippers and given them a further bashing on heads and bodies with those. Monika and Um-Mohammed felt sorry for the women. The bedouin wanted to return the already purchased trouser suit as a punishment for them, but Monika did not agree. The man, all out of breath, swore at his wives in Allah's name and cursed the day he had married them. He said they were ruining him and his life. He said he had had to take a third wife because Allah had prevented the first two from bearing him a son; he had six daughters already.

In Kuwait live many Palestinian refugees, almost outnumbering Aseel Kuwaitis. Because they produce so many children, they were very good customers at Domino. Wondering why they were breeding like rabbits in a strange country where they were looked upon as third-class citizens with no possibility or hope of returning to their homeland, she asked a Palestinian father who entered with four small kids and a pregnant wife one day.

"I have got six children now, three boys and three girls. The girls don't count now, but they can bear boys later on. I expect that at least two of my boys will die in our fight for the cause of winning back our homeland Palestine. Then, we will be left with only one boy, do you see? The more children we bear, the greater our chances of going back home one day." Understandable Palestinian theory. Let's hope they will be able to go home one day soon and that their determination is not fostered in vain.

CHAPTER TWENTY-TWO

A CANCER SCARE AND OTHER CLOSE CALLS

Monika's poor health went from bad to worse. Stomach pains developed. She did not feel like getting up in the mornings: she saw no point at all in living through the day, and when her poor children (who were well looked after by nannies) wanted to be near her, she even sent them away out of the room because she didn't want them to see her so low and in pain. Her nights were totally sleepless. She felt hoards of imaginary ants swarming all over her skin, which increased to such an extent that she sometimes sat in the bathroom most of the night not to wake Abdulla with her scratching. She scratched at her body furiously, wishing she could get her hands on a wire brush—that's how bad she felt. She lost her appetite and vomited continuously. What started as mild headaches had turned into raving migraines that persisted for days. The pain was so intense that she simply wanted to die. She wanted to close her eyes, never to open them again. If she walked, she felt a massive, heavy burden hanging onto her chest like a 10 kg iron weight pulling her to the floor. Completely drained, she had now lost all interest in the shop and gave instructions to her assistant, mostly by telephone, while Abdulla went to check the books and collect the money. Monika spent most of her time lying in a darkened room. What was now left of her was a tired, ill, haggard wreck of bones and skin that bore no resemblance whatsoever to the once pretty, bubbly, fresh girl who had entered Kuwait so full of life and enthusiasm over twelve years ago. Now Monika was convinced she had cancer and that no man would waste a second look on her, and if so, then only out of pity.

The in-laws rattled away, taking the greatest pleasure in spreading the news of Monika's ill health all over Kuwait.

"She has got cancer and the doctors cannot help her anymore!" reached Aya and other friends of Monika by word of mouth. The origin of that rumor was, of course, the al-Amahanis in Keefan. Some women who hardly knew her came to visit Monika on orders from the in-laws, to keep a close check on how Monika was progressing towards the grave or out of sheer nosiness.

Monika gave her servants instructions that she would see no one. While in the past she enjoyed a tipple, now she drank vodka and gin like lemonade, calling these spirits her best friends. And while she had never before missed Vienna, her instinct and senses directed her back home to her mother, to whom we know she had never been especially close. Even Abdulla looked worried and thought she might have cancer, although he didn't say as much since none of his doctor friends could make head nor tail of her case. He encouraged her to go for a proper check-up in Vienna, following her own suggestion and to have her off his hands. It was acceptable in his books to accompany his precious sister abroad for special medical evaluations and treatment, but not his wife. As usual, Monika—in need, even desperately ill and half dead—had to fend for herself. She didn't dare dwell on what would become of her children if she'd pass on. For all she knew, her in-laws, especially Sabiha (who, if stupidity had wings, would fly through the room like a pigeon), sat together already, making plans to reorganize her house and take over her children in the near future, after she had gone.

Monika bet herself that mother-in-law was planning to move in with Abdulla. Her own house was no comparison to what Monika lived in and had helped to create. The old wicked witch often asked Abdulla which room in the house she would occupy once she got too old to manage her Keefan house by herself. To which question Abdulla always answered sugary-sweetly, "Any room you want, Mother dearest. The whole house is at your service. You know that. You are the head of the heap, and I, my wife, and children are all at your feet."

"Feet, my foot!" Monika thought to herself.

Dentist Pavlik and brother Werner looked straight past Monika at the Vienna airport. They did not even recognize her when she stood right in front of them and looked them in the eye. Her voice was what startled them into an awareness of who she was. After they exchanged greetings, Werner closed his hands with lots of space left around Monika's tiny wasp waist and joked that he had always dreamt of clasping a female like that. He was trying hard to underplay her skeletal appearance. On the way home, he had to stop the car three times to let her out to throw up. The plane trip to Vienna had made her delirious. Monika was pleased that it was behind her. Dentist Pavlik sat next to her daughter, crying and preaching to her about the Arabs she had warned her against in good time while Werner, with a cool head, told his mother off.

"If you cry and scold her, it won't help to make her better, Mother, you know. For Christ's sake, act and think positive. She came home for help, not to be cried at."

Dentist Pavlik must have seen the point. She suppressed her tears and dried her eyes immediately, gearing the conversation to the medical appointments she had prearranged, starting the next morning with Doctor Huber, who had been their family doctor since Monika could remember.

Only a couple of hours in Vienna and Monika felt better already. The peaceful, quiet atmosphere in which people lived there, compared to where she had just come from—hyper-noisy Kuwait—had its first pleasant healing effect on her.

Doctor Huber greeted her warmly. After listening patiently to all her complaints and symptoms and the fear she had of cancer, he told her not to think so pessimistically.

"There are one thousand and one possibilities as to what your problem might be—besides cancer—problems that can be medically treated or be operated on to make you a healthy being again," he reassured her. The doctor made half a dozen appointments with various specialists, for X-rays, blood tests, tissue tests. She had to see a gynecologist, a psychologist, a heart specialist. He told her to come and see him again in two weeks, for by then all her tests should have reached his desk.

For a week, Monika rushed from one doctor to another and lived on her nerves in fear of negative outcomes for a week after that. When she finally saw Doctor Huber again, he greeted her right away with the words: "No cancer anywhere to be detected, young lady." A mighty stone fell off her chest. "Please sit down. Make yourself comfortable on my couch. What we will do now is going to take a while. We will sit us down and do a bit of talking. Now, I know you are married to an Arab, but I want to know more. I would like you to tell me the story of your life in Arabia. Tell me, under what sorts of circumstances do you live there, in Kuwait, and try to be thorough."

Monika didn't need much coaxing. It was a welcome invitation to open up her heart and talk about her life to the doctor. She told him of her weak husband, of his latest affair, the nasty in-laws, the way she felt trapped in that new house in Kuwait, that she couldn't leave Abdulla because of her three children. Monika got everything off her chest, and it did her the world of good to have an understanding, distinguished person listen to her troubles. When she had finally finished, the assistant served herbal tea. And then it was the doctor's turn to speak. He gave her a long lecture.

"Now listen to me carefully, Monika. You will be surprised at what I have to tell you. There is nothing at all physically wrong with you except for a spastic colon, which can be treated with patience, and some ulcers in your stomach that seem to be healed up; but what is drastically wrong with you is your marriage to that Arab in Kuwait and your in-laws. That unhappy marriage has made your mind ill, which in turn has made your body ill. Body and mind go as one. They are indeed one."

Monika didn't quite get it. How can one's mind make the body ill? Was that really possible? She let the doctor speak.

"If you go back in memory, you remember that you told me you were very enthusiastic and willing and positive up until you moved into the new house, despite all the troubles you went through; and then you gave up. Shall I tell you why you gave up? You gave up because your last hopes, the hopes you put everything into, of freeing yourself from the in-laws were broken. Right up until then you always lived with hope. Having none left is what has made you ill, made your elastic finally snap. And you worsened your condition further by fearing that you might have an incurable cancer sitting somewhere in your body. You were convinced you had a fatal illness, and your fear made you lose touch with reality. You became totally incapable of coping. Now, Monika, just in time I have saved you from a complete, what we call, nervous breakdown. After today you will discover that most of what you thought were symptoms of a cancer are no more than the effects of prolonged physical tensions and continual anxieties under which you have lived for so many years, for such a long period, in Kuwait, in your prison of depression because you could not see how to make any changes in the way you lived your unhappy life.

"You tell me you are financially dependent on your husband and therefore think that without his help and 'okay' you would be lost. Once you are convinced that what I am telling you is really the core of your problem you will be half way towards recovery. You have to make up your mind. If you carry on like this, you will become a worse wreck than you are already, with the possibility of maybe really developing cancer, and then, as you know, you won't be any good to your children. So you see, you don't do them a favor by carrying on where you have left off.

"Or you can do as I advise you to do: you wake up, get a grip on yourself, and join the world out there, young lady. You fight for your rights and beliefs, don't lay your heart on a golden platter and let those dunderheads misuse it. You were raised to live among civilized people, and when you live among those people, you have to give as good as you receive. I know it is not what you were brought up to do, but you have to learn. Once you get the hang of it, it is easy. Don't hold anything back. Next time mother-in-law enters your home and insults you, you take the next best chair and chase her out of the house. If your husband gets in the way, go for him, too. You have to convince him you mean business. You have to let the anger out of your system and not leave it there suppressed, or you will never get your health back to normal. Fight for what you believe in, muscle them. It's a great pity, but you have lost faith in yourself completely; and that you have to get back, starting from now, this very minute, once and for all, never to lose hold of it again.

"Now, let's analyze your migraines. Let me explain. Your migraines are an escape route of the soul. In 90% of all migraine cases I get, no organic reason can be found. Very dutiful, correct, ambitious people just like you are especially susceptible. Usually, the reason for them is a situation or conflict that seems unsolvable, either in one's job or private life. So the illness serves them as a rescue path for the soul. Through it one escapes all annoyance and bother and feels consideration of one's fellow man, which in your case isn't even the case. The pain deafens one's burdens and thoughts. The problem is pushed aside, out on one's consciousness, and now you know how the rabbit runs with you, my dear. It's nothing that cannot be repaired by you with your own tools. Every problem is solvable. It might need patience. And if not today, then things will surely happen tomorrow. But you have to take the initiative and help it along.

"Many people underestimate their inner voice and don't know that we live through our soul, only because one day the rest is doomed to death. So, you, my child, go back to Kuwait and remember that you have to feed and care for body and soul, too. Be strong. Don't commit emotional suicide.

"As for the sex, try looking upon it as something you indulge in only for your own benefit and enjoyment for the time being. Think not that he uses you, but that you use him for your own needs. Close your eyes and imagine you lie there with the man of your dreams—not your cheating husband but someone you fancy. That can't prove too difficult a task for you, can it? And let fantasy help you along.

CHAPTER TWENTY-THREE

BACK IN KUWAIT AND SMARTER ALL THE TIME

Dr. Huber had asked, "Why shouldn't you betray him in your mind when he has done it in mind and body?" He had also said, "You are a very attractive young woman. The whole world is still at your feet, and tomorrow when your children are grown up—and time flies, my child—then you come home to Vienna where you belong and start a whole new life. But remember your old doctor's advice: think positive, act positively, and attack the problems by their horns as soon as they arise instead of brooding over them. So, you see the solution. The key to your health rests in your hands." The fatherly Dr. Huber had ordered Monika to keep a strict diet for the following three months to get her colon back to normal, and he had prescribed some tranquilizers to be used for emergencies only.

The very moment she had gotten up from the consultant's chair, Monika was already a healthier person. The more the doctor had spoken and advised, the more he had convinced his patient that his diagnosis was dead right. Monika had left the consulting room walking on air, feeling happy to be alive—in strong contrast to the condition she had been in an hour or so earlier when she had walked slowly into it, dragging herself along with heavy steps, as if her legs had been filled with lead, a sharp pain lying heavily on her chest, expecting to be given a death warrant. Dentist Pavlik had been, of course, relieved, too, and had wanted to keep her daughter in Vienna for another week, but Monika had to go back. An invisible magnet pulled her in the direction of her children. Reflecting on these matters, Monika actually enjoyed her return flight. She was going back to Kuwait relieved that she was after all, thank God, not seriously ill. The trip to the doctor in Vienna had been as good as a holiday because in the short time home she had managed to get together with some of her friends, she had gone for motorbike rides with Werner, which had brought back happy memories, and at night they had hit the town together. All of it had helped her to collect new zest for life. In Austria she had been able to discuss her troubles with intelligent beings and had been given lots of advice—well meant—by everybody. The problems no longer loomed as huge monsters she had thought couldn't be conquered. They actually shrank—and considerably.

Doctor Mardetschläger, a respected lawyer in Vienna who mainly handled divorces and was a close friend of Monika's mother, had told Monika that in Catholic Austria saying one's marriage vows in church was no guarantee either of a marriage "happy ever after." As a matter of fact, he had added, Austria is a front runner among countries that have the highest divorce rates, and a happy marriage was to be found like a needle in a haystack there, too, as the saying goes. Monika thought about that, too.

If one thinks about it logically, she concluded, it's practically absurd—impossible really—to vow to love, to obey, and to care for someone for a whole lifetime, until death parts. It's like making a promise never to fall ill, which is, of course, quite impossible, too. It's a stupid, man-made, old cobbler's work. Don't lawyers do well out of it, though? Was this institution discovered by lawyers—does anybody know?

Abdulla and the kids met Monika at the airport, where she discovered in grief that the big trunk filled with toys and clothes she had bought with great love and care for the children—worth hundreds of pounds—was missing. She was told there was hope that it could still be traced, but Monika's intuition told her she could make a cross over it right there and then—and she was proven right. It had apparently got nicked in Lebanon, where she had been in transit.

Back in Kuwait, Monika cut out the drinking, stuck rigidly to her diet, took an active interest in her dress shop, and felt her health and self popping back to normal—while all other things continued as before. The relatives still telephoned and came, and Abdulla was never at home, and when he was, his moods were as unpredictable as ever. The servants were relieved to have their Madam back, for mother-in-law had busied herself every day at the house, ordering them around and even taking them back to her own house to do all sorts of dirty jobs there.

As she was departing for Austria, Monika had told Sakia to lock the bedroom every day after Abdulla had gone to work and after the room had been cleaned and to keep the key in her pocket and unlock it only when Abdulla returned home. Monika had thought it out that way to keep her in-laws from sniffing through her most private possessions and to prevent their spreading their curses and potions among her things. Yet, she might as well not have said anything. The first day after Monika took off for Vienna, the in-laws all came around—even Sabiha—and demanded, first of all, the bedroom key! Sakia, bless her, had refused. So they were immediately on the phone to Abdulla at the hospital, and he ordered Sakia to open the door for them at once. They entered falling over themselves, as Sakia reported, and ordered Sakia out of the rooms. After they had gone, they left a mess that looked like a place that had been ransacked by thugs—turned upside down—just as in the films, Sakia said. They had gone through *everything*—clothes, makeup, drawers, and photographs (of which they took—they stole—almost half). Monika had anticipated exactly what the sisters might be up to in her absence and had kept jewelry and important papers well under lock and key in a secret little drawer. They had tried on all her clothes in her absence, never having gotten the message that it was not the dress but the figure that counted. They thought, by buying and wearing as she did, they would look like her, too!

But, on her return, Monika made the greatest effort not to let anything affect and trouble her. She was doing quite well, considering the crazy things going on all around her.

Out of the blue Abdulla came home one day and announced that he had been ordered by the Ministry of Health to the United States for a six-month medical course in glamorous California at the Presbyterian Hospital. Monika knew he had applied for it behind her back because the Ministry does not give such orders to any Aseel Kuwaiti without his willingness and explicit consent, but she didn't care a fig. She knew this could become the real test period for her newfound strength: facing the in-laws alone. Several days had passed since Abdulla's departure when one night Monika was taken by surprise to hear the cow Sabiha's voice on the phone after Monika had ignored her now for years. Really, this female had neither self-respect nor pride at all! She said her brother had not phoned and that her mother was worried. Had he telephoned Monika?

"Yes, he has," answered Monika. Then there was silence, after which mother-in-law came on the line wanting to know why she, Monika, had received a telephone call and not his mother. The old woman's tone was accusing. Monika responded that she did not know the reason and, what's more, did not care. Mother-in-law moaned into the receiver that Monika was callous and didn't appreciate nor deserve to be living in such a splendid house and that she only dared to be so cheeky to her because Abdulla was so far away and could not protect his mother.

"Do you really think your son Abdulla was born with the gift to protect the devil?"

What courageous Monika had just had the guts to say needed some time to sink in at the other end of the line. They were not used to hearing her talk like that. Mother-in-law interpreted to her daughters, and Monika could hear the family gearing up for a real good row as all of them shouted abuse at her at the same time and left her with the good news that they would come around and sort her out. Monika slammed the phone down. She remembered her sweet doctor in Vienna and that gave her the strength she needed.

Fifteen minutes later mother-in-law, Diba, who had much recovered from the stroke, and Tamader, grown into a spoiled young woman who fancied herself the most beautiful thing in this world, walked hurriedly from their black limousine, plastic bathroom slippers on their feet, black covers loosely thrown over their night clothes and blowing in a warm, humid breeze. They entered through the open gate like a bunch of enraged pilgrims with hot chili peppers up their arses. Monika stood, arms crossed over her chest, expecting them. She had her Elvis music on Loud, purposely because they hated it, and Senta standing close by, not wagging her tail because they hated her, too, and the feeling was, of course, mutual. The three boys surrounded their mother closely. None of them moved to give their grandmother the false kiss that never came from the heart but that they had been trained like dogs by their father to give her. They didn't offer the false kiss because Abdulla was not there to order it and because, with him gone, they did not have to expect punishment.

"Why doesn't anybody kiss me?" the old dragon stood and shouted. "*You*, Hamra, are the reason! You turn the children against me!" She ordered Sakia: "Turn off that screeching sound! It gives me a headache."

"You leave my music alone, Sakia," came Monika's loud, clear voice. To the intruders she said, "This is my home here and I play what I like. You go and give orders in your house."

"You dirty hamra, you! You will not succeed in taking my only son and turning him against me! In our veins runs the same blood. We all look upon you as a big mistake Abdulla made—an outsider, here today and gone tomorrow. Tell your children to kiss me! Teach them manners. Teach them that I am the head of this family and that neither you nor anybody except God can change that! Haven't you realized that by now!"

Monika stood with a slight smile on her face, not moving an eyelid, watching the performance. Whatever mother said was repeated eagerly by her daughters, the sound trailing behind like echoes.

"I will put salt in your pants, make no mistake, you daughter of a dog! This house will never be yours to rule in and order about. It is my son's and mine and the girls', and one day I will come here. I will move in because this is where I will spend my days when I am old—with my son!"

Patient till now, Monika thought it was about time to speak, especially a she thought of something fitting to say.

"Go and look at your house in Keefan, lived in by four women who have servants to clean for you and yet it still looks like a pigsty. If I were you, I would think twice before deciding to live here in my house, because in my house it is much too clean for your lot. From what I have seen, you've all got an allergy against cleanliness; it makes you ill. Since you come here to create trouble, you'd better go now. None of us is keen to see you, you black-hearted lot, and because your hearts are so black, none of you are happy. You just go around begrudging other people's happiness. If any of you sees me holding hands with Abdulla, it makes you ill with jealousy!" Monika had started to speak in a normal, collected voice, but she had lost hold hallway through and had ended up at the top of her voice.

"You bloody bitch, you hamra, who are *you* to insult my poor mother!" Tamader shouted. "Nobody dares to speak to her like that! You just wait till Abdulla hears of this!"

"That mother of yours and the whole lot of you had it coming since I first set eyes on you. Go away, live your lives, and let me live mine! I am married to Abdulla and not to any of you, and now I ask you—for the last time—to leave. We are invited out for supper. I won't let my friends wait." With that little white lie to tease them, Monika finished off her polished speech. Her courage surprised her as much as it knocked them for six. Under further rude remarks, the three troublemakers had no choice but to turn towards the door; and, as Sakia closed it behind them, she clapped her hands in admiration.

"Bravo, bravo, Madam, well done! You should have done that a long time ago."

The children joined in, too, and Senta wagged her tail busily. She knew everybody was happy and gave a little bark. Monika sat down on her wine-red telephone table in the blue room and booked a call to Abdulla in California. He was jolly, right through to the end of the ultimatum she delivered to him—which was that his mother, sisters, and any others of that vile category he called his family and their friends were never to telephone or visit at the house again unless explicitly invited; and then were to behave in a civilized manner, as she did when he dragged her along to visit the in-laws; and if he did not call them at once to tell them so, she was packing to make room for them and taking the children with her to Europe; they would not die; somehow they would survive there without him; he had his choice. And to Monika's surprise, Abdulla was very understanding and even said he sympathized with her.

"I don't blame you, Sweetie," he said. "If they get on your nerves, I will phone them straight away and tell them to stay away from your house. It is your house, Sweetie." Monika did not believe her ears—and luck. For once, Abdulla was cordially in her favor. He was understanding and on her side, and that was such an uncharacteristic sign in Abdulla that Monika had to find a reason, some explanation, for it. She had probably interrupted him in bed with some pussy or another, but the time it would have mattered to her was history. Nothing he did could resurrect her dead emotions, after Fawzia. On second thought, Abdulla's abnormally normal behavior—such a surprise—might probably (and more likely) be due to the fact that he was out of his family's reach and, therefore, not brain- and body-washed with evil elixirs.

After that showdown with Abdulla over the phone, his family stopped phoning and coming over to the house. A welcome calm fell upon the house, a calm that Monika had never before experienced in Kuwait. It was thanks to her waking up and finally putting her foot down. Monika the latecomer who had been raised to obey blindly and ask no questions had finally arrived: she had at long last broken their hold on her, even if she hadn't broken the hold they had on Abdulla, something she had no interest in doing. For all she cared, he could live and sleep with them, too. The only reason in this world that she was still where she was, that kept her in Kuwait, was her children. If only she had delivered an ultimatum years ago, she thought; maybe then, if she had had the courage or if someone like Dr. Huber in Vienna had egged her on earlier, she need not have gone through endless problems and heartaches at the new house. It was easy to be wise in hindsight. Monika had never asked Abdulla what his message to them from America had been, but it was obviously effective. In a way, it proved he cared for her more that she had thought he did because now, away from her, he put her before his family. It was the first time he'd taken so major a position in her favor when he could easily have said to her, "Take your children and go! See how far you get." All he had to do to stop her from leaving the country would have been to instruct the airport authorities by telephone not to let her and the children leave, have her passport confiscated, or even make her leave by force and keep the children behind—as at least two Kuwaiti men whom Monika knew well had done to their wives. One was an Aseel whose wife, a German, tried to leave with her daughter without her husband's knowledge and approval. Renate had packed everything removable from the flat the couple shared. She wasn't lucky. He got wind of it through his family, by whom she was spied on like Monika, and she had to leave all her luggage behind at the airport. Renate's husband had a Kuwaiti wife Number One and three children by her who didn't let the German woman have peace of mind for one minute. For instance, when it had been Renate's turn to sleep with her husband, his teenage children took turns banging at her bedroom door all night long. The Kuwaiti had met Renate in Germany where he had gone to study. He made the working-class German girl pregnant, married her in Germany, and brought her back to Kuwait, where she was faced with the nasty reality that he—surprise, surprise!—already had a wife and several big kids.

The other victim was an English woman married to an Irani Kuwaiti. She had a young son and was highly pregnant when she tried to flee Kuwait in desperation. Poor thing. The authorities in the airport informed her spouse by telephone and then acted on her husband's behalf. He had instructed them to keep his son and the luggage behind and let her go on alone. The screaming boy was dragged away from his mother, after which she decided not to go if she had to leave the child behind. But even here she was thwarted: she was told that her husband did not want her in Kuwait anymore, and she was put on the plane to England by force.

Life writes the most bizarre stories and makes interesting reading, doesn't it? Each one of us at some time or other has read or heard of a sad story of some European girl's bad luck in a Middle Eastern country, maybe a story, indeed, similar to the one told in this hook that your nose is buried in at this very moment! Isn't it just one long stirring story with, so far, no happy ending in sight?

Then, just as Monika—at long last— thought she could enjoy her new-found peace and quiet in her own home, someone (or rather, a couple of 'someones,' male and female) started to play absolute havoc with her telephones at the shop and now at home, too.

Females spun through "Domino" like a whirlwind, only to insult her and then leave the store, and the telephone calls she was now receiving were of a different nature, more personal than the kinky ones she had gotten up to that time. Before, they had been sex calls '*a la* Kuwait,' but now someone was really trying to get at her. The male and female voices were saying that while Abdulla was in the United States she should stop pretending that she had no one in the meantime to fuck her, that she should stop acting the lady, that a *ghaba* like her couldn't do without it. They said things like "if yogurt turns to milk again, a prostitute like you will go straight" or "Tell us, how does it feel to be tossed off by a dog?—that's why you keep a big one like that, isn't it, your filthy whore?" or they would say, laughing, "Abdulla gave me permission to fuck you while he is away. I'll be with you tonight. Get ready!"

What agitated Monika most was that the callers always knew her exact whereabouts, just as if she'd been shadowed by some detective. As soon as she stepped into her house or the shop, the telephone began to ring and she'd he told where she had been, what she had bought, and what she was wearing; and that situation got her down. It felt ever so eerie, to say the least. One didn't need to he psychic to realize this harassment was an in-law-instigated hate campaign against her. Her common sense—and she had plenty of that—told her so. In their primitivism, they knew no barriers; they recognized no bars to their desire to get back at her for having to keep their distance from her house.

Even so, all of a sudden, Monika felt really trapped; it was one of her mother-in-law's particularly toxic, especially evil spells. She firmly sensed it, for what happened to her—the way she now felt—was not of a normal nature. She felt restless, feverish, and nervous, felt scared but did not know of what (there was really nothing to be scared of), felt unsure of herself, and her skin had gone goose pimply. To cut a complicated story short, she felt and lived with the feeling once again of being the victim of an evil spell, of sitting on a time bomb ready to explode at any minute. She was so fully occupied and absorbed by the unreal situation she found herself in that she hardly thought about much else. She could not free herself of that thick, heavy foreboding, sensing everywhere invisible eyes watching. Meanwhile, faithful Um-Mohammed sprinkled the shop with Holy water to destroy the power of whatever strange force it was that was bothering Monika and advised her, after two weeks of sheer havoc, to stay at home for a couple of days, to take the telephone off the hook, and to relax. At least that way nobody could get near enough to get at her. Monika agreed and thought it a good idea to stay inside her own four walls to unwind, relax, and escape.

That night on her way home, she was involved in the strangest of car accidents. As she drove, she wondered if anybody was following her and then she wondered who it might he. At the red traffic lights, she had stopped in the middle lane, had come to a complete halt, when a school bus shot up on her right side, rammed her car, squashed its right side like a tin of sardines, pulling and carrying her along right on through the red lights. After a couple of meters, the bus slowed down. Its driver put the bus into reverse gear, lurched, then put it into reverse a couple more times, until Monika's Datsun stood clear of it, after which the bus took off like a torpedo. Feeling like she'd been stung by a huge bee, she followed that bus with her left hand pressing hard on her car's horn. She had her foot on the gas, and her car gave all it had while other cars on the road made way for her; and when she reached the bus she drove up close, overtook it, and put herself right in front of it, forcing the bus to halt. Enraged, she got out of her wrecked vehicle—and who do you think drove the bus? A bunch of school kids, that's who—twelve- to fourteen-year-olds on a joy ride. The Kuwaiti boys looked remorseful and apologized. Monika, thinking of Nabeel and Sulaiman, took the bus's number and drove home shaking like a leaf—wondering, of course, if that strange accident had anything to do with the wicked, invisible influence she was under.

When she got home, put her car keys down, and was just starting to tell her children and servants what had happened to her, the telephone rang. She lifted the receiver and a male voice said, "If you had had a proper fuck by me that accident tonight would not have happened. Don't you..." Monika didn't let him finish, but put the receiver down and lifted it again and put the receiver on the table. She was flabbergasted. What the bloody, fucking hell was going on here? That influence was one of the strongest and worst she had encountered in Kuwait. Feeling that she had no privacy and that she was safe nowhere, she had to talk about this to somebody who understood her, so she phoned across the street to Laila's mother and announced herself. The old woman said that Monika's condition was a typical one and that she would need a white plate that nobody had yet eaten from and that she would then write something from the Holy Koran on that plate for her, which would protect her from the worst. All Monika had to do was pour soup into that plate and consume it, making sure the writing had all very well dissolved and disappeared into the liquid and down into her stomach. Monika wasn't quite in tune with the idea but promised to buy a plate. She felt much better after talking about her problem. The woman also told her that if she were to cross the sea by ship or plane, then all spells put on her would be automatically broken. Now, that made her think! That made sense to her. Hadn't Abdulla flown to L.A. en route to which he had crossed the ocean? Was that why he was so nice and understanding and on her side against his family? Because the evil spells mother-in-law had put on him were broken and he was now in his right mind? Who really knows! An amateur on the subject, Monika could only do guesswork.

Yet on her foggy future sky neither plane flights nor ship journeys were anywhere in sight, and not to be expected in the near future either. For three days after the smash up, Monika stayed safe in her house. The car had been taken for repair. With the phone off the hook, she felt a bit better now. When the time came, she drove Abdulla's pure, pure red, lovely Chevrolet to her shop. On her way she stopped—don't laugh—to buy a white plate, and she put it on the seat beside her. In front of her drove a small, yellow mechanical digger—rather slowly. Monika overtook it and drove on as normal, but that mechanical digger didn't want to be overtaken by her and came up noisily to overtake her. The driver in green overalls turned around, giving her a provocative dirty smile, driving in front of her very slowly while he made some smoke come out of some thick exhaust pipe right next to him. Had he known that what he had dared to tease here was not just some white woman but the wife of an Aseel Kuwaiti, he would not have dared to wink at her with one eyelid. Agitated, Monika was ready to take off again. He realized this and gave gas, too, and didn't let her pass him. And once again she was overcome by that strange sensation that had the power to sink deep right into the very marrow of her bones and made her wonder what, for heaven's sake, it was. All the way, that mechanical digger played games with her and didn't let her pass. She had to drive by stops and starts. Close to "Domino" now, she was annoyed to say the least, and as she gave her left turn signal and started her turn that fucker did likewise, turning left to continue his game with her. He now drove close up to a wall thinking Monika had parked somewhere to the right or left behind him and so spun his machine around a half turn, not realizing that Monika stood right behind him, close up, where he could not see her and where she had put herself because she thought "He's not going to get away unpunished" and had in mind to call the police. Yet, instead, fast, like a sword's edge, the sharp iron teeth sliced the brand new, beautiful, red Chevy open from its front in a straight line right through to the back, with the ease of a cook slicing fish—after which one could see right through it. The white plate lay broken in two. People near the shop knew her, of course, and called the police and made sure that the culprit couldn't escape. Monika was shaken and confused. She found herself in such an unreal situation, here, that she felt paralyzed and speechless. The last time she drove, her car got it; and now this. When and where is it going to stop? Was the power of mother-in-law's or whoever's witchcraft really that powerful? Or was it just a bit more coming her way of what she had already had plenty of?—sheer bad luck!

Up to now, she had never caused nor even been involved in the smallest of fender-benders, not in all of her twelve years of driving in Kuwait. After halfway having gotten over the shock, Monika stepped out of the car still very dizzy, to approach the living reason for the smash up. Now the driver stood there innocently, as if butter wouldn't melt in his mouth, looking very scared and presumably sorry for what he had done.

"Radi!" shot Monika's angry voice at him, "I can't *believe* it. It's you! How dare you, you dirty little rat."

Before her stood a man she knew well, for he was the Palestinian kitchen helper she had employed previously at her restaurant for a short time and had then fired because he wasn't any good.

"Sorry, Madam. I didn't know it was you. I didn't recognize you."

"So bloody what! You didn't recognize me—is *that* your excuse? What makes you think you can drive around Kuwait teasing white women?"

The police came, took details, and carried Radi away with them. In the middle of the bustle of Monika's bewitched life, she entered the shop very low key, and yes, you've guessed it, the phone rang—mind you, she actually expected it—and a by now familiar voice spoke, "Silly girl, silly girl, you just don't listen to me. That's why you will never learn. That's your second accident within a week. All because you are so frustrated. Let me give you a good fuck before the third accident happens. You don't want to die young, do you?"

Monika had so much to say to him, yet she was lost for words. She had no reply. What was the use? What had happened to her was so unreal. Those stupid Kuwaitis gave her hell, and there she was powerless with no way she could have gotten hold of them because they were Aseels. What a laugh for the civilized world! Monika phoned Laila's mother to tell her what had happened this time.

"My child, you need strong protection. It is a bad sign to me that the plate you bought was broken. I better take you to a very respected wise old man who has a good reputation. He will be able to help you more than I can, but that will cost you. He is not cheap."

"No, thank you. It is very kind of you, but visiting a witch doctor isn't really me, to be honest." Monika was of two minds about meddling with the supernatural. She would have tried the trick with the plate. Maybe it would have proven positive, but she wasn't to go any farther with potions, drinks, little poems that she would have to blubber numerous times a day and to have to pay dearly for it as well. Monika thought back, remembering that often, when she had lived with the in-laws, they sat in a circle discussing how to get rid of Diba's alcoholic, sex maniacal husband, who could get no hard on because of his drinking and therefore could not satisfy Diba. He molested male and female servants sexually and therefore no servant stayed for long. It was very hard on Diba, especially after her illness. But worst of all, he grossly mistreated the children and Diba. He would bash them about like tennis balls. If a child wet his bed, he would burn his penis with a match and let him stand naked, freezing, in the hallway's draught. Then there came a time when one of his teenage sons had to sleep in the nude with him and tell his father stories, actual children's stories, to send him to sleep. It was no unusual event for Diba to be hit black and blue and then thrown out of her house by him. Abdulla had tried fruitlessly with his wastas to put his brother-in-law into a mental hospital, but had failed because the maniac was related to sheikhs who had stronger wastas. When Abdulla had to go and fetch Diba and bring her back to their mother's house where the women would sit together holding council on how best to get rid of him, even kill him after all the spells they knew and had cast upon him to cause his death had proven useless, they began to talk of killing him themselves. There was the poison that was considered. Or no, maybe better to hire a killer. Or let one of his boys, who hated their father, shoot him with one of the many guns the maniac kept in the house and with which he frightened them all the time; then afterwards the son could just pretend it was all an accident. So, if they were not able to get rid of him by curse, Monika thought, then I needn't worry about myself that much really, do I?

She also remembered how she had inwardly laughed at them and thought them nitwits with their spells—but not anymore. She wouldn't say "What piffle!" now, after her experience with those strange encounters she felt on her own body. Now she thought twice. Once a non-believer, now she was convinced.

Monika's Sulaiman had come running to her once after a visit to mother-in-law's house, telling her, out of breath, "Mum, mum, do you know what Diba's son did to the goat? He held his dishdasha up and put his willy in her bottom, pushing it in and out very fast, and in the other hand he held a cigarette. What was he doing, Mum? He told me, when he saw me, not to tell anybody." Like father, like son? Little Sulaiman was only nine years old at that time. Lots of stories of sexual encounters of the unnatural human-animal kind sweep Kuwait. With women being so strictly kept, wrapped away out of sight and out of reach, any hole served some of the men as a welcome, substitute relief.

Abdulla's six months in the U.S.A. ended. For his arrival back home, the whole house was alight and decorated with balloons, messages, and jokes by Monika, the children, and the servants—as for some big party. The decoration didn't stop at the house but spread all over the garden, which was blazing alight with multi-colored outdoor light bulbs, the kind used for Kuwaiti weddings. Does absence make the heart grow fonder? I suppose it does. As a lark, his sliced open Chevrolet stood painted all over in the brightest watercolors, like something out of Disneyland. On its trunk were written the telephone numbers dialed between Kuwait and America. Monika wrote a little poem about Linda Lovelace and the film *Deep Throat* (in which Linda Lovelace starred) because Abdulla had seen the film in L.A., had thought it great, and had written home about it. The children were overexcited that their father was coming back, and Monika—to be honest—was somehow pleased, too, because since he had gone she had had those nasty calls and adventures while he phoned regularly home from America and had been behaving like the nice person he always was when he was alone with his wife and kids in London away from the in-law interference. He was actually pure honey in telephone conversations and letters to Monika, never mentioning a word about his mother or sisters.

    On the day of Abdulla's arrival, late in the evening, Monika drove the kids and Sakia to the airport in that sensational car. Cars driving alongside slowed down to take a look at the strange-looking vehicle. No one in Kuwait had ever seen a car like that before. An ideal parking space was found near the terminal's main entrance and from far one could hear Abdulla's noisy sisters and their children's carrying on inside. Mother-in-law sat ensconced in a chair like a throne. Monika's eyes, hidden behind the dark lenses of her sunglasses, pretended not to see them. She made herself busy with Luay, who sat in Sakia's arms. She could hear the bitches criticizing her dress and their purposely-loud giggles meant to attract her attention, but she ignored them with steely determination. She was very good at that. She had had loads of practice and, besides, knew she looked good, very good. She had gained weight and was her old self again at 54 kilos while the blown-up balloons were jealous of her looks and trim figure. After having waited for a long period, at last they saw Abdulla. In backcombed Afro hairstyle, he stepped through the automatic sliding glass doors, dressed in a white suit, white tie, and black shirt that all matched his black locks. He looked really smashing. Along with proper behavior in public and a couple of other virtues, Monika had taught Abdulla fashion sense, and he stuck to the rule never to wear more than three colors at a time. He stood there smiling, looking around, searching for something, and when he had found that something, he made a beeline for his mother. He kissed and hugged her, saying how much he had missed her, after which it was his sisters' turn, and then their children's, after which he shook hands with their driver and finally came over to kiss his own children.

Monika was attended to last, very coldly, as always when the in-laws were present: he blew a superficial kiss on her cheek, accompanied by a "hi," after which he ran back to his mother to walk her to her car. He gave all his attention to mother while Monika trailed behind like the fifth wheel on a car, feeling totally out of place. Once outside, when they got to see the painted car, naturally all the fun it was supposed to generate was, of course, ruined. His mother stood with her hands on her head hysterically shouting abuse at Monika as if she were their bought slave, and her daughters did likewise, pleased to have found a reason to have a go at her and so to make up for the past inactive months, feeling strong with Abdulla at their side.

Monika was sick to the stomach and wished she could do a disappearing act as Abdulla just never mustered the guts to show Monika any kind of affection in his family's presence. It was at that moment—when his mother pulled at his sleeve to drive home in her car—that it first sprung to Monika's mind that her in-laws were just like the nasty stepmother and the three ugly sisters of "Cinderella"—hence the title of this book!

Mother-in-law hissed at Abdulla: "You're not going with her in this disgraced car! It's scandalous! Think of the people who will see you. Everybody knows you. Aren't you ashamed? What am I going to say? Tomorrow all Kuwait will talk. Come with me. Don't let her ruin you like that car." That's how the old rattlesnake shook her rattle nonstop—for she had about six months of nastiness to catch up on, and she did a jolly good job. She hadn't lost her touch.

Abdulla was always, always ready for a good joke and a laugh, however stupid, and Monika knew that if the in-laws hadn't been there to stir trouble and shit, Monika, Abdulla, and the kids would be having massive fun now. Wishful thinking! That was just not to be. Instead, Abdulla, wound up, was actually furious at Monika and told her off, while she in turn wished that he hadn't come back, that he were still away and would never have to come back, now or ever. And she felt sorry, of course, for having made so much fuss over his homecoming. It was just no use. She was happiest alone with her poor children.

On the way home, a fight erupted in the car, and she felt like getting out halfway, which was impossible for a woman without a cover, unless in the shopping area, because every male driving by would stop and chat her up for sex.

Abdulla was surprised and pleased to see the house alight and decorated in his honor, but the atmosphere stayed thick and lay low. Everything was ruined, even for the kids. Monika picked up a crystal tumbler and poured herself a gin and tonic to soothe her nerves, something she hadn't done for months, not even after all those phone calls and accidents. "Don't be stupid, Monika," a voice inside her spoke, "what did you expect? A changed Abdulla with a halo over his head just because he has been six months in America?"

"I know he will never change," she told herself, with a faint smile and pity for herself.

Abdulla had brought with him the most expensive and, even in Kuwait, unimaginable presents, mainly from California's Rodeo Drive. The children got electronic gadgets, toys, clothes, and caps; and Monika was presented with diamond jewelry, and a suitcase full of chic clothes, and matching shoes and bags. That first night Abdulla didn't stay long, didn't even touch the food that was especially prepared for him because—yes, you've guessed it—he had to pay his homage and respects to his mother, eat there, and spend the rest of the night with them, too. That was how another day that had started so promising— one more day in Monika's ongoing fight for the survival of her sanity— had taken a bad course instead.

After that lukewarm start, Abdulla was back to his normal abnormal behavior, but the in-laws stayed away, thank heavens for small mercies. For that, he solemnly blamed Monika; but she didn't give a hoot and fought him with all she had, just as her doctor had advised her to do. And would you believe it? After some time his unjustified outbursts became far less frequent. Still, it was everything but a joy to live alongside this man who lived spellbound under his mother's hexes like a zombie. In a way, he was pathetic, and Monika often pitied him. Yet, the affair with Fawzia was of his own doing. He had always been a bit of a ladies' man, ever since they got engaged. She should have known better; and, therefore, he lost her love . . . or, could it possibly be? Had his mother something to do with Fawzia, too? Could that love affair be traced back to her? We will never know. That answer is written in the desert winds, amidst many, many more.

Tamader, the last spinster among Abdulla's sisters, somehow got hold of a very nice young man somewhere in Kuwait and fell head over heels in love with him, Farouk. Young people are not seen courting openly in Kuwait, but they have their ways of getting to each other, believe you me. They have to, or run the risk of being bundled off into an arranged liaison without love. The telephone, the girlfriend, a car, and the desert play a big part in secret courtships. To start with, one usually meets at one of the supermarkets, just to talk between the peas, crisps, and bog rolls. There one can stand side-by-side, touch hands by picking up one and the same thing off a shelf, as if by accident. Quite romantic, don't you think? And then they take it from there. The girls wear, of course, their black abayas, the ideal disguise.

Farouk, a Kuwait University graduate, was of a much darker skin color than the average Kuwaiti because his mother was of black African origins, Africa being where Kuwaitis went to buy slaves. She was made pregnant by an Aseel Kuwaiti, who denied fatherhood although everybody close to her knew who exactly had fathered Farouk. Tamader's mother was dead set against such a liaison.

"Farouk is the bastard son of a Negro slave," she said, "without a penny to his name. If that Negro bastard ever enters my house, it will be over my dead body. I prefer you to die of cancer than shame me and bring me that disaster and let me live in shame, having to hide my face until my dying day. How dare you even speak to a person like him! You are from an Aseel family!" Now, a time came when there was good reason for mother-in-law to work on her fake heart attacks. For the first time Monika could well imagine how his mother first received Abdulla's news of his marriage to a foreigner. He must have been to hell and back.

Usually sisters stick together in such situations, but not in the al-Amahani clan. Sabiha was of no help at all, quite the opposite. She told Tamader heartlessly, "If you marry that piece of coal, my Fahad is going to divorce me and marry someone else. He won't stay married to a wife whose sister goes off with a slave's son." That's how heartless Tamader was treated by her near and dear—as if she were their enemy number one and not their own flesh and blood, the so important flesh and blood that they kept talking so much about. They had no compassion whatsoever.

Mother-in-law's, Sabiha's, and Diba's cruelty surprised Monika. She knew they had black hearts towards her and others, but never thought them capable of such cruelty towards Tamader. By all the laws of humanity, the way they tried to solve a problem bordered on the inhumane and belonged to the dark Middle Ages, but then that's where Kuwait's roots still lie today in lots of ways, ways that clash head on with the newly acquired, oil rich modern way of life that young people crave but cannot have because they are suppressed by the old society that weighs them down heavily under the strong influence of Kuwait's fundamentalism, that fanatical Muslim power. One wonders whether Kuwait will get away unscathed with Ayatollahs on the scene. Let's hope it will for the sake of future generations—Monika's grandchildren and their children and everybody else. Mind you, the situation looks very bleak, but let's leave politics out of it. Let's just hope that fundamentalism never swamps this pro-Western outpost. That's what I hope, yet my instinct tells me the opposite is likely to be true.

So, now, Tamader stood tormented, all alone, like a lone cross on Mount Everest, with her heart overflowing with love and love's heartache, with for once—just like Monika—no one to turn to. She couldn't even risk confiding in girlfriends because it's no secret that Kuwait's females can't keep a secret. If anything leaked out prematurely, all the other relatives of the al-Amahanis would join in negative campaigns and then her reputation would really be out the window. So to whom do you think she chose to turn to in her misery?

None other than Monika.

Surprised? After a short telephone conversation, Abdulla said to Monika one afternoon, "Sweetie, Tamader is not well. She is doing rather poorly. You know how mother treats her over Farouk. She just asked me if she could come here and talk to you about it. She wants to apologize for her behavior towards you in the past. It wasn't really her. She was influenced by mother and Sabiha. She wants you to know this. Is it okay if she comes now?" And without thinking twice, Monika said automatically, "Yes, of course." Monika knew that Tamader, although bad, wasn't evil like mother-in-law and Sabiha; neither was Diba. Those two were just very spoiled, robot-like, mindless, easily influenced brats who were envious, sarcastic versions of their mother with less evil. Monika knew that if Tamader and Diba showed more compassion for her, they would be on bad terms with mother and Sabiha instead. So they preferred to join them all the way. Many a time Monika had the desire to line the four of them up and slap them until she was exhausted. Just slap their faces one after the other through the row! That thought really satisfied her. Merely the thought of doing it made her feel good. And yet, when Tamader came, Monika took pity for she looked very low and humble with a drawn, pale face, the black mascara from her tearful eyes smudged all over it. She made her welcome, offering black tea and nuts. Soon Tamader sat there, a heap of sadness, pouring her heart out. They sat chatting like old friends. Tamader said that Farouk would kill himself if he could not get her, and she said she would kill herself if she could not get him. They had made a death pact. Tamader told Abdulla that not her mother but he, the only man in the family, stood in the position of her father, and that only his word counted regarding whether she should be allowed to marry Farouk or not, according to the Islamic law in Kuwait.

See here, up to now Abdulla had been made to hide in the background. Now, though, with his sister's love affair, his word was law. Abdulla came out of the shadow feeling sorry for his sister and agreed to oppose his mother by agreeing to meet Farouk, whom he liked at first sight; and after many more wrangles with his family, Abdulla dared to go over his mother's head and write a marriage contract between Farouk and Tamader. But before that, the lovers often met in Abdulla's house, the only safe place for them in all of Kuwait. After that, they were very quietly married and moved into a flat of their own among foreigners in Salmiya. Because of their strong opposition to the marriage, her whole great family circle set itself against Tamader, for she had brought shame upon all of them. Tamader and her husband were shunned by close and not so close relatives, who gave Abdulla and his mother a real dressing down for allowing Tamader to bring Farouk into the Aseel family clan. Nine months later, Tamader had a little girl, and that occasion was for many members of the family a good enough reason to forgive and forget and let grass grow over their differences. Most of her relatives visited Tamader at the hospital, and so Tamader and Farouk were slowly accepted, in good time.

As for Tamader, she grew fat and fatter after her first child and was not a nice person to be with at all while Farouk was and still is a real "lulu" (pearl), who is now a VIP on Kuwait's top list. He made it from nothing to everything on his own; and, see here, now that he is somebody, all the al-Amahanis are mighty proud of him and can't drop his name often enough. Now Farouk gives wastas to the al-Amahanis-among other favors—simply because he has got the power. He is more influential than they are. Well done, Farouk! But if he eyes other females, it is not surprising. He is a good looker who cares for his appearance while Tamader simply doesn't care nor look after herself for her man.

After 27 months of complaining from aches and pains during her three pregnancies plus her continuous nagging and shouting, she is retired on the scrap heap with her two sisters.

Soon after Tamader was furtively married, it came to light that a very wealthy Kuwaiti man old enough to be her father had asked through females for her hand in marriage. Tamader's mother heard "rich and wealthy" and was fire and flame. She was all set to sell Tamader off, never mind her happiness, which shows that mother-in-law's greed for money knew no boundaries. It was typical of her.

Nowadays, the three ugly sisters feel deprived and unloved, something Monika can sing a song of, too; yet, unlike her, they try to substitute activities that are nothing to he proud of for the love that's missing in their lives. Their bad characteristics worsened considerably.

Monika, who also craved love, understanding, and a close relationship she never had, fell, without then realizing what pushed her, into a habit of going on compulsive, mad shopping binges in hopes of getting her some of what was missing in her life, especially since money had become no object. Since she had "Domino," she bought designer clothes, accessories, bags, and lots of jewelry as if there were no tomorrow, as if that would help to transform her emotional unhappiness into bright sunshine. Her huge wardrobes were stuffed to the brim with merchandise. She would bring it home without really wanting to wear any of it. It can get rather dangerous if a woman with little money available develops such a mania, for then she sits in an even worse rut than before. To be quite honest, for a couple of hours (it may even last longer), this seemingly innocuous vice can help replace the alcohol and Valium, but it does not help to solve a thing! Many mad shopping trips later, Monika came to see the light on that subject and wished she had stuffed the little fortune she blew (and flushed down the fashion drain) into a bank account instead. Nowadays, once bitten, twice shy, this lesson is just another one of many she learned that will stay with her forever.

One sunny, funny day interrupted her rotten days. Monika got a letter from America addressed neatly to her at her new house's address. Opening it, Monika wondered who had sent it. She supposed it might be a chain letter, for she didn't know a living soul in America. After unfolding the thin, fine, peach colored writing paper, her eyes searched first for the signature, which read "Bettina." Only then did she read the contents:

> *Dear Monika,*
> *I write to you to warn you, your husband Abdulla has been going steady with me for five months here in California and just before he left for Kuwait we got engaged. He told me he loves me and that he was going to divorce you and send you back to Vienna. I agreed and was quite willing to look after his three boys, but since he has left for Kuwait I have not heard from him once, nor had a reply after repeated letters I have written to his hospital. When he hears my voice on the telephone he hangs up on me, but I am not the 'One for the Boys' type and I am very, very hurt that somebody should play such a dirty game with me, believe me. I feel used as a sleeping carriage by Abdulla. The Kuwait Embassy is of no help at all and I am really devastated after having made so many arrangements to live in Kuwait according to and following Abdulla's wishes and promises. Now I realize of course that he has made a fool of me and you, because some Kuwaiti I met told me that Abdulla is happily married and he would bet anything that he'd never divorce his wife. That's why I thought you should know what sort of a rat you are married to, and that you can keep him with my blessings. I don't want*

him for all the tea in China. Up until now I didn't experiment with cheats and liars such as Abdulla. I didn't know such creatures walked on our planet. Good luck to you. You will need all you will get,

In deepest sympathy,
Bettina.

At the end of the letter, Bettina had written her address and telephone number and also that she hoped for a reply.

She is still waiting.

After reading the letter, Monika put it down and smiled, amused, as if she had just read a jolly joke. It didn't leave the shadow of a bad after-effect on her at all, which surprised her and pleased her. The urge to cry and fight over Abdulla was well and truly out of her system, and the time for jealousy was all over. That letter just proved it. Nothing hurt any more. Abdulla wasn't worth it. That stern fact had finally reached all her senses and left her floating above and aloof.

After her illness, Monika used her cigarillos sparingly. She often decided and dreamt wide-eyed of giving up smoking, that filthy habit, altogether, but there was time enough for that. Now was an occasion to light one up and enjoy one with a cup of coffee and read the letter once again. After having read it for a second time, she felt like a protective mother figure towards Abdulla. Bettina had complained to her about Abdulla in the hope that Monika would punish him for his naughtiness and rotten behavior towards Bettina. Monika already knew how he would apologize after finding out—just like one of her sons after having been naughty, and then find a stupid excuse as to how none of it was his fault, that it was all the girl's doing, that he was totally innocent, after which he would go out to buy her another piece of expensive, eye-catching bribe jewelry, thinking, "That's it—now I have paid for it," and feeling certain as he always did that everything was repaired and that life would be back to normal again—until the next time around.

"While my hands are tied and I can't change a thing about it now, I might as well sit back and collect bribe jewelry," she debated with herself. A faint smile passed over her face and a giggle left her lips. She wondered how many more exquisite pieces of girl's-best-friend diamond sparklers were still to join her by now superb collection in that ever-growing jewel box of hers, where her pearl-encrusted engagement ring, that more or less had started it all, was kept, too, bringing back bits and pieces of the past every time she looked at it. Sometimes she took it out and thought, Mother was so right about pearls. You've really brought me nothing but tears and bad luck.

We have now a wide-awake Monika. It took her a long time. She had come a long way, but only because she gave life a little more time to make something worthwhile of her. She knew Bettina wouldn't be the last female escapade in Abdulla's life. There would be many more Bettinas, Fawzias, Kikis, and SuSus to help brighten Abdulla's sex life and boost his ego. Abdulla, like most men (East and West), will always need other women. So, after all, this time it finally came home to her that that husband of hers was the type of man who could be compared to children entering a toy shop taking blonde, black, red haired dollies off shelves to take a good look at them, play with them, and then put them back, having lost interest. Abdulla was like his father, who knew no barriers when it came to ladies. Or he could be compared with the majority of Kuwait's male population (after all, he is one of them!). They were all the same! Monika's theory out of sheer experience convinced her that men don't have stronger sex drives than women; they are just weaker. But honestly, which male would admit to that? And since all laws and propaganda are built by men, they have spread the word that *they* are sexier, which sounds so much better than being weak. It lifts their egos considerably, no end.

Talk to *any* male and collect the evidence for yourself. Men think after they leap, while a woman uses her sex machine with her head, which is a plus and doesn't mean she is less sexy than men are. It's women who keep the family together: a world left entirely to men would he a right chaos. And while we are at it, don't forget: behind every great man stands an even greater woman, who often stands in the shadow. A woman cannot do without her man, and man cannot do without woman. That's how Father Nature—or is it Mother Nature?—plays the game with all of us. I wish we could question Our Creator on that one!

Monika slid Bettina's letter between the pages of Abdulla's daily paper, which he was in the habit of reading after lunch and before he took his siesta. After he discovered it and read it, he showed immense surprise that Monika could stay so calm over it, even refusing to want to hear his side of the story, although there is usually another side to the medallion. But her Abdulla was an exception to that rule because he was not in the least bit acquainted with the truth; he had no ground to stand on, yet he told his lies anyway if only to relieve his guilty conscience, telling her that Bettina worked at the hospital's laboratory. He danced with her at a party given in honor of some big shot there and that from then on she started to take her coffee break with him. Sometimes she gave him a lift home in her car, which suited him fine and that, would you believe it, according to him, was all. Mind you, he said he promised her some presents from Kuwait and because he hadn't sent her even a stamp, she was seeking revenge and wanted to make trouble for him. After he had finished dishing up that crap, Monika said, "It's an insult, you weakling! Don't hold me for so dumb. Let me tell you something for nothing. You are a born liar and, like Kleenex, soft and disposable. When I dispose of you, you won't know what you have had until you have lost it. The day will come. Remember that."

Bettina sent a second letter and a third, with more accusations and listing still more promises that Abdulla had made to her. After the third letter, Abdulla instructed the servants to collect the mail and hand it to him first—without Monika's knowledge—for vetting. Later on, one of her servants confided in Monika that Jilted Bettina had written two more letters—five in all. Monika felt that Bettina was writing the truth. Maybe Bettina really was in love with Abdulla or maybe it was revenge, who knows? Who cares?

Doesn't time fly! Three and a half years had passed already since the family had moved into the new house, yet it seemed as if it was only yesterday that Monika had dubbed it the "Emotional Death Chamber Castle in the Desert." It wasn't just Monika who did not live happily ever after in it. Although it was very, very beautiful and hyper-modern, her children and often the servants, too, scattered like chickens catching sight of a fox when Abdulla had one of his unpredictable, shitty moods—when he would have a go at anything and anybody that crossed his path, looking for innocent victims on whom to let loose his mother-injected frustrations, which he could not hold bottled inside of him.

Since her enlightenment and having grown stronger as a result of it, Monika didn't keep mum and polite for peace's sake, as she used to do. She stopped pussyfooting. She gave Abdulla as much mouth as he gave her and shouted back at him every time. She told him to go to his dominant mother, the sole reason for his outbursts, and live and sleep and let the fur fly there. Abdulla inwardly knew he was doctored by his mother and could not set himself free, and he knew Monika knew that he knew, and that fact actually bothered him greatly—weakling! But what could he do? God had created him like that. Even his friends teased him about his iron-maiden mother. They said things like, "Abdulla, are you sure that under that black abaya of the person you call 'Mother' there isn't actually a man hidden?"

CHAPTER TWENTY-FOUR

TRANSITIONAL TENSIONS

And now, hold on, for one smiling day—just as in a children's story—a thundering bright light shot like one of Robin Hood's precisely aimed arrows—bang!—into the middle of Monika's darkness long after she had given up hope. A miracle occurred, which came, as lovely things and good luck usually do, out of the blue, when one least expects it. Abdulla was offered a post at the Kuwait Embassy in London, thanks to his Irani Kuwaiti friend Abou Amer, who had recently become the new Minister of Health in Kuwait.

It was high time to let a new wind blow through that ministry, for the sake of its mostly foreign staff, if for no other reason. Doctor Amer had all the know-how, personality, and qualities that a minister should have and that the previous one had never, ever even heard of.

How Amer's predecessor had made it to Minister remains a mystery, the only possible explanation to the puzzle being that he was appointed to the position for which he wasn't the slightest bit qualified through a first class *wasta* from some powerful sheikh. Full of alcohol, the Health Minister's Undersecretary Berges used to chase nurses through hospital corridors and up staircases at night in hopes of getting (or demanding) a bit of "on the side." Once during the holy month of Ramadan, the whole hospital talked, for the Undersecretary chased and grabbed and tore a nurse's uniform while she was struggling to get away from him.

She had not submitted; so, a week later, she got the sack. It was back to Cairo for her. Everyone knew that he—and not she—was grossly in the wrong, but so what? Who dared complain? And if so, to whom? He himself was the all-powerful Health Minister's Undersecretary at the top of the pile and his employees, mostly subservient foreigners.

Female hospital staff quite often got a job or were reappointed for another year by being nice—or lost their bread and butter by not being nice and refusing his advances. Yarka, a forty-five-year-old, single, Czech woman radiotherapist didn't get her work permit renewed by the Undersecretary because he had repeatedly asked her to invite him to her house, something she politely refused to do.

"Before I lose my self respect with that pig, I take the chance of losing my job," Yarka had said. Yarka meant what she said, and lost. That pig, as Yarka had very fittingly named him, looked like one, too, but had a very nice, young, beautiful wife, most probably obtained through an arranged marriage, for no pretty girl of Kuwait in her right mind would marry such a grotesque being of her own free will. (You'd be surprised in Kuwait at the number of good looking women married to ugly men—and vice versa—through arranged marriages.) That Undersecretary's looks well matched his actions and character as well. After her first encounter with his wife, Monika needed a lot of convincing to believe that the beauty really was the pig's wife. Marriage in Kuwait is like throwing dice—some are lucky, some under ice. The first time Monika had the pleasure of meeting Mr. Piggy himself was at a doctor's farewell party, where he was the guest of honor. He came up to Abdulla to discuss unashamedly the anatomy of females present at the bash as if he were in Hamburg's Herman Strasse to choose some professional easy lay, which made Monika blush on his behalf. Even before that—first thing on sighting Monika by Abdulla's side, he came over and said, "*Halla, halla,* nice piece! Where did you find her?" and looked her over with his beady, greedy eyes that flickered like two candles in the dark. Then he started to talk such filthy talk about what was in his mind, not having the faintest idea that Monika was understanding every word he said and was having a hard time believing that such a fart was really Undersecretary and for the Ministry of Health on top of it all. She had to ask a bystander if it was really true that this foul, fat man was who he was said to be, because Monika was thinking that Abdulla had played another one of his practical jokes on her.

After the Undersecretary decided finally to move on, Abdulla fantasized aloud about what he would do with that vile, fat piece of meat if, let's say, he weren't his boss because Abdulla, like everyone else in Kuwait's professional world of medicine, had no respect whatsoever for Mr. Piggy. Abdulla couldn't stand his guts.

After a self-service buffet and numerous speeches by different medical personnel, the Undersecretary approached Abdulla once more. He came close up and ordered him to wait until he had reached a certain well proportioned lady he pointed out in the large crowd and then to go and switch off all the lights in the hall for him. "I've got to sink my hands into that dreamboat of a maqua. I want you to help me to get a good grip on that fat arse," lusted the Undersecretary of Health, drunk, deeply lost and drenched in lust and sin.

Just as Monika had had a hard time getting through the night due to illness, now Monika had a hard time sleeping because of her overwhelming happiness over her new prospects of freedom. Freedom was in sight, beckoning, and waiting in London for her. Maybe she wasn't born with a plastic spoon in her mouth after all. But first she had to wait another six months before it was actually all going to happen. She lived through that time rather fearfully and worried because—as fate had it with her—it could all be canceled at the last minute.

Abdulla was on the lookout for suitable tenants to live in the house during the absence of the coming years. He was very happy about his sudden promotion and said to Monika just as soon as he had learned of it, "Sweetie, you really have telepathic gifts. You always told me I would make it big. How did you know? How could you have been so spot on?"

"I wish I knew. It puzzles and frightens me sometimes." Those funny feelings she was overcome by and things she dreamed that later turned out to be realities—she herself could not explain them yet, and it often worried her, especially during her early life. Through reading about it here and there, she realized later that what she had was to be looked upon as a gift not everybody possessed. Monika knew that Abdulla was the ideal person for a diplomatic job. He was born for it. He was a charmer and had the hang of dealing with European and Arab people and knew their customs. He was made of the ideal material to represent Kuwait. His combination of professionalism and affability made him the ideal man for such a top job. Monika had always sensed, even if only subconsciously, that she would not spend her last days in Kuwait, and she knew, too, that the next time she returned to Europe with her children would be the last time she would see Kuwait as a resident. The jug that fetched the water had broken, was irreparable, and her marriage was stone dead.

Monika often said to her friends, "I shudder when I have to think I might have to live the rest of my life in Kuwait and then be buried in a desert cemetery where wild dogs roam at night, with my head towards Mecca and a stone on top of it to mark the position of the body." In Kuwait, only males attend the burial of the dead, whose bodies are first oiled with a special potion and then wrapped in snowy white linens. There are no coffins. The dead are covered with earth, and then *basta*— you're on your own. Nobody comes to visit, to put down flowers. During the day, the sun burns down, the sand storms dance, and, as I said, barking wild dogs pass at night to lift a leg and sniff each other. Even if our souls go to another world (for there is life after life) and our bodies become as one with Mother Earth's earth, one's body should be put to rest in dignified surroundings, too; that's Monika's view.

Abdulla had no trouble finding suitable tenants for the beautiful house and made sure that the American couple came to view it in between prayer times at the mosque next door, whose blaring cacophony through the loudspeakers might have scared them off. The Americans, the first couple to view the house, fell in love at once, but said they were not used to living among such exquisite, leisurely surroundings and furniture and wanted to bring their own. They had two small children and loved to give parties, too, like all foreigners in Kuwait, but didn't want to take responsibility for the al-Amahani household furnishings. Huge trunks were bought and everything removable—even the crystal lights—were dismantled by workers and packed away professionally and stored along with the furniture in Abdulla's nice Aunt Fatma's house since she had many empty rooms. The room at their disposal was then locked, and Monika was in possession of all the keys.

Within a week the al-Amahanis moved out and the Americans moved in. Abdulla rented a flat in Salmiya, a mixed neighborhood where many foreigners lived, for the couple of months until the time for their departure was ripe. The rent Abdulla collected for several months in advance was very high, and he promised Monika on the death of his children and of his mother and sisters, too, that once they were settled in London, he would give Monika half of the rental money every month "Because without you I probably wouldn't have had a house and wouldn't be where I am now. By myself, I could not have done any of it. You have made me what I am." He praised her enthusiastically. "You are the one who got me through my exams, who again and again stopped me, relentlessly, from drinking and smoking. You are the one who helps and advises me through all my problems. You have been an excellent wife to me and the best mother to my children. You are the one who had to swallow and tolerate my family's jealousy where a Kuwaiti woman would never have stood for the half of it, and when I have been unfaithful, you always got over it in your own way." Little surprise!—that crap, spoken in a happy mood and in haste, was to be just another empty promise Abdulla made. Maybe he meant it while he said it. All the same, Monika never, ever got to see one single penny of the rent from that house although she had put everything she had into it.

With Monika's help, all her servants found new jobs with nice people, except for little Gloom. Gloom was an Indian boy who was brought to Kuwait through an agency by one of Abdulla's friends to help look after visitors in their douvaniah. But when Abdulla's friend set eyes on Gloom for the first time, that was it. Poor Gloom. He didn't want him. "That Indian monkey frightens my visitors away," he joked. Gloom was very dark, almost black, very small for his age, a bit of a midget really, and his teeth were brown, which was a telltale sign of malnutrition. He was sixteen yet had the figure of a nine-year-old and hadn't the slightest notion about how to behave among civilized people. He acted exactly as one might expect a jungle boy to act. Since his arrival in Kuwait, he had been with five families within two months "Everybody sends him back to me. Nobody wants him," Abdulla's friend said. Monika—one to make up her mind quickly—said, "Bring him to us. I'll teach him how to work." Abdulla's friend's smile shone brightly all the way to his ears. He was ever so pleased at the offer—and good riddance. It was decided that Gloom would be sent to her after 5 pm the following evening, but the fellow couldn't wait to get rid of little Gloom. It was as early as 10 am when a chauffeur rang the bell and made his delivery.

Gloom was a skeleton, all skin and bones, and to Monika's surprise could speak a bit of English. Well, he came from Bangladesh and, therefore, no great wonder—it was once British, wasn't it? Yes, once, the sun never set on Britain's dominions. Otherwise, Gloom looked just as described to her. She introduced him to the other servants and showed him to his room, and then she felt as if she had just adopted a delinquent child. Three months passed and Gloom still hadn't a clue how to hold a broom, let alone sweep a room. He was of absolutely no use whatsoever, except to play with the children. So she took him along to her boutique, to try her best to awaken some easy-task cleaning buds in him there. Yet, again, to no avail. Gloom brushed the dirt up one end of the dustpan and off again at the other side and back onto the floor while his face, with his nose sticking out, was high up in the air looking at customers or watching people and cars passing by outside. Gloom acted as if he had been absent when God was parceling out the brains to people. Four months later, Monika heard of a family looking for a servant where his only job would be to bring and take away an old, blind man's meal trays, help him wash his hands, and lead him to the toilet.

"That's ideal for Gloom. He's capable of doing that," thought Monika and told him of the new job. "Get your seven plums together and then I will drive you there. You can come to visit us on your free day off if you want to." A couple of hours later Monika went looking for him and found him sitting on top of his little bundle of personal belongings. "Are you ready, Gloom?" Monika asked. "Yes, Madam," he answered, half swallowing his words. He looked at her with tears in his eyes, searching in hers for mercy. Monika's heart missed a beat.

"Don't you want to leave our house?" she asked.

"No, Madam." The little unfortunate soul shook his head wildly and broke out into a flood of tears.

"Okay, okay, take it easy." She patted his curly head. "Unpack. You are going nowhere. You stay right here with us," she told him. She just could not bring herself to turn that poor being away, and when Abdulla came home that night, she told him that Gloom was staying. "I know he'll be only living, eating, and sleeping with us for otherwise he is useless, but let's just say that in keeping him on we are doing a good deed for our children. We have got a deposit with God." And would you believe it possible? As if to thank her, Gloom—left unnoticed to one side—developed into the most hardworking, honest, thorough, faithful, trusted servant the al-Amahanis had ever had, as good a helper as anyone would wish for and a staff member that other families were jealous of, especially the in-laws. He learned to clean, cook, and do the gardening as well as all the others, if not even better. He was loved by the children, who grew to think of him as a brother. Monika had a stepson. And now Gloom was chosen, the only one, to come along to London. That's a happy ending for you!

With great sadness, a new home had to be found for doggy Senta. Abdulla—the boss and sole person in charge of how his income was to be spent, just like his mother—was dead set against paying for a dog's fare and accommodations for the six months quarantine required by British law for animals brought into Great Britain. Abdulla stuck stubbornly to his guns. He was *not* paying. He didn't want Senta in London in the first place. "You are crazy if you think I will pay a six-month hotel bill for a dog!" Monika's and the children's please were to no avail. The children's playmate had to stay behind in Kuwait with a very nice, animal-loving foreign couple who promised to take Senta back to Holland after their contract in Kuwait had expired.

Monika's boutique "Domino" was by now a little gold mine. So the couple decided that—to start with, at least—the business there should continue with Um-Mohammed in charge and a close friend of Abdulla's acting as Mr. Monika. Monika would come to see her shop every six months or so and bring new stock on those trips from England.

The day of departure finally arrived. Goodbye, Kuwait, and thanks for nothing! Abdulla flew to London to arrange suitable living accommodation and to get the hang of his new job, which was mainly to see to it that Kuwaiti patients, who could not receive treatment for their ailments in Kuwait because the medical skill needed was not available there, saw the right doctors and were put under the proper professional care. It was almost left entirely up to Abdulla and his good judgment to determine to which specialists those patients should go.

Abdulla's kids, Monika, and Gloom flew to neutral, red-white-red Austria for a glorious three months holiday amidst the woods, mountains, farms, and fishing spots. Never before in all her life did

Monika appreciate the green, green grass of home as vigorously as on that landing at Vienna's Schwechat Airport. Up to then she hadn't realized how much she had really been missing the green and how soothing it was just to look at it. It made her feel calm inside. It was balsam to the eyes. The children spoke English and Arabic and only a smidgen of German they had learned from their mother, mainly baby talk, but in Austria they picked up the language with such speed from children they met that Monika stood back in amazement and was happy although, mind you, much of what they learned was slang that did not particularly please her.

Back smack in the middle of European civilization, Monika's past— her ugly past—followed her like an invisible dark shadow. She had not given tit for tat, and the deep-rooted desire for revenge lurked in her subconscious, just waiting for a chance to burst out and repay the guilty parties for all the injustice that was piled and piled and piled upon her by those nasties in the desert. Yet, at the same time, she wanted Kuwait, the Kuwait she had gotten to know, to sink into oblivion. She was eager to forget that long nightmare once and for all, to enjoy every minute of the peaceful, very much appreciated "now" that opened so promisingly into a totally different direction: a life as a diplomat's wife.

Would she fit into high society among London's social upper crust? She wondered uneasily whether she was up to scratch, fit for a diplomatic life in London, which would, she knew, involve plenty of socializing—even with royalty. Did she have what it takes? (Good God, she needn't have had qualms and doubts about that, she was soon to find out!) One thing she was sure about: tomorrow she was never going to look for yesterday! She left Kuwait educated in the knowledge that one has to take defeat in life because it is part of life. It's what helps to make us what we call "grown up." Do we ever get there? Are we ever grown up? Monika's message for Kuwait's majority who treat foreigners of all nations as doormats is this: "What you don't want to happen to you, don't bring upon nor wish upon others either. Love your fellow human beings as you love yourselves. Do less kneeling on your prayer carpets on show in public. And if you live a bit more according to you own Holy Koran and treat each other and foreigners, too, according to its teachings, then Kuwait, with all the riches God has bestowed on it, could be a blessed Kingdom to live in, with happiness for everybody. God has done his bit. Why don't you do yours, too? And, while we're at it with God, do respect other religions. Yes, it's a tall order for you, but it tells you so in your Holy Koran, you know.

Monika is convinced that all religions on our planet strive towards one and the same almighty force we call God. It's common sense. Every religion's, every sect's ground rules are, when it comes down to it, the ten commandments, which is exactly what a normal human being's instinct—without being preached to—knows anyway. Shirley MacLaine's theory that the church is not an arbiter between God and us is Monika's, too. Our inner voice always tells us what's right and what's wrong. So let's listen more often to that perfect judge, our valuable inner voice. Since religion and war—institutions that ambitious men have made—always go hand in hand, it should make us think where their ambition has gotten us. All of us, every one of us, at this very minute has in the back of our minds the fear of a Third World War, a nuclear war, that might erupt at any time—thanks a lot to you bunch of past and present, misleading, egghead leaders. A fine mess you have gotten us and yourselves into. Small wonder, for politicians are only philosophers who use the rich to keep them and the poor to vote for them while promising to protect the one from the other.

The three months in Austria had passed like sweet music on the wind, and behind her were the times when Monika had felt like a dazed sand corn on a lonely beach.

She, her children, and little Gloom sat on a First Class flight from Vienna to London. From now on everything was going to be First Class all the way—priorities and privileges no end for Monika—except, naturally, Abdulla's behavior. That was—and would stay—classless.

CHAPTER TWENTY-FIVE

DIPLOMATIC IMPUNITIES

On the tarmac at London's Heathrow Airport, standing proudly like a peacock at the bottom of the plane's staircase, stood Abdulla as his family emerged, and instead of going through passport control and customs with the rest of the passengers, they were driven to Old Cock and Browns VIP Lounge in an American, long, black, chauffeur-driven limousine with diplomatic license plates. There the reunited family relaxed in privacy and were served sandwiches, tea, coffee, cookies, and light beverages, while their passports were taken away and attended to, which did not take very long, and it was back into the car. A second limousine and a Buick station wagon took care of the luggage—and London 1976, here we come!

Abdulla was full of talk of the swell, colorful, London diplomatic life, day and night that he had never even dreamed of living and now was a part of thanks to his bosom pal Abou Amer. In Kuwait one doesn't say "bosom pals"; one says "two bottoms in one pants." Monika had sensed right that her Abdulla would end up Top Dog somewhere, someday. She wrote on his entire luggage from Kuwait to London "Top Dog A. al-Amahani" just to remind him.

Attentive, trying hard to please, Abdulla took his family to a lovely, three bedroom flat overlooking six tennis courts and a bowling green he had purchased smack in the middle of London, a stone's throw away from his Kuwaiti Embassy, where he worked.

As soon as Monika had laid eyes on Abdulla at the airport she had noticed how smartly turned out he was and that he looked years younger, certainly sprouting vitality and zest for life. "Diplomatic life in London must be a fountain of youth. I wonder what it will do for me," she thought, "uprooted once again, this time out of the desert sands and set into rich dark soil." So, let's wish her that only the best may come of it. She well deserves a better, happier life.

Nobody would have believed that Abdulla and Monika were the parents of those three strapping, handsome youths Sulaiman, Nabeel, and Luay, who were as completely different as chalk and cheese in looks and characters, too. In Austria, at playgrounds and parks, people would come up to Monika to ask if she really was the mother of those three big boys they had heard calling her "Mum." And now it started to be fun (and Monika was proud) to look younger than her actual age. Had she lived a happy life in Kuwait during the unlucky thirteen years she had vegetated there, she might have looked even better.

Abdulla's new post had power and brought money—and money is the root of all evil in the East, the West, the South and the North. No matter who possesses it, whether the clever, highly educated have it or it is in the hands of illiterates and idiots, money has the strong power to corrupt the majority of people from all walks of life, who are also (sadly) the ones who need a lifetime to find out that they are mortals, too, and can't take it with them when they have come to the end of the road and are lying on their death beds and it is too late for making changes and they can only leave a great chunk to a good cause in the desperate hope that they can thus buy themselves a piece of Heaven at the last minute. Why are so many people born with so little insight or foresight that they cannot, during a lifetime dominated by greed for more and more (never mind how they get their hands on it so long as they get it in the end), see how corrupting money can be? Is it the individual's fault to be born with these characteristics? If so, how? Sulaiman, Nabeel, and Luay strive out in totally different directions. They have totally different ideals, beliefs, and characters, yet they have and were raised by the same parents. So how we are can't have much to do with the way we were brought up. Whatever it is that molds people into what they are still puzzles Monika and I bet many of you readers, too. Are you any the wiser as to why some human beings are born saints and others—the majority of others—reckless, greedy bums, with a thin layer of people sandwiched in between who don't care either way, and the corrupt sods keep trying to hide at the bottom of the thick dark pile?

The following eight years of married diplomatic life the al-Amahanis spent mostly in the company of other Arabs, with whom Abdulla felt much more at ease and who, to Monika's surprise, were treated like royalty wherever they turned up—by the same British, mind you, who only ten years earlier had openly showed that they didn't want colored people living in their flats or to associate with them in any other way either, but who now (like everyone else in the world) had cottoned on to the fact that the Arab Gulf States were unimaginably rich and their people overly generous. The word got around and many a German, Austrian, French, English (you-name-it) individual, not to mention government, from then on—having a chance to associate with someone like Abdulla al-Amahani—put a veil of disguise over their prejudices against the filthy, dirty, desert race and arse licked no end for no other reason than that they had hopes of gaining financially thereby. And the truth is, of course, that they often obtained richly fruitful results that way.

Monika witnessed that kind of game again and again just about everywhere she went, and it pissed her off. She was very disappointed that European people like herself were capable of such hypocrisy, but in time worked that one out for herself and came to the conclusion that she had been convent-drilled and disciplined "to perfection" and therefore expected a much too flawless, immaculate behavior from her fellow human beings, too. Yes, well, not just in Kuwait; in Europe, too. It's a cold, hectic world everywhere out there for a decent human being to live in.

In complete contrast to what she was permitted in Kuwait, Monika was now able to choose almost daily which bash, party, or charity dinner she'd like to attend with Abdulla; and if none of these took her fancy, she could always accompany him to one of the many night clubs or casinos Abdulla had joined or had been made an Honorary Member of. She once counted up his membership cards and came to well over thirty in all. And because you have to be one to know one and Monika wasn't one, it took her some time to see the light shining on the fact that most invitations she and Abdulla received were not issued because people liked their faces but only because they were after what they could get from being associated with the now influential al-Amahanis. Once Monika saw right through that wide-faced, false socializing, accepting an invitation became a pain. There weren't any genuine ones, except with Abdulla's Kuwaiti friends, mostly Embassy staff.

When these Kuwaiti men and women sat together, humorous, fun-loving Abdulla, still the heart and soul of every gathering, and his witty Austrian wife who could crack a joke on herself and others in Arabic with a Kuwaiti accent usually ended up entertaining the whole group. Her behavior was usually forced though, especially when she felt like going straight home after she had only just joined them because they simply could not accept her as one of them, even after all those years amongst them. Remarks were made not just by her in-laws but by all Kuwaitis. They often let go in her presence about the bloody British or Europeans in general, looking at her as if she were one of them, or behaving as if she were not present at all. Even so, they were a much more refined group than Monika had had the pleasure of associating with in Kuwait. It was what traveling the diplomatic circuit does, one should think: it educates—and always in the right direction.

Even other Arabs living in London who invited and made a fuss over Abdulla and Monika were out to pick up a crumb at the Gulf's dinner table. The party slowed down considerably for Monika when she realized all that, but not for Abdulla. He loved it all too much, especially (since Monika increasingly preferred to stay home with the children) he was free to go alone and drink as much as he felt like drinking, which was always too much, diplomat or no diplomat, and chat up the ladies who were laid on thick as bait wherever Arabs came and went in parties, at clubs and casinos, and even by some of the medical profession—but to that we will come later.

What do Gulf Arabs go for? Yes, I thought you knew. Alcohol, women, food, and gambling—provide any of these and you are in business, in good business. Some of their suppliers had started with nothing and ended up often richer than some Arab himself. Monika loved the theater, the cinema, and a little opera, while Abdulla hated it all and would only take her if she insisted, cursing her all through the show for leading him to sit among "peasant" people who were beneath his diplomatic norm while she sat there boiling, not enjoying any of it and feeling sorry for having insisted on going in the first place. And when they went home, she had to pay him for his sacrifice with sex or he cashed in on it before they left. If she dared to refuse him because she considered it bribery and blackmail, he would say, "You're fit enough to watch a show, so you must be fit enough to give me sex."

Sex was the weapon Abdulla, still dead jealous, employed to cut Monika down to size, especially now that high-powered males he respected complimented him on his wife and he saw what kind of wives some of the other diplomats turned up with. He was proud of witty, popular Monika, who was now in her early 30's but didn't look it. She could match and mix with anybody in any given circumstances. Still, she was not allowed to go out alone to a casino or club, nor to the cinema, not even with another women, not unless, Monika supposed, she was his sister.

A propos sisters, have you missed them yet? They'll be dropping in on life in London soon enough, never fear. That circus show goes on as usual.

Monika had not a single club or casino membership in her own name, which she would have liked and could have used during Abdulla's frequent absences on diplomatic missions abroad and his solo pleasure trips—trips that, loving himself most of all, he often indulged in, while for her it was always, "No, no, no, you stay at home when I am not around, like all the other Kuwaiti wives in London, who are never taken by their husbands to clubs and casinos like you in the first place. Do you ever think that they are not so fortunate as you are? If my friends were to see you out at night alone, they would think you were a prostitute looking for men when I am not here, and those rumors would spread to Kuwait in no time." The self-appointed lord had spoken.

Forever trying to avoid trouble, Monika had no choice but to live by his word, which she did with the help of the bright light of insight, not too far away now, that came closer and closer through that once so bleak, long, dark tunnel of faith. She had her plans. Patience does it! Be patient, little ram. Be humble still. You'll get there eventually. After serving time in Kuwait, your day is sure to come. Have faith in God and in yourself. You are moving in the right direction!

For people who have never been inside a casino or very seldom might see one for what it is, or isn't, here is a bit of an eye opener on the way Monika got to know casino life. She started off by going to the fanciest London casinos every day of the week and drinking champagne there. "A little caviar for Madam? Smoked salmon?" and "Please, Sir, try the grilled meatballs. They are delicious, made especially for you. There were cheeses matured to perfection and strawberries and cream in season." "With your pink champagne, Madam." And you sit there and think, "Wow! It's great, this life," but after some time, when you've been to and seen through those exclusive rip-off joints—unless of course you are very, very stupid—then you begin to recognize the masks those clowns wear and see the deep lines in their faces, put there by a thousand artificial, false smiles a night. Watch out, they don't give a fuck about Madam and Sir. It's your money they are after with all the tricks of their trade in an ever so sugar-coated, sweet and civilized a manner. Abdulla was often greeted and addressed as "His Excellency" by doormen who didn't need a crash course to find out how to make their way around Arabs and were rewarded with big, generous tips of paper money, especially after one of them had had a lucky hand. Punter Abdulla was in the habit of tipping heavily. He dearly loved all that artificial, superficial chitchat and razzmatazz glitter and falseness, and in no time at all was addicted to London's nightlife and everything that went with it, much of which is at first sight hidden from the eye, the Sodom and Gomorrah aspect of it.

At the beginning, before the people at the nightspots knew who Monika was, she was looked upon as just another one of the many classy escort girls who decorated an Arab's arm at night, and she was treated accordingly, without much respect, by the nightlife serving class. Numerous times during her years in London with Abdulla, other Arabs would slip her a telephone number or make a pass at her in the very presence of Abdulla. She always replied, annoyed, with a rude, loud answer in Arabic. This pleased Abdulla, but he never spoke up for her on such occasions. It really used to get up her nose to get taken for some tart by that out-for-fun, stuffed-with-money ignorance. That's why Monika made sure she was known as Mrs. al-Amahani as soon as possible wherever they went and why she made a point of speaking only in Arabic when she was with Abdulla—to protect herself. In the 60's and early 70's, one could go to any night spot and would find that a good 75% of the customers were the wealthy Gulf Arabs in the company of their bit of crumpet or crumpets for the night, and since those girls were dressed, coiffed, and bejeweled like ladies of the manor, thanks to the generous clients they had, it was difficult to put a tag on them and not Monika. Arabs, especially Gulf Arabs, don't even introduce their wives to night clubbing—with very few exceptions—because nightclubs are considered male only territory, very much like the douvaniahs in Kuwait. Monika met many friends of Abdulla and Embassy employees, whose wives she knew well, in the company of good time girls. One might have thought these men would be embarrassed, but no, the opposite. They were proud to be seen with pretty faces, as if those girls weren't with them just for their money, and that was their ignorance shining through. Sometimes Abdulla's married friends would phone Abdulla well in advance to find out if and where he was going with Monika that evening just to make sure not to bump into her with their floozies.

London's nightlife, the way Abdulla led it, did nothing for Monika. She yearned and strove for deeper fulfillment in life, especially after Kuwait. In those casinos, the drinks of eligible gamblers and big punters were heavily laced—a single whisky became a triple, or a quadruple without the client's being aware of it. Chatting away with a friend or the bartender, one would be apt not to notice. Many of Abdulla's first-time-in-London, first-time-in-a-casino friends thought it ever so generous of the club, not suspecting the club's policy and practice—that by the time they got to the gaming floor they should be smashed out of their brains, ready and willing to lose, egged on even further by the smiles and come-on looks of the prettiest croupier girls, to whom they handed over their money.

Weak at the knees Abdulla was a most welcome sight to every casino manager's eye because Abdulla always brought wealthy Kuwaiti punters with him and, yes, as they say in America, "Jesus saves, Moses invests, and Arabs spend, spend, spend." Check-cashing facilities were available for the good customers, where some good people's daily limit could be 500,000 pounds sterling; for others (the well-known faces at the club and their deep pockets) no limit was set. Abdulla's wasn't that much, but when full of drink, fruitless gambling nights ran easily into thousands of pounds on any single occasion. Abdulla's highest loss in

Monika's presence was 60,000 pounds sterling a night, but sometimes it was more. He tried to avoid playing big money when she was with him because she wouldn't cease nagging him-unsuccessfully!—to get help to curb his gambling fever, even suggesting hypnosis to chuck it altogether, but the lower the stakes the less excitement it had for Abdulla. Monika might gamble 50 or 100 pounds or a little more sometimes, but always stopped when she won and put her winnings in the bank the following day, more often than not having to hide her winnings from Abdulla at the club, for if he lost, he would insist on taking her winnings to lose that, too. He would become, literally speaking, claustrophobic upon knowing Monika had some money tucked away, while it made Monika sick to her stomach to watch him throw all that money away at the same time that he was granting her a very meager allowance of pocket money. Monika would have to manage for a month on what a club doorman collected from him in a couple of days for calling him "Excellency" and parking his car. Even in London, she was never handed any housekeeping allowance. No sir, and if he did give her money for expenses, on the odd occasion, she had to show the receipt to account for every penny of a five- pound note—and that, after sixteen years of marriage and three children. Gloom and even the maid Josephine, who had been flown in by the al-Amahani family from the Philippines, were put in charge of the housekeeping without having to own up to specific expenditures. When the money was finished, they just had to ask for more. The servants commanded more trust and respect from Abdulla than his wife. What did this mean?

    Mind you, he at least now began to realize what Monika was to him. She was the one who felt quite at home on London's diplomatic circuit. She knew what the social scene and the job required of her, as if born into it, while he felt and often acted unworldly, mixed up, fidgety, and uneasy to start with. Yes, Abdulla had discovered much too late what an asset his wife was—in Europe, at any rate. If a man paid her too much attention at a party, restaurant, or club, he would tipsily chirp up quite out of line with, "Hey, hey there, Um-Sulaiman, Monika!" He would shout across the room or table and unashamedly address the male he thought had gotten too close to her. "Excuse me," he would say, while she, knowing what was coming next felt hot under the collar, "but that's my wife you are talking to," looking at, or whatever. In this manner, Abdulla dropped clanger after clanger, while he himself simply could not resist and had to chat up every pretty face and always insisted on sitting not just next to but close to one, too. Good thing it left Monika cold. For a jealous woman in love, it would have been hell. After Abdulla had insulted her, Monika made her repair rounds, saying her sorries—"My husband had a very trying day. He has taken the unwinding process a bit too far. He must have looked too deep into his whisky glass. Please do excuse him"—to injured parties who were actually hardly ever offended by him.

He prevented Monika from smoking in public and, being quite a heavy smoker, she found it necessary (as any of you smokers out there can well understand) to retreat numerous times a night to the ladies' room. She was well aware that people in their company must have thought she had a weak bladder or a dysentery problem.

In Kuwait, Monika often contemplated divorce, had fantasized about it when it seemed like the only answer to her problems, but now in London she was in no hurry. She knew she could (and had to) cope with Abdulla's moods a couple of years longer, while his job, friends, casinos, clubs, and women kept him away from home most of the time. In the meantime, she was patiently waiting and preparing for the right moment to jump off the wagon in style. Planning well and far ahead, she counted on making her getaway around the time when Luay, her youngest son, reached the sensible age of fifteen, which she took to be the right age, for then he would be grown up enough and would understand his parents' break up. She judged this from Sulaiman's and Nabeel's general state of mind and outlook on life when they were at about that age and stage of their young lives. Once Luay was also old enough, Monika wouldn't need to pussyfoot around and dance to her desert hubby's ill-adjusted fiddle any longer.

The children, who had experienced family discord from a very early age and survived the endless fights of their parents and in-laws, always urged their mother to leave Abdulla, not realizing nor understanding what a big part the resources of the Kuwaiti government played in their lives then. In London, the generous Kuwaiti bureaucracy took good financial care of her children's educational fees and clothes. They could have private tuition, guitar lessons, lessons in whatever took their fancy. The good old government would pay for it, no questions asked. Comparing her own childhood with that of her kids, Monika thought a million times how financially fortunate they were, but what a great pity it was that they couldn't really appreciate it because they just didn't know what it felt like to have to save up for something, wait for it, or bring home good school reports to earn what one got. Monika's children's childhood was something I am sure they would rather forget, but—in contrast—Christmas came once or twice each month of the year. Let's hope they can keep up the financial lifestyle they were born into right straight through to their dying days, for it is easy to have been without and come into money, but very difficult to have had it all and end up with nought. Of course, their mother hopes they live life not giving money too much importance, raise happy families, be more spiritual than material, value their health, and bring happiness to others. They already know that money does not bring happiness but, even without being a substitute for it, helps a great deal to put one's mind at rest, and—mind you, no denying it—money brings you respect. If Monika had had the money, Abdulla would have greatly respected it and treated her accordingly.

In the casinos there were other things besides the gaming tables. There were the most exquisite foods—prepared and cooked by talented gourmet cooks—much tastier than at the fanciest restaurants. Good customer Abdulla seldom paid when the bill was handed to him in a thick, leather-bound folder. It was usually pure formality as he signed and slipped in a fair number of money bills, tips for the over attentive waiters. Generally, the tip was large enough to have covered the cost of food consumed that night. Wherever Abdulla went, Abdulla—like all rich Arabs—received First Class treatment. As long as he kept his money on show, everybody was ever so obliging and delightful. The power money has makes one sick at times. The only thing they came short of doing to Mr. al-Amahani was to ask politely if they could clean his bottom and powder it for him, maybe give the hair there a little trim, too, Sir?

Nowadays, Monika prefers not to think about the many houses, cars, riches, Abdulla let go down those many, many money slits in London's casinos; and although she now felt that time had nearly run out for her and her husband, she still felt something for him. It certainly was not love. That had died back in Kuwait—when she had discovered Fawzia. If anything, it was some sort of motherliness towards him. He was her biggest, naughtiest child, more childish than her youngest child Luay. She talked her throat dry trying to persuade him to invest in London's 1970's property market or to make investments in his or their children's names—to no avail.

Abdulla was everything but business-minded, although he had many (and loved those so popular) business lunches in Britain with businessmen who wanted him involved as middle man in numerous big projects and dealings between London and Kuwait, Kuwait and London, but nothing ever came of any of them. A person able to switch off shop completely after office hours, Abdulla wanted only to have fun, and that's exactly what he continuously had, non-stop.

When the bank manager noticed endless checks covering huge amounts continuously cashed from Abdulla's expense account by various of London's casinos, he gave Abdulla well meant, unasked for, fatherly advice. He told him to think long term and to curb the vice once and for all. He made some suggestions as to where he might invest wisely, but this caution was also to no avail. The good resolutions Abdulla was full of after such a meeting might have lasted a couple of days, alter which he became very fidgety and nasty at home, and it wasn't long before he would be back to his normal, nightly gambling habit. It was in his blood. Mind you, to be fair, some of the fault lies with ever-pursuing Kuwaiti friends, who often led him on, especially those visitors from Kuwait who were strangers to London's nightlife. They had the money to gamble away but no memberships and therefore no access to those Top Dog clubs and casinos where members are well vetted before they are accepted.

The bartenders who mixed those generous drinks were also most obliging in fixing customers up with the right girl for the night. All a randy guy (and all of them were randy at all times) had to do was to slip the bartender a large denomination note, and the bartender would bestow you with some dolly's number, a dolly tailor-made to your sexual preference—blonde, black, thin, fat, bust size "boy" or 38-40 C-cup, whatever!

For Monika, casinos are a waste of space and of sole bomb benefit to the owners. Nobody ever wins in a casino in the long run, and if he says he does, he is a liar, unless, of course, he owns one. A well-known British multi-millionaire newspaperman had the habit of putting the highest bets, mounting into the thousands at any given time, on two or even three tables, playing them all at once, and therefore not being able to be at every gaming table when the little white balls fell into the winning numbers. (Let's call him Robert Maxwell, for that was his name. Mysteriously dead since, God save his soul.) Monika witnessed, time and time again, how the croupier quickly pulled back a couple of that unsuspecting fellow's winning stacks of chips while the dupe was busy at another table and then paid him out far less than he had actually won. On a couple of occasions, Monika was dying to let the victim know what was going on, but Abdulla's chicken cluck prevented her. Abdulla was afraid he might be banned by the management for squealing, so Monika was obliged to leave it at that. But it killed her, believe you me.

London's casinos were then, and still are today (although a bit less so), heavily frequented by Arabs, and if they stayed away, many a casino would be forced to close shop. One can recognize the same faces of the compulsive gamblers—men and women—night after night. Monika often stood just watching people's expressions and reactions after winning and, much more interesting, after losing, pitying those poor souls—some, like children, who would curse the casino staff as if the staff had forced them to lose their money; others, usually husband and wife teams, who would fight with each other; a woman with a handbag full of winning chips denying to her spouse that she had any; and losers approaching winners with outstretched hands, behavior that just did not fit with the outer layer of sophistication that so many of them cultivated. For those rich human beings, there seemed to be no hobbies, kicks, or enjoyment left after sex, food, and drink except casinos. What an empty life so many poor rich people must lead—sleeping the beautiful, fruitful day away only to sit on their arses losing money all night. Now and then, an ambulance had to be called because some player's body and nerves couldn't cope with the strain of financial loss and the individual sustained a coronary thrombosis or a mild (or even, sometimes, a fatal) heart attack. Those collapsed victims, though, are never Arabs but mostly older Jewish people, a manager once assured Monika, as she witnessed a man in his forties being carried out on a stretcher. He had lost well over £150,000 that night. His wife trailed behind in tears.

In Monika's casino days through the crowds of regulars there moved an extremely elegant, attractive, bejeweled Iranian lady who always wore a neatly coiffed chignon decorated with diamond jewelry. She smoked her cigarettes through a long platinum diamante cigarette holder. Nightly she changed her massive, precious jewelry the way other people change their socks, therefore came and went with two burly, poker-faced body guards. That lady made her rounds through London's clubs always surrounded by a big crowd and by favored gentlemen, who were even more regular than Abdulla. She always caught Monika's eye, for she reminded Monika of the late Shah Reza's last two classy, beautiful, unfortunate wives, Princess Soraya and Princess Diba. Looking night after night like a fairy princess on the catwalk, this all-time elegant roulette-, poker-, and dice-playing lady seemed to be very much in the same class as those princesses so often photographed and written up in high society magazines during and after the unfortunate Emperor Shah Reza's reign. Only a couple of years later, after having given casino life more or less the boot altogether except for an occasional flutter once in a blue moon, Monika saw that very same female, who in the meantime had cruelly slipped from riches to rags. There was nothing that reminded one of the once so grand lady she had been. Now she looked like an everyday, hard-working, ordinary woman. God, had she changed! She was hardly recognizable. Her shoulder-length hair hung down, most unruly. Gone were her brilliant sets of jewels. Now she wore only a thin wedding band, a watch on a black leather strap, and a tiny golden Koran around her neck. She was alone and looked and acted very nervous. She hadn't bothered with make-up, except for some lipstick. The simple brown dress she was clad in was something Monika would not wear to do cleaning chores in. All the glitter that once had surrounded that grand pearl of the night had disintegrated, and there was no evidence left to prove who she once had been, except for her impeccable manners. Now, that's sad. That once sparkling, proud, respected, mysterious lady of the night had been rudely pulled off her throne by nothing other than addictive gambling fever. She had become hopelessly hooked. The millionairess was broke and all alone, and with the money had gone the pride and self-respect. Now, she borrowed and begged money—£50, £20, it varied—from fellow members. From Abdulla, too—which, of course, he never saw again.

Is one supposed to feel any compassion for that weak victim? It depends a lot on the upbringing which that lady of rich Iranian background had. Was she pampered in cotton wool all her life? Could she have been strong and immune and any the wiser after the overthrow of the Shah's regime when that event snowballed her in the direction of Great Britain? Had she had something like Monika's strict convent upbringing behind her, there might well have been a greater chance of her doing other worthwhile things in life with her money. And to think that half of the population of this world is unhappy because they can't have what makes the other half unhappy. We individuals have much too little general knowledge of life as it is lived in our world and, therefore, yes, for every big fool there is an even bigger one somewhere amongst us, or out there somewhere. Thank God for that!

One of the casinos down London's Park Lane that hit the headlines before it had to close down for the unlawful way it lured its customers away from other clubs had once been a rather nice, friendly place as London's casinos come. Long before the club made big news, big bad news, Monika had witnessed strange goings-on. In the small, long dining hall's center, two tables, each seating twelve, were sometimes extra-attractively laid out, but only on one of them stood a prettily arranged bouquet of flowers. At around 9 pm, slowly arriving Gulf Arabs—always conspicuously first-time visitors—and cheap-looking call girls would seat themselves at those tables, led there by Vico, the over-the-top, attentive Italian head waiter himself. The girl bait gathered, chatting excitedly, at the flower-graced table; the Arab victims, at the other table. As the restaurant was very small and the Arabs were talking very loudly in their native language, Monika had no choice but to pick up their conversations. Their talk revolved around the girls, who winked at and charmed the men, chatting primitive, suggestive crap across those tables in English as if they were in some brothel, while the men discussed the girls quite openly and rudely and coarsely with each other as if there were nobody else in the room who could understand their Arabic. They would argue about who would lay whom. "This one? No, I don't want her. She is too thin. I don't want to fuck a boy," one would say. Another, "Look at that one in the red dress. I don't know who is going to end up between her legs, but it is not going to be me. Her mouth reminds me of our cow's cunt, and if her mouth looks like that, what do you think her cunt looks like?" "I want the one with the huge meatballs. I love to lose myself in big tits. I'll spunk all over them," another one would wince, and after each brilliant remark, loud *kah-kah-kah* laughter would follow, as each was trying to outdo the other.

On another occasion, a table full of primitive guys from filthy rich Qatar walked in with their interpreters. Their European suits were awfully ill fitting, and none of them knew how to eat with cutlery. They reached for and grabbed everything with their fingers, so the waiters jumped to their rescue and showed them how it's done—to piles of laughter, the Arabs' and the other guests'. At moments like this, Monika was "bang" back in the middle of her in-laws when she first arrived in Kuwait; and she resented the fact (accepted in Europe) that—never mind who you are, who you are not, what you don't know, and how you do it—bullshit walks, money talks, and there was no getting away from it.

Many a finger bowl of lemon water for cleaning fingers has been drunk out of ignorance just as many a neatly folded napkin with the club's initials was used as a handkerchief. And those girls, in spite of their profession, wouldn't have smiled so sweetly, nor would the management have laid on the free "do" (to lure the rich patrons as future customers, of course) if they had understood half of the filth that was discussed because, not Monika alone but all the other Arab customers also understood what was going on and glanced at each other meaningfully, especially when after the sweet trolley had made its rounds, the noisy folks at the two center tables were (all together) ushered out and up a staircase like a herd of sheep—for coffee, they were told, to disguise the actual, complimentary, free fuck they were now entitled to, compliments of the Club upstairs. That accomplished, the girls went on with their rewards to another job while the stinking rich, primitive-acting, oh-so-important VIP Gulf Arab crowd, heavily induced and impressed by all the bravura laid on for them so generously by the *Ingilesis*, was gently ushered to the tables of loss, where, high rollers that they were, they did the management proud.

It was the same management that got in trouble with the law by not being able to wait for the goose to lay its golden eggs and so forced its way up the goose's bum to grab the golden eggs and pull them out. They lured those punters away from other casinos with the illegal help of officers of the law who were, of course, financially rewarded. They made sure that the sets of set-up Arabs who got the special treatment were the wealthiest ones, even if they didn't look the part (having, to start with, trouble with Western dress, language, and behavior), and also smart enough to learn to blend in fast and to spend their money in no time flat better than anyone. In short, the manner in which the private addresses of those wealthy Arabs were procured by that club's management was unlawful and could be heard and read about in the British media later on. Arabs are strange: they hate being taken advantage of, they love arse lickers, yet they are greatly offended at the same time if they don't receive the most obsequious treatment wherever their money takes them. It's a story of greed feeding on vanity and vanity feeding on greed and of East and West never truly meeting.

If it were decided that Monika should catch up with Abdulla in one of the casinos stiff with Arabs, or if she changed her mind and decided to follow him after all, instead of staying home for the evening, she was usually obliged to wait in the lobby of the casino and told, "We beg your patience, Madam, while we are going to check for Madam if Sir is here."

"Of course, he *is* in here," she would answer. "I know he is. His car is parked right outside." Or she would say, "Why not make it simple and take a look in your guest book where you will find his signature!" still annoyed at the silly policy which made her wait like a fool before being let through. It was the club's policy always to inform its gambling members first of the arrival of a visitor before inviting someone in, for maybe a member did not want his wife, friend, or whatever to know that he was there in the first place or to be discovered gambling big money or to be caught in the restaurant or at the roulette table with a butterfly of the night by his side. To avoid such nasty little shocks and embarrassments, the well-heeled punters were well protected and considerately taken care of and decently warned in advance so that they had time to adjust. Ahhh—isn't that all so nice and thoughtful? Is that English etiquette and decency? A pretty female receptionist would come up to Abdulla, bend down low so that he could watch her bells ring, and (while his eyes would pop) would whisper in his ear, "Sir, excuse the interference, but your wife is in the lobby. Are you here?"

Abdulla was a good customer and had to be protected accordingly from his wife because it was no secret to the people in the circles he moved in that he was a great admirer and lover of a whole range of day and night butterflies, for all colors and sizes and shapes took his fancy. If losing his money was no skin off Monika's back, the countless affairs everybody knew that silly outlander heavily indulged in really got up her nose. It was the shame of it all that got under that skin of hers and settled there to stay. Even if Abdulla's womanizing left her now emotionally cold, thank God, it mattered to her how (in what light) decent people saw her because it would have been quite easy to assume either that she was an easy lay like him or that she was a brainless property of Abdulla strictly incapable of using her own mind and individuality. She resented being made out to be a non-person like any other Arab's robot wife, who was forced to be her children's father's lackey "flunkey."

The curvy, sexy magnets of mostly Egyptian or Moroccan origin, hired by casinos to attract Arabs, come to Britain under false pretenses. Acting as bait for the rich Arabs, they buzz around tables to suss out a good bet for themselves. They settle closely beside high skating punters, who soon throw at her a couple of chips to try her luck with, which at the same time are meant to tell her that she is "on." Then the pair might disappear for thirty minutes or so for a quickie, after which they come back, he to the table to lose some more, and she, on the lookout for another lay. London's nightlife is working overtime and doing fine. If Abdulla happened to be spoken to in Monika's presence by one of those (to him very familiar) high-class hookers, he would look right past her, pretending he didn't know her, and address his wife in loud Arabic Um-Sulaiman fashion, the secret code to let the hussy know that he was with his wife and that the hussy had to keep away for once.

Abdulla had (and Monika discovered) one blissful affair after another, nonstop. Within no time she had solid proof of nine involvements, excluding his one-night stands, within their first seven years in London. Had she been anything like him, she would have had more than enough opportunity to do likewise without having to pay for it with hard cash as he had to do—but she never did. She looked forward to and prepared for the day she'd finally divorce Abdulla, after which she promised herself to compensate for what she had missed out on in her life with Abdulla, in every field where she had been unfulfilled and neglected in marriage, emotions, tenderness, companionship, and sex (of course) included. Arabs and Europeans alike, in typical male fashion, thought that if Abdulla screwed about so openly, she must be made of the same clay and tried it on with her, which insulted her.

All of Abdulla's extramarital involvements were with money-seeking, money grabbing females who sold themselves and let themselves be used just like doorknobs. They went from one hand into the other. Never once did Abdulla give Monika reason to be jealous over what he picked up because it was always rubbish that he had to feed, show a good time to, and pay for as well. Let's face it: a man who has got to pay for his company and sex is not a proud man. As a matter of fact, he is only a very little bit of a man. While it's hard to find virtue in all this, allowances might be made, of course, under certain exceptional circumstances in which prostitutes do a very worthwhile job within our sick society by helping to prevent rape and, often, murder, too, although many people don't see it that way; but that's exactly how it is.

The average official term in office for Kuwaiti diplomats is four years, but since Abdulla's friend, the Minister of Health Dr. Rezza Hashemi, was elected again and again by Kuwait's parliament and because his bottom was in the same pants as that of his friend Abdulla, Abdulla 'stayed put' in his London post far beyond the first four years—for a second term and a third four-year term as well. And his private, promiscuous, turbulent, colorful day- and nightlife didn't bother nor offend his superiors in the least bit because none of them was any the better; nor was Abdulla any worse than any other high ranking Kuwaiti so-and-so's that he mixed with, although they are all such excellent pretenders and actors trying hard to give the impression of God-fearing, decent, considerate, deeply religious God's children while, in reality, thanks to the money that puts them on the thrones from where they reign, it's God first and the Kuwaiti second, but only if and when (Monika got to know some of them) it really wasn't possible to put themselves first and God second. Non-Kuwaiti Arabs say, "Kuwaitis have no mothers; they are the only people who give birth to themselves." In other words, what they are trying to say is that they think their shit doesn't stink. Abdulla was even admired by the Kuwaitis for the way he managed to keep his nice little European wife and play about so freely at the same time. He was always approached for his valuable knowledge as to where to find well endowed, big-titted, large bottomed crumpet supplies for some of his top superiors. That friendly free service came more or less with his job, whenever they came on official or private visits to London.

Monika never got to the roots of something that puzzled her. From where did Abdulla get, all of a sudden, that money to which he had unlimited access in London? Had he finally gotten his hands on his inheritance at long last? Wherever it came from, he stayed firmly in charge of it all, threw it about, showed off with it, and enjoyed it immensely. Whoever ate at a restaurant in Abdulla's presence knew the meal and everything that went along with it was paid for already. It seemed as if he were out to buy his friendships and attention, of course. He always had a couple of guys hanging around whom he would openly order about and who were beneath his social standing and who sponged off him. Monika well remembers the time when Abdulla seemed to be so put off by show-offs of the sort he now was, but his apparent disgust, as it turned out, had been just a charade, for it became apparent in time that he would have wanted to, but couldn't, do likewise then; he caught up fast, however, and became one of the biggest show-offs of all! Now, Abdulla, the professional joker, couldn't get enough of telling whoever was willing to listen just how much he was worth, exaggerating extensively, which was partly the fault of those who believed every word he was saying just because they could see that he was a diplomat. People would stand or sit all ears and slack-jawed, listening spellbound to every one of his words, as if in a trance.

It's amazing how many Westerners believe that almost every Arab is wealthy or a millionaire. That's why Abdulla had fun no end, leading many a doctor, director, or manager—and, of course, many a pretty girl—into his non-existent fantasy world of how unbelievably rich all the Kuwaitis were and how and on what they spent their money so leisurely; and then he and his Arabic friends would be tickled pink for having successfully led them astray. It was such easy play.

The staff of a well-known superstar hotel on London's wealthy Park Lane walked for three weeks in awe, curtsying with back pain from bending down for a Saudi Arabian prince and his entourage of about eight people, up until the day they all disappeared into thin air, after living it up, leaving behind unpaid bills that ran into the thousands—because that prince was no prince at all, but the crooked look-alike of a Saudi prince who often resided at that hotel (and was therefore well known), but was actually in Saudi Arabia at that particular time. The pranks some Arabs get up to in London could fill a joke book.

Abdulla's gleaming black limousine that came with his job was equipped with two car phones, and when a couple of pretty girls came his way—no matter whether his wife or kids were with him or not and knew exactly what was to happen and crouched down in shame at the back—Abdulla would pull up both receivers, one on each ear, and smile broadly at the passing females, making sure his Swiss Piaget diamond watch was well on display, too. Yes, this time in London with almost any luxury at hand that money could buy in the flick of a finger, Abdulla worked hard on being the center of attention. He made every effort and wanted to be looked at and admired. He turned out to be altogether a very selfish human being. For himself, nothing was too good, nor too expensive, while his wife, who always worked hard, brought and shared her money with him from the time he first set eyes on her. She still had to account to Abdulla for every penny she spent in order to "keep her in her place," as Abdulla put it.

Abdulla had a huge oil portrait painted of himself sitting majestically in his native dress, a white dishdasha and brown-gold trimmed cloak. It was by the well-known British painter Hailstone, who had painted Her Majesty the Queen and many other members of the Royal Family. To his delight, "Abdulla in Oil" was exhibited for a couple of weeks at a gallery in Pall Mall, close to Buckingham Palace. Abdulla loved watching people admire the work of art that portrayed him. There were one or two nasty remarks made that he overheard, like "Those bloody Arabs are everywhere," but then the people who made those remarks didn't know that that very Arab sitting high up in all his glory stood close by disguised in an Italian designer suit, observing and eavesdropping on them.

Once, as Abdulla was being chauffeur-driven to the Kuwaiti Ambassador's residence, where diplomats were to meet prior to an audience with her Majesty the Queen, Abdulla sat sunk in the soft comfortable leather back seat of his sleek black limousine, dressed in his Arabic robes and smoking a huge cigar when the car stopped at a red light and up pulled a double-decker bus. Abdulla noticed smiling passengers crowding at the windows, so he smiled back and waved at them. What do you think he got in return? Well, almost everybody poked a tongue at him and gave him the finger. Poor Abdulla, they had really hurt his ego! He talked about it for days after. I mean, there the almighty Kuwaiti was, stepping down to those mere mortals, and they didn't know how to appreciate it! The reserved English people don't warm easily to foreigners.

Abdulla indulged heavily in food and drink, put on weight, and then went for two to three weeks at a time to some fancy health farm on London's periphery to get back into shape in comfort and the company of British upper crust, where sex is not mentioned but is nonetheless practiced. Nothing was too expensive or outrageous for himself.

He had his head eternalized in bronze by a lady artiste, and he went to the U.S.A. on the QE2 with a married friend of his, who had at least six children back home in Kuwait and was old enough to be Abdulla's father. It had been prearranged that Monika and Abdulla would take this holiday together, but then the plan was changed and Monika would follow solo by plane after the two of them had taken their freedom and had done, first, what they felt like doing undisturbed by her presence, which was of course having lots of sex American style. On the day of Abdulla's and his friend Salam's departure, Abdulla, waiting for his driver, was dressed from head to toe in a brand new jeans outfit, cap and all. Happy and excited, he danced the twist to Monika's Elvis music, which she was playing because she, for one, was happy to have him off her back that morning and for some time to come and, for another, was— m spite of that—feeling distressed with the hypocritical life she was still living and Elvis's music always helped her along in sad as well as happy moments. She stood mixed up—should she laugh or cry?!— not knowing what to make of that husband of hers leaning against the lounge door when he remarked, still dancing, "My friend Salam is old and looks it, too, so how are we going to pick up pretty birds, I ask myself?—Oh, I know, I'll tell them he is my bodyguard! That should do the trick." Abdulla was so wrapped up in himself that he was not giving his kids nor his wife the slightest consideration. And as Monika watched and listened to him she thought what she had thought sooo many times before: "Good God, that's my *husband*. I feel like I am his mother."

Monika didn't follow Abdulla and Salam by plane three weeks later, as priorly arranged, after all, for once in America Abdulla changed his mind—or had it changed for him yet again. "Sweetie, if you come, my friend will feel like a spare tire. I'll take you next year to America. I promise."

Monika's plane ticket for the holiday in America did not go to waste. It landed with poisonous-snake-in-the-grass, chauffeur-butler-pimp, I-do-anything-for-money, British, simple-minded-but-also-sly Gregory, who worked in Abdulla's office. Abdulla and Salam had decided to rent a car and let Gregory drive them along America's southern coast in style. And it was California, Nevada, Las Vegas, San Francisco, and much more for Abdulla—in style; meanwhile Monika and the kids were left behind with few European friends.

Monika had tried to befriend Europeans in London, but Abdulla always put a stop to it with his appalling, often drunk, insulting behavior. When people began to make friends with Monika, he put them off on purpose, for he couldn't stomach her making friends with anyone other than Arabs, and then only with the ones of whom he approved and singled out for the purposes. Despite all of that, she felt newly born in London and ever so free.

Two months later, three very eccentric, very unusual diamond rings, purchased at the Beverly Hills Hilton Hotel's jeweler in California were presented to Monika as a consolation bribe for being ditched. As if she were just any poor, neglected, typical, Kuwaiti Muslim wife! But that's how Monika's collection grew and expanded! She would soon be able to open a jeweler's shop of her own, providing Abdulla's roving eye and sexual libido stayed active and she survives it by his side a bit longer.

And if ever she dared to challenge Abdulla on how Abdulla had singled himself out for all the superior treatment he granted himself, his answer was almost always the same: "I am a man. You're a woman. You have food, clothes, jewelry, and a pillow to sleep on. What more do you want? Count your blessings and shut up. Don't try to shit on my head!"

Being married to a Muslim like Abdulla can really brainwash a human being into believing that God created woman solemnly to multiply and please man, the superior creature, but not to have any fun or indulge in any enjoyment of our beautiful world because enjoyment is strictly reserved for the male population. The female species is unworthy of it all!

Almost as soon as Abdulla was off on his American bachelor holiday, unfortunate Monika found herself pregnant for the fourth time! She had no idea how it could have happened as she was always so careful—but, obviously, not careful enough. Knowing that another child would set her many unhappy years back, she did something she never thought herself capable of. She hurriedly arranged and had an abortion, and when Abdulla came back, he was none the wiser—until two years later when Aya made a mistake and let it slip. Abdulla was furious and threatened to sue the doctor who had aborted his child without his consent. Monika told Abdulla to go right ahead.

"You are not capable of being a father to the three boys you already have. What would you want with a fourth one? You sue the doctor, and I will prove to the court that I did the unborn child a favor."

Abdulla kept his promise and took Monika on a trip to American one and a half years later. They toured New York, Washington, Los Angeles, Las Vegas, and San Francisco, and stayed one week in a dream of a hotel in Waikiki, Hawaii—and that was fabulous: the scent of native flowers in the warm breeze, the lovely music, and such exotic foods to choose from! It must be heaven on earth—if you happen to be fortunate enough to be there with the right person, that is.

Tell me, what's a journey to America worth for a nutty Elvis Presley fan such as Monika without at least a short side-trip to Memphis, Tennessee, to view Graceland, his home, where he lies buried near his swimming pool and next to his Mamma Gladys? Monika also went on a sightseeing trip to his out-of-town ranch on which a huge white cross stands erected, reaching far into the sky. On that ranch, Elvis had his own gas station, where six of his cars stood on show, including the one that bears the famous bullet holes. Many of his fabulous fringed, rhinestone-covered stage clothes were on display there behind huge glass cases, too, among other Elvis memorabilia. Around Elvis's house you find nothing but shops that sell Elvis souvenirs—as far as the eye can see. Some are tasteful, others downright tasteless.

Monika expected much more glamour in California, but that was because she was spoiled by what she had seen in Kuwait. The houses of those big Hollywood stars cannot be compared with the luxury and grand style in which modern Kuwaiti houses are built. Monika's own Kuwaiti house would have been a showpiece among those of the Beverly Hills residents, believe me.

America was a pleasant experience, but Monika couldn't say, when asked, if she ever wanted to live there because a tourist never gets the proper insight into any country unless he or she stays amid its people; and from her visitor's perspective, she found it a little lacking in etiquette and discipline; but maybe she got the wrong impression, as one often does visiting a country for the first time. One thing she couldn't get over, though, was how many fat, grossly overweight people walk America and don't stop eating. You see a fat person from the back in America, and you can be sure that he is holding a Hot Dog in his hands when you get to see them from the front—not very health conscious, although USA aerobics apparently has swept the continent. If Monika hears of America, it brings to her mind endless paper cuts, plastic glasses, plastic cutlery—everything is fast; the key idea, convenience. The Statue of Liberty, at least, was impressive.

Sly, white faced, British, barely educated Gregory, who couldn't spell his own name properly, had worked in London's Kuwaiti Embassy as a "boy do anything" for a couple years prior to Abdulla's arrival and was well skilled in how to get to and around the Kuwaitis to benefit financially for himself. He lived in a council-owned house with his wife and three children, but thanks to Abdulla's generosity and the generosity of some other Kuwaitis, he was able to call that house his own property four years later. Kuwaiti patients and their companions were fetched from London's Heathrow Airport by a fleet of drivers from the Embassy's Health Section, of which Abdulla was the boss. The drivers were British or of Arab origin but never from Kuwait, for it would be beneath a Kuwaiti's dignity to be a chauffeur, and drove American station wagons, in which they took arriving patients to lodgings or hotels according to prior arrangement. Patients sent by the Kuwaiti Government had to fly the flag and always arrived by Kuwait Airways, but if they traveled on their own accounts, it was by the much-favored British Airways—for its alcohol trolley, of course, which was missing from their dry-as-their-arid-desert Kuwaiti Boeing 747. The patients in critical condition were taken by waiting ambulances straight to the hospital especially reserved for them.

Gregory had no trouble at all in sussing out who the Aseel Kuwaitis, the ones whose names stared with "al-" were, on the arrival lists, the ones that were the best tippers, and he made sure he got to drive them, to make friends with them, and to look after their London-owned flats and their cars; for in the late 60's and early 70's it was the "in" thing for Kuwaitis to own a flat or house somewhere in London, which called, of course, for someone to take care of things in their absence. The lower part of London's Edgeware Road, for example, is mainly owned by Kuwaitis, especially the block of flats behind the Safeway supermarket. If you stroll down that road on a warm summer's night, you might think you are in Kuwait. (It's perhaps of interest to mention here that Edgeware Road is now cockroach-infested!) Gregory had a way of convincing the Kuwaitis newly turned into London-property owners that he was their man, someone who knew how to take care of business, so he was always in demand.

From the start, Monika had no trouble in seeing right through Gregory with her intuitive X-ray eyes and soon had him sussed out. Gregory, who made easy game of naive, softhearted Abdulla, was a two-faced rat in human disguise. What sex-starved Kuwaitis yearned for was, of course, sex, and Gregory knew that. He had his man in Kuwait and shipped—charging double and often triple for his services and goods—trunks full of sexually explicit magazines and sex aides to Kuwait's big screws, who themselves carried influential wastas and so were completely immune from Kuwait's sanctions against the importation of anything sexy and from the usual, strict Customs Checks. Gregory and some other drivers also made a pretty penny on the side by being at all times well equipped with video machines and hardcore "blue" films stocked in the trunks of their cars. It needed painfully little coaxing to sell the videos to those poor, shriveled, sex-starved, deprived Arabs. That 'little' big business was booming, not interfered with for years, until a strait-laced Kuwaiti who was approached to watch one of those films took offense, and Abdulla finally was obliged to put a stop to it.

Birdy-song ringing telephones that were pinched from the British G.P.O. (and sold at twice their normal value to unsuspecting patients and their companions) were also a part of the illicit commerce that went on for years as a business side-line among Kuwaiti Health Office drivers—until the long arm of the law, British law that is, put a stop to it and marched off some of the enterprising to prison.

Primitive Gregory, who was born to arse lick without shame, was to become Abdulla's most trusted confidant at the office and in private. He knew Abdulla's secrets, business, and current girl affairs; and the trusted snake often accompanied Abdulla—so much so that Abdulla's friends teased Abdulla saying that Gregory was Abdulla's wife Number 2, his shadow, or his gay love. In no time, Gregory knew how the wind blew in Abdulla's and Monika's marriage and played it safely both ways. He made Abdulla believe he stood his ground with Abdulla, taking sides against Monika, while he kept creeping to Monika behind Abdulla's back, bringing her all the information on everything she wanted to know and on all that she had had no idea Abdulla was up to, too. Monika played that game with Gregory although it was not really "her"—just one among many games she had to participate in and was forced into, thanks to Abdulla. Deep down, she despised Gregory, but taking Gregory's information was the only way she would ever know what Abdulla was really up to. Gregory's services did not come free, no sir. She had to make him feel important and paid him for his betrayals with 22-carat gold jewelry from Kuwait, watches for him and his family from Switzerland, fur hats from Austria, clothes for him and his family, and hard cash when he kept moaning how eternally short he always was. Once Gregory had left Abdulla behind with one of his girlfriends somewhere and, as happened often, came back to Monika to deliver his report on Abdulla, calling Abdulla names and swearing at him; and that's when Monika plucked up the courage to tell Gregory something he had had in store for him for a long time.

"Abdulla is a naughty, weak, spoiled, easily-led-astray, selfish brat who's not fit to be a husband nor a father, but when he is compared with you, with your character, you, Gregory, aren't even fit to polish his shoes! I just want you to know that."

Gregory took Monika's statement with a pinch of salt. He smiled and said, "A man's got to make his living. I am solemnly on your side because I feel sorry for you. You deserve much better. A European man would lick his ten fingers if he had a wife like you. If you don't tell him, he will never know. I don't harm him. If he is a fool, then that's his business, isn't it? If I want the nice things in life, I've got to work for them the way I know best. I haven't learned a profession. What I know best is how to drive a car. I wasn't born into money like those Arabs, you know. It makes me truly sick when I see how they throw it about, and I admit that—yes—I want to get some of it. The money is in the wrong hands among that ignorant bunch, and they don't know how to use it."

Not just Gregory, but many intelligent, highly educated Westerners have the same attitude towards the Middle East's riches, believing that the wealth is in the wrong hands, which is, of course, total rubbish, for who says who is entitled to have the money and who is not? And who is qualified to say how and by whom it is to be spent? Tell me, I ask you, dear readers, is the money with which the crowd of well-heeled sleuths fought in grand style (though so discreetly and elegantly) in Switzerland in 1987 over the Duchess of Windsor's jewels in the right hands? Or the money in the hands of the people who occupied the seats at Sotheby's so stylishly to bid for van Gogh's Sunflower canvas (the canvas he painted in Arles 99 years ago)—is that money in the right hands? Yes, it's an unjust world with the modern and uncivilized, influential, rich society gone and going further O.T.T. (over the top). Stinking rich Arabs and wealthy Eurotrash are in the same bag. Allowance might be made for the desert Arabs; the Eurotrash has no excuse. Children starve and old people die of dehydration all over the world. If you ask me, the enormous amount of excess money some people dwell in often comes through illegal deals or the hard sweat of others. It should all go in the direction of the Bob Geldorfs of this world, and then it would be in the right hands. Do darlings, let the Arabs spend, spend, spend their money according to their whims, wishes, and desires, and let them be happy throwing it about. Don't begrudge them the money. Let them have it. We have glorious freedom that their and nobody's money can buy them. Kuwait is not a democratic country, you know that, don't you? By now we have well established that money doesn't bring happiness. If you've never had wads and wads of it, you might not appreciate my view. Yet, believe me, the lucky, fortunate West can live life so carefree—blessed with delightful, delirious love, for to love and be loved is the most blissful state of existence imaginable, something most poor Kuwaitis know nothing about and die never having known. What their money can buy them is sex with a piece of meat, not love.

Love is what most of us instinctively seek more than anything else, even if our eyes are often blinded by the materialistic. Money, success, and power and all the other goals we set for ourselves are often just substitutes. Let's face it and admit it, and we are halfway to understanding ourselves better. What's all the fame and money worth if at the end of the day you sit alone between four walls of a lonely, cold, oh so lovely art deco room—although the central heating is on High—like so many of the rich, talented, and famous who are surrounded by locusts who want to feed on them. Yes, Sandie Shaw, for my money you can sing out loud "Long Long Live Love"!

Have you ever noticed how happily and cheerfully the hand-to-mouth working class lives compared to the rich hobnobs? You pass a building site and you'll hear a happy, jolly whistle come your way. These people work for their weekly pay and are happy and much closer to nature, too. A 9-to-5 hungry secretary enjoys her 45p ham sandwich much better than the person who eats a $50-to-$100 gourmet lunch every day of the week, is raised on *a-la-carte* grub, and thinks the word "hunger" is a city in Germany. And while we are comparing, next time you walk down London's Knightsbridge or Oxford Street, do look in the faces of the active, busily rushing about, white skinned working women and then compare what you see there with what you see in a fur-coated, bejeweled, or wrapped-up-head-to-toe rich Arab woman's troubled face. That tells you all.

Except for Gregory, all approximately thirty-six of Abdulla's employees—who were mostly of English or Arab origin—were a likeable bunch. At times some of them took liberties but couldn't really be blamed because Abdulla their boss had such a weak personality.

Instead of letting his staff greet him the boss, he used to tour the office saying his Good Mornings. If the staff had some complaints, he used to apologize to them. Yet, the whole office feared influential Gregory, who let them know—being in favor with Abdulla—that it was up to him who would get the sack and who could stay on; and, if indeed anybody did have to be given the sack, gutless Abdulla left the dirty task to Fouad, his second man in charge. Only at home did Abdulla become ten feet tall and play the tyrant and let the devil out of the sack.

After a couple of years of artificial, diplomatic razzmatazz, the charm of life in these so-called diplomatic circles wore off for Monika because it did nothing for her to be among people who pretended the night away. She was forced to play along and to associate with a crowd that she was increasingly fed up with and tired of. She grew increasingly to hate having to portray the good little obedient Muslim housewife by day and the live decoration on the arm of playboy Abdulla by night. She became sick to the teeth with her "diplomatic" life, which required her to be dolled up at night and to look good for Abdulla's sake. She might as well not have had a brain. She kept telling herself she was enduring this married life for the sake of her children and looked patiently and longingly forwards into the future when the time would be right and ripe for a divorce.

Sleeping in different bedrooms helped Abdulla to develop a stupid habit which otherwise-alert Monika took some time to cotton on to. After he, or both of them, had come home from an evening out, usually in the wee hours of the morning, and had said their goodnights, he would retreat to his room, where he quietly got dressed once more to sneak out behind Monika's back and meet with friends or girls at a discotheque or whatever. He was often seen by mutual friends, and most of the time, when friends made passing references, Monika thought that they had made some mistake, or that Abdulla had a jolly good double.

Monika loved dancing and Abdulla knew it. She often begged him to take her out to dance, but he always replied that dancing was unfit for a Muslim woman of her age and mother of three children and that she should be ashamed of wanting to cha-cha-cha on display and of wanting to shake her body in public.

"Watch it, don't try to get too big for your boots," he would say to her while she thought to herself, "Up yours, you selfish bugger! It won't be much longer now, and then I'll cha-cha-cha until I drop!"

CHAPTER TWENTY-SIX

MONIKA'S EMBASSY JOB AS INTERPRETER

Having more or less thrown in the towel on her fruitless nightlife, the nightlife that other females envied and wished they were in her shoes for, Monika once more felt a bit useless and cut off from the outside world. As she was driven around London in limousines, Monika constantly noticed people looking longingly at and into the cars—sometimes, even, touching them. "If you'd know my true lifestyle, you wouldn't look so envious," Monika thought to herself. Yes, the grass always does look greener on the other side of the fence. So, as before, she started once more to work gently on Abdulla to reach his agreement that she be allowed some daytime occupation. And, since he would not hear of anything that would throw her amongst European people during the day because, as he said, they all wanted to fuck her (a notion he had because he thought everybody was like himself), Monika gladly accepted his offer, which was to work with and for him in the Kuwaiti Embassy's Health Office and which was better than sitting at home brooding and rotting. Monika joined the Embassy Staff—as interpreter—and was put in charge of six more translators, for the next approximately five years.

Monika's job—and that of her staff—was to visit the Kuwaiti patients in hospitals and clinics scattered all over London and to report to the Embassy office how the patients were progressing, how they were treated, whether there was anything they needed or wanted. It also involved doctor-patient interpretation. Monika enormously enjoyed doing her job. She loved to help the patients, for whom it was no easy task being so ill, lying in a strange land, often without companionship and not speaking one word of English. And the patients liked her in return, for numerous reasons, which they expressed in many ways—but maybe first of all because she was Diplomat Abdulla's wife and came to see them personally, something an Aseel Kuwaiti woman would never do; and, secondly, because she always got them what they wanted, which was easy for her because her husband was the boss and because she could get her wastas from him.

Some privileged patients came to London with two companions; others, always the poorer version, with none and no money either—like the poor alcoholic guy who drank mentholated spirits for years in Kuwait and, therefore, developed gangrene. He had already had four toes and three fingers cut off and didn't have any money to buy cigarettes. Sometimes she forked out a bit of her own while pressing on Abdulla to speak to his Minister friend Dr. Rezza to get official permission to finance a weekly allowance for such cases, which were plentiful.

When the Minister of Health came to London, which was very often during the year, he loved to eat Monika's Arabic cooking.

"If one can eat food prepared by Um Sulaiman's hand in London, which idiot would choose to go to a restaurant instead," he would say. At just such a meal, eaten Kuwaiti style right on the floor, the Minister said to Abdulla, "You better watch out. I get more patients who enter my office back in Kuwait to thank me for what Monika has done than for your services rendered."

Abdulla always gave his job 100%. The Minister and everybody else in Kuwait knew that, too. Abdulla was definitely in the right job. It was rewarding for Monika to enjoy her work and get acknowledgement for doing so. It pepped her up. Yes, people were satisfied and very thankful for all the help and often, too, the tips she gave. Soft-hearted Abdulla also dipped into his own pocket, sometimes very deeply, or spoke to his Ministry to help out a poor Kuwaiti bedouin who came for private treatment on his own account and not the government's because he was either too proud to ask or he had asked and had been turned down. Like everything else in Kuwait, who could be treated expertly in Britain under the world-famous, first-class British medical care and have three companions all expenses paid, and who could not, very often had a hell of a lot to do with a good wasta. Officially there was a special Committee of the Ministry which was set up to discuss every patient who might be sent abroad for medical treatment, but many of those receiving government funding were filthy rich and could easily have afforded to foot their bills themselves but came to London all expenses paid, thanks to an unofficial wasta. Who was sent and who wasn't and why and by whom were always widely discussed topics among the Kuwaitis living and working in London.

Apart from learning a lot relating to the medical field, Monika encountered a few unusual experiences in her years among the medical professionals and her official charges. So, let's look closer at a couple of them. Saddest of all were the little cancer and leukemia kiddies at the Great Ormond Street Hospital, who were always so friendly and polite and never complained. Those children took their fate in so much more dignified a fashion than the sick grown-ups did. They appeared to Monika to be living already in another world, of which they had a sort of second sight and so were not afraid to die. Every time Monika left the children's cancer ward, it set her thinking: they were all such brave little angels. One week you see them as normal and lively as any healthy child and wonder what they are doing in a hospital, and the next week they have become much quieter, their little faces thinner and yellowish, hair loss now evident from their medication. The week after, you might find them lying quietly, looking you straight in the eyes from their white-sheeted little beds, crusts of blood forming around their noses, their colorless, thin lips quivering. You know then that that little darling hasn't long to go. And the next time you make your visiting rounds, the bed is empty, or another child has taken it over. It's sad. Awfully sad. And yet, what can one do but count one's blessing and go on living? Among all the illnesses of human nature, Monika's tragic life was not tragic at all—not compared to this.

The greatest gift on earth is health. God bless people like British cricket ace Ian Botham for his unselfish part in children's cancer research in Britain. Isn't it sad to know approximately how much money is put into the Super Powers' Star Wars game and how little in comparison is available for research on cancer, among other ailments including the latest, AIDS.

Monika often had to deal with complaints by the nursing staff about the patients, and vice versa. Those Arabs who flashed their hard-on willies at nurses and at Monika remained on the amusing side of things. That practice wasn't taken too seriously by anybody unless the horny, kinky guy got out of control, in which case he was reported to the Health Attaché Abdulla, who would warn him personally that he was on the next plane homeward bound if he did not henceforth restrain himself.

There were the two fanatical religious Islamic brothers with long beards. They were in their thirties. One of them had an incurable disease. Now, that patient wouldn't allow a female nurse to get close to him because, he said, the nurses wore perfume and wanted to seduce him. So Abdulla hired two male nurses from a private agency—one for day, one for night—to make him feel more comfortable. When Monika came to visit, he quickly hid under the blankets and only spoke to her from behind the bedclothes because she too was a devil in disguise.

When the attending physician discharged this patient and it was time for him to go back home to Kuwait even though there had been little real improvement in his condition, the brothers refused to leave. They thought that Abdulla didn't like them. The patient's brother came to Abdulla's office and attacked him with a huge knife that ripped through Abdulla's jacket but got stuck in a pillar that Abdulla had leaned against and not—thank God!—in Abdulla's stomach, the intended target. Abdulla had been alert enough to jump aside in time, and his quick reaction had saved him. Retrieving his knife, the bedouin ran into the street, where it took two policemen and some bystanders quite some time to overpower him and, most difficult of all, to get that weapon out of the bedouin's iron strong fist. White-faced Abdulla was of course left shaken. Once in London, all patients wanted to stay on for as long as possible, all expenses paid, with daily pocket money from their generous Government. Their stay was often a welcome holiday after their recovery. It was always up to the attending physician and Abdulla to determine when the patient's time in London was up.

The doctor would almost always receive a worthwhile "thank you" gift from his Kuwaiti patients. These were often used as bribes for a longer convalescent period, for these needed to be authorized by their doctor. The presents ranged from golden Cartier pens to diamond-studded gold Rolex watches or even a set of jewels for the wife, Czech cut-lead crystal ornaments, and so on. Abdulla was presented with "thank you" gifts as well, sometimes by recuperated sheikhs, of whom he had had to take the best care, of course, as was only to be expected. Monika didn't go unnoticed either. Some things she accepted, others she rejected politely. She did once accept a golden pendant with a little diamond that a young Irani Kuwaiti who had an incurable liver disease and who had come all alone on his own account and had gone out to buy for her, knowing that he would die.

Many patients were allowed to stay on after one doctor had finished with them because that first doctor couldn't find a cure, or because doctors could find nothing wrong in the first place, to have a second and a third opinion. Some patients were treated on the private account of a generous sheikh. Once a whole family got the green light to go to London, be treated, and live on the Crown Prince Saad al-Saad's account, where they were seen by other Kuwaitis collecting discarded receipts from the floor at Harrod's, London's biggest and most exclusive store—receipts which they handed to Abdulla a couple of days later in an envelope, saying that they had bought the goods and asking that the money be reimbursed to them from the sheikh's account.

A close Kuwaiti friend of Abdulla who awaited an operation at the Wellington Hospital had handed out £6,000 in tips to the nursing staff within the first three days of his hospitalization and before he had his operation. And that's no good either because, here again, tipping corrupts and spoils the nursing staff. It's natural that Sister Pat would enter a generous patient's room more often and show more patience in his case than she would to the frail little bedouin who isn't quite with it in his head, poor chap. Just as Monika was walking into such a person's room, she heard the nurse shout at the patient rudely, "Shut up, you stupid camel!" The nurse was of course reported to the sister in charge, for if any hospital had trouble with the Kuwaiti patients, all they had to do was ask the Health Office for a special, private nurse.

When such incidents happen, one can hardly blame the patient or the nurse. Culture clash—they were different people from different worlds, and it was often difficult for both to cope with each other. The bedouin would look upon the nursing staff as his private servants, paid for by his government, and the nurse would run out of patience if the patient repeatedly shit in the bidet or stripped his bed completely to make it where he was most comfortable, which was the floor. Yet, all patients—modern Kuwaitis and their old-fashioned bedouin brothers alike—greatly respected their doctors.

Monika opened the door of a Wellington suite once and walked in on "nurse on top of patient." The patient was a man she knew well from her Sea Club days and whose son was a friend of Sulaiman. The nurse, dressed in the crisp white uniform of a private agency, jumped up but couldn't get her dress down in time. Monika saw her black stockings held up by white suspenders. She wore no panties—convenient, in her case. Monika didn't mind the nurse so much but wasn't impressed by the patient's need for "sex with danger," so she said in Arabic, "Oh, please, carry on with your medicine" and left a startled, embarrassed twosome behind.

On browsing through London's hospital wards, Monika was to meet many an unfortunate Kuwaiti woman who was, as she had once herself been, afflicted by illnesses that were traceable back to the way their husbands treated them. It was really quite unbelievable. When she translated for those patients and their doctors, the doctor would say, for example, "Here we have a classical example of a woman who is allergic to her husband, and if I were an excellent doctor I would have to tell her, Get a divorce or you'll never get better!—but how can I do that? We'll just have to treat that poor soul like all the others, which is a waste of good time and money, after which we will have to send her right back home to continue her ordeal."

Monika knew exactly what the doctor was talking about.

In London's Harley Street work—no doubt about it—many of the best specialists in the medical profession world wide, doctors who have cured patients who were given up as incurable by others. But there are also a handful of cowboys who have put themselves in the same neighborhood but who now and then give the good old establishment a bad name. Here, again, those few are mostly not ethnically British; some are Arabs. Arab patients, especially those who come on their own accounts and branch out to find their own specialists, are often taken for a ride. Some doctors rent rooms for a couple of hours a week in fashionable areas near Harley Street and then hold "surgery" there. These are cases where a patient often pays in advance hundreds—sometimes thousands—of pounds for treatment (often an operation) he or she doesn't even need. Sometimes a couple of people are involved in such a racket, many working for commissions, starting with the one who is on the lookout for the sort of patient who would go for this kind of doctor; and then it goes on and on from there.

There are doctors who do not hesitate to lay on the music, wine, and women, and maybe throw in the wife, too, for contacts like Abdulla—to lure him into letting him have plenty of patients in return. One such doctor's wife is the private fuck of a high, high up Kuwaiti top dog—with her husband's blessing. She's got enough jewelry and possessions to prove what she is up to and, being rather careless, not just Monika knows about it. Other doctors offer handsome commissions; these are the same doctors who have charged a Kuwaiti and other Gulf patients almost twice as much for an operation as they charge an English Harley Street society patient.

One evening, Monika got herself ready to attend a Harley Street specialist's private party and was quite smitten with the notion of going to it. As she and Abdulla got there, loads of people, mostly British, had already arrived and were all over the place. All the guests looked their "cream of society" parts. In the middle of every room of this doctor's luxurious house sat a fur-covered waterbed on which people had gotten comfy, and the air smelled sweet. Yes, grass was being smoked and passed around—never mind that. As Monika tried to listen to the words of the music that a He and a She were singing (and doing enough groaning for a 100 multiple orgasms, too), Monika realized that this record was probably meant to be a "turn you on" piece. As in a kaleidoscope, people moved closer together and Abdulla stood over-protective near Monika while male eyes viewed and smiled at her as they did at all the other females, who seemed to be beguiled by it all and smiled broadly and invitingly back at the fellows. Just as Monika said to Abdulla, "It's a strange party," the host, who could hardly lift his tongue when he spoke, so heavily was he under the influence of drugs, came up close to Abdulla and mumbled, "Any minute now, my friend, and the fucking is going to start. Whom do you go for? Have you made your choice?" Monika couldn't believe her ears, and Abdulla answered, "I am taking my wife home. Next time you have a party like this, warn me and I'll come alone."

"Abdulla, what are you talking about?" the doctor grabbed his arm. "Without fucking it's not going to be a bloody fucking party, now is it? You've got to create the right atmosphere. You're not in Arabia. Come on, why don't you and your wife enjoy it! Don't be so bloody fucking old fashioned."

Abdulla pushed Monika towards the exit. She had wondered, and now she knew why all the ladies, some of whom were quite old but kept surgically young-looking, wore short two-piece or silk pajamas while the men were dressed very casually. The clothes were, naturally, most convenient for easy access to the male and female sexual organs and tits, let's face it. Oh, well. Good luck to them . . . birds of one feather flock together. Monika was very broad-minded, but more than two people involved in a sex session wasn't her scene. That doctor wasn't British, but he had a British passport.

A young Harley Street dentist, who was a drug-taker and over-active in London's nightlife—once again a British citizen, but not an ethnic Brit—had at some point introduced Abdulla to a pretty, young dental nurse who had formerly worked for that dentist and who was now on holiday in London from Australia. Abdulla fell for her. He urged her to give up her job in Sydney and to come live in London, where he would set her up in a flat as his mistress. The silly girl flew home and was back a couple of weeks later to take Abdulla up on his word, but he got cold feet and didn't want to do it anymore. So, to start with, the girl threatened to tell his wife, Monika, to which he responded that she could save her breath because he would tell Monika himself, and tell her he did. Monika took it in stride—one more, one less, what did it matter? The next thing that girl did was to get herself a lawyer, who tried to make it clear to Abdulla in a written statement that the girl had given up a well-paid job—and her nursing career back home in Australia to accept his promised offer—to which the dentist was a witness. Lucky Abdulla was in the clear, for the law couldn't touch him with its little finger: he was a Diplomat! My God, didn't he just live like one, too?

If you hear through the press that somebody worth mentioning has died of natural causes, it doesn't always mean you are being told the truth. Abdulla was once called to a top London hotel's most lavish suite, where a Kuwaiti sheikh sat in a chair with a needle up his arm and close by was a big wide-open traveler's bag filled to the brim with—you name it—all sorts of drugs. The seated man was a dead man and, being discovered rather late, had blown up to twice his normal size after rigor mortis had set in. Nevertheless, in the papers the next day you could read a story in which the only thing that related to the truth of the matter was his name. It was reported that he had died of a heart attack.

As most Kuwaitis are completely lost in London, knowing little or no English, Monika was frequently asked to accompany women on their shopping sprees. As soon as they got to know her a little, the first thing they wanted help with was finding out where to buy blue films and sex aides. Monika took them straight to Anne Summers' sex boutique, where the poor dears spent a fortune, ashamed of what comes naturally to all of us, always saying (and stressing the point) that what they were purchasing was not for their personal use but that a friend had asked them for it all. Monika got quite expert in buying and asking for all the possible aides available because there was no way any of those women could muster the courage to do it for themselves.

One day Monika helped a woman to purchase a three-piece suit in a Bond Street boutique in the West End, only to discover that the same suit (a few blocks down in Fenwick's) not only was actually much cheaper but consisted of five pieces, which included a matching hat and shawl. Monika returned with her shopper to the first shop and the manager there "discovered" that the two missing items had been "accidentally" left downstairs in the storeroom. He also approved a reduction in price, but only after and not before Monika mentioned the Consumers' Council. Many London shops didn't and still don't display prices, and this practice gives a dishonest sales assistant a chance to overcharge, especially when the easily recognizable, wealthy Arab males and females couldn't read price tags even if they had existed.

The Kuwaitis were very generous and very careless with their money in the 60's and 70's although nowadays they are becoming more and more aware of the pitfalls of extravagance, especially in view of the increasingly uncertain political future of Kuwait. After the Iran-Iraq War and the Gulf War that followed it, Kuwait will never be what it was in the 60's and 70's. Restaurants were great at adding £25 or more to a bill without the customer ever knowing. If the waiters were caught out once in a while, as they were from time to time (especially when Monika was present and checked the bill), the most that could be hoped for from the manager she then insisted on seeing was, "We are so sorry . . . an error, we beg your pardon, madam." Monika was amazed how foolish restaurateurs and shop staff and even some hairdressers could be, for what they obtained dishonestly by taking advantage of ignorance they could have multiplied by being honest. Gulf Arabs—and in particular Kuwaitis—will trust you and send you their friends if you are honest, but once you are caught cheating them, you'll never see them or their money again.

One morning, as she got out of her car in front of London's Wellington Hospital, which is more like a five-star hotel than a hospital, Monika heard and then saw five masked Arab women from Qatar clad in long dresses standing beside a taxi, their voices raised in Arabic at the cabby:

"*Bess, bess, harami!*" (stop, stop, you thief!), they yelled.

Monika walked up to them and saw that a young Arabic girl had been holding out a roll of twenty-pound notes in her hand and the driver had been helping himself by pulling note after note from the small fortune offered to him in this manner. The women were pleased when Monika turned up and explained that every day they had paid under three pounds for the fare from the Churchill Hotel to that hospital, but that this time they had got a greedy taxi driver who had taken much, much more than he was entitled to. The cheeky taxi driver's excuse was, "This horde of messy, noisy women are a bloody nuisance! If I charge them a bit more, it's because after the likes of them I have got to go and have my cab cleaned out before I can pick up a new fare." Even so, if London's taxis have a choice between an Arab and a white face, they almost always stop for the Arab because he tips well or, out of ignorance, pays too much.

Do you know why the statistics show up such a high rate of Arab shoplifters? You might think because they are guilty, but that's not always so. Arab Embassies advise their nationals to plead guilty and pay the fine, for if they try to fight the claim to prove their innocence, not only would there be circumstantial evidence against the defendant, the defendant would have to wait in London for the case to come up before a Magistrate. Passports would have to be surrendered to the authorities until after the case had come to trial. Apart from the cost of lawyers and translators, there would also be the cost of staying in England, sometimes for as long as six months.

A pregnant young Kuwaiti mum who had come to London to do her layette shopping for the new baby in London at "Mothercare" on Oxford Street held a couple of chosen goods over one arm when she turned around and her three-year-old daughter was nowhere in sight. The mother searched, irritated, everywhere, and then ran out into the street to look there when she was rudely grabbed by the wrists and pulled back into the shop, where she saw her daughter sitting on the floor playing happily with coat hangers. That young woman's English got her nowhere; so she, too, joined the queue of those who pleaded guilty—just to have it over and done with.

During Monika's spell at the Embassy, reports of Kuwaiti patients and visitors to London whose handbags (containing their money and jewelry) and their passports had been snatched out of their hands in London's streets, big stores, and small shops, flowed in regularly. The victims were sometimes left holding just a strap while the bag had been cut off and had vanished.

Accommodation, too, can be a real problem. Whether they choose to stay in a rented luxury flat or in a suite at a celebrated hotel, Arabs—especially the very richest ones—are nowhere safe. Not even when they put their trust in the hotel's safe, where one Kuwaiti sheikh deposited his lolly and found it gone; and another victim: his diamond jewelry (purchased for his fiancée as a wedding gift), and found it gone, too—when he came to collect his property. Seldom was it the ethnic British who indulged in break-ins and robbery, in back-to-back selling, and, of course, the popular practice of commission offering and taking—but mostly other Arab brothers of lesser financial fortunes, whose businesses flourished in Great Britain and who could tell a Kuwaiti by his accent.

Those other Arabs in business do rather well on the London property market, owning flats that are only rented out to wealthy Arabs. It is understandable that the Kuwaitis and other Arabs on a trip to London, a strange world to them, are happier and more at ease if another Arab stands waiting for them at Heathrow Airport with a friendly "*Marhabba*" greeting than a white-faced Englishman with his "Hello, lovely day, isn't it? Shall we have a cup of tea?"

Monika became attached to an out-of-the-ordinary, very pretty sixteen-year old Kuwaiti girl who had lost all willpower to live. She lay absent-minded and listless night and day in her darkened hospital room, covers pulled high over her head. That pretty, unfortunate maid was not only injured—body, mind, and soul—but really wanted to die, for she was the victim of incest with her own father and a twenty-year-old brother, too. It was hard work, to start with, for Monika to get her attention, not to mention a single word out of her—like squeezing blood from a stone. Yet, after lots of patience and gentle coaxing, Monika was rewarded with a confession, which contained information very necessary to the girl's attending physicians, of course, and helped her and, in the end, did her a lot of good. The patient had been sent to London, like so many other patients, because in Kuwait the doctors could find no explanation for what was the matter with her.

The first thing that poor girl said to Monika was "Give me a gun. Bring me a gun. If I could get my hands on a gun, I would shoot myself!" Her medical file was classified as 'Very Confidential' and kept out of the girl's room. After the doctors had convinced her that they could help her, she slowly cheered up a bit, especially after she was sewn back up into a virgin. Repaired in body but not in soul, she dreaded going back home.

"My father keeps phoning me. He is going to leap on me like a mad, wild dog the day I get back home. He is already waiting for me," she said. To avoid that, Abdulla arranged for her to return to some of her relatives without her father's knowledge. The trouble was that that father of hers was some influential so and so, too; and, therefore, that poor girl knew it was no use to pluck up the guts to complain about him to anybody. She knew it would be fruitless and would only succeed in bringing her and anybody who tried to help her more trouble from him. Those other relatives of hers promised Abdulla they would work hard and do their utmost to help her quickly into an arranged marriage, which was the only way to set her free from the two bastards she called father and brother. Hopefully, the plan worked, for (although the girl promised to keep in touch) Monika never heard of her again.

During this time more or less, Abdulla helped to purchase the Arazi Hospital in London's Devonshire Street for Kuwait. In that hospital lay one of the wives of the Emir of Kuwait, Sheikh Sabah al-Sabah. Abdulla and Monika were frequent guests at his beautiful summer residence in England's fashionable Sunningdale. The Emir liked to be entertained by

Monika's Kuwaiti-accented Arabic, and Abdulla was pleased as punch that he could so please his Emir with his wife. But, back to the hospital. There, one of the Emir's wives lay bedridden with cancer. Monika made her almost daily rounds to her bedside, too, and was always received with open arms and shiny eyes by her daughter Mouneera. Mouneera chain-smoked and took drugs, was about 38 years old—and was a lesbian. Every Kuwaiti Aseel seemed to know that except Monika. Mouneera offered chocolates, tea, coffee, and so forth to Monika and insisted that Monika should visit her in her London apartment for supper. Mouneera smoked her cigarettes and blew the smoke into Monika's face, looking deep into her green eyes with her black ones. She became physical and kept touching Monika, the first couple of times casually, then later round the waist. She brushed her big breasts against Monika's. That was when Monika talked to Abdulla about it and found out that Mouneera's sexual orientation was lesbian. Being who she was—the Sheika and a royal princess—Mouneera could let her wastas dance; so Abdulla suggested someone else should visit the patient, the Emir's wife, and her randy daughter. To start with, Monika had been very pleasantly surprised, naturally, that Mouneera was so friendly and sweet, especially since she was a member of the royal family, who are usually very stuck up, distant, and unapproachable. They are the sort of people who look down on others if they are not royals, too. If they mix with Kuwaiti Aseels, the Royal Family still stay on their thrones.

The doctors, administrators, and nurses at the hospitals where Kuwaitis were admitted and treated got to know Mrs. al-Amahani better than they knew the Health Attaché himself, with whom they mostly talked over the telephone or communicated by letter. It was, therefore, quite natural that hospital personnel sometimes phoned the Kuwait Health Office, asking for and preferring to speak to Monika than to Abdulla over some patient's matter. And so Monika the 'action woman' was famed for getting things done and always fulfilled what she promised. People knew that her word was honorable.

But her being thus favored found no approval with the all-time jealous, bossy, domineering Abdulla, who showed his displeasure by rebuking his wife, by acting high-handedly with her, and, even more shabbily, by trying to squeeze her into some fitting place of disgrace. For example, he stubbornly played deaf unless she addressed him as "Sweetie" all of the time. At home, he didn't accept food unless it was served to him from her hands—not even a cup of tea. When he shouted out "I want tea" and the servants brought it, he would send it back saying, "Let my wife bring it to me!" He once again started to whistle for his and his friends' refills of alcohol, reviving the past and breaking a promise he had sworn to, this time after taking a shower, never to do again in the presence of strangers. And he overstepped the mark at all times by bragging in public and in her presence about how many girls he had had besides her. "I don't know why I got married. I must have been drunk," he'd say. "If you want a pint of milk, you don't have to buy a cow." To such insults, Monika responded by trying to play things down with something a bit humorous, like "Abdulla, my Sweetie, let me tell you a bit of home truth for free. The girls you get are the ones who keep falling, hook, line, and sinker for your money. They are the ones whose sole motive with you is 'this time it's love, honey, next time you pay for it.' Or: "Abdulla, you're welcome to each one of them. Have lots of fun, Sweetie. You have all my blessings."

After his late nights out on the town, he would bang his fists on her bedroom door, demanding sex. "You are my wife! I am a Muslim, and so are you. According to the Koran, you have to give it to me any time I want!" He shouted, crazed by alcohol, the door cracking and splitting in all directions, which not only woke the children and the servants who then stood shivering and watching the unfolding drama, but made the neighbors knock on their walls with broomsticks and sometimes inspired them to complain in person or to write warning notes that they would then push through the mail slots the next day saying that they would be reporting the noise to the police the next time they were disturbed by it.

One time, Monika was sitting on the toilet when he came home from a merry night out. He waited for her—to have sex—so she stayed in the loo, locked in for well over an hour. Abdulla—fed up, still waiting, having talked pointless bullshit for an hour—started to kick at the door with his feet. For the neighbors' sake, because she was ever so ashamed, she opened the door, hoping wrongly that she would be able to reason with him. He leaped at her and forced her baby doll panties down to her knees with iron strength and in full view of bystanding Gloom and her kids. She pushed him quickly back and retreated into the loo, banging the door shut as hard as she could. But the door didn't close quite and a loud shout of pain erupted from Abdulla on the other side. Monika had caught Abdulla's hand in the doorjamb so hard that the door had made a big cut in the palm of his hand. It quieted him down some, but now she had to get dressed to take him to Saint Mary's Hospital where he had to have six stitches.

It was not the first time she had rushed her sweetie to that hospital for stitches. One time he woke her up at 3:30 in the morning, drunk as usual, with a bleeding gash wound just above his eyebrow. His story was that he and a friend were at some restaurant where that friend of his had made passes at a girl whose boyfriend was Irish. The Irishman followed Abdulla's friend to the toilet and Abdulla smelled foul play. He followed and was injured trying to help defend his friend. The police were called, and in the police car the three of them took a ride to Paddington Green Police Station, where lucky Abdulla could claim diplomatic immunity and was released; but his friend, who apparently wasn't even injured, was kept there for the rest of the night. Now, don't forget—that's Abdulla's story. How much truth is there in it? All those adventures didn't throw Monika off balance, for they were more or less typical of the sorts of shenanigans that Abdulla was always pulling and that she had gotten accustomed to and had lived through over the years.

And then he did one thing that really got to her. Behind her back, he told the six official hospital visitants over whom she was in charge to ignore his wife, to take no instructions from her, and not to report to her in the future, but to his Deputy instead. He said nothing to her about this order. Now, that hypocritical, impotent action of a jealous weakling cut her pride deeply! So she sat down straight away and wrote what Abdulla had probably been waiting for some time—her resignation. She handed it to him as a late Christmas present.

And so ... it was back to the home front once more, to occupy herself domestically in who knows what—with hardly a worthwhile thing to do, having two servants in the house to manage it all.

CHAPTER TWENTY-SEVEN

A FEW LAST STRAWS

Now, let's get into how Abdulla's top job in London affected the in-laws. To start with, they were busy with great bravura all over Kuwait, letting everybody know how powerful and influential they—along with Abdulla—now were. If you are a Kuwaiti multi-millionaire, you are not so well respected as you are when you have an influential post with the Government, such as Abdulla had been appointed to. Government jobs are power jobs, wasta jobs. No sooner had Abdulla taken up his London-based job than his shit-stirring mother and sisters and their children (who were no bother) began appearing on the scene, too.

By the way, which loony is on record for saying that men choose wives who resemble their mothers? What bloody, insulting nonsense that one! When Monika first laid eyes on her in-laws in London, she thought, What the heck are they doing here? Are their cages being cleaned? And so the eternal triangle proceeded. Thank God, though, that Monika's flat was not big enough to accommodate them. Abdulla had to arrange lodgings for them close by.

They loved, they enjoyed, the country of the "hamra-gahba brigade" enormously, you know. And if anything hurt or bothered them, doctors of the same race they had previously called the "bloody fucking English" came in handy now to treat them and nurse then back to health. Abdulla ran circles around them, taking great pains to fulfill their every wish—which were plentiful (no change there!). It was expected of him, and he dutifully obeyed. In return, never once did Monika or her boys receive a nice present from her in-laws, something that they would have wanted to keep, nor did Abdulla either. It was always rubbish you would be ashamed to offer to the servants.

When Monika took a trip to Kuwait to sell off her boutique "Domino" because it had been increasingly difficult to run it successfully from London, she was informed over the phone by a tired, hard-working Gloom that Sabiha and Fahad were roosting in Monika's London flat in her absence and slept in Abdulla's bedroom while Tamader and her husband, who was under medical care and had had a biopsy taken of a glandular tumor to check if it were cancerous, occupied Monika's bedroom. Gloom's bed was rolled out every night on the sitting room floor—often very late, after everybody had gone to bed; and Abdulla, the diplomat, slept in his servant's bed in the kids' room.

Monika felt betrayed by Abdulla once again, who kept treating her like thin air. There was no end to it. She was furious. She knew the noisy parkers were sifting through all her stuff without hesitating or thinking twice about lifting something if it took their fancy. Monika had known the sisters were in London when she left for Kuwait, but Abdulla had once again lied to her when he told her they would all be staying at the posh, exclusive Churchill hotel.

Gloom complained to Monika over the telephone, saying, "Madam, they have turned the flat upside down and shout and order me about all day. I am standing on my feet since 7 am, in the kitchen, following their cooking orders and washing their clothes. It is 5 pm now, and I didn't have a minute to sit down yet. They even invite their friends to your flat to eat their rice dishes I have to cook here, too." Poor Gloom.

Monika hated the fact that those nasties should have the benefit of Gloom and Josephine, the servants she had trained to perfection. (One of the first things Monika had done for Gloom when they had first arrived in London was to arrange to have his brown front teeth capped, which made him very happy and improved his self-confidence. He looked so much better!) Now, all she could do was to comfort him by sympathizing over the phone.

Angry, Monika shouted justified abuse at Abdulla over the long-distance line, telling him that his sisters had no business sleeping in her bed and that she wanted those leeches out of her flat as fast as possible.

"Sweetie, they just walked in! How could I have turned them away?" came his lame excuse.

"Abdulla, you always want to run with the big dogs, yet you still piss like a puppy," she told him in a temper that was rising fast along with Kuwait's immense heat, and she slammed down the receiver.

On her return to London, they were gone, but only just gone. They had left the flat at the very last minute before her arrival, and the flat was still in a bloody mess, which Josephine and Gloom were trying to erase. The women's long, thick black hair was everywhere for ages after. Monika joined in to clean after the bold-faced, ignorant scroungers, who had plenty of money they were too mean to spend on themselves, just like their mother. Why go to a hotel and pay for it if you can push your way into a ready-made nest like a cuckoo—with well-trained servants, who are so much cleaner and tidier than you yourself are, at your fingertips and ready to wait on you? The kids, along with the servants, bombarded Monika with typical "ugly aunt" stories. Monika found a photograph pinned to the wall of her bedroom that was taken during the period just before Nabeel's birth. It showed Tamader, Sabiha, Abdulla, Monika's mother, little Sulaiman, and a pregnant Monika. On that photograph they had completely scribbled out Monika with a Biro pen. Monika pulled it down, tore it into little bits, and then burned it in an ashtray. Who knows, she thought, what evil spell that tampered-with photograph might carry?

In London, mother and sisters demanded—and got from the Embassy—a limousine with the driver of their choice to cruise them about in. It was at their disposal twenty-four hours a day, and it was okay; but when one of Abdulla's own sons, almost grown up by now, asked occasionally to be driven to, say, Oxford, where both boys now and then took courses, all hell would break loose.

"Take the train or the bus," he'd yell at them. "I can't let you use my office transport. People will talk, and when the Ministry finds out, I'll be in trouble."

The times when Abdulla's mother and sisters were in London were always the worst ones. That's when Abdulla, doctored by them, acted like a maniac at home. He forced his kids and wife to be subservient to his family, or they would be deprived of their pocket money. He didn't speak to Monika, but hissed. Monika, in turn, did things her way and succeeded with the tried and true, as in Kuwait. She got around him with her only weapon—sex—if she wanted something because she just couldn't even pretend to be nice to his next of kin anymore and because at the very sight of them (even if all she did was hear their voices) her stomach heaved a turn and her skin turned cold, showing goose pimples. In those situations, a gin and tonic often did the trick, as in Kuwait.

It was the same story with the telephones, the bills for which were, like everything else in the diplomat's life, paid for by his Government. Abdulla would regularly bring home his mother and sisters and often their friends, too, to make private phone calls to their friends and family members back in Kuwait. They wanted mostly just to exchange gossip and to relate the goings-on of other Kuwaitis in London, and to brag about what they had bought in the London shops. But if Abdulla's kids lingered too long on the telephone with their friends or if Monika called Vienna now and then just to inquire how her mother was, Abdulla would pace nervously up and down in front of them, interrupting nonstop, urging them to "Go on, go . . . go, finish!" and saying, "That's enough! Stop now! The Ministry has already complained about my telephone bills." And that's when Monika felt like chucking the phone into his face or to get a good grip on his balls, for he only behaved that way to irritate, to disturb her. In response, she and the boys had made it their regular routine to hold their telephone conversations before Abdulla re-entered the house, often having to slam down the receiver on hearing his key turn in the lock, and so to avoid provoking the completely unnecessary upheavals. Monika had personally asked the Ministry's deputy about the phone bill, and he had laughed in her face. "Don't be silly! Who would complain?" he had said. The fact was quite simply that, because Monika gave Abdulla no genuine reasons for disapproval, Abdulla was constantly on the look out for ways of trumping up trouble for her and his own three sons, knowing (as he did) that one of the easiest ways to get at Monika was through them.

Abdulla took many short, First Class trips to Kuwait. As his close chum and shadow, Gregory, drove him to the airport in a limousine, a station wagon packed with trunks-full of goods for his sisters and mother always followed. Now, Monika wasn't supposed to know that secret, but—yes, as you have probably guessed—it was Gregory who, of course, squealed it to her.

What really killed the ugly, fat sisters and their mother was that slim, pretty Monika's picture was frequently taken at Embassy parties and appeared in magazines all over Kuwait. It was Monika who was invited—and not they—to attend Her Majesty Queen Elizabeth's garden parties and other auditions at the Palace and in other high places. Monika had the good fortune and the pleasure of meeting all of the popular, close members of the Royal Family at such do's, except for Lady Diana, who was pregnant and not by Prince Charles' side when he remarked once on Monika's hat, saying, "Oh, I like that hat! My wife is very much into hats, too. Are you in the medical profession?" When Monika answered, "No," Prince Charles continued.

"This must be your husband?" He smiled, indicating Abdulla.

"Yes, it is," answered Monika.

"Well, I can see you have your hands full with looking after him," remarked the Prince and moved on.

Prince Charles is in the habit of adjusting his shirt cuffs as he speaks to people with that lovely voice and excellent English of his! Wouldn't it be nice for all of us who speak English to speak like that? Come on, you lot, why not? I can see some of you—especially you Cockneys—don't at all agree! Why is that? Let me guess! . . . Anyway, Monika, like everybody else who has met the Queen Mother, was quite smitten with that lady.

The first time the Kuwait Embassy Delegation—with Monika and Abdulla included—was presented to the Queen and Prince Philip, charming Prince Philip, as etiquette dictates, addressed the Ambassador while looking at Monika, who stood in the line-up with the rest of the Kuwaiti diplomats. The splendid audition hall sported polished parquet floors, and its walls were plastered with Old Masters' canvases of past Royals and new portraits of present Royals—all with their animals and children—among other opulent works of art. The delegations customarily stand along the two sides of the huge chamber, and it's anybody's guess which side Her Majesty the Queen chooses to address on entering the receiving hall; so, while she has a friendly word and a smile for each of the Embassies standing on the left side of the room, the right side is left standing in envy, on the outside so to speak, looking in. Prince Philip, gazing at Monika (who stood out blonde and white-faced against the black-haired, milk-chocolate-faced Kuwaiti delegation), addressed the Ambassador and asked, "Do I detect a new face or two amongst you, Ambassador?" Monika got ready to answer Prince Philip in German, because she knew he could speak it, when the absent-minded Kuwaiti Ambassador said, "No, we have no new additions to our staff," so Prince Philip just nodded at Monika, and she gave him a broad smile, tennis-at-Wimbledon-like, instead of a bit of German.

Ascot, too, was on Monika's yearly "with it"-list, where strawberries and cream, washed down by champagne, were served in private enclosures after lavish meals. Monika had flutters on numbers 7 and 9 at Ascot, her lucky ones, and often won. Once Abdulla was invited by a businessman friend, who asked him to come wearing his national costume. The party arrived by helicopter, and Abdulla's outfit alerted journalists and photographers, who of course pushed up for an interview with him. Prankster Abdulla told them that Monika was his private secretary and that his four wives were on their way, bundled into helicopters which would be arriving at any minute. His bull was taken down seriously in notebooks, while he walked off, having the time of his life. And so did Monika, who appeared on British TV, thanks to her white all-lace dress, sun hat, gloves, matching umbrella, and fancy little shoes.

Another time Abdulla invited Tamader and her husband to come along to a reception at a big hotel. Small Tamader was very pregnant and very fat. She looked and waltzed like a penguin, while her slim, good-looking husband by her side could have been mistaken for a male model. They were seated at the Managing Director's table with the hotel's PR's. When the after-dinner coffee was served, the conversation turned to Abdulla's family and to how many sisters and children he had. The Director complimented Abdulla and said, "You're good looking, and, with such a pretty wife, I'll bet your three sons are all very handsome boys that the girls will all go wild over some day."

"No, they're not!" butted in Tamader in a loud voice. "My sister Sabiha's sons are the most good looking ones. My brother's sons are nothing special."

Everybody was quiet and a bit embarrassed, while it satisfied Monika that Tamader had put her own foot in her mouth. Tamader's *faux pas* actually did Monika a world of good. The Manager politely changed the subject, and Tamader's rudeness was ignored; but Tamader wasn't going to take that slight lying down. Somebody had paid a compliment to Monika, and that civility disturbed Tamader's system and rankled her. After the dinner, as the little party stepped into the hotel's elevator, an agitated Tamader held her nose shut with her fingers, saying, "Pooff! It stinks in here. Somebody is wearing Tea Rose . . . it's so out of fashion . . . my servants wear it. Get me out of here! I feel sick!" The bitch knew, of course, that Monika was wearing that lovely fragrance, for there was no other woman in the lift.

Yes, jealousy raged now more than ever around Monika, who was the common Enemy Number One of her in-laws, but she didn't give a shit anymore! She felt safely a couple of cuts above that ignorant lot, who, if they had the chance, would drag her back to the Stone Age by her thin blonde hair. Soon Monika would have nothing at all to do with them. Soon she'd be out of that liaison altogether. She deserved an Oscar for sticking it out this long, for hanging in where angels fear to tread, as the saying goes. Her marriage (what a laugh, marriage!), no doubt about it, would amount to the Death of Hope for anybody. Her liaison, as anybody could see, was just another form of Hell on Earth. Anybody less strong than Monika was—or maybe less lucky—would have been (it's a safe bet) driven to suicide by the likes of it. Monika dreamed of getting away. She wanted to get away from feeling she was marooned, all alone, eternally vexed, in the middle of nowhere in her life. She needed a change, to get on the mainland, to be rescued. And the time for that, she felt, was very, very ripe. The feeling returned every time she had anything to do with the in-laws. She was fed up with Abdulla and his harem.

Harem! In the West, thanks to a lot of misinformation, the word means different things to different people nowadays. Say the word Arab, and images of the harem spring to mind, especially to the male mind, well before the Arab's thoroughbred stallions do, am I right? To most of you, a harem brings to mind a roomful of young, scantily clad or naked, hot-blooded, mysterious, bronze or milky-white, always smiling and willing females, who seem to enjoy foreplay and actual sex even more than you do.

The first questions that Monika was asked—bombarded with—by men (after they found out she was married to an Arab from the Gulf) were always the same:

"Tell me, what's it like, living in a harem? What number of wife are you, then? How many wives does your husband keep? How do you get along with his concubines?" Unbelievable, the tactlessness! And Monika was really taken aback by people's ignorance, too, especially by the ignorance of the English, for Britain had given Kuwait its independence in 1961, yet didn't know a lot about it. Some had not even heard of it before at all—and that's the upper crust we are talking about. You had to explain that Kuwait was a country in the Arab world.

Now, I have to apologize to all you men folk, but I am about to spoil your illusions and burst the bubble for you because a harem in the sense you've all dreamed about just doesn't exist in the real Arab world at all. The harem is very much there, but as I said, not in the way you have been brought to believe. It doesn't function as you probably imagine. Be honest. It rather tickles that "fancy" of yours, doesn't it? Am I right, my friend?

The place—it may be at the seaside, in a tent, or in any other room or space where women meet or gather at any given time—is automatically (becomes automatically) "the harem" when women are in it. Males are "strangers" to it. Males, even one's own family members, above the age of fourteen don't burst in on the women without first giving a coughing warning sign, which is meant to give the women enough time to cover up whatever they wish to cover, before a man enters their presence.

A Kuwaiti's harem is made up, quite simply, of all the female members of his immediate family. So, all you misled Western men, think of Abdulla's harem and tell me what's so appealing about it? And what's so sexy? I know, I know! You're now a pleasant fantasy the poorer, instead of which you might have still harbored the hope that you, too, might one day have a chance to be spoiled in a delightful harem. After all, dreams do come true, don't they? Not this one, though.

Well, supposing that every Kuwaiti had a harem full of willing sex slaves, it would be heaven on earth, wouldn't it? What about those chosen few, the oil rich? Nothing is 100% perfect for any of us down here, on this huge round ball we live on like ants, believe you me.

So the next time you fantasize how some lucky Sheikh of Arabia lies half naked on a chaise lounge draped in red velvet, flanked on his right side by full-bosomed Samia, her black hair loosely cascading way down past her waist like some waterfall, teasingly covering that prominent high cheeked, silky, olive-skinned arse of hers, to which the longest, loveliest, well-formed legs are attached, whose feet stand in golden high-heeled sandals, and who is also the owner of pouting pure, pure bright red glistening lips and the longest red nails that match those lips and promise to scratch you in just the right spot at the right moment but now feed that lucky-in-heaven, outstretched pasha grapes and passion fruit... On his left appears light skinned Faheda, her henna red hair pulled up high, held together by a golden, bejeweled clip. She bends over him, her bare full breasts—huge nipples pointing straight ahead, sprouting like rosebuds on a summer night covered in dew—now touching that lucky bugger's hairy chest... and you float on air as you imagine it's not him at all, but you, lying on that couch. She kisses you, not him, softly on the lips. She slides her wet tongue between your lips for the split part of a second, only to withdraw it almost instantly, leaving you to wonder if you really felt it touching yours or were imagining it. Her sweet smell of jasmine that arouses your senses helps to put you in a deeper trance. You notice that she has cute light brown freckles on her half turned-up nose and remember that you always fancied girls with cute freckles but never actually had one and, as if she knew what you were thinking, she smiles at you innocently. The girl may look it, but is no innocent. She knows damn well what she is doing as she fixes her eyes firmly on your manhood, her slender light skinned, skilled fingers massaging you teasingly from the neck over the chest slowly, oh so slowly, down and down, and then up again and then further down, much further down; and when you think you can't hold yourself any longer and this is it, you're ready to explode, the vixen abruptly stops altogether, pretending to adjust her thin, see-through black veil that's draped carelessly around her slender hips . . . ; then her fingers slide between her legs and start to rotate slowly, very slowly up and down and further inside the moist atmosphere while she groans and moans as . . . Oh no! . . . on-coming, belly dancing Soraya interrupts the show, a black G-string and rotating tassels on her tits, wearing nothing else. She is the third beauty who comes to please you. She sports pitch-black hair cut in a bob, a fringe reaching deep into her narrowly slit, emerald green eyes. She has not only eyes but a body, too, like that of a dangerous black panther. God, great Architect of the Universe, help me, you think, wondering and hoping that she holds what her appearance promises to give, when at the bottom of your rest bed, that has turned into a pleasant torture chamber, a sweet smiling strawberry-blonde angel in a white see-through tunic appears and offers you a water pipe for the price of a kiss on her oriental, musky oily, glistening, bejeweled sexy belly button. It's smooth . . . and oh so sexy. You're floating and your inflated manhood is floating with you, threatening to lift you to the ceiling. You get a bit embarrassed when four hands all grab at it at the same time...

   Now, stop! Wake up! Carry on reading. The rest of the way you have to go it alone because this is not a do-it-yourself help-along, you know. You're supposed to be reading the sad life of Cinderella in Arabia, remember?

   Well, I'm just enlightening you a bit and letting you know that if that's what you think an Arab gets in his harem every time he craves it, he'd have to arrange it, first, then pay for it, every time—just as you'd have to do if you wanted something like that. Want to take my advice? Watch it on a video and use your imagination. That way your kinky "harem" kicks are cheaper and more accessible. Okay, just trying to help.

The fact that Muslims are allowed to be married to four wives at a time (but actually to as many as they want to, in the long run) is crucial. It puts a whole new complexion on relationships. Even if a man doesn't marry a second time, polygamy creates the sorts of conditions—as in Monika's case—where a man's consorting with mistresses at a "Mezraha" or abroad is not considered wrong but just part of a normal process. It happens often enough that some man marries a young wife, hides her away in an apartment somewhere, and says nothing to his current wife or wives because he wants to avoid the jealousy a younger competitress always creates. People are well aware of the difficulties that polygamy causes, but still continue to practice it without notable restrictions or restraints. Most often, if they can afford to do it, Kuwaitis buy and gobble up every willing pussy that takes their lusty fancy and do so without much feeling or emotion besides self-satisfaction. For them it's the meat that counts, not the woman as such. And, although it's forbidden in the Koran to lie with a woman other than a wife, well…

As everywhere else in the world nowadays, such fuck-all lads will have to restrict themselves to their (once virginal?) wives, who are going to get far more respect and attention from their spouses (and good for them!), or those men will drop like flies under the killer spray of AIDS as time goes by. Mankind is forced back into faithfulness by nature, which after all is God, too. God—let's call it nature if you like—always has the last word, which takes most people longer to realize than we like to admit, but in the end nature (God, the truth) catches up with all of us.

When Monika first came to Kuwait in the 60's, there was no evidence to be seen of what was going to happen in the 70's, when a fanatical religious fever started to infest Kuwait and sweep over it, as it swept over so many other Islamic nations. All of a sudden, out of nowhere, just like overnight mushrooms, up sprang the new fashion. Many of Kuwait's womenfolk, who up to then had bought everything they wore from *haute couture* designers, the same women whose farts would have borne Yves Saint Laurent labels if they could have managed it, exchanged all that savvy for huge scarves knotted most unattractively around their heads to hide their black hair and straight, long-sleeved, unsightly, disfiguring, loose-fitting clothes to cover their bodies from neck to the tip of their toes. Nowadays, these are the figures and the outfits you will see in society's shopping centers.

Did you know that they look upon Western women—those of us who fail to cover ourselves similarly— as painted floozies who invite sexual assault? Do we know that—going about our own home towns dressed as we do—our dress shouts out, "Come and rape me"? Absurd, do you say?

Those poor Muslim women are being tricked into servility by their fervently traditional but weak menfolk, who can't be bothered and don't even try to control their own sex drives. So they make it easy for themselves by ordering their poor women to wrap themselves up like bunches of mummies.

Have you any idea what it means to live like than in the desert? The sacrifice is not required of them by the teachings of the Holy Koran (the Islamic bible), you know. Many Islamic women are made to assume the slave's role, not because of religion, but in reversion to stone-old traditions that seem to be coming back stronger by the day—from the past. Such repression is very much in evidence nowadays. It all began in Iran. A religious fad has brought about that revolutionary change. The females are brainwashed into this tyrannical male nonsense. All that the Prophet Mohammed asked was that when women go to pray they don't look sexy; all they need to do is to cover their legs and arms and put a scarf over their hair. Other than that, no woman is obliged by the Koran to wear a scarf, veil, or mask. Women who mutilate themselves in order to prevent men from getting turned on and randy, instead of dressing to please themselves, are (to start with) a sure turn-off to their own husbands and (secondly) a sure bet to send their husbands astray. The perversion could be compared to a beautiful garden's flowers being purposely covered over by dead leaves. Do you think that such a twist was our Creator's intention—what he had in mind when he designed us?

"Who wants to fuck a fat, ugly drum like the mother of my children?"—or something like it—is what some of those Muslim men used to say to Monika when she caught them out with a bit of crumpet. At least they were honest. So, when she watched programs on television in which Muslim men and women were invited to speak their minds, Monika felt that nearly always the men were speaking exactly (or, at least, as much as the political situation allowed) what was on their minds, yet the women wouldn't dare do any such thing. Everything they say is a front. They always say only what they believe people expect them to say.

If you ask me, the revolution in the Islamic world today is the beginning of the Islamic War, which according to Nostradamus's prophecies (and all the other predictions, too) is the first glimpse of a Third World War that's not too far away. So brace yourselves. You have been warned. I hope I am wrong. As we said all along, it's very much a man's world and especially in Kuwait. And Monika is well aware of how lucky she is to have borne three sons and not to have given life to slave girls.

Starting with Kuwait's Emir, who has fathered approximately seventy children, a handful of Kuwaiti sheikhs (and a few other men who have the money and the inclination) are known to divorce their wives weekly, each man paying off his current wife only to marry another straight away, always making sure it's another virgin, often chosen for that purpose from the bedouin tribes in the desert, sometimes proceeding in this manner for long, long stretches of time—and always claiming to be living and abiding by the protection of the Holy Book which they forcefully bend to their wills in order to satisfy their animal instincts, never considering anything (or anybody) else. The last thing they are concerned with is the female who has been put to use like a match to light their fire.

That kind of marriage is called a "muta" marriage. The muta marriage has its roots in the past, and was designed for such times as a husband might be parted from his wife or wives for a considerable period of time, especially if he was a merchant or a soldier. Just in case the muta woman becomes pregnant from this type of brief union, the man is obliged to pay her upkeep for at least three months and ten days after the muta marriage contract has been terminated; but if the woman is indeed pregnant at the end of the three months and ten days, the man must continue his payments. I'd say a muta marriage is little more than prostitution. It doesn't say anything in the Holy Koran about where a legitimate wife may turn for sex when her husband is absent. No muta marriage for her, is there? Yes, it's easier for a camel to go through the eye of a needle than for a rich man to enter through the golden gates of Heaven. Jesus said that.

Jobless, restless Monika had coaxed Abdulla successfully into letting her build a small house in Austria's beautiful countryside, 45 minutes by car to the south of Vienna, on a plot of land her father had left her. No, it wasn't just Senta, the Dalmatian doggy, that Monika had inherited from him after all. As she had done in Kuwait, Monika designed her house in Austria, too. She didn't need an architect to construct it—just builders.

For about two years, Monika traveled to and from Austria, giving instructions and paying bills until it stood ready. Her inheritance, her five years' salary plus her casino winnings—all the money she had managed to save in London—went into that house, and Abdulla, who couldn't get used to it at all that she had her own property, nevertheless chipped in when he felt like being generous—or maybe to say, as he did when it stood ready, "I have built her a house in Austria."

Abdulla, Monika and the children had planned a journey to Italy. When mother-in-law heard of it, she, too, wanted to come along. Abdulla was completely opposed to (and actually scared of) the idea of taking his mother to Italy—to start with, for the simple reason that she didn't know how to behave in public and, accustomed to eating with her hands, couldn't manage her food with cutlery.

At that time, Monika had set her eyes and heart upon owning a restaurant in London's Baker Street. She dreamed of transforming it into an eatery where only Kuwaiti national dishes would be served. It would be the first of its kind in Britain.

But to make that dream come true, as always, she had to work her way around Abdulla first.

Restaurant in mind, Monika agreed to take care of, feed, and look after Abdulla's mother on a journey that was better not discussed afterwards. Apart from her bossiness and ignorance, everything mother-in-law saw mother-in-law wanted—not once, but four times over. One of everything was for Diba, one for Sabiha, one for Tamader, and one for mother-in-law herself. Everything, of course, was paid for out of Abdulla's pocket—naturally. In Venice, mother-in-law insisted on buying a lilac glass coffee set, but Abdulla, stretched to the limit, lost his temper and told her, "Why do you sit on your money? I know you have plenty of your own. You could buy the whole of Venice with it. Next time you come from Kuwait, bring some with you. I don't shit mine, you know."

To start with, as usual, Abdulla was dead set against the restaurant idea, but Monika didn't give up, and in no time everybody at the Embassy knew that Monika wanted to open a Kuwaiti restaurant. Everybody encouraged her. The Ambassador promised to send her customers from Bahrain, too, where he had previously been stationed. Under so much positive pressure from all except a few jealous Kuwaitis, with the in-laws out of the way in Kuwait, Abdulla finally gave in, and Monika was happy.

She knew she would be successful in that business because, to the Kuwaitis, food is their religion. No restaurant in all of London prepares the rice dishes the Kuwaiti way, and Monika knew how to do that. In fact, Most Kuwaitis hire holiday flats instead of hotel rooms when they are in London because that's where they can cook. Eating at some Lebanese restaurant or Indian curry house is the closest substitute for Kuwaiti cuisine. Italian, English, French restaurants provide what Kuwaitis consider just snacks and do nothing for a Kuwaiti appetite. If you live in London you might have gotten used to the sight of Arabs crossing the street or hailing taxis holding huge aluminum cooking pots wrapped in cloth; that's when they are off to some other Arab's lodgings or hotel with the rice because it is their turn to cook dinner that day, and they're always taking turns this way out of desperation. It's been known to happen that a pot of rice makes a plane journey to nearby France or Ireland to somebody who is zealous to indulge in his own cuisine. Arabs in general do lots of food carrying on their travels, and a Kuwaiti's rice eating plays a major role in his daily life and is of immense importance. If he hasn't eaten rice for a day, he says he hasn't eaten at all and is very bad tempered. Like Abdulla.

It had occurred to Monika to open a Kuwaiti restaurant when she realized that all the Kuwaitis in London—businessmen, visitors and patients—had nowhere to go to eat the food they were used to and loved. They complained endlessly of their deprivation. London is full of Kuwaitis and of other Arabs all year round, and those well-heeled people would well appreciate genuine Gulf cuisine and be willing to pay for it, provided the restaurant was well run. With Monika managing it, the restaurant couldn't help being a financial success—success was already guaranteed!

Abdulla and Monika opened a joint bank account at the London branch of the Bank of Kuwait, and the manager congratulated the couple on a great idea and wished them luck. Once more Monika pushed her sleeves up and went happily to work, and in no time she had a manageress, a wine waiter, and a headwaiter, who was willing to give up his job at a casino and work for her. A couple of Arabs who were cooks at first-class establishments were ready to jump over, lured by a fatter salary. Things were going fine in all directions, and Monika's mind was happily diverted from her "Marriage." Having her time occupied with business made her life easier, but the happiness was short-lived.

Ten days before the restaurant contract was to be signed and finalized, Abdulla got cold feet and went back on his word. He—or somebody—changed his mind completely.

"If I let you run the restaurant, you won't need me anymore, and you will stay in Britain if the Kuwait Government sends me back home."

Monika left no stone unturned, yet she couldn't convince Abdulla that she wasn't after the financial independence—only after achieving success in business. It had first been agreed that ownership and everything would be 50/50 between them; so, now she offered to step down and suggested she'd accept a monthly salary and that everything else would run through lawyers in his name. Still, he didn't budge. Abdulla—stone cold—canceled the bank arrangements and everything lay kaput.

And what a bloody let down that was for her. Abdulla had now royally screwed and messed her up once too often, and this time it was to affect her so much that she decided enough was enough. She wasn't going to take any more of that immature shit from her undiplomatic diplomatic spouse. Not in Europe. So now was as good a time as any to make a final U-turn out of that messed up life of hers.

Having married under both the British and Islamic law, she had to consider two divorces in order to regain her full freedom, which would not be easy. Nothing was easy, nor came easily to her. She had gotten used to that by now.

It was the story of her life.

CHAPTER TWENTY-EIGHT

BYE, BYE, ABDULLA

She decided to begin by getting out of her Islamic liaison. The English divorce would be simple to get because of the extra-marital evidence against Abdulla; procuring it would be child's play. Monika thought wrongly.

The British law may be widely known as just, but for a lucky, carefree diplomat, the law has all these fantastic loopholes, which come under the Diplomatic Immunity Act, you know.

After having repeatedly threatened Abdulla with a divorce all through their marriage, Monika had a hard time convincing him that this was it. He naturally thought nothing of it when she really, finally meant it.

From what she had seen and heard in Kuwait, Monika knew damn well that the Kuwaiti Islamic law might be on her side in the Holy Koran and on some paper documents, but in real life she wouldn't have a leg to stand on as a woman and a foreigner, at that.

Abdulla, who didn't want to know anything about a divorce, and got up to walk away whenever she stated to mention the subject, was the strong one with all the favors at his disposal. He was the male Muslim, a powerful diplomat. He had loads of wastas on his side, and that's what counts in a Kuwaiti divorce. It would have been a different story if Monika had been a native Kuwaiti of some influential wasta family, too—in which case she would only have gotten married after working out and signing some marriage contract that awarded her family the power to file and arrange for a divorce should the need ever arise. At first, Abdulla blindly refused even to consider a divorce. When he realized that Monika was serious, he launched into tirades.

"If you want a divorce, go to Kuwait and get one," he said. "But don't forget... As for money, forget it! According to Islam, I don't have to give you a single penny if we get divorced, which won't happen. If we do get divorced, I will say it's because you refused me sex, after which I would have to keep you for another three months, just in case you are pregnant, after which I have got nothing to do with you. Then you can go back to your mother, like our Muslim women. And then you're second hand—and disgraced for life, like a prostitute." Abdulla spoke only his native, typical Kuwaiti mind. Yes, it's true a divorced woman is looked upon as a prostitute in Kuwait. And that's the sole reason why many a poor soul sticks, in ill health, to a miserable life. It's preferable to live miserably than to live the rest of one's life in disgrace with one's totally disgraced mother and father.

After giving up on talking Abdulla into agreeing to an amicable divorce, Monika pulled herself together and took a hopeful pilgrimage to the friendly Kuwaiti Ambassador, convinced he would be of help and advise her on how to go about things. Monika didn't ask for much. All she wanted was a divorce and a small settlement of money that Abdulla wouldn't even feel—to keep her going modestly, far below the high lifestyle she was used to living with him and didn't care for. Freedom was much, much more precious to her. And now, more so than ever before, she was determined and willing to work hard.

The Ambassador was one big let down. Even after Monika told him some of the worst pranks Abdulla had been up to during their marriage, he thought she should think of the children and gave her a lesson on how to stick it out by his side.

"My children are grown up, and they themselves urge me to get divorced because they can't stand to see their mother suffer any longer. I've been waiting for years for the right moment, which is now," she told him.

Reminding her again to consider the kind of uproar her divorce could arouse, he concluded the discussion, reminding her of all the good points in Abdulla's favor.

Monika was disgusted with the Ambassador's view. According to him, the way Abdulla lived was okay. It serves you right, you stupid cow Monika. What did you expect, confiding in someone who himself keeps a secret hideaway flat for his bit of crumpet on the side?

Monika's next attempt to secure help with that wretched divorce from Abdulla was to see Abdulla's boss, the Minister of Health Dr. Rezza Hashemi. He was conveniently on one of his official London visits, and Monika arranged what she thought would be a heart-to-heart discussion. She was convinced she was on the right track with him. It was he, if anybody, who would channel nutty, high-wire Abdulla into a decent, "grown up" divorce, especially after he'd be disgusted when she told him about a couple of things Abdulla was up to in London and about what she had endured all those years with him. Doctor Rezza projected to Monika the air of a fair judge who stood with what was right even though many of Monika's patients and lots of other Kuwaitis were not at all keen on him, for the simple reason that he was originally a Persian and looked Persian, too. His mother couldn't even speak Arabic. The prejudiced Aseel Kuwaitis thought a Minister's job should stay within the tight Aseel Kuwaiti circle. Would his background make him sympathetic to Monika's cause?

Abdulla was often teased by his Aseel friends that he took orders from some Persian, which Abdulla always warded off with jokes. To Monika, all that meant nothing. What always counts in the end is never one's looks, nor origin, but an individual's character. Right?

In London, Abdulla had met and made friends with Italian businessman Lorenzo, who had for sale an Italian painting with a price tag on it reaching into the millions and who was out to find a suitable buyer, maybe a Kuwaiti, through Abdulla. Lorenzo was married to a German girl, Helga. They had an eight-month-old baby. Whenever they were in London, they stayed in a suite at the Churchill Hotel. One day, Monika received a call from Helga to come and visit her at their suite, as she couldn't make it down to the lobby with the baby. Because of the Arabs, London's hotels were prostitute-infested in the 70's, and security staff kept a close watch for trespassers of that sort. As Monika entered the hotel's lobby and made her way to the elevators, she saw one security guard wink to another and both came marching on the double towards her. Monika, you have had it, she thought; they think you're a prostitute, blinking cheek! Both men entered the lift behind her. Halfway up to Helga's apartment one of them addressed Monika.

"Madam, are you a resident at this hotel?"

"No, I'm not," answered Monika, feeling the heat of annoyance rise up. "I know why you follow me, which is okay because you're doing your job. But can't you wait to see where and to whom I am heading before insulting me by assuming that I am a prostitute?"

The two—one a small, cheesy-white-faced short and stumpy bloke, and the other, long, thin-faced, mustached, neither of them of good breeding as you could tell from the dialect they spoke—were astounded that Monika was defending herself. After fruitless arguments that got her nowhere, while pressing ascendant and descendant buttons with them in turn, she demanded to be taken to the Hotel Manager. The whole episode was proving embarrassing for her because every time the elevator door opened and a guest wanted to enter, the guards, who flanked Monika's right and left side, asked the person to use other available lifts. Surely all of them must have thought, Aha, jolly good work, they've caught a prostitute here! Elevator now on the ground floor, a small fat Hotel Manager dressed in a gray pinstriped business suit walked grinningly in her direction. She stepped out and met him halfway. She handed him her diplomatic I.D. card and explained herself. Can you imagine her state of shock when he, cheeky-faced, stuck by the security, insisting (sneeringly smiling) that the room number she was intending to visit was that of a single gentleman?

Monika—in disgrace—stood in a cold sweat, surrounded by a wheel of onlookers. She made a last attempt to defend herself by asking the Manager to use the house telephone. That bloody bastard kept repeating that the room number was a gentleman's, and didn't she say she was on her way to a woman friend? The Manager enjoyed what he was doing and spoke in a very loud voice. Cornered, Monika told the Manager he would hear from her lawyer and stormed out of the hotel, but not before making a loud comment on the piece of ear lobe that was missing from one of his ears. Pointing at it, she said, "How does the saying go? Beware of people who are marked by God, isn't that it?"—after which she jumped into her car, lit up a menthol cigarette, drove home (which was just down the road), and phoned her lawyer.

The Assistant Manager (as he turned out to be) had to apologize to her the next day, as ordered by the Hotel's Management, but according to law, they had a right to turn away people who are non-residents. The newspapers got hold of and reported the story. They even came to take a photograph of her, which was taken in Abdulla's office. Abdulla, of course, was of no use at all in the matter—as he was always inadequate when she needed a man's help. The following day one could read in the *Daily Express* something like "well-endowed, attractive Austrian-born so and so, wife of Kuwaiti Diplomat stormed out of the Churchill Hotel, enraged and embarrassed, accusing the staff of having mistaken her for a prostitute"—and so on.

Anyway, Doctor Rezza got hold of that story, too, and telephoned Monika from Kuwait to tell her he was annoyed with her and that she would have to fight the case and prove her innocence with the help of the Embassy's lawyer at hand, or Abdulla would have to pack in his job, and both of them would be called back to Kuwait. Can you believe that? Monika was just as disgusted with Rezza then as she was with that cheeky, insolent hotel employee. But in the end she managed to convince the Minister of Health as to what was the true story, and he apologized.

Apparently the false story had been mentioned in Kuwait's Parliament and the allegations thrown in the Minister's face; and he had been made to feel responsible for sending a Kuwaiti with his scarlet woman, a European woman who dirtied the good name of Kuwait in Britain.

Remembering all that now, Monika was sure it would be sufficient to give the Minister of Health, who seemed to care and to be fair (he was "the Minister of Justice" to her now), just one of Abdulla's woman-stories to taste. Monika had decided on the one involving Egyptian girl Badria. Monika looked upon Rezza as an open-minded Muslim, or Persian. Surely he, as a doctor, would understand how she felt during and after Abdulla's escapades when Abdulla demanded sex from her and she couldn't stand his hands on her body anymore. She hoped that Rezza would understand that she, too, needed love, attention, and, of course, sex; and that she had the right to function as a normal, happy human being just as all the Arab men did.

Monika kept three different gynecologists on Harley Street because she was ashamed to go repeatedly to one and the same when she was in need of prescriptions to cure the infections that Abdulla kept passing on to her. So Monika told the Minister all about that, including the latest story about Badria, whom Abdulla had put up in the Royal Lancaster Hotel's Penthouse Suite—on the top floor, overlooking London—for a luxurious two whole weeks. Monika had found out all about it, thanks to scandal-leaking Gregory. Monika had taken a private detective along to get more proof in black and white for her forthcoming divorce proceedings. After the two weeks of luxury at the

Royal Lancaster, Abdulla had lodged his Badria in a flat that belonged to a friend of his. It was there that Monika had decided to pay Badria a surprise visit. Monika pretended to be an employee of the huge building's landlord. Armed with a small hidden tape recorder, whose microphone she had clipped onto her sleeve to collect solid evidence, Monika rang the doorbell, holding a huge official-looking clipboard in her hand. The chained door was opened a crack, and a foreign female's voice said, "Yes?"

"Excuse me," Monika began. "I am here to check on all the flats in this block. If it's not convenient right now, I can always come back later. All I have to do is to count the rooms in your flat, madam."

"It's all right. You come in," and the door opened.

"Good morning, Badria! I am your lover Abdulla's wife," Monika announced in Arabic while walking over the threshold.

The pretty but sluttish-looking girl's dark hair was set in huge rollers. She stood open-mouthed in a red, revealing, see-through nylon nightie under which she wore nought. She sported huge black nipples on massive tits, and one could easily make out that in true Islamic fashion she, too, had shaved her pubic hair down there. Monika knew from Gregory that Abdulla's drivers were fighting with each other to be the one to deliver anything to her, and now Monika knew why. Monika made it clear to a scared, stunned Badria that she could have Abdulla for keeps, with all Monika's blessings.

"If Abdulla says he loves you but that he can't get rid of me, you'd better know he is lying. He's just using you for sex. I want to get rid of him. If you can get him off my back, you would be doing me a big favor. And don't look so scared; I won't bite you, darling."

Triumphantly smiling, Monika made her exit with solid evidence and proof on her tape. The poor girl, whose job was fucking, but whose fault it wasn't, was left behind frightened. She had talked like a waterfall. What Monika expected next happened. Badria, of course, got straight away in touch with her darling Abdulla, who in turn got in touch with

Gloom to check what Monika was wearing that day. Gloom only confirmed what Badria had already said and described a red fox fur jacket, matching fur hat, and jeans. Poor Abdulla strained his brain on how Monika could have found out about that one. He still had no idea—and wouldn't for a long time yet to come—that his private fox Gregory had let the cat out of the bag and betrayed him.

Before that Badria visit, the moment that foxy Gregory had moved the Egyptian girl under Abdulla's instructions from the Lancaster Hotel to the flat, nosy Monika was at the Lancaster Hotel, watching it all close by; and once Gregory and Badria took off, Monika asked at the reception to see that specific penthouse suite.

"Madam, it was just vacated a minute ago. The suite has not been made up yet."

"Oh, that doesn't matter at all. My parents lived in it two years ago, and as they are considering booking it for two months this time, I just wanted to have a quick peek at it."

With "Very well, madam" and a uniformed porter who held the keys, she was on her way to view the love nest of her Sweetie. Golly, what a kick! Romantic, isn't it? She just wanted to know for what style and atmosphere Abdulla was willing to pay 150 pounds a night to fuck his current choice of Egyptian pussy. As usual, Abdulla didn't disappoint her. Nothing but the best was good enough for him. The door was opened and Monika stepped into a beautiful, friendly, bright, two-roomed, spacious, sumptuous apartment that seemed to be put together of windows and deep pile carpet alone. From the unmade, king size brass bed in the bedroom two or three stairs led up to the lounge, from which a corridor led to a dream of a bathroom. Charlie, the heavy perfume favored by the lower class of Arabs, lingered in the air. It must have been Badria's. And there (what a laugh!), white, long-stemmed lilies, the flowers of innocence and purity, stood on a table in a massive green-on-white, dragon-painted vase. A basketful of exotic fruit that was hardly touched rested on a side table under a wide, square, massive gold-framed mirror. Looking at that mirror, in which the huge bed was reflected, Monika thought, Ah well, yes, Abdulla always appreciated mirrors in his lovemaking. And so did she. The Harrod's label attached to the fruit basket swayed in the breeze that entered through the open windows and ruffled the crisp, satin curtains. "Must have been well to do folks who have moved out of here today," said Monika to the porter.

"Some Arab and his woman," answered the man. "They're the ones who have got all the money, aren't they, young lady, but they are very nice, no complaints. Those people are the best tippers. You can bring me an Arab anytime, and to be quite honest, I wish we could swap them with the miserly Germans, too." Both laughed, while Monika couldn't resist a little lark.

"How dare you say a thing like that? I am German, too, you know. I come from Hamburg." But when she saw his face, poor guy, she quickly put him at rest, tipped him, and left.

Monika's reward from Abdulla for finding out about Badria was a diamond-face Choppards gold watch, about which Gregory couldn't resist commenting, "You owe it to me. Thanks to me, you've got that watch." The fox was dead right.

Abdulla's friend Dr. Rezza, who proved this time that his bottom really was in one and the same pants as Abdulla's, was not in the least bit impressed with Monika's Badria story—or with any of Abdulla's other escapades, like his drunkenness—and got very cross with her for wishing to file for a divorce and wouldn't hear of it. And, would you believe it? Instead of getting him to influence Abdulla positively, Monika had to hear him try to frighten her with childish things—like, if she divorced Abdulla, her husband would take their teenage son Luay from her; Monika would never see Luay again; Abdulla would confiscate all her jewelry, furs, and clothes, and give her no money, and then the British police would be called to come and throw her out of the country. Rezza just couldn't stop himself from piling it on and on and was talking with an amazing confidence about throwing her out of Britain, as if Great Britain were his.

Monika was speechless at this man's simple-mindedness. This time her gift for seeing through people and into their characters had really let her down badly. She was left amazed and insulted by the way this otherwise intelligent man had so grossly underestimated her intelligence.

"Look, Rezza, forget it. I see I've knocked on the wrong door (the toilet!). I'm not a bedouin, you know, and may I remind you we are in Europe and, thank God, not in Kuwait where Abdulla with a couple of wastas could, no doubt, have me thrown out." And that was the end of that trip into disappointmentland.

Her next attempt towards procuring her Islamic divorce and annulling her Islamic marriage was to drive to the St. Johns Wood Mosque to seek the help and advice of a sympathetic mullah, who himself could do very little, but gave her the address of an Egyptian lawyer. Before she left, that mullah, who had plenty of experience with Islamic divorce cases in Britain, sternly warned her not to expect miracles, especially being married to a Kuwaiti. The law in Kuwait, he said, is the Koran, but sad as it might be the Koran is open to interpretation, and those with wealth, influence, and connections (wastas) can bend what it says into almost any shape that pleases them. Yes, well, what the mullah had to say here was no news to Monika. She was well acquainted with that bit of bad news—and had been all along, well in advance.

The Egyptian lawyer, a bear of a man who had a big impressive, typical, Egyptian-styled office in the City, greeted her in a very friendly manner; and as she was dressed in a Tyrolian outfit, addressed her in fluent German: "*Sind sie von Österreich gnädige Frau?*" meaning, "Are you from Austria, Madam?" and so broke the ice. After having listened to an account of her twenty-three years of marriage to a Kuwaiti, that lawyer assured Monika he indeed could help her to a fair Islamic divorce. It might cost, but he would get her through. He bent forwards and reached for a golden pen to take down the necessary details. "Your full name, please?"

"Monika al-Amahani," she answered.

"Al-Amahani?" the lawyer repeated slowly, in a questioning tone. "Tell me, is your husband related to a Kuwaiti called Mohammed Yusuf al-Amahani?" he asked awkwardly.

"He is my husband's uncle."

"Oh. I see," said the lawyer, put his pen down, leaned back in his posh leather chair, and was a changed man. "The best advice I can give you is to talk to your sons, who are quite grown up, to convince their father to give you a divorce on fair terms. I've always found that to work best in practice. I can't help you any further, I'm afraid."

Monika didn't argue with the man. She knew instinctively that the lawyer had big transactions going with substantial, big spending Kuwaiti clients like Abdulla's uncle, whose name he had just mentioned and who might get annoyed upon finding out that his lawyer was defending a mere foreign woman against the family. Besides, Monika was, she knew, just a little financial fish for the German-speaking Egyptian lawyer, just an insignificant hamra for whom it was not worth risking the big wheeler-dealing, worthwhile financial shark accounts. Yes, Kuwaitis' wastas reach like octopuses' arms far into the civilized world.

Growing increasingly impatient, Monika gave up the idea of handling the Islamic divorce herself and put greater pressure on Abdulla instead, until royally pissed-off he finally boarded a plane to divorce her in Kuwait. On his return he threw the divorce papers in her face—and that was all that the mother of his three sons ended up with after twenty-three years of grooming Abdulla and helping him to get where he was.

According to Kuwaiti Islamic justice, a woman married even that long had fully served her purpose when her husband was finished with her, and her man didn't owe her anything after he had reaped all the benefits of their marriage. For all the law cares in Kuwait, she could now end up in the gutter!

Abdulla put his divorce papers proudly on show under the glass top of his office desk and bragged to everybody that he, fed up with that bloody foreigner, had divorced her to live life a little and have fun. After all he was getting on a bit and wanted to enjoy his money in grander style. That's what he told people. Still married to Abdulla under British law, Monika intended to carry on living in their Government-owned and -supplied luxury flat until her British divorce came through. Just then, a letter from the Kuwait Embassy reached her that said that, since she was now divorced and the flat belonged to the Government of Kuwait, she was to move out within the next three weeks, or action would be taken. That formal letter, which was written by somebody who had called himself her friend not long ago, bore not a word of sympathy, nor even a signature, just the official stamp of the Embassy, bloody cowards. And to think that such people were responsible for the welfare of Kuwaitis like Monika who were living in Britain!

Monika had gotten no end of telephone calls from Kuwaiti men and women who offered their congratulations on the divorce. Many of them were people Monika barely knew. They cheered her up and said "good riddance to bad rubbish" and "everybody knows how many affairs he's had" and "you're much too good for him" and so on. Although Abdulla had tried hard to give people the opposite impression, everybody knew it was Monika who had divorced Abdulla, and those telephone calls proved it.

Although divorced, Abdulla still thought he owned her and got dead jealous when a number of Kuwaiti males tried to make contact with divorcee Monika. They asked for her at the Embassy and phoned her to such excess that Abdulla had the telephone number changed; but he needn't have worried and should have known that, after what she had been through with an Arab man, she was cured of them for life. Amen.

Now, don't you go thinking that getting a good British lawyer is child's play either. First, Monika came across this older, absent-minded woman lawyer, a spinster who bit her fingernails and couldn't answer a single one of Monika's questions without looking up the answer in her law books first. Then Monika moved on to a middle-aged, bespectacled, fat baldy of a lawyer who resembled a spotty, scruffy school kid that's always picked on by others, and she just couldn't get 'warm' with that one either. It's very important to have a lawyer you respect and are in tune with, especially in the case of a divorce.

But then it happened. Through a friend, she got to know that superduper whiz kid of a lawyer Alan Lowe, who didn't just look and speak the part, but acted it, too, and got her through her British divorce with flying colors—as far as the law permitted it, that is, for (old story again) Abdulla the Diplomat couldn't be touched by Courts (only cunts). According to the British law, Monika shouldn't have gotten a divorce altogether, but her canny lawyer had the divorce papers served to Abdulla through personal contact and Abdulla happily signed them, thinking the document was something else. His signature was all-important, and it was what was needed and what counted. Monika was now Scot-free again—exactly the way she had been when she had met him twenty-four years earlier. And the three sons that nobody could take away from her were all she—the innocent, suffering party—had to show for the union. There was to be no financial settlement, no monetary support—and this, despite her going through two divorces and Abdulla being guilty all the way. How does that strike you?—those of you acquainted with a Kuwaiti male right now? Females, be careful! You have been warned.

As grounds for the divorce, Monika had cited nine of Abdulla's extramarital affairs, to which he afterwards said, "You stupid, only nine? After ten years in London? That just shows that you don't know a thing about me. If you had added two zeros after the nine, it would have been much closer to the truth." Abdulla's pride was deeply hurt that Monika had left him, that his marriage to her was finally over. So, as a way of getting over his distress, he did what he knew best. He threw himself even more heavily into wine, song, and women to hide his hurt pride.

All the while that she had been living through the past several years in London, which were spiked with draughts no end of Abdulla's nasty family, his women, and those false, unreal, high society soirees—Monika had put all her trust in getting a fair British divorce, which would leave her not affluent, but definitely fairly well off. Instead, she was left to look through her fingers while Abdulla launched himself into throwing his money about as never before—to tease her. He gave the impression that he sweated money. His hangers-on multiplied. And he walked the nightclub scene like a pimp, surrounded by his bodyguards.

Now, just think, and tell me. Can what happened to Monika—and I'm sure to a thousand more out there—be called fair? Is the law that was invoked to protect Abdulla a fair British law? How many crimes get away Scot-free thanks to diplomatic immunity, which should really stop at political matters and not have the power to reach deep into a marriage? Forget about the barbaric unfairness of Islam to women. That British diplomatic law is not any better. It didn't protect her, the innocent party. She got married at a Registry Office, and over twenty-three years later, she can't even initiate a divorce against her grossly philandering, marriage-law flouting husband because he is a *Diplomat*! Surely any right-thinking person must agree that that's a very unfair, stupid law—and should be changed immediately; for it left Monika, after all the good she did and the suffering she endured, without a penny's worth of compensation—just as the barbarous Islamic divorce law had done. If she didn't have a little bit more than average up top, she'd be doomed by that Diplomatic Immunity Act to be a dishwasher in some hotel now, or something along those lines—and, my oh my!—wouldn't that please those in-laws? On second thought, someone like her—minus her brain—was at least as well endowed to earn her living like Badria or some of Abdulla's other floozies, in which case she'd certainly have the advantage of knowing exactly where the readiest and most extravagant clients were to be found! Or, as a Madam.

Monika moved with Luay, her youngest one, back into their old flat, a flat that Abdulla had bought when he first came to London. The in-laws couldn't wait to move in with Abdulla, taking her place. It wasn't easy. And it took Monika another two years of patient work on Abdulla to put the flat she lived in, at least, in her name. She also had to pussyfoot gently around for another four years after her divorce so that Abdulla would continue his voluntary payment of a regular check for Luay and her living expenses, every first of the month. Abdulla also paid the flat's taxes, telephone bill, and electricity, but Monika often had to ask and ask again for that pittance and might not get it until well into the middle of the month. Abdulla loved putting Monika through this sadistic ritual. He throve on hearing her ask for it again and again; her pleading was music to his ears, but it made her feel degraded, especially when he would say to her, "Aren't you ashamed to ask me for money? You're a grown up woman. When are you going to start earning your own money?"—after which she would slam the phone down.

The only reason she put up with that bad aftermath of a rotten marriage was Luay, or she would have been off like a shot long before. But Monika wanted Luay to have the same luxury and benefits that his two older brothers had had at his age. He was much too young to be left with his careless playboy father; so, for Luay's sake, she sacrificed a couple more years. It wasn't that difficult, for at least now she had freedom—even if it was not freedom with a capital F, not yet. For, had Abdulla ever seen or heard of her with another man, he would have stopped his money supply dead on. So Monika had to be careful and polite—and have you any idea how bloody hard that was?

But what is it that a real mother doesn't do for her kids? In return for her renunciations, Monika reaps deepest love and devotion from her three cavaliers, who, she can be sure, will never let her down. All her marriage sacrifices were well worth sons like those three troopers of hers. Needless to say, she is very proud of them.

As soon as Monika was divorced, the Kuwaiti Embassy confiscated her diplomatic I.D. card and her diplomatic passport and handed her an ordinary one, in which it was stated that she was the divorced wife of a diplomat and with which she had great difficulty entering Britain every time she traveled abroad. The problem was soon overcome because she applied right away for her Austrian identification papers and passport; and, with them in hand, she had no further trouble at all. The Immigration Officers turned from nasties into friendly, smiling gentlemen and ladies. Friends and acquaintances, upon hearing of Monika's ordeals at the hands of some overzealous British Immigration Officers, some of whom were often extraordinarily rude and completely out of line with her, advised her to buy herself a British Citizenship or long term visa for £5,000 that would provide her with the contacts right inside the Home Office who would be glad to make the arrangements. Their unwritten law says, "You bring the money, you get the goods, and fuck the law, man." And that is just about how it is all the world over, I can tell you.

In fact, there is amidst the London night scene an older, quite notorious "Madam"—as she likes to be called—who supplies nightclubs in London and Paris with the best pieces of moving flesh that her clients' money can buy. Having her fingers in many pies, she is also very influential. So much so, that she also supplies people with legal documents of their choice, but, of course, only if they pay up and meet her demands. Monika is not a person to meddle in things that are against the law because she well knows that crime is going to catch up with its perpetrator, if not today, then tomorrow, just as it has to catch up with Abdulla one of these days. And, mark my words, it will. Those who walk with forged passports, visas, and citizenship documents don't sleep well at night. They can't. It's human nature, isn't it. Bad conscience!

Before her Islamic divorce, Monika had a tooth capped out of vanity. It was badly done and caused an abscess at its root. The tooth had already been operated on twice when that dumb abscess, which was very painful, re-occurred for the third time—right at the time of her Islamic divorce. She went to Harley Street to have it seen to, as usual, and expected it to be paid for by the Kuwait Government, also as usual. But Dr. Rezza, no longer her friend, refused her. He asked Monika to bring a letter of justification from her treating dentist, only to scrawl across it that her case was not a matter of life or death and could be dealt with in Kuwait. Now, didn't that action just stink to heaven? She was divorced, yes, but she was still a Kuwaiti citizen and still married to Abdulla according to British law. Monika felt there was something criminal about it. The Minister put many Kuwaitis on the Government's medical payroll, people who, without the permission of some Committee that was set up in Kuwait for the purpose, were not entitled to stipends—like, for instance, Abdulla's mother and sisters and many others; yet, Monika, who used to cook for and feed that traitor and had the right to be granted financial support of this sort, on account of being a Kuwaiti citizen at least, was ousted and refused. She was treated like a leper.

The Kuwaiti Ambassador and the Minister of Health blew out of the same horn. Whenever Monika asked for something, they would say, "Go to Kuwait and see to it there." The Ambassador told her—after her divorce, when she came to ask what funds she should live on from now on—to go to Kuwait and live there in her house because that was hers and her children's by law now, and not Abdulla's. Fat chance she would have trying to attempt that one! Wasta working, they'd have stamped her right into the desert sand without leaving a trace that she'd ever existed. Yes, it was (and still is) wastas all the way! Who wants to know or cares about what's right or wrong? In Kuwait, qualifications take you nowhere. Wastas, kickbacks, bribery, and commissions are what get you anything, everything, everywhere. In a world like this, it seems the easiest way to live is by joining in, too, which would have been no hard task for Monika. All she would have to do was to give in to one or a couple of those big knobs' sexual desires, and she, too, could have gained those wastas and be in the big money—but that just wasn't her. Instead, Monika sat down and did it *her* way. She wrote a letter to "His Excellency The Minister of Health" and told him exactly what she thought of him and sent it off by Diplomatic post, after which she felt tons of unjust weight lifted off her chest.

Remember Monika's strange perceptions and those dreams of hers that came true? She was to find out more about them after she was introduced to Great Britain's Psychic Research Center in London's Belgrave Square. It was there she met other people with the same gift, but who were fully developed psychics. Meeting them helped her also partly to get over her divorce blues, which were much heavier and harder to live through than she would have anticipated, but which did not outweigh her heavenly peace and new-found feelings of freedom. Needless to say, it was quite difficult for Monika to start her new life on her own. It was something like learning to walk on crutches after some horrid accident.

It was not easy—after twenty-three years of having been taken care of financially and of giving orders to servants and employees wherever she moved. Monika didn't even have experience in dealing with some of the most simple, everyday things in life that every housewife has to deal with—like, for instance, how and where to pay for the parking tickets she was issued after her diplomatic license plates had been confiscated, too. Monika cottoned on quickly, and she was as proud as can be every time she achieved each little bit of real independence. Silly, isn't it?

It took some time to make new friends, who mostly turned out to be younger than herself. And that's exactly how Monika likes it because she is very young at heart. The few European-twilight contacts she had while she was married to Abdulla stayed behind, of course, where the money was, which was to be expected. Isn't it difficult to find genuine friendships? There are the users, and there are the pretenders and the posers, and there is painfully little in between. Before wasting time with a roomful of artificial, affluent folk whose favorite pastime (and only interest in life) is showing off their wealth because that's all that counts for them, Monika prefers to keep herself to herself. People who live to impress are just not her cup of tea. She enjoys down-to-earth straight talk with a farmer's wife much more than having to chat to some society lady who is in her seventh heaven with her newly acquired set of emeralds from Cartier, which the poor skin simply can't stop showing off.

Monika, too, has had the furs and the jewelry necessary for moving in and about London's diplomatic high society, but all of that left her unfulfilled and unimpressed. Abdulla's nice cousin Sabiha, who was the one who impressed Monika the first time she met her way back in Kuwait, came often to London because one of her rebellious daughters, Agbal, who hated everything about Kuwait except its money, loved everything about England, where she studied and settled. Monika asked Sabiha once if she had ever really said that her forehead looked like a monkey's bottom, as Tamader had reported. Sabiha admitted, "Yes, I did say that, but only to please Abdulla's family." Ah well, let bygones be bygones. Anyway, sticks and stones may break your bones, but words will never harm you.

Agbal, Sabiha's very Europeanized daughter, who started to visit Monika after Monika's divorce, invited her for a big meal at their home, where Agbal lived all hush-hush and secretly with her much older Continental husband Catholic Carlo and their love child. Agbal's parents, it turned out, ashamed that their daughter had married a non-Muslim and a European to boot, had spread the misinformation in Kuwait that their daughter had married a Moroccan Muslim who lived in Britain.

Later, Monika repaid Agbal's hospitality with one of her typical, Kuwaiti rice dinners. The three of them seemed to get on well, until

Monika served the sweet. While she was eating it, she felt Carlos' foot in sock slide half way up her leg. She looked at him, but all his interests seemed absorbed in his pudding. No. It wasn't on purpose, she thought. Things like this do happen, sometimes quite unintentionally.

After the dinner table was cleared, Monika served Arabic coffee with Turkish delight and After Eights. Carlo paid her a compliment on her poison-green velvet tunic, which was heavily embroidered in gold thread.

"Do you really like it? I have six different ones in different materials and patterns," Monika said.

"Oh, please, may I see them?" said Carlo, who had opened his belt and slipped off his shoes to make himself comfy after the sumptuous meal. If Monika could do one thing, it was cook a good meal. When the naive noodle re-entered the room with all her caftans slung over one arm, Carlo had his right hand down the open front of his trousers and was playing with "IT."

"Lovely, lovely. Go on, put that see-through on for me. I'd love to see you in it. You really turn me on," he said while his Agbal helped Carlo to encourage a stunned Monika.

"Yes, go on, Monika! Put it on. Let's have some fun together."

"What?" she answered in disbelief. "You want me to do a striptease for the two of you? You're joking, surely!"

"No, we're not joking! Look!" Carlo stripped off his trousers, shirt, underpants next, and white socks, too, tossing each item high up in the air.

Monika was so surprised and taken aback with the unexpected development that she needed more time than usual to think how to handle the situation. By now, Carlo sat on her beige velvet settee under Tutankhamen's picture, stark naked, with his hairy white legs wide open, invitingly outstretched, vigorously stroking and working on his very medium-sized willy with his nail-bitten fingers. He looked like a plucked chicken, a pitiful sight, and a safe turn-off. Agbal chased after

Monika and tried to lift her tunic, but when Carlo joined in and got hold excitedly of her suspender strap, she had to shout out a Sergeant-Major-like, authoritative-sounding "Stop it at once!" to prevent them from stripping and raping their hostess in her own flat. They both sat down.

"I told you Monika is more Arab than an Arab," said Agbal to Carlo, without the slightest sign of shame. Monika turned to Agbal.

"If I agreed, you would really let Carlo make love to me?"

"Of course I would. He likes your figure. I make a good model. I look good in clothes, but when I take them off, there's nothing for a man to hold on to. I have no bum, nor tits, like you do, and Carlo loves your kind of figure."

"And what would you have done if I had agreed to have sex?" asked Monika.

"Then I would have joined in, too. It's only human. We are both very open-minded about it," she said.

"And what if Carlo liked our lovemaking so much that he comes sneaking back for more behind your back?" Monika wanted to know.

"Then I'd get a divorce," she smiled. "But we have an agreement."

"Holy macaroni, I don't believe this!" Monika said and really believed she was dreaming. "If you really have that opinion that every European indulges in sex with just anybody at any time, you've got it all wrong about us, Agbal; and if I weren't a nice, understanding person, I would be offended now by the two of you." Monika reached for her dust brush beside her open fire place and handed it to Carlo, who was still working on his meat and two veg and said, smiling, to him: "Here you are, something to tickle your fancy with. Maybe it helps."

Carlo looked a heap of shame. He put his clothes back on and said, "Well, nobody can say I haven't tried. Monika, with whom do you have sex now? Do you have any at all?"

"That's my private affair, and that's the way I'd like to keep it, thank you very much."

Monika never socialized with them again. That episode goes to show just what sort of behavior restricted girls brought up in Kuwait are capable of when they're let loose in the West, and what kind of man they go for. They really do think that being European means acting as Agbal and Carlo did. It was bad enough that Kuwaiti men and one or two lesbians had tried in the past to have a go with Monika, but Abdulla's cousin's daughter, too? Monika had never expected that, and that's the race that has the nerve to call every white female a prostitute or scarlet woman! What a crazy, crazy, interesting world.

For some Arabs, a close second in line to London's escort agencies are the attractive, alluring, pretty girls at the make-up and perfumery counters at London's top stores such as Harrod's, Harvey Nichols, Selfridges, Debenhams, and so on. Many an Arab has quite willingly let such a girl talk him into buying hundreds of pounds worth of Estee's newest spring make-up or scent, goods he doesn't even need, that he gives away afterwards to some other girl, or takes home as presents for his sister. All of it is done in hopes that sooner or later the salesgirl may let him lay her. Some men go around handing out presents to those girls, gifts such as pretty lighters or gold jewelry and perfume that they have brought with them by the dozens from Arabia. Some of those young ladies—especially the prettier ones—get daily offers and have the pick of the crop, if they want to take advantage of the situation and play the game. Do they want to? Yes, they do. Plenty of them do. Horny Abdulla had some of them right through the row and then recommended them to his friends. That's true friendship, isn't it? Yes, well, those girls are noted amongst the Arabs as cleaner and cheaper fucking material than the outworn agency girls. But don't go thinking that every girl who works at such a counter is easy game—of course, not. But for those who are made of that material, men have an eye, don't they? Ah well, let them love and give. Good luck and a good fuck to all of them. We're not begrudging folks, are we? Of course, not.

To sum it all up, Monika is forty-plus nowadays. When one door closes another opens. She is free, single, and still pretty enough to attract attention. Female vulnerability at forty-plus is great, but Monika doesn't want to learn someone else's habits and foibles. She's had enough of that from Abdulla to last a lifetime. She doesn't crave the white heat of passion that she might encounter in another steady relationship. She's had all of that and children, too. But if love does happen all over again, it's because it's meant to be. It's impossible for a human being to swear an affidavit today on how she's going to live the next 10, 20, or 30 years.

Monika has learned from the Arabs not to take life too seriously, as so many hard working Europeans do who hardly ever play. Life is what you make it, and work is only intended to help you to afford to have a lot of fun. We were not put by God on this planet to work till we're dead for a room and a bed and a life full of misery. Have you noticed that nearly all the badness we have to deal with in all of our walks of life is self-inflicted, by 'hu-men' beings?

In Monika's age group a woman realizes that what she was searching for in the past perhaps doesn't exist, so she gives up looking for it and tries to make the best of what is actually available to her. It also hasn't gone unnoticed that men want attractive, intelligent, and brave women, but whenever they finally find one, they just don't seem to know what to do with her. So once we women have got ourselves accustomed to the fact that all men, however great their names and reputations may be, are little boys who don't grow up, it's much easier for us women because we have to make do with them, you know, like it or not. We (most of us) have no other choice.

Out of each horrid experience, there is always a lesson to be learned, and Monika is a good pupil who has become streetwise. She has had to pay a price for the glorious freedom she intends to hold on to for keeps. Now, that it's all over and she's made it, she feels no bitterness towards the past. London's Battered Wife Refuges are filled to the brim. Who knows what would have been in store for her had she married one of her own kind? Now, the world is her oyster. She has got another chance and is not likely to make another mistake. The strong and clever take the steering wheel to reach their aims; the weak and the simple-minded follow the leader.

Only determination will get you there, and now I am speaking to the hundreds of thousands of trapped women who go along all alone in a "Cinderella in Arabia" 'shituation' at this very moment, just as Monika once did. Your road may seem—and be—dark, long, lonely, and littered with obstacles, too, that you think you will never overcome, and you might want to give up, but don't ever give up and follow the leader. Always have faith in God and yourself, as Monika did. She knows what she is talking about. She has been down your road, remember? Don't ever lose your faith in faith, and one day it will happen for you.

Unfortunate Abdulla, poor chap, was a victim of time. The once peaceful-living Kuwait is a victim, too. The more those wealthy people have, the greedier and meaner they become. Many have dipped their hands deep into the Government's kitty. Monika was well acquainted with some of those thieves, but because *everybody* did it, nobody could point a finger. People who live in glass houses can't throw stones. Had Abdulla's little country not been disturbed by the wealth of oil through the British, he would have married his own kind, maybe one of his cousins, and never known that England and Monika existed and be far happier today, for Abdulla was only exhibiting happiness on the outside but wasn't deep down. May he, too, find his happiness, whatever that may consist of. Painfully little is known, researched, or written on the feelings of a couple that has lived together for a long time and then parted because they couldn't master life together. Yet, there lingers that certain bond that one doesn't count on when one is dying for a divorce—which, in a way, is some form of love, and not just because a man is the father of the woman's children, as in Monika's case.

Now, folks, this story that you have read almost didn't happen—by a hair's breadth because during World War II Mrs. Pavlik took her children for a short period to Czechoslovakia, their father's country, where it was safer and dairy products and meat were more easily available than in Austria, while Dentist Pavlik served in the Army where he did his job by being a dentist. When the situation got more dangerous in Prague than in Austria, Mrs. Pavlik bundled her children together to make her way back to Vienna. The bus they traveled in to the border was held up half way by Czech soldiers, and all the passengers were ordered to leave the vehicle for inspection. German speaking Mrs. Pavlik and her two children were singled out to one side, while the rest were allowed to continue their journey. That day, Czech soldiers had shot a playing Czech child, mistaking it for German. To compensate for that mistake, they had decided to shoot the first German family that came their way and which they thought they now had found with the Pavliks. The children were taken from their mother and put in a van while Mrs. Pavlik was placed against a wall. Shots were aimed around her head. They rang out loud and died in the soldiers' cheers before she was to receive the planned, fatal bullet, which was reserved for the one who had earlier killed the Czech child. Next in line for slaughter would be Werner and Monika. Little six-year-old Monika fainted, but her brother, nine-year-old Werner, screamed his lungs out, which saved their lives because his screams attracted the attention of a passing Military Policeman on a motorbike, who interrupted the festive sacrifice to investigate and came as a Guardian Angel. After examining Friederike Pavlik's identity papers, that policeman discovered, of course, that the children they were detaining were half-Czech, too, and so they were all set free to cross the border. Dentist Pavlik was carrying a leather case full of her jewelry and valuables, which she then handed to her lifesaver. From the case she took only her legal papers. Monika remembers her mother telling that story again and again to people all through her childhood in Austria. "I will never forget the sight of the white gloved hand of that policemen who saved us from being shot—not as long as I live," she would say time and time again.

So you see, Monika was meant to live through her ordeal in Arabia, too; and now, as it's all over, she can only go one way, which is Up, and in order to go UP, you have to be DOWN first. So, goodbye, ground, and make place up there for her as she goes UP AND UP AND UP to the heavens above.

DEDICATED WITH LOTS AND LOTS OF LOVE
TO
SANALU
I LOVE YOU

HEY, ELVIS, THANKS FOR YOUR MUSIC IN THE BACKGROUND
OF MY LIFE
STAY WITH ME

P S The added scar my son Nabeel got as a twenty-year old he acquired, of all places, in Oxford. He got it bravely warding off five blacks who came out of nowhere and surrounded Luay, his youngest brother, who sat peacefully on a bench to enjoy his MacDonald's Quarterpounder with french fries. They were after Luay's thick gold chain, and trooper Luay refused to give it to them. Nabeel, who saw they were outnumbered and in danger, begged Luay, urging him to let them have that silly chain. Luay hung on to it. "Who's got the knife?" one of the thugs shouted. Following a click, Nabeel saw a sharp blade going towards his brother's chest. Quick as a flash, Nabeel put his arms around Luay to protect him, and instantly felt heat on his left arm. The five took off running. Heroic Nabeel had the tendons of his left arm cut and will never again be able to move his fingers properly, like you and me. Luay feels ever so guilty and awfully sorry for being the cause. From what I have observed as a mother, this incident has brought the two brothers closer together. There is this accident bond. Having nothing to lose, however, Nabeel did agree to a name change and to the killing of a lamb on his twenty-first birthday. Let's wish him luck and protection from above! May he live to be a hundred.

Post Script

Dear Reader

You will have realized that I have not written specifically or extensively on my three mixed-race sons—Sulaiman, Nabeel, and Luay. There is, of course, a reason for it, too. No, I am not a self-centered person, to bring only my own circumstances to the surface. I was especially asked by the trio to leave them "OUT OF IT," and true to my word, that's what I've done. How could I not? They don't want to be associated with their parents' "crap," as they call it, very fittingly.

This book was written in the Austrian countryside. The manuscript was finished in 1987—yet it never saw daylight in book form until now, 2001. Since 1987 so much "out of the ordinary" has happened to me and to Kuwait – who knows, I might share my experiences with you at a later date

If you have read and enjoyed *Cinderella in Arabia*, let me say a hearty 'THANK YOU!'

Monika

Printed in Great Britain
by Amazon